Assessment Report on Chinese Primary School Students' Academic Achievement

Huisheng Tian · Zhichang Sun

Assessment Report on Chinese Primary School Students' Academic Achievement

4 Subjects of Grade 6 in Primary School Taken as Examples

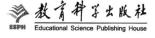

Huisheng Tian
National Center for School Curriculum
and Textbook Development
Ministry of Education
Beijing, China

Zhichang Sun
Institute for Educational Research
Beijing, China

Translated by
Na Wei
National Institute for Curriculum
and Textbook Research
Ministry of Education
Beijing, China

ISBN 978-3-662-57528-4   ISBN 978-3-662-57530-7 (eBook)
https://doi.org/10.1007/978-3-662-57530-7

Jointly published with Educational Science Publishing House, Beijing, China
The print edition is not for sale in China Mainland. Customers from China Mainland please order the print book from: Educational Science Publishing House.

Library of Congress Control Number: 2019932605

© Springer-Verlag GmbH Germany and Educational Science Publishing House 2019
This work is subject to copyright. All rights are reserved by the Publishers, whether the whole or part of the material is concerned, specifically the rights of translation, reprinting, reuse of illustrations, recitation, broadcasting, reproduction on microfilms or in any other physical way, and transmission or information storage and retrieval, electronic adaptation, computer software, or by similar or dissimilar methodology now known or hereafter developed.
The use of general descriptive names, registered names, trademarks, service marks, etc. in this publication does not imply, even in the absence of a specific statement, that such names are exempt from the relevant protective laws and regulations and therefore free for general use.
The publishers, the authors, and the editors are safe to assume that the advice and information in this book are believed to be true and accurate at the date of publication. Neither the publishers nor the authors or the editors give a warranty, express or implied, with respect to the material contained herein or for any errors or omissions that may have been made. The publishers remain neutral with regard to jurisdictional claims in published maps and institutional affiliations.

This Springer imprint is published by the registered company Springer-Verlag GmbH, DE part of Springer Nature
The registered company address is: Heidelberger Platz 3, 14197 Berlin, Germany

Preface

Students' academic achievement is the developmental level reached by students in the aspects of knowledge, skills, affect, attitude, etc., through learning activities with teachers' direction, based on prior experience. With the background that the world countries generally stress, explore, and carry out the macroscopic educational quality monitoring and with the premise that "Two-Basis" has been realized, quality education is in thorough implementation, curriculum reform is ongoing, and the problems of school running condition and financial devotion have been basically solved, it has vital theoretical meaning and practical value to do the studies on students' academic achievement. On one hand, it can monitor students' academic achievement at the national macro-level, which is good to thoroughly, objectively, and truly know and master the quality of our country's basic education, to genuinely and effectively implement quality education, to provide feasible and reliable evidence for the policy-making and management of educational administrative departments and to accelerate the realization of the goals of educational fairness and balanced development. On the other hand, it can provide scientific foundation for the modification of curriculum policy, formulation of curriculum standards and curriculum implementation, to make assessment play the function of accelerating students' development and teachers' improvement and improving teaching, to feasibly advance the deepening of basic education reform, and to improve educational quality.

The participants in the present survey are primary school students in Grade 6, and the subjects surveyed include the four subjects of Chinese, Mathematics, Science, and Morality and Society, mainly aiming at knowing students' academic achievement on Chinese reading, Mathematics, Science, and Morality and Society. Student questionnaire and school questionnaire are also employed to explore the factors influencing students' academic achievement.

The present academic achievement survey mainly employs the mode of criterion-referenced assessment, based on Full-time Compulsory Education Curriculum Standards (Experimental version) (Curriculum Standards in abbreviation hereinafter), and develops the basic assessment framework from the two dimensions of subject content and subject competency to form the two-dimensional table of specifications. The test instrument for each subject is developed according to the classification of learning outcome of SOLO (Structure of the Observed Learning Outcome) taxonomy. The development of test instruments includes the procedures of preparation, construction, modification, pilot test, re-modification, and final draft formation. Strict training, organization, and management system has been built for the holistic test process to ensure the test scientificity.

With the employment of the method of stratified random sampling in the present survey, more than 18,000 primary school students in Grade 6 are selected from 31 districts and counties out of 8 provinces in the east, middle, and west of the country. The situation of students' academic achievement on the four subjects of Chinese reading, Mathematics, Science, and Morality and Society is investigated, in order to know to what extent their academic achievement has reached curriculum standards and to deeply analyze the factors influencing students' academic achievement, with the aim to provide scientific basis for the decision-making of education administrative departments and to provide feedback information for subject teaching and students' learning, and then to improve subject teaching quality and to accelerate students to do self-orientation and self-monitoring learning.

The present research is the fruit of the project team. The project host, research fellow Tian Huisheng, has organized and led the project research from the beginning to the end. The associate team leader and secretary, Sun Zhichang, has assisted the project host to carry out the research. And the core team members are Chen Qin, Liu Fang, Cai Yonghong, Ren Chunrong, Hu Jun, Chen Xiaodong, Yang Lijuan, Zhang Pengju, Ma Xiaoqiang, Ma Yanwei, Yang Baoshan, Jiang Ming, Feng Xinrui, Wang Xiaoxia, and Li Jiajun. The division of the present report writing is as follows: Preface and General Report on Students' Academic Achievement are written by Tian Huisheng and Chen Qin; Assessment Report on Chinese Reading is written by Zhang Pengju and Wang Xiaoxia; Assessment Report on Mathematics is written by Chen Xiaodong; Assessment Report on Science is written by Hu Jun and Yang Baoshan; Assessment Report on Morality and Society is written by Yang Lijuan; Survey Report on Factors Influencing Academic Achievement is written by Ren Chunrong; and Test Instruments are finished based on cooperation between each subject team and the general project team. The final compilation and editing of the holistic report is responded by Tian Huisheng, Sun Zhichang, and Chen Qin. Although many efforts have been made, mistakes and defects are hardly avoided. Comments and criticism are greatly welcome.

The publication of the present report gets the strong support from Educational Science Publishing House. The seriousness and strictness of editing staff makes the report more polished, and we would like to express our appreciation herein together.

Beijing, China

Huisheng Tian
Zhichang Sun

Contents

1	**General Report on Students' Academic Achievement Assessment**	1
1.1	Students' Academic Achievement Assessment—Objective Need to Deepen Basic Education Reform and to Improve the Quality of Education	1
1.2	Research Basis and Main Content of the Present Academic Achievement Assessment	4
1.3	Research Methods and Instruments	4
	1.3.1 Development of Each Subject's Assessment Framework	4
	1.3.2 Technological Line of Assessment—Theory and Method of SOLO Taxonomy	5
	1.3.3 Development of Two-Dimensional Table of Specifications	6
	1.3.4 Development of Test Instruments	6
	1.3.5 Content of Assessment Instruments	8
1.4	Implementation of Students' Academic Achievement Assessment	8
	1.4.1 Selection of Participants	8
	1.4.2 Implementation Procedures	9
	1.4.3 Data Analysis	9
1.5	Quality Analysis of the Present Students' Academic Achievement Assessment	10
	1.5.1 Retrieval Rates of Test Papers and Questionnaires	10
	1.5.2 Analysis of Validity and Reliability, Item Difficulty, Discrimination, and Item Characteristic Parameters of Test Papers	10

1.6	Analysis of Students' Academic Achievement Assessment on Each Subject		12
	1.6.1	General Situation of Students' Academic Achievement Assessment on Each Subject	12
	1.6.2	Specific Analysis of Students' Academic Achievement Assessment on Each Subject	16
1.7	Analysis of Factors Influencing Students' Academic Achievement		22
	1.7.1	Analysis of Basic Condition of Factors Influencing Students' Academic Achievement	22
	1.7.2	Multilevel Model Analysis of Factors Influencing Students' Academic Achievement	43
1.8	Research Conclusions		48
	1.8.1	Students' Academic Achievement	56
	1.8.2	Factors Influencing Students' Academic Achievement	56
1.9	Countermeasures and Suggestions		57
	1.9.1	Drawing Lessons from International Advanced Experience to Implement the Quality Monitoring of the National Education	57
	1.9.2	To Build the Quality Monitoring System of the National Education to Carry Out Continuous Monitoring of the Quality of Education	57
	1.9.3	To Further Transform Students' Learning Way to Improve Students' Ability to Comprehensively Solve Problems	58
	1.9.4	To Improve Schools' Teaching Efficiency and to Reduce Students' Learning Load	58
	1.9.5	To Strengthen the Continuing Education Training of Teachers in the West and in the Countryside and to Improve Teachers' Professional Literacy	59
	1.9.6	To Pay Attention to the Teaching of Science and Morality and Society and to Improve Teachers' Professional Literacy	59
2	**Chinese Reading Assessment Report**		**61**
2.1	Research Background		61
2.2	Theoretical Framework		62
2.3	Research Method and Instrument		65
	2.3.1	The Bases of the Instrument Development	65
	2.3.2	The Procedures of the Instrument Development	66
	2.3.3	Construction of the Two-Dimensional Table of Specifications	68
	2.3.4	The Test Item Writing	68

		2.3.5	Pilot Test and Modification	73
		2.3.6	The Characteristic Parameter of the Test Instrument and Measurement Index of the Test Paper	73
	2.4	Analysis and Discussion on the Reading Test Results		76
		2.4.1	The Overall Complexion of Student Ability Distribution	76
		2.4.2	The Grouping Analysis on Student Ability Performance	78
		2.4.3	The Proportion of Students in Different Ability Groups and the Tasks That Can Be Accomplished	80
		2.4.4	The Corresponding Analysis of Students' Practical Ability Performance and Item Target Test Level	82
	2.5	The Main Findings		88
		2.5.1	The Overall Complexion	89
		2.5.2	The Positive Aspects	90
		2.5.3	The Aspects Which Are Not so Satisfying	91
	2.6	Countermeasures and Suggestions		92
		2.6.1	To Strengthen the Reading Ability Practice and to Optimize the Classroom Teaching Efficiency	92
		2.6.2	To Develop Colorful Extracurricular Reading Activities and to Actively Build Schools with Book Fragrance	92
		2.6.3	To Strive to Form Family Reading Atmosphere and to Build Parent–Offspring Reading Space	92
		2.6.4	To Vigorously Advocate the National Reading to Comply with the Needs of the Information Age	93
3	**Mathematics Assessment Report**			95
	3.1	Research Background		95
	3.2	Theoretical Framework		95
		3.2.1	Definition of Subject Competence	95
		3.2.2	The Present Research Complexion of the Subject Competence Assessment	98
		3.2.3	The Requirement of the New Curriculum Reform for the Subject Competence Assessment	105
	3.3	Research Method and Instrument		107
		3.3.1	The Instrument Development and Its Reliability and Validity	107
		3.3.2	The Testing Time	118
	3.4	Analysis and Discussion on the Test Results		118
		3.4.1	The Overall Complexion of Student Ability Distribution	118
		3.4.2	The Grouping Analysis of Student Ability Performance	119
		3.4.3	The Tasks That Can Be Accomplished by Students in Different Ability Groups	120

		3.4.4	The Corresponding Analysis of Students' Practical Ability Performance and Item Target Test Level	120
	3.5	The Main Findings		133
	3.6	Countermeasures and Suggestions		135
		3.6.1	To Improve Mathematics Curriculum Standard	135
		3.6.2	To Further Transform Students' Learning Approach	135
		3.6.3	To Emphasize and Strengthen the Teaching on Mathematical Thinking Methods	136
4	**Science Assessment Report**			137
	4.1	Research Background		137
		4.1.1	The Development of International Science Academic Achievement Assessment Research	137
		4.1.2	The Development of National Science Academic Achievement Assessment Research	145
	4.2	Theoretical Bases and Main Analysis of the Research		148
		4.2.1	The Theoretical Bases	148
		4.2.2	Definition of Basic Concepts	150
		4.2.3	Reference for Research on Science Subject Competence Assessment	151
		4.2.4	New Requirements for Science Subject Competence Assessment from Our Country's Educational Reform	152
		4.2.5	Specific Requirements for Science Subject Competence Assessment from Our Country's New Curriculum	152
		4.2.6	Basic Views	154
	4.3	Research Aims and Methods		155
		4.3.1	Development of Assessment Framework and Test Instrument	155
		4.3.2	The Characteristic Parameter of the Test Instrument and Measurement Index of the Test Paper	168
		4.3.3	The Testing Time	170
	4.4	Analysis and Discussion on the Test Results		172
		4.4.1	The Overall Complexion of Student Ability Distribution	172
		4.4.2	Distribution of Student Scientific Ability Performance	172
		4.4.3	The Proportion of Students in Different Ability Groups and the Tasks That Can Be Accomplished	175
		4.4.4	The Corresponding Analysis of Students' Practical Ability Performance and Item Target Test Level	179
	4.5	The Main Findings		179
		4.5.1	Overall Complexion	187
		4.5.2	Aspects Improved	189
		4.5.3	Aspects to Be Emphasized	190

	4.6	Countermeasures and Suggestions	191
		4.6.1 To Pay Attention to Science Education in Compulsory Education from the Perspective of "Developing the Country Through Science and Education" Strategy	191
		4.6.2 To Enhance Students' Practice and Mastery of Scientific Basic Knowledge and of Basic Abilities	192
		4.6.3 To Develop Students' Ability to Comprehensively Apply Multiple Skills and to Solve Complicated Problems, and to Thoroughly Improve Students' Comprehensive Quality	192
5	**Morality and Society Assessment Report**		193
	5.1	Research Background	193
	5.2	Theoretical Framework on Students' Social Development Assessment	194
		5.2.1 Taking Students' Social Development as the Basic Assessment Scope and Competence of Morality and Society Subject	195
		5.2.2 Conception Definition and Content Structure of Curriculum Standard-Based Social Development	196
		5.2.3 Visualization on Students' Social Development	199
	5.3	Development of Test Instrument and Test	203
		5.3.1 The Theory and Method of SOLO Taxonomy	204
		5.3.2 Development Procedures of the Test Instrument	205
		5.3.3 Construction of the Two-Dimensional Table of Specifications	206
		5.3.4 Test Item Writing and Examples.....................	206
		5.3.5 Pilot Test and Modifications........................	214
		5.3.6 The Characteristic Parameter of the Test Instrument and Measurement Index of the Test Paper..............	215
		5.3.7 Analysis of Students' Responses to Typical Items	220
	5.4	Analysis and Discussion on the Test Results	227
		5.4.1 The Overall Complexion of Students' Social Development....................................	227
		5.4.2 Grouping Analysis of Students' Social Development Performance	227
		5.4.3 The Proportion of Students in Different Ability Groups and the Level Description of Their Academic Achievement....................................	229
		5.4.4 The Corresponding Analysis of Students' Practical Ability Performance and Item Target Test Level	233

5.5 The Main Findings 245
    5.5.1 Students' Social Development Level Almost Reaches the Requirements of Morality and Society Curriculum Standard, but Students' Holistic Social Ability Is Slightly Low 245
    5.5.2 Students' Mastery of Each Content Domain Is Fairly Balanced, with the Weakness in the Domain of Geography and Environment 246
    5.5.3 Students' Mastery of Basic Knowledge and Basic Skills of Society Is Fairly Satisfying, While the Ability to Solve Problems by Comprehensively Applying Acquired Knowledge Is to Be Improved 247
    5.5.4 The Social Development Test Paper Has Fairly High Stability and Is Quite Scientific 248
5.6 Countermeasures and Suggestions 248
    5.6.1 To Emphasize and Strengthen Morality and Society Curriculum, and Its Teaching and Learning, to Effectively Guarantee the Subject Position 249
    5.6.2 To Build Fairly Stable Teachers' Team and to Improve Their Professional Development 249
    5.6.3 To Transform the Beliefs and Approaches of Teaching and Learning and to Pay Attention to the Development of Students' Internal Thinking Level and the Ability to Comprehensively Solve Problems 250
    5.6.4 To Build the Management Institution of Monitoring and Assessment on Subject Teaching and Learning Quality and the Sustainable Assessment System 251

6 **Survey Report on Factors Influencing Students' Academic Achievement** 253
    6.1 Introduction 253
    6.2 Results and Findings 254
        6.2.1 Holistic Distribution Feature of Students' Academic Achievement 254
        6.2.2 Students' School Learning Situation and Environment 256
        6.2.3 Factors Influencing Students' Academic Achievement—Analysis Based on Multilevel Model 285
    6.3 Conclusions 299
        6.3.1 Influence from Student Individuals and Family Is Stronger than That from Schools for Students' Academic Achievement 299

	6.3.2	Students' Learning Load Is Too Heavy and Their Learning Time Is Not in Direct Proportion to Students' Academic Achievement 299
	6.3.3	The Education Efficiency of Middle and Western Regions Needs to Be Improved 300
6.4	Problems Found in the Survey 301
	6.4.1	Some Teachers Do not Follow Curriculum Plan and the Academic Achievement of Students in Regions with Classes Added or Reduced Is Significantly Lower than That of Those in Regions Where Classes Are Given Seriously Based on Curriculum Schedule 301
	6.4.2	The Aspects of Teaching Way for Self-access Learning and of Teaching Norms for Subjects of Science and Morality and Society Needs to Be Managed with Emphasis................................. 301
	6.4.3	The Quality of Science Teachers' Team Needs to Be Strengthened 301
	6.4.4	There Is Aging Tendency for Teachers' Team in Western Schools...................................... 302
	6.4.5	Western and Countryside Teachers Lack Opportunities of Continuing Education 302

Appendices Sample Items of Assessment Instruments 303

References 347

Chapter 1
General Report on Students' Academic Achievement Assessment

1.1 Students' Academic Achievement Assessment—Objective Need to Deepen Basic Education Reform and to Improve the Quality of Education

In the recent years, with the rise of governments' recognition for the quality of education in countries, it has been a mega trend that real and thorough information of the quality of education and students' development is acquired with scientific research and assessment system to better provide policy foundation for education reform and to provide basis for students' personalized development and sustainable development. The evaluation for the quality of education, i.e., the educational level and degree of its effectiveness, is mainly centralized at learners' developmental level and the academic achievement is the core index to represent the developmental level.

Academic achievement is the developmental level reached by students in the aspects of knowledge, skills, affect and attitude, etc., through learning activities with teachers' direction, based on prior experience.

Regarding the survey and assessment on students' academic achievement, large quantities of theoretical researches and practical exploration have been done nationally and internationally. At present, the fairly influential researches on students' academic achievement are the international comparison researches carried out by the two international organizations of IEA (International Association for Educational Assessment) and OECD (Organization for Economic Co-operation and Development). TIMSS and TIMSS-R programs, hosted by IEA, are mainly to assess students' academic competence in Science and Mathematics. Three types of participants are included in the assessment. The first type is the students aged 9 (in Grade 3 or 4); the second type is the students aged 13 (in Grade 7 or 8) and the third type is the students in the last Grade in secondary school. And TIMSS-R mainly does researches on the second type of students. While PISA (Program for International Student Assessment), hosted by OECD, mainly emphasizes students' competence for practical life when they are adults, including reading literacy, mathematical literacy, and scientific literacy. And the participants are students aged 15. The two programs have great influence internationally due to the strict and delicate assessment dimension, index, instrument, and normative assessment procedures. Besides these programs, many countries regularly carry out students' academic achievement survey on subjects to build national norm and do longitudinal comparative studies, such as NAEP (National Assessment of Educational Progress) in the US, British APU (Assessment of Performance Unit), Japanese National Assessment of Academic Ability, and Cyclical national norm modification in countries of Australia, New Zealand, Switzerland, etc. Abundant experience on knowing the complexion of students' academic achievement and leading students' learning with assessment has been accumulated through these researches.

Due to various reasons, our country does not participate in the survey or research on students' academic achievement carried out by the international assessment organizations, such as IEA and OECD, as a whole entity. Although there is university entrance examination at national level and senior high school entrance examination at district level, their main function is screening and selection. Since 1990s, our country has begun to make some progress on the survey of students' academic achievement. The sampling survey in eight provinces carried out by the union of the previous Department of Basic Education of Ministry of Education, UNICEF (United Nations Children's Fund), and UNESCO (United Nations Educational, Scientific and Cultural Organization) involves 24,000 students in Grades 4 and 6 from near 1300 primary schools and more than 6000 teachers, which is the first macroscopic monitoring on primary school teaching and learning quality in our country.[1] In the recent years, "Research on Primary School Students' Academic Achievement Assessment Reform", the "10th-Five Year" key project of Ministry of Education and "Beijing Assessment of Educational Quality" (BAEQ) program authorized by Beijing Municipal Education Commission, sponsored by Beijing Academy of Education Sciences, "Study on the Academic Management and Assessment in the Implementation of Quality Education in Primary and Middle Schools", the "10th-Five Year" key project of Ministry of Education, sponsored by Shanghai Huangpu District Education Bureau, "Academic Achievement Research of East Asia-Pacific Students", UNICEF program sponsored by Department of Basic Education of Ministry of Education and "National Assessment of Basic Education Quality" program carried out by the National Assessment of Basic Education Center of Beijing Normal University, etc., all do exploration and researches on students' academic achievement. However, these researches lack

---

[1]Shen BY, Meng HW (1996) The present situation of our country' primary school students' learning quality. Yunnan Education 5: 20 (Page quoted. Ditto).

continuing extension or emphasize microscopic aspect or just start, which makes that there is a big distance to build national norm and database reflecting the situation of students' academic achievement in compulsory education.

To sum up, at present, our country lacks a national survey, research, and assessment on academic achievement. The existing academic achievement assessment is still "learning for testing, teaching for testing", in which the theories of psychological and educational measurement are not applied enough and the construction of assessment instruments is mainly based on experience, in deficiency of theories and norms,[2] and the assessments dwell in the survey of the present situation, without much attention to how to accelerate the teaching improvement and students' development. Therefore, against the background that the worldwide countries generally stress, explore, and carry out the macroscopic educational quality monitoring and with the premise that "Two-Basis" (Basis of knowledge and Basis of skills) has been realized, quality education is in thorough implementation, curriculum reform is ongoing and the problems of school running condition and financial devotion have been basically solved; it has vital theoretical meaning and practical value to do the studies on students' academic achievement, to construct fairly high-quality assessment instruments reflecting the situation of local students' development, to carry out students' academic achievement assessment of national basic education period and to analyze the factors influencing the development of students' academic achievement.

On the one hand, students' academic achievement can fill in our country's statistical blank in the national macro-level academic achievement assessment. As a decisive factor to improve the country's competitiveness, the quality of basic education is an important signal of a country's comprehensive national strength. To thoroughly, objectively, and truly know and master the quality of our country's basic education can genuinely and effectively implement quality education to provide feasible and reliable evidence for the policy-making and management of educational administrative departments and to accelerate the realization of the goals of educational fairness and balanced development. On the other hand, it can accelerate the improvement of education and teaching and students' development. Evaluation of students' development, curriculum goals' achievement, and curriculum teaching could be made through large-scale students' academic achievement survey and then scientific basis could be provided for the modification of curriculum policy, formulation of curriculum standards and curriculum implementation, to make assessment play function of accelerating students' development and teachers' improvement and of improving teaching practice, to feasibly advance the deepening of basic education reform and to improve educational quality.

---

[2] Xin T (2006) Academic achievement against the background of new curriculum: value of measurement theory. Journal of Beijing Normal University (Social Sciences) 1: 56.

1.2 Research Basis and Main Content of the Present Academic Achievement Assessment

Regarding students' academic achievement assessment, there are two main types: norm-referenced assessment and criterion-referenced assessment. Norm-referenced assessment is designed to explain individual student's performance or test results by linking with that of an appropriate previous peer group, which is called norm group and the explanation is comparative. And criterion-referenced assessment makes an explanation of individual students' performance or test results in relation to specific standards or performance objectives, not in relation to other students, which is also called absolute assessment. The present academic achievement research mainly employs the mode of criterion-referenced assessment, based on curriculum standards, to carry out national-wide academic achievement assessment of primary school students of different regions and genders in city and countryside. The assessment is to investigate the situation that to what extent students' academic achievement has reached curriculum standards and to deeply analyze the factors influencing students' academic achievement, in order to provide scientific basis for the decision-making of education administrative departments and to provide feedback for subject teaching and students' learning, and then to improve subject teaching quality and to accelerate students to do self-orientation and self-monitoring learning.

The main content of the present academic achievement includes: 1. to construct the index system and instrument suitable for the academic achievement assessment of four subjects of Chinese reading, Mathematics, Science, and Morality and Society of primary school students in Grade 6 in the national context; 2. to carry out the national-wide academic achievement assessment of Chinese reading, Mathematics, Science, and Morality and Society subjects of primary school students in Grade 6, building the database of primary school students' academic achievement to set the foundation for the development of national norm of primary school students' academic achievement; and 3. to analyze the relevant factors influencing primary school Grade 6 students' academic achievement, in order to provide feedback for subject teaching and students' learning, accelerating the improvement of teaching and learning.

1.3 Research Methods and Instruments

1.3.1 Development of Each Subject's Assessment Framework

The present academic achievement survey takes the subjects' requirements for students' development in the two dimensions of subject content and subject competency as basis to develop the basic assessment framework. Subject content means the basic content of subject students should master obviously regulated in curriculum

1.3 Research Methods and Instruments

Table 1.1 Basic assessment framework of primary school Grade 6 subjects

Subject	Content dimension	Competency dimension
Chinese	Characters and words	Recognition and reading
	Sentences and paragraphs	Understanding
	Chapters	Application
Mathematics	Numbers and algebra	Knowledge and skill
	Space and shape	Mathematical thinking
	Statistics and probability	Problem-solving
	Comprehensive application	
Science	Life world	Presentation
	Physical world	Application
	Earth & cosmos world	Inquiry
Morality and Society	Citizen and society	Cognition
	Health and safety	Understanding
	History and culture	Application
	Geography and environment	

standards and subject competency is the level of mastery students should reach required in curriculum standards. The assessment framework of each subject including dimensions of content and competency could be seen in Table 1.1.

1.3.2 Technological Line of Assessment—Theory and Method of SOLO Taxonomy

The present academic achievement survey employs SOLO taxonomy as the basic technological line of each subject's assessment, based on which the index system and instrument of each subject's assessment are constructed and developed. In terms of the complexity of the thinking structure reflected from students' answers to questions of a subject, students' performances are classified into five structural levels by SOLO taxonomy, which are pre-structural level, uni-structural level, multi-structural level, relational level, and extended abstract level.

1. Pre-structural level (P)

Students mistakenly understand questions and lack of the simple knowledge needed to answer the questions. They are obsessed with the prior irrelevant knowledge learned, paying attention to the bits of unconnected information and their answers are not organized and make no sense.

2. Uni-structural level (U)

Students pay attention to topics or questions, but immediately jump to the conclusion with only one relevant cluc or resource.

3. Multi-structural level (M)

Students use two or more clues or resources, but the meta-connections between them are missed, so is their significance for the whole, representing that students can connect a number of isolated events but lack the ability to organically integrate and often give some fragmented information.

4. Relational level (R)

Students are able to use all the available clues or resources and appreciate the significance of the parts in relation to the whole, which becomes the structure with internal consistency within the known system, representing that students can imagine various events and link them to answer or solve fairly complicated concrete questions or problems.

5. Extended abstract level (EA)

Students go beyond the given area, in a new reasoning approach, and generalize some abstract features, representing that students can induce questions and generalize and consider new and more abstract features in induction and the conclusions are open and more abstract.

Primary school students' thinking structure is mainly represented in the three structural levels of uni-structural level, multi-structural level, and relational level. Test items reflecting the three structural levels are designed and constructed by subject experts to assess students' learning outcomes and then the situation of students' academic achievement in the subject could be known and acquired.

1.3.3 Development of Two-Dimensional Table of Specifications

According to the assessment framework, key content goals are selected from the content domains of the subject's curriculum standard. With the combination of ability requirements in curriculum standard, the content goals are transferred into the expected students' learning outcomes, which are marked with the ability classification based on SOLO taxonomy, and then the two-dimensional table of specifications (see subject report) is developed and test items are to be written. Based on SOLO taxonomy, uni-structural (U), multi-structural (M), and relational (R) level test items are designed with the proportion of 2:2:1 in each subject.

1.3.4 Development of Test Instruments

The development of test instruments in the present academic achievement survey includes the procedures of preparation, construction, modification, pilot test, re-modification, and final draft formation.

1.3 Research Methods and Instruments

Preparation period: It is to clarify research aim and research method, to learn SOLO taxonomy, to consult the research results of the related international and national programs, such as IEA, PISA, to analyze the belief of new curriculum reform and Curriculum Standard of every subject, and to make discussions and communication.

Construction period: Based on curriculum standard requirements and SOLO taxonomy, it is to construct the cognitive structural framework of every subject for the primary school Grade-6 students, including the related content domains, curriculum standard requirements, requirements on student ability, and the uni- structural, multi- structural and relational level items with certain proportions.

Modification period: Based experts' discussion and communication, it is to adjust and modify the content in the cognitive structural framework and the predicted difficulty structure design. Regarding the fairly difficult items, it is to make modifications based on students' pilot test results, and to modify the sequence of items and the sequence of options in the items.

Pilot test & re-modification period: It is to choose a number of primary schools in Chaoyang district in Beijing to do the pilot test. According to the analysis results in the pilot test, it is to re-modify and to re-select the content in the cognitive structural framework. Items which are not easily understood or are with too much difficulty are deleted and the quantity of items which is 1.3 times as needed is reduced to be proper. Adjustments on item difficulty structural levels are made as on the sequence of options in the items. The rating scales are modified at the same time.

Final draft period: It is to form the final draft of the cognitive structural framework of the four subjects for primary school Grade-6 students, test items, rating scales, to solve the problems in the layout design and printing in order to make ready for the formal test.

The principles complied with for the development of test instruments in the present academic achievement are as follows:

1. To comply with students' cognitive law and features for their age.
2. To thoroughly consider the content of every domain in the curriculum standard and to select the key requirements of the domains.
3. Stem language should be brief and the illustrations should be clear, with the aim that all-level students can understand the items' requirements, and the language of options should be accurate and have equivalent lengths.
4. The items' structural levels, proportion, quantity, time consumption, and rating scales should be well designed.

1.3.5 Content of Assessment Instruments

The assessment instruments in the present academic achievement survey mainly include test papers of the four subjects of Chinese, Mathematics, Science, and Morality and Society, student questionnaire, and school questionnaire. There are 22 items in Chinese test paper, 37 items in Mathematics test paper, 42 items in Science test paper, and 42 items in Morality and Society test paper. Student questionnaire contains 27 items in which there are 132 subitems in total and school questionnaire contains 30 items. The testing time for Chinese and for Mathematics is 60 min and 50 min for Science and for Morality and Society, respectively. The time to fill in the student questionnaire and school questionnaire, respectively, are 40 min and 20 min.

1.4 Implementation of Students' Academic Achievement Assessment

1.4.1 Selection of Participants

The present academic achievement survey employs the method of stratified random sampling. 18,600 primary school students in Grade 6 are selected from 31 districts and counties out of eight provinces in the east, middle, and west of the country and the number of students finally participated in the test is 18,226, including 68.5% of students from city and 31.5% of students from countryside and 46.6% of students are boys and 53.4% of students are girls. Individual students participate in tests of the four subjects of Chinese, Mathematics, Science, and Morality and Society. The

1.4 Implementation of Students' Academic Achievement Assessment

participants for the student questionnaire are all the students participating in the tests and the participants for the school questionnaire are all the schools participating in the tests, which are 372 schools. The implementation of the present academic achievement has been carried out in May 2009.

1.4.2 Implementation Procedures

Strict training, organization, and management system have been built for the assessment of the present academic achievement survey.

1.4.2.1 Two-Level System of Test Training

First, the national-wide training of test implementation was given by program experts. The specific content of the training includes: Test aims, thoughts of item writing and assessment framework of Chinese, Mathematics, Science, and Morality and Society; organizational requirements of test implementation; composition of test sample and development of student code; the manipulative specifications and problem-solving in the process of test implementation; retrieval and posting of questionnaires and answering to test questions for particular areas. Then, the training of test implementation was given to test schools and participants, which was organized by districts or counties. The specific content of the training includes requirements of test implementation, plan for student code, invigilation arrangement and requirements, etc.

1.4.2.2 Strict System of Test Organization and Management

There are a series of working organization and requirements, including preparation, formal test, check after test, sorting and aggregation, etc., to guarantee the effective retrieval of test papers and to ensure the authenticity and scientificity of the test.

1.4.3 Data Analysis

Item Response Theory (IRT) is applied to calculate the parameters of test papers and student ability in the present academic achievement. With the direction of IRT and one-dimension one-parameter scoring model (Rasch model) as the basis, the analysis of the test quality at the test paper level is done. The indices for the test paper mainly include validity and reliability, item difficulty, discrimination, item characteristic parameters, etc. The analysis of students' academic achievement mainly is to analyze students' overall competence level, situation of subjects' academic achievement and the difference of academic achievement between different regions, city and countryside, genders, etc., based on students' ability parameters.

1.5 Quality Analysis of the Present Students' Academic Achievement Assessment

1.5.1 Retrieval Rates of Test Papers and Questionnaires

In the present academic achievement survey, 18,226 test papers of the four subjects including Chinese, Mathematics, Science, and Morality and Society, 18,226 student questionnaires and 372 school questionnaires are distributed. The retrieval rate for the four subjects is 92.2%, 98.2%, 89.9%, and 98.9%, with 94.6% and 83.3%, respectively, for student questionnaire and school questionnaire (Table 1.2).

1.5.2 Analysis of Validity and Reliability, Item Difficulty, Discrimination, and Item Characteristic Parameters of Test Papers

The present survey results show that the test papers of the four subjects including Chinese, Mathematics, Science, and Morality and Society all have fairly good validity and reliability. The reliability of the four subjects' test papers is above 0.80, with 0.99 or 1.00 as the mean of the infit index, indicating that the content structural validity of the test papers is high, in accordance with the hypothesis of one-dimension ability in Rasch model (Table 1.3). The correlation coefficient between subjects also reaches high significance level (see Table 1.4), which indicates that the test results of each subject's test paper reflect the same type of students' ability.

Table 1.2 Retrieval rates of test papers and questionnaires (%)

	Chinese	Mathematics	Science	Morality and Society	Student questionnaire	School questionnaire
Retrieval number	16,799	17,898	16,378	18,024	17,244	310
Retrieval rate (%)	92.2	98.2	89.9	98.9	94.6	83.3

1.5 Quality Analysis of the Present Students' Academic Achievement Assessment

Table 1.3 Parameter analysis of test papers

	Chinese		Mathematics		Science		Morality and Society	
	Mean	Standard deviation	Mean	Standard deviation	Mean	Standard deviation	Mean	Standard deviation
Infit index	0.99	0.07	0.99	0.07	1.00	0.07	0.99	0.17
Difficulty	0.00	2.38	0.00	1.07	0.00	1.01	0.00	1.03
Point-biserial correlation coefficient	0.16	0.13	0.39	0.08	0.35	0.07	0.27	0.09
Discrimination	1.00	0.11	0.99	0.10	0.98	0.19	1.00	0.06

Table 1.4 Correlation coefficient between test papers

	Chinese	Mathematics	Science	Morality and Society
Chinese	1.000	0.503[a]	0.429[a]	0.473[a]
Mathematics	0.503[a]	1.000	0.601[a]	0.611[a]
Science	0.429[a]	0.601[a]	1.000	0.707[a]
Morality and Society	0.473[a]	0.611[a]	0.707[a]	1.000

Note [a] means reaching significance level of 0.01

From the perspective of the item difficulty, among the four subjects of Chinese, Mathematics, Science, and Morality and Society, the mean of the Mathematics, Science, and Morality and Society item difficulty is 0.00 and standard deviation is approaching 1.00, indicating that the distribution of item difficulty is fairly good and wide; the mean of the Chinese item difficulty is 0.00, and the standard deviation is 2.38, indicating that the distribution of item difficulty is fairly wide.

From the perspective of the item discrimination, except that the point-biserial correlation coefficient of Chinese subject is fairly low, the point-biserial correlation coefficients of the three subjects including Mathematics, Science, and Morality and Society are fairly high, indicating that the item discrimination is fairly good. Meanwhile, the mean is above 0.98 of the four subjects, approaching 1.00, indicating fairly good item discrimination, in accordance with the prediction related to item difficulty in Rasch model.

From the perspective of the item characteristic parameter (see subject report), except some items, almost all the item characteristic curves of items of the four subjects of Chinese, Mathematics, Science, and Morality and Society accord with the IRT model, representing that the higher student ability is, the higher the possibility they can accurately answer the more difficult items, i.e., the probability to respond items with larger difficulty is higher.

1.6 Analysis of Students' Academic Achievement Assessment on Each Subject

1.6.1 General Situation of Students' Academic Achievement Assessment on Each Subject

1.6.1.1 Students' Academic Achievement on the Four Subjects of Chinese, Mathematics, Science, and Morality and Society Basically Reach the Requirements of Curriculum Standards

According to their mastery of curriculum standard, students' performances are classified into five levels of excellent, proficient, qualified, basically qualified, and unqualified in the present survey. Unqualified level means that students have not reached the basic requirements regulated in curriculum standards; basically qualified level means that students have basically mastered the basic knowledge and basic skills required in subjects, but improvements are still needed for some aspects of knowledge and skills; qualified level means that students have fairly thoroughly mastered the basic knowledge and basic skills of subjects, owning basic subject competence; proficient level means that students can comprehensively apply the knowledge and skills acquired to analyze and solve problems; and excellent level means that based on proficient level, students can creatively think and solve problems.

The survey results show that percentages of students reaching qualified level and above exceed 60% on the four subjects of Chinese, Mathematics, Science, and Morality and Society, and the percentages of students reaching basically qualified on the four subjects exceed 90%. And over 95% of students reach basically qualified level and above for the three subjects of Mathematics, Science, and Morality and Society, with less than 10% of students at unqualified level. This indicates that primary school students in Grade 6 all basically reach the requirements of curriculum standards of the four subjects including Chinese, Mathematics, Science, and Morality and Society.

1.6.1.2 The Percentage of Students at Qualified Level and Above Is the Highest in Mathematics and the Lowest in Chinese

The present survey finds that among the four subjects, the percentage of students at qualified level and above is the highest in Mathematics, intermediate in Science and Morality and Society and the lowest in Chinese. From Fig. 1.1, it could be seen that the percentage of students reaching qualified level and above is the highest in Mathematics, which is 78.3%; the percentages for Science and Morality and Society are, respectively, 71% and 67.3%; and the percentage for Chinese is the lowest, which is only 62.8%. Around 30% of students are at basically qualified level for Chinese, i.e., the mastery of some basic knowledge and skills is deficient.

1.6 Analysis of Students' Academic Achievement Assessment on Each Subject

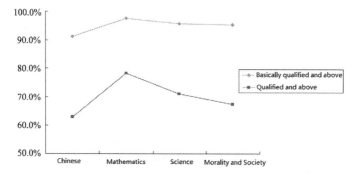

Fig. 1.1 Distribution of students' academic performance on four subjects

Thus, it should get the general support of all society to pay attention to students' mother tongue learning and to improve students' Chinese competence.

1.6.1.3 Students Owning Comprehensive Problem-Solving Ability Are Fewer Than One in Three

The ability that students flexibly apply subject knowledge to solve problems in daily life is an important aspect emphasized in new curriculum standards. The present survey finds that the percentages of students reaching proficient level and above, i.e., students who can comprehensively apply basic knowledge and skills to analyze and solve problems, on the four subjects are all below 30% (see Fig. 1.2). The subject of Science is taken as an example. Only about one in three students can accurately read the temperature of the four types of liquid measured with a thermometer and order them in the sequence from low to high. For the subject of Morality and Society, only 31% of students can flexibly make judgment on school's

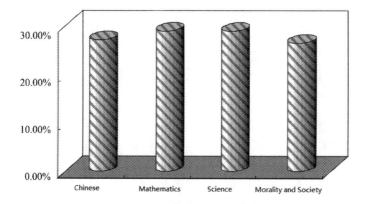

Fig. 1.2 Percentage of students reaching proficient level and above on each subject

practical location based on the position of the Sun in illustration, and then accurately solve problems and find the best way. Therefore, it is important to pay attention to the development of students' ability to comprehensively solve problems in the modification of new curriculum, which should be further emphasized and clarified in the specific curriculum standards.

1.6.1.4 Students' Academic Achievement in the East Is Obviously Higher Than That in the Middle and West and Students' Academic Achievement in the City Is Higher Than That in the Countryside

The present survey indicates that students' academic achievement in the east is obviously higher than that in the middle and west and the difference between them is significant (F = 113.014, P =< 0.05), while the difference between students in the west and in the middle is not significant. From Fig. 1.3, it could be clearly seen that although the percentages of students at basically qualified and qualified levels in the east, middle, and west are almost the same, the percentages of students reaching proficient and excellent levels are obviously higher than that in the middle and west, especially that the percentage of students at excellent level is higher than that in the middle and west both by around 10%, and the percentage of students at unqualified level in the east is obviously lower than that in the middle and west both by near 15%. This indicates that the development of students' ability to comprehensively apply is obviously higher than that in the middle and west.

Second, students' academic achievement in the city is obviously higher than that in the countryside and the difference between them is very significant (Z = −6.63, P = 0.00 < 0.01). From Fig. 1.4, it could be seen that the percentages of students reaching proficient level and excellent level are higher than that of countryside students by near 3%, and the percentages of students at basically qualified level and

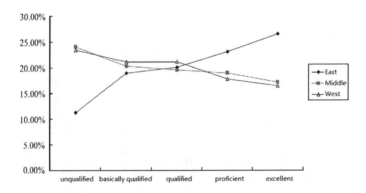

Fig. 1.3 Comparison of students' academic achievement in the east, middle, and west

1.6 Analysis of Students' Academic Achievement Assessment on Each Subject

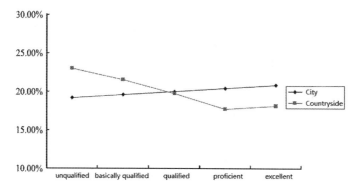

Fig. 1.4 Comparison of students' academic achievement in city and countryside

unqualified level are both lower than that of countryside students, especially that the percentage of students at unqualified level in the city is lower than that in the countryside by near 4%.

To reduce the influence of sampling error, the variables of region and city and countryside are put into multilevel model together to be tested. The model only includes constant, variables of region and city and countryside, and the data stratification is designed into three levels of sample district or county, school, and student. The test results indicate that students' academic achievement in the east is significantly higher than that in the middle and west by 1.755 standard marks (standard error = 0.718, $P < 0.05$) and 2.134 standard marks (standard error = 1.024, $P < 0.05$), and the difference of students' academic achievement in the middle and west is not significant, with 0.379 standard marks (standard error = 0.96, $P > 0.05$) as the difference coefficient. In the same region, countryside students' academic achievement is lower than that in the city by 0.735 standard marks (standard error = 0.335, $P < 0.05$).

1.6.1.5 There Is no Significant Difference Between Male and Female Students' Academic Achievement

The present survey, with non-parameter test, finds that there is no significant difference between male and female students' academic achievement on Mathematics ($Z = -0.10$, $P > 0.05$), male students' academic achievement is higher than that of female students on Science ($Z = -3.86$, $P < 0.05$), and female students' academic achievement is higher than that of male students on Reading and Morality and Society ($Z = -11.48$, $P < 0.05$; $Z = -2.19$, $P < 0.05$). However, with further test of effect size, the findings show that there is no significant difference between male and female students' academic achievement on the four subjects of Chinese, Mathematics, Science, and Morality and Society on average. From Fig. 1.5, it could be clearly seen that the percentages of male students and female students reaching

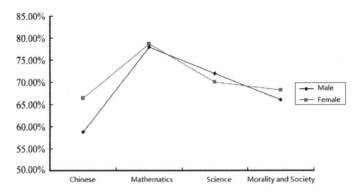

Fig. 1.5 Comparison of students reaching qualified level by gender

qualified level and above are almost equivalent on the three subjects of Mathematics, Science, and Morality and Society. For the subject of Chinese, the percentage of female students reaching qualified level and above is higher than that of male students, indicating that female students' Chinese reading competence is slightly higher than that of male students, but the difference between them is not significant.

1.6.2 Specific Analysis of Students' Academic Achievement Assessment on Each Subject

According to curriculum standard and assessment framework of each subject, based on the analysis of general situation of students' academic achievement, further analysis has been done for each subject from the two dimensions of content and competency, which is mainly through the comparison of students' scorings in different domains and performances on some typical test items to know students' learning situation on each subject.

1.6.2.1 Chinese Subject

The content dimension in the assessment framework of academic achievement on Chinese subject mainly includes the three domains of "Characters and words", "Sentences and paragraphs", and "Chapters" and the competency dimension mainly includes the three domains of "Recognition", "Understanding", and "Application". Students' scoring in different domains could be seen in Table 1.5.

1.6 Analysis of Students' Academic Achievement Assessment on Each Subject

Table 1.5 Students' scoring in each domain of Chinese subject (%)

	Content domains			Competency domains		
	Characters and words	Sentences and paragraphs	Chapters	Recognition	Understanding	Application
Scoring	81	59	63	82	76	27

- Students' performance on "characters and words" is obviously better than that on "sentences and paragraphs" and on "chapters".

In the content domains, students score highest on "characters and words" and the scorings on "sentences and paragraphs" and "chapters" are comparatively low. This indicates that students' performance on "characters and words" is obviously better than that on "sentences and paragraphs" and on "chapters". For example, most students "can accurately understand the definite meanings of words in the language environment" and "can accurately understand the particular meanings of idioms", while about two out of three students "can accurately extract related information from narrative texts", "can accurately understand the main content in the poem", and "can accurately tell the pronunciation of the polyphonic and polysemous characters in the context", and no more than one out of ten students "can accurately understand and use their own language to summarize the main content of the texts" or "can learn from experiencing the expressing effect and evaluate it in their own language".

- Students own the basic abilities to recognize and to understand, while the ability to apply is still to be improved.

In the competency domains, students score highest on "recognition" and "understanding", while the scoring on "application" is comparatively low, and the difference reaches the level of very significance. This indicates that students have already owned the basic abilities to recognize and to understand, but the ability to judge, infer, and apply based on feelings, experience, and comprehension is still to be improved, which is also represented on the tasks that can be completed by students in different ability groups. Students in basic qualified group can understand and apply words and sentences and search information from chapters based on requirements, such as "can accurately apply conjunctions" and "can accurately understand the definite meanings of words in the language environment", etc.; students in qualified group can extract and integrate information in the text and understand the main content of the texts, such as "can accurately extract and integrate related information from the expository texts" and "can accurately understand the main content of the poem", while only students in excellent group can understand and apply in texts, such as "can accurately judge, infer, and express in their own language".

1.6.2.2 Mathematics Subject

The content dimension in the assessment framework of academic achievement on Mathematics subject mainly includes the four domains of "Numbers and algebra", "Space and shape", "Statistics and probability", and "Comprehensive application", and the competency dimension mainly includes the three domains of "Knowledge and skill", "Mathematical thinking" and "Problem-solving". Students' scoring in different domains could be seen in Table 1.6.

- Students' performances on "numbers and algebra" and on "space and shape" are obviously better than that on "statistics and probability" and on "comprehensive application".

In the content domains, students score highest on "numbers and algebra" and "space and shape" and the scorings on "statistics and probability" and "comprehensive application" are comparatively low. This indicates that students' performances on "numbers and algebra" and on "space and shape" are obviously better than that on "statistics and probability" and on "comprehensive application". This is also represented on the specific tasks that can be completed by students in different ability groups. For example, tasks requiring to "indirectly obtain the information related to speed from the time-distance figure", to "obtain the accurate implicit information from the time-distance figure", and to "make calculation based on the numerical relationship in the statistical figures" can only be completed by students in proficient group or above and task requiring to "calculate the circumference of a half circle" can only be completed by students in qualified group or above.

- Students own the basic abilities of "knowledge and skill" and "mathematical thinking", while the ability to solve problems with the application of mathematical rules is still to be improved.

In the competency domains, students score obviously higher on "knowledge and skill" and "mathematical thinking" than on "problem-solving", and the ability to find mathematical rules and to make mathematical inference is still to be improved. This is represented on that task requiring to "make inference based on the found rules" can only be completed by students at qualified level or above, while task requiring to "use the comparison of fraction to make inference" can only be completed by students at proficient level or above. There are more examples, such as that 92% of students can obtain the unknown number based on the equivalent relationship, while only 61% of students can apply equations to solve problems, and

Table 1.6 Students' scoring in each domain of Mathematics subject (%)

	Content domains				Competency domains		
	Numbers and algebra	Space and shape	Statistics and probability	Comprehensive application	Knowledge and skill	Mathematical thinking	Problem-solving
Scoring	81	74	66	65	80	78	64

1.6 Analysis of Students' Academic Achievement Assessment on Each Subject 19

that 82% of students can answer the calculation question on "the situation students meet the basic requirements in the test with the full score unequal to 100", while only 66% of students can solve the practical problems related to fraction.

1.6.2.3 Science Subject

The content dimension in the assessment framework of academic achievement on Science subject mainly includes the three domains of "Life world", "Physical world", and "Earth & Cosmos World", and the competency dimension mainly includes the three domains of "Presentation", "Application", and "Inquiry". Students' scorings in different domains could be seen in Table 1.7.

- Students' performances on the three content domains of "life world", "physical world", and "earth & cosmos world" are quite equivalent.

In the content domains, students score higher on "life world" and "earth & cosmos world" than on "physical world", but the difference is not significant. This indicates that students' performances on the three content domains of "life world", "physical world", and "earth & cosmos world" are quite equivalent. However, comparatively speaking, students' attention to life health and general knowledge of sanitation are more satisfying. More than 80% of students can identify that smoking a lot is most likely to enhance the risk of suffering from bronchitis; 80% of students can realize that it is most likely to cause diarrhea by drinking polluted water; over 70% of students can accurately identify the feature inherited from parents. It could be seen that through Science education, it is beneficial for children, from childhood, to develop good sanitation and living habits, to pay attention to healthy life, to respect life and love life, accordingly to realize people's comprehensive development.

- Students own certain abilities to observe, to analyze, and to solve problems, but the ability to solve fairly complicated practical problems with application of multiple skills is still to be improved.

In the competency domains, students score higher on "presentation" and "application" than on "inquiry". This indicates that students have already owned certain abilities to observe objects, to read diagrams, to analyze data, and to solve simple scientific problems with scientific knowledge and principles, but the ability to analyze and solve fairly complicated practical problems with application of various types of knowledge and multiple skills is still to be improved. For example, 86% of

Table 1.7 Students' scoring in each domain of Science subject (%)

	Content domains			Competency domains		
	Life world	Physical world	Earth & cosmos world	Presentation	Application	Inquiry
Scoring	69	63	68	68	71	60

students can find the main differences between organisms in complete metamorphosis and in incomplete metamorphosis through illustration observation; 70% of students can observe a map and judge the position relationship of three objects; near 60% of students can read line chart and find the relation between time and temperature for a metal to change into liquid from solid; 75% of students can accurately use thermometer to measure and read its display, etc. However, when recognizing the edible part of which common vegetable is root, only 56% of students answer accurately. Although students can identify the features and functions of the six organs of typical plants demonstrated in class, they cannot fully make use of the relationship feature of root and stalk to identify in practice when linking with life; only half of students can find the most efficient method to cool soda water; near half of students cannot find the methods to help reduce friction in daily life, to which near 20% of students mistakenly think that it is to reduce friction when turning with dry cloth on the soft drink bottle; there are 34% of students who choose metal rather than plastic for the material of power switch box, indicating that they cannot choose accurate option by making use of the knowledge acquired that metal is appropriate for electricity conduction material, while plastic, etc., nonmetal materials are appropriate for insulating materials. Only 35% of students can accurately read the display of thermometer and order the temperatures of the four types of liquid in the sequence from low to high; and near half of students cannot analyze experimental data of groups or to make fairly complicated inferences and cannot analyze the relation between three or more members in the food chain.

1.6.2.4 Morality and Society Subject

The content dimension in the assessment framework of academic achievement on Morality and Society subject mainly includes the four domains of "Citizen and society", "Health and safety", "History and culture", and "Geography and environment", and the competency dimension mainly includes the three domains of "Cognition", "Understanding", and "Application". Students' scoring in different domains could be seen in Table 1.8.

- Students' performances are better on "citizen and society", "health and safety", and "history and culture" than that on "geography and environment".

In the content domains, students' scorings on the four domains all are not reaching 70%, indicating that students' academic achievement is holistically low. And the

Table 1.8 Students' scoring in each domain of Morality and Society subject (%)

	Content domains				Competency domains		
	Citizen and society	Health and safety	History and culture	Geography and environment	Cognition	Understanding	Application
Scoring	64	65	64	59	76	57	59

1.6 Analysis of Students' Academic Achievement Assessment on Each Subject

scorings on the three domains of "citizen and society" (64%), "health and safety" (65%), and "history and culture" (65%) are fairly equivalent, indicating that students' performance on the content below is fairly good and quite balanced, such as national sense, globalization sense, consciousness of social rules, and sense of democracy participation; knowing related knowledge of law; mastering the knowledge to keep health and safety; knowing the representative world historical culture; understanding historical knowledge, knowing and understanding important historical events and their influence to analyze and judge historical subjects, etc. Among the four domains, the achievement on "geography and environment" is the lowest (59%), indicating that students' performance on the content below is fairly weak, such as mastering basic geographic knowledge and skills; knowing some basic geographic complexion about China and the world and understanding the relationship between natural environment and people's life; and understanding some environmental and resource problems human beings face.

- Students know fairly well the basic and general knowledge and basic skills of sociality, own initial ability to analyze and to think problems, but the depth and width of thinking are to be extended and the ability to solve problems with flexible and comprehensive application of knowledge acquired is still to be improved.

In the competency domains, students score obviously higher on "cognition" than on "understanding" and "application" and the difference reaches the level of high significance. This indicates that most students have quite satisfying knowledge of sociality and basic skills such as international knowledge, knowledge of law, historical facts, geographic knowledge, life skills, etc. The scorings on the aspects of understanding (57%) and application (59%) are fairly low, not reaching 60%, which indicates that the two abilities are quite weak. Among the two parts of items, it has been found that students' scorings are generally high (over 60%) on items closed to their life experience (such as the rules of democracy in class, issue of quality protection period, safety skills, and results of global warming), on items with fairly direct and singular relationship between subjects (such as the relationship between attitude and temperature, and the relationship between climate and crops, etc.) and on items with the representation of illustrations and diagrams (such as acquiring information on telephone development from the statistical chart and acquiring information related to the relationship between smoking and health from the statistical chart), while the scorings are not high (less than 60%) on the items which slightly surpass their realistic life and present experience (such as earthquake and escaping method, relationship between living way and environment), on items of which the internal logic relationship within subjects is complicated, multiple, and abstract (such as the understanding conceptual meaning of "B.C. and A.D.", relationship between human being and nature, relationship between the price change and supply–demand, and relationship between climate and human being activities) and on the items requiring students to solve problems by flexibly and comprehensively applying various types of knowledge and various abilities (such as the position identifying in combination with realistic situation, choice of self-protection in dilemma, and extracting effective information to do future prediction). This indicates that students have the ability to do initial analysis and thinking of subjects and phenomena by making use of life experience with the help of diagrammatic information. However, the width and depth of their thinking need to be improved and the ability and sense to flexibly apply knowledge acquired and to comprehensively solve problems are to be strengthened.

1.7 Analysis of Factors Influencing Students' Academic Achievement

Regarding factors influencing students' academic achievement, analysis of basic condition of influencing factors has been done first, based on which, analysis with multilevel regression model on these factors is done.

1.7.1 Analysis of Basic Condition of Factors Influencing Students' Academic Achievement

There are various factors influencing students' academic achievement. The present study mainly has done analysis on the basic condition of the four aspects including students' family socioeconomic situation, students' learning, schools' teaching, and management.

1.7.1.1 Family Socioeconomic Factor

Regarding the family socioeconomic status, five aspects including family materialistic condition, parents' educational background, children of floating population, home–school distance, and parent–child interaction are mainly investigated.

1. The general situation of students' family materialistic condition is good. Family materialistic condition in the east is obviously higher than that in the middle and west and family materialistic condition in city is higher than that in countryside.

The present study finds that most families can provide fairly good learning environment and condition for students. The percentage of families with more than 25 books is approaching 70%, while the percentage of families with fewer than 10 books is less than 10%. Families owning a desk specialized for students' study, a quiet place for study, reference books for learning, dictionaries, literature books, poetry works, magazines or newspapers, computer, recorder or audio player in series of MP3 are reaching 70% around and some reach 90% above. The percentage of families with computer access to Internet is near to 50% (Tables 1.9 and 1.10).

1.7 Analysis of Factors Influencing Students' Academic Achievement

Table 1.9 Quantity of books in students' family (%)

Quantity	Overall	School location		Region		
		City	Countryside	East	Middle	West
0–10 books	9.78	4.90	14.40	5.40	12.10	11.90
11–25 books	22.69	16.10	28.40	17.60	25.60	24.70
26–100 books	40.47	41.50	40.50	43.10	38.60	40.90
101–200 books	15.55	20.70	10.90	19.70	13.20	13.80
More than 200 books	11.5	16.70	5.90	14.20	10.50	8.80

Table 1.10 Students' family materialistic condition (%)

Cultural status	Overall	School location		Region		
		City	Countryside	East	Middle	West
Desk for learning	87.54	93.30	81.60	91.90	85.80	82.90
Place for learning	88.26	91.80	85.40	93.20	85.60	86.00
Reference books	85.22	88.70	81.80	87.50	84.60	81.90
Dictionaries	99.06	99.50	98.60	99.40	99.00	98.50
Classical literature books	76.15	86.80	65.90	82.60	75.20	63.40
Art works	56.79	64.90	49.20	66.50	51.10	53.70
Poetry works	69.78	77.80	61.90	76.70	68.30	58.20
Magazines or newspapers	61.77	74.10	49.00	71.60	59.70	44.80
Computer	72.91	82.50	62.70	79.60	70.60	65.00
Access to internet	46.80	64.20	30.90	61.20	40.30	35.10
Recorder or MP3, etc.	75.67	84.65	67.16	80.27	74.81	67.44
Family car	31.05	39.36	22.78	40.27	25.10	30.07

Meanwhile, the present study has also found that learning environment and condition provided by families for students in the east is obviously better than that in the middle and west, among which, the percentage of families owning books reaching 25 or above in the east is reaching 77%, higher than that in the middle and west, respectively, by 15% and 13%. Regarding the aspects of families owning a desk specialized for students' study, a quiet place for study, reference books for learning, dictionaries, literature books, poetry works, magazines or newspapers, computer, recorder, or audio player in series of MP3, the percentage in the east is higher than that in the middle and west from 3 to 27%. Especially on the two aspects of magazines or newspapers and computer access to internet, the difference between east and middle and west is huge. Although family materialistic condition in city is better than that in countryside, the difference is not as obvious as regional difference. On the three aspects of magazines or newspapers, computer, and access to Internet, the difference between city families and countryside families is highly significant.

2. Parents' education level is generally low. Parents' education level in the east is higher than that in the middle and west and parents' education level in city is higher than that in countryside.

The present study finds that the education level of primary school students' parents is mainly junior high school level and senior high school level or technical secondary school level, and the percentage added of both is reaching near 2/3 (about 64.3%), while the percentage of parents with education level at junior college level or vocational technical college is less than 30%. Parents' education level is generally low.

From the perspective of region, the education level of primary school students' parents in the east is mainly junior high school level and senior high school level or technical secondary school level, and their percentages are basically equivalent, while the percentage of junior high school level is higher than that of senior high school level or technical secondary school level in the middle and west. Meanwhile, the percentage of parents with education level at junior college level or vocational technical college in the east is 33.4%, higher than that in the middle and west by 8 or 9%. Especially for parents' education level at undergraduate level and postgraduate level, the percentage is obviously higher than that in the middle and west. From the perspective of city and countryside, parents' education level in city is obviously higher than that in countryside. The education level of students' parents in city is mainly senior high school level or above and its percentage exceeds 70%, while the education level of more than half of parents in countryside is at junior high school level or below. The difference between city and countryside is highly obvious (Table 1.11).

3. The number of students going to school in city with their parents who leave hometown for the city to work is increasing and this phenomenon generally exists in the east, middle, and west.

Table 1.11 Analysis of parents' education level (%)

Education level	Overall	School location		Region		
		City	Countryside	East	Middle	West
Primary school level or below	0.93	0.37	1.36	0.32	1.04	2.08
Primary school level	6.37	3.30	8.73	3.45	7.08	11.19
Junior high school level	34.23	21.38	46.70	30.25	35.97	37.95
Senior high school level or technical secondary school level	30.07	32.39	29.45	32.60	30.05	23.73
Junior college level or vocational technical college	11.19	15.67	6.73	11.90	10.27	12.77
Undergraduate level	13.37	20.37	6.28	16.78	11.93	10.01
Postgraduate level	3.83	6.52	0.76	4.70	3.66	2.26

1.7 Analysis of Factors Influencing Students' Academic Achievement

Table 1.12 Floating population's children (%)

	Overall	Region East	Region Middle	Region West
"Left-behind" children	6.31	4.40	7.40	7.00
Children going to school with parents	12.28	13.70	11.00	13.50

In the recent years, with the number of people who leave hometown for the city to work increases, education receiving of the "left-behind" children whose parent(s) go(es) to city to work and students going to school in city with their parents who leave hometown for the city to work gets the general attention of society. In the present survey, 6.31% of students are the "left-behind" children and 12.28% of students are the children going to school with their parents leaving hometown for the city to work. The percentage of these students in the group of city students reaches 16.4%. Meanwhile, the present study finds that the phenomenon that children go to school in city with their parents who leave hometown for the city to work generally exists in the east, middle, and west (Table 1.12).

4. The distance between students' home and school is generally short, and students in the west spend more time on the way to school than students in the east and middle.

In the present survey, the time spent on the way to school is within half an hour for most students and the percentage is 91.5%. This indicates that the distance between students' home and school is generally short. From the perspective of region, students in the west spend comparatively more time on the way to school. The percentage of students spending more than 30 min on the way to school is 12.95%, higher than that in the east and middle by about 5%. From the perspective of city and countryside, city students and countryside students spend basically equivalent time on the way to school (Table 1.13).

Table 1.13 Time spent on the way to school from home (%)

Time spent	Overall	School location City	School location Countryside	Region East	Region Middle	Region West
Within 10 min	42.47	43.37	42.91	41.55	43.99	39.13
10–30 min	48.99	48.97	47.93	49.86	48.69	47.93
30 min–1 h	7.45	6.96	7.67	7.71	6.38	10.71
More than 1 h	1.10	0.70	1.49	0.89	0.93	2.24

5. Communication and interaction between parents and children are fairly deficient. Parent–child interaction in the east is more than that in the middle and west and parent–child interaction in city is more than that in countryside.

In the present survey, communication and interaction between parents and children are fairly deficient. Although 70.1% of parents can often encourage children to well behave themselves in school, the percentage of parents who often talk about what happens in school with children is only 42%, and the percentage of parents who often talk about the national and international social affairs with children is only 26.8%, and parents who help children with their homework are even fewer, only 11.22%. This indicates that communication between parents and children is mainly simple requirement and encouragement, while parents equally talking with children and helping with their homework are fairly few (Table 1.14).

From the perspective of region, regarding parents' encouragement and help with children's homework, the difference between the east, middle, and west is not obvious. However, regarding the equal communication and interaction, the percentage of parents in the east is obviously higher than that in the middle and west by 10–18%. Meanwhile, the percentage of parents who can equally talk with children in city is obviously higher than that in countryside (Table 1.15).

Table 1.14 Parent–child communication and interaction (%)

	Never	Seldom	Sometimes	Often
My family or friends help me with my homework	24.47	34.75	29.56	11.22
My family encourages me to behave myself in school	2.99	7.20	19.75	70.06
My family talks about the things happening in school with me	8.30	18.38	31.32	42.01
My family talks about the national and international social affairs with me	18.32	27.40	27.49	26.80

Table 1.15 Parent–child interaction (%)

	School location		Region		
	City	Countryside	East	Middle	West
My family or friends help me with my homework	12.60	10.15	12.32	10.88	9.74
My family encourages me to behave myself in school	69.95	70.31	73.69	67.51	70.40
My family talks about the things happening in school with me	49.30	34.47	49.67	39.59	31.93
My family talks about the national and international social affairs with me	34.15	19.66	35.18	23.10	19.62

1.7 Analysis of Factors Influencing Students' Academic Achievement

1.7.1.2 Students' Learning

Regarding students' learning, four aspects including students' interest in learning and devotion, self-access learning, sense of self-efficacy, and learning load are mainly investigated.

1. Students like Chinese and Mathematics much more than Science and Morality and Society, and the time spent is correspondingly more.

The present study finds that out of the four subjects including Chinese, Mathematics, Science, and Morality and Society, 43.64% of students like Chinese most and 44.42% of students choose Mathematics as their favorite subject, while the percentages of students enjoying learning Science and Morality and Society, respectively, are 7.40% and 4.60%. From the perspective of time spent on learning, students spend most time on Chinese and Mathematics, which, respectively, are 42.60% and 47.70%, while the percentages of students spending time on Science and Morality and Society are only 6.80% and 2.90% (Table 1.16).

Regarding the favorite subject, students' teachers own the features as follows: be very responsible for students' learning, can teach based on students' features, their classes are interesting, immediately give positive feedback for students' progress, pay attention to individuals' learning, give extra help to students when they need, have patience and seldom get annoyed to students, etc. (Table 1.17).

However, the present study finds that it is not totally consistent between students' favorite subject and the subject on which they spend most time. Only 38.10% of students spend time most on their favorite subjects.

2. Students' self-access learning ability still needs to be improved.

The present study finds that overall students' self-access learning ability still needs to be improved. Although near three out of four students (73.6%) can actively review the reasons for mistakes in their exercises and test papers and modify them, new curriculum fairly emphasizes the combination of knowledge and life, for example, the percentages of students who often can "actively find examples or evidence of knowledge learned in daily life" and can "manipulate what teachers deliver in class at home" are only 43.70 and 35.0% and over 20% of students never or seldom do

Table 1.16 Students' favorite subject and subject on which time spent most (%)

Favorite subject	Overall	Subject you spend time most			
		Chinese	Mathematics	Science	Morality and Society
Chinese	43.60	39.80	51.00	6.70	2.60
Mathematics	44.40	45.90	44.60	6.50	3.00
Science	7.40	42.70	45.70	9.20	2.40
Morality and Society	4.60	39.50	47.90	6.20	6.40
Overall	100.00	42.60	47.70	6.80	2.90

Table 1.17 Teachers' features of the subject students like (%)

	Complete in accordance	Most in accordance	Partial in accordance	Little in accordance
I like this teacher	74.90	20.30	3.50	1.30
He/she is very responsible for our learning	86.10	11.80	1.60	0.60
He/she can teach based on our features	58.50	30.20	9.30	2.00
His/her classes are interesting and students are very active in their classes	56.80	28.50	11.30	3.40
In this subject classes, I can learn knowledge which could be used in life	75.20	20.60	3.50	0.80
He/she can immediately give positive feedback for my progress, which raises my confidence	67.60	23.70	6.80	2.00
He/she pays attention to individuals' learning	77.30	17.20	4.20	1.30
He/she gives extra help to students only if we need	65.00	25.30	7.30	2.40
He/she has patience and seldom gets annoyed to us	53.30	31.90	10.50	4.20

these. From the perspectives of region and location, self-access learning ability of students in the east is obviously higher than that in the middle and west, and self-access learning ability of students in the middle is significantly lower than that in the west; self-access learning ability of students in city is obviously higher than that of students in countryside (T = 8.12, df = 14299, p = 0.00).

3. Students' sense of self-efficacy is fairly good generally.

Results of the present study indicate that, on the whole, students have a quite good sense of self-efficacy and most students think that the subjects are not difficult and they have confidence for learning and can quickly learn the content required in curriculum. With Mathematics as an example, 73.87 and 91.36% of students think "I find Math difficult to learn well" and "I am confident in learning Math well", 91.26 and 72.20% of students "can learn quickly in Math class" and "can understand even the most difficult question". Meanwhile, among the four subjects, the sense of efficacy for Morality and Society is highest (the average score is approaching 10), and then are for Chinese and Mathematics, and the sense of efficacy for Science is the lowest (the average score is less than 9) (Table 1.18).

4. The problem that students' learning load is too heavy generally exists and there is a difference between the learning load of students in different regions and of students in city and countryside.

The present study finds that it is still a problem that students' learning load is too heavy. There are only 32.8% of students who spend less than 1 h on their school

1.7 Analysis of Factors Influencing Students' Academic Achievement

Table 1.18 Sense of efficacy for each subject (%)

		Levels (%)				Average score
		Complete in accordance	Most in accordance	Partial in accordance	Little in accordance	
Chinese	I can quickly understand the authors' feelings or thoughts	48.03	42.93	8.00	1.04	9.16
	I can understand difficult passages in the textbook	28.60	47.89	20.04	3.48	
	I find Chinese difficult to learn well	6.86	13.79	29.76	49.59	
	I am confident in learning Chinese well	69.62	23.42	5.80	1.16	
Mathematics	I can learn quickly in Math class	55.46	35.80	7.92	0.82	9.01
	Compared with my classmates, I find Math difficult to learn well	9.39	16.74	28.72	45.15	
	In Math class, I can understand even the most difficult question	25.51	46.69	23.80	4.01	
	I am confident in learning Math well	67.64	23.72	6.73	1.92	
Science	I can learn quickly in Science class	44.39	39.21	12.93	3.47	8.87
	I can fully understand the knowledge delivered by teachers	44.75	38.86	13.04	3.35	
	I find Science difficult to learn well	8.24	16.67	34.05	41.03	
	I am confident in learning Science well	55.57	29.54	10.59	4.30	

(continued)

Table 1.18 (continued)

		Levels (%)				Average score
		Complete in accordance	Most in accordance	Partial in accordance	Little in accordance	
Morality and Society	I can learn quickly in Morality and Society class	62.53	29.37	6.21	1.88	9.76
	Since I took Morality and Society class, I have begun to pay more attention to the society and events taking place in the surroundings	59.33	30.86	7.66	2.15	
	I find Morality and Society difficult to learn well	6.14	11.24	29.96	52.66	
	I am confident in learning Morality and Society well	64.43	26.23	6.97	2.37	

Note The full score of students' sense of self-efficacy is 12 and the lowest score is 0

assignment, only 34% of students who never participate in out-of-school training classes or reviewing schools, only 44.40% of students who read extracurricular books from 1 to 2 h, only 32.20% of students doing sports from 1 to 2 h, and only 46.60% of students whose sleeping time can reach 9 h or more every day (Tables 1.19, 1.20 and 1.21).

Meanwhile, the present study finds that there is a difference between the learning load of students in different regions and of students in city and countryside, which mainly reflects in the aspects as follows.

Table 1.19 Students' extracurricular time allocation (%)

	None	Less than 1 h	1–2 h	2–4 h	More than 4 h
Doing housework	12.59	60.26	22.87	3.06	1.22
Doing sports	14.20	45.75	32.19	6.03	1.82
Reading extracurricular books	5.18	33.59	44.44	13.22	3.57
Surfing on the Internet	63.70	22.39	9.80	2.67	1.45
Doing homework	0.61	32.78	43.77	17.57	5.27

1.7 Analysis of Factors Influencing Students' Academic Achievement

Table 1.20 Whether students participate in out-of-school reviewing or training (%)

	Overall	Region			School location	
		East	Middle	West	City	Countryside
No	34.00	44.90	28.30	30.90	28.90	48.20
Yes	66.00	55.10	71.70	69.10	71.10	51.80

Table 1.21 Students' sleeping time (%)

	Total	Region			School location	
		East	Middle	West	City	Countryside
6 h or less	2.40	1.20	3.25	2.13	2.14	2.77
7 h	8.70	6.26	10.72	7.23	8.73	8.51
8 h	42.30	38.38	45.27	41.14	41.43	42.37
9 h or more	46.60	54.16	40.77	49.50	47.69	46.35

- The load of school assignments for students in the middle region is the heaviest. The percentage of students spending over 1 h on school assignment reaches 73.80%, higher than that in the east and west by 18% and near 7%. The school assignment loads for students in city and countryside are almost equivalent.
- Students in the east spend more time on reading extracurricular books than students in the middle and in the west, and students in city spend more time on reading extracurricular books than students in countryside. The percentage of students in the east spend 1 or 2 h on reading extracurricular books, respectively, higher than that in the middle and in the west by about 6% and 3%, and the percentage of students who do not read extracurricular books in the east is lower than that in the middle and in the west by 3%. The percentage of students in city spend 1 or 2 h on reading extracurricular books higher than that in countryside by 8%, and the percentage of students who do not read extracurricular books in city is lower than that in countryside by near 14%.
- Students in the east spend more time on out-of-school reviewing than students in the middle and in the west, and students in countryside spend more time than students in city. The percentage of students in the east participating in out-of-school reviewing and training is near 45%, higher than that in the middle and in the west by about 15%; and the percentage of students in countryside participating in out-of-school reviewing and training is 48.2%, higher than that in city by about 20%.
- Students in the middle spend least time on sports, and the percentage of students who do not do sports or who spend less than 1 h on doing sports is as high as 62.40%, respectively, higher than students in the east and in the west by 4% and 7%. Students in countryside spend less time than students in city, and the percentage of students who do not do sports or who spend less than 1 h on doing sports in city is higher than students in countryside by near 14%.

- The time students in the middle and in the west spend on surfing on the Internet is obviously less than that in the east, and the time spent by students in city is less than that in the countryside. The percentages of students who do not surf on the Internet in the middle and in the west are as high as 67.50% and 70.40%, respectively, higher than that in the east by 12% and by 15%. The percentage of students who do not surf the Internet in city is 57.5%, lower than that in countryside by 18%.
- Time of sleep for students in the middle is obviously less than that in the east and in the west, and there is no significant difference between the time of sleep for city and countryside students. The percentage of students sleeping 9 h or more in the middle is lower than that in the east and in the west by near 15% and by 9%, which is related to the reason that the quantity of school assignment is too large in the middle (Tables 1.22 and 1.23).

1.7.1.3 Teaching in School

Regarding teaching in school, three aspects including teachers' teaching way, class arrangement, and interpersonal relationship are mainly investigated.

1. Support from the teaching of Chinese and Mathematics subjects for students' self-access learning is obviously stronger than that from the teaching of Science and Morality and Society subjects. Support from teachers' teaching in the middle for students' self-access learning is lower than that in the east and in the west, and support from teachers' teaching in city is higher than that in countryside.

The present survey has found that overall, among the four subjects, support from the teaching of Chinese and Mathematics subjects for students' self-access learning is fairly high, while support from the teaching of Science and Morality and Society

Table 1.22 Students' extracurricular time allocation by city and countryside (%)

		None	Less than 1 h	1–2 h	2–4 h	More than 4 h
Doing housework	City	14.15	60.14	22.28	2.34	1.10
	Countryside	9.81	60.45	23.71	4.47	1.56
Doing sports	City	12.21	43.34	35.72	6.73	2.00
	Countryside	18.05	50.92	25.26	4.43	1.35
Reading extracurricular books	City	4.20	29.82	47.42	14.70	3.86
	Countryside	6.98	40.71	39.40	10.06	2.86
Surfing on the Internet	City	57.47	26.39	11.39	3.12	1.63
	Countryside	75.96	14.64	6.64	1.83	0.93
Doing homework	City	0.58	32.42	44.13	17.42	5.44
	Countryside	0.64	35.87	43.19	16.10	4.20

1.7 Analysis of Factors Influencing Students' Academic Achievement

Table 1.23 Students' extracurricular time allocation by region (%)

		None	Less than 1 h	1–2 h	2–4 h	More than 4 h
Doing housework	East	8.62	64.74	22.99	2.72	0.93
	Middle	15.64	57.85	22.31	2.91	1.29
	West	11.30	57.95	24.60	4.48	1.67
Doing sports	East	9.81	48.55	34.26	5.72	1.66
	Middle	17.35	45.02	29.71	5.98	1.95
	West	13.58	41.53	36.17	7.00	1.72
Reading extracurricular books	East	3.11	33.01	48.03	12.92	2.94
	Middle	6.34	33.62	41.91	13.92	4.20
	West	6.10	34.90	44.79	11.40	2.82
Surfing on the Internet	East	55.35	29.39	11.70	2.42	1.13
	Middle	67.53	19.67	8.46	2.80	1.55
	West	70.37	15.01	9.96	2.82	1.85
Doing homework	East	0.46	43.83	41.99	11.52	2.19
	Middle	0.72	25.47	44.47	21.78	7.56
	West	0.58	32.14	45.62	17.15	4.51

subjects for students' self-access learning is comparatively low. With the example of "encourage students to propose questions", Chinese teachers who can often do this are 69.10%, Mathematics teachers are 60.10%, Science teachers are 44.90% and Morality and Society teachers are 47.30%. With another example of "organize students into groups to discuss questions", Chinese teachers who can often do this are 51.30%, Mathematics teachers are 45.10%, Science teachers are 36.40% and Morality and Society teachers are 35.00%.

From the perspectives of region and city and countryside, support from teachers' teaching in the middle for students' self-access learning is slightly lower than that in the east and in the west, and support from teachers' teaching in city is higher than that in countryside. With the example of "encourage students to propose questions", the percentage of teachers of the four subjects who can often do this in the middle is lower than that in the east and in the west by about 3–10%; and the percentage of city teachers is higher than that of countryside teachers by about 6–8%. With another example of "listen to teachers most of time in class", the percentage of teachers who often do this in the middle is higher than that in the east and in the west by about 5–12%, and the percentage of city teachers is lower than that of countryside teachers by about 2–4%; the phenomenon that teachers in the middle and in countryside do class cramming is fairly common (Tables 1.24 and 1.25).

Table 1.24 Teachers' teaching ways of each subject

		Level			
		Never	Seldom	Sometimes	Often
Chinese	Teachers encourage us to propose questions	2.25	6.99	21.69	69.08
	Teachers guide us to read out passages in textbooks in different ways	2.71	8.57	22.34	66.39
	Teachers require us to silently read passages in textbooks independently	1.97	8.44	28.09	61.50
	Teachers guide us to grasp key sentences or words to understand the main idea	0.75	2.30	10.85	86.10
	Teachers divide us into groups for discussion	4.81	13.65	30.26	51.28
	Teachers allow different understanding of the texts in class	4.59	9.41	26.29	59.71
	Teachers give us instruction to read extracurricular books	2.71	8.03	22.44	66.82
	In class, most of the time is devoted to listening to teachers	6.83	17.23	33.47	42.47
Mathematics	Teachers encourage us to propose questions	2.26	8.90	28.80	60.05
	Teachers encourage us to solve problems in different ways	0.99	4.21	18.89	75.91
	Teachers encourage us to talk about our thoughts bravely	1.56	3.55	9.67	85.22
	Teachers can elicit mathematical questions from our learning and living environment	1.99	8.24	27.68	62.09
	Teachers divide us into groups for discussion	6.86	17.21	30.86	45.07
	Teachers always tell us the key to the question in a hurry	65.09	25.87	5.32	3.72
	Teachers ask us to find examples in daily life when delivering new knowledge	2.20	7.73	27.71	62.37
	In class, most of the time is devoted to listening to teachers	5.54	19.20	34.97	40.29

(continued)

1.7 Analysis of Factors Influencing Students' Academic Achievement

Table 1.24 (continued)

		Level			
		Never	Seldom	Sometimes	Often
Science	Teachers encourage us to propose questions	10.27	19.31	25.48	44.94
	We observe teachers conducting scientific experiments	13.69	21.59	27.85	36.87
	Scientific experiments or investigation plans are made under teachers' guide	15.01	20.86	26.85	37.28
	We do experiments or investigations independently	18.32	27.29	28.36	26.03
	We form groups with classmates to do experiments or investigations	17.35	20.68	25.62	36.35
	We make a note of the process and the result of experiments and investigations by ourselves	17.09	23.62	26.66	32.64
	We give a report and share our achievements in class	15.91	20.35	24.55	39.19
	In class, most of the time is devoted to listening to teachers	7.73	17.82	31.86	42.60
Morality and Society	Teachers encourage us to propose questions	10.49	17.61	24.65	47.25
	We learn this subject on our own by reading books	23.42	29.53	27.46	19.58
	We usually do self-learning or do homework of other subjects	44.73	25.40	16.34	13.54
	Teachers ask us to look for materials and give a report and share with other students in class	13.87	18.29	31.21	36.63
	We form groups with classmates for discussion and for doing social investigations	18.65	21.66	24.68	35.02
	The entire class goes out for visits or does social practices together	38.51	24.11	18.50	18.88
	Teachers organize students to do role-plays or practice according to what we learn	30.16	24.52	22.27	23.05
	In class, most of the time is devoted to listening to teachers	9.32	18.17	30.86	41.66

2. The phenomenon that class hours are used for other things is still generally common.

The present survey has found that teachers of the four subjects including Chinese, Mathematics, Science and Morality and Society who can follow class hour regulation to teach are only about 60% and the phenomenon that class hours are used for

Table 1.25 Teaching ways by region and location (%)

			Region			School location	
			East	Middle	West	City	Countryside
Teachers encourage us to propose questions	Mathematics	Never	1.86	2.69	1.62	2.16	2.30
		Seldom	8.16	9.18	9.69	8.14	10.27
		Sometimes	27.45	29.89	28.12	27.76	31.21
		Often	62.53	58.24	60.57	61.94	56.22
	Chinese	Never	1.46	2.93	1.70	2.29	2.10
		Seldom	5.96	7.69	6.94	6.48	7.87
		Sometimes	19.80	23.57	19.48	19.96	24.97
		Often	72.78	65.81	71.89	71.28	65.06
	Science	Never	7.14	12.98	8.07	10.06	10.57
		Seldom	17.62	20.47	19.26	17.52	22.60
		Sometimes	24.57	25.77	26.71	24.51	27.60
		Often	50.68	40.78	45.97	47.91	39.24
	Morality and Society	Never	7.56	13.05	8.34	10.64	9.79
		Seldom	15.98	19.21	15.73	16.53	19.43
		Sometimes	23.87	24.86	25.82	23.06	27.74
		Often	52.59	42.87	50.10	49.78	43.03
In class, most of the time is devoted to listening to teachers	Math	Never	6.64	4.64	6.13	6.29	3.90
		Seldom	22.16	15.75	24.55	19.89	18.37
		Sometimes	35.77	34.32	35.39	35.13	35.51
		Often	35.43	45.30	33.93	38.69	42.22
	Chinese	Never	7.27	5.64	10.13	7.95	4.81
		Seldom	20.46	14.49	19.25	17.40	17.63
		Sometimes	34.33	33.21	32.30	33.51	34.35
		Often	37.93	46.66	38.33	41.14	43.22
	Science	Never	7.97	7.83	6.79	8.46	5.30
		Seldom	19.88	14.96	23.20	18.64	17.23
		Sometimes	32.72	31.24	31.99	31.45	33.11
		Often	39.44	45.97	38.03	41.44	44.36
	Morality and Society	Never	9.36	9.53	8.42	10.27	7.21
		Seldom	19.72	15.48	24.22	18.88	16.94
		Sometimes	31.24	30.29	31.98	30.20	32.75
		Often	39.68	44.70	35.37	40.65	43.10

other things is still generally common. For Chinese and Mathematics subjects, the class hours are usually added, which are 41 and 36%, while the class hours of Science and Morality and Society are usually reduced, with the percentages of 40 and 42%.

1.7 Analysis of Factors Influencing Students' Academic Achievement

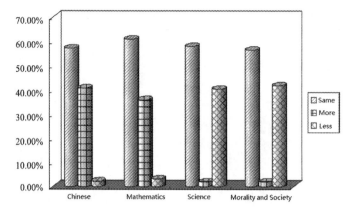

Fig. 1.6 Situation of each subject's actual classes

From the perspectives of region and city and countryside, the situation that teachers in the middle follow the classes planed in schedule is the worst, the percentages of the class hour addition for Chinese and Mathematics are higher than that in the east and in the west by about 10%, and the situation that class hours for Science and Morality and Society are reduced is serious. The percentage of the class hour reduction for Science is higher than that in the east and in the west by 16% and by 14%, and the percentage of the class hour reduction for Morality and Society is higher than that in the east and in the west by 18% and by 11%. The situation that class hours for Chinese and Mathematics are added and class hours for Science and Morality and Society are reduced in countryside schools is more serious than that in city schools (Fig. 1.6 and Table 1.26).

3. Students have a quite good interpersonal relationship in schools and have a sense of safety.

The present survey has found that most students have a sense of safety in schools and have a quite good interpersonal relationship. About 90% of students reflect that they feel safe in schools, it is easy to make friends, schoolmates like them and they are treated equally; teachers care students, can have conversations with students in an equal way, can promptly give a hand to students when they have difficulties and can give students appropriate praise and encouragement, etc.

Meanwhile, it has been found that about 10% of students do not feel safe in school. And 12% of students think they do not get equal treatments in schools and what is more, over one third (36.35%) of students think that there is bully or insulting phenomenon among students. These negative feelings are fairly obvious for the group of students with low academic achievement. Therefore, it is an important issue for school development to strengthen the development of school atmosphere and to create fairly good interpersonal environment for students (Table 1.27).

Table 1.26 Comparison on actual classes between different regions and city and countryside (%)

		Region			School location	
		East	Middle	West	City	Countryside
Actual classes of Chinese subject versus class schedule	Less	1.75	2.95	1.34	1.76	3.47
	Same	68.36	49.04	58.29	59.21	54.76
	More	29.89	48.01	40.38	39.03	41.77
Actual classes of Mathematics subject versus class schedule	Less	1.90	3.64	4.77	2.28	4.60
	Same	71.50	52.38	66.21	63.85	58.86
	More	26.60	43.98	29.03	33.86	36.53
Actual classes of Science subject versus class schedule	Less	31.47	47.56	34.76	36.37	44.82
	Same	67.30	49.91	64.32	62.04	52.81
	More	1.23	2.53	0.92	1.58	2.37
Actual classes of Morality and Society subject versus class schedule	Less	31.62	49.48	38.55	40.21	42.75
	Same	66.98	48.33	59.57	58.11	54.94
	More	1.40	2.19	1.88	1.68	2.30

Table 1.27 Students' interpersonal relationship in schools (%)

	Totally agree	Agree	Disagree	Totally disagree
I can easily make friends in school	61.90	30.92	5.68	1.49
It seems that my schoolmates like me very much	36.64	47.47	13.30	2.59
There is no bully or insulting phenomenon among students	33.07	30.57	26.63	9.72
I can get an equal treatment in school	53.67	34.19	8.99	3.15
I feel safe in school	58.60	30.90	7.86	2.64
I feel that I am an outsider in school	5.29	6.11	24.34	64.26
I like my school	64.51	32.26	2.31	0.93
Teachers care students much	65.21	31.66	2.33	0.80
Teachers can have conversations with students in an equal way	51.56	37.51	8.96	1.97
When I have difficulties, teachers can give a hand promptly	60.09	33.87	4.96	1.08
Teachers give me appropriate praise and encouragement	62.27	33.23	3.62	0.88

1.7.1.4 School Management

Regarding school management, four aspects including quality of school principals, quality of teachers, condition for school running and teaching and research activities and family-school communication have been surveyed and analyzed.

1. For principals, the percentage of female principals is fairly large, age of principals has the tendency to be younger, and principals' degree is generally high.

The present survey has found that the percentage of female principals in primary schools is gradually higher, primary school principals are becoming younger and principals' degree is generally high. Among the 303 schools in the present survey, the percentage of female principals is 37.10%, with the average age of 43.8 years and average teaching age of 23.8 years, and 59.6% of principals have bachelor's degree or above.

2. The degree of city teachers is apparently higher than that of countryside teachers and the degree of countryside Science teachers is fairly low.

The present survey indicates that no matter in countryside or in city, the academic qualification rate of primary school teachers reaches 99% and teachers with bachelor's degree or above also reaches 45.50%. However, the percentage of city schools with teachers owning bachelor's degree or above is 50.40%, while that for countryside is 32.40%. Meanwhile, further comparison on teachers' academic qualification of different subjects between city and countryside shows that regarding the teachers owning bachelor's degree or above, the total percentage of Chinese teachers is 40.80%, with 42.60% and 35.90%, respectively, for city and countryside; the total percentage of Mathematics teachers is 33.80%, with 36% and 27.90%, respectively, for city and countryside; the total percentage of Science teachers is 31.70%, with 37.60% and 23%, respectively, for city and countryside; and the total percentage of Morality and Society teachers is 37.30%, with 43% and 27.20%, respectively, for city and countryside. It could be seen that Chinese teachers' academic qualification all comparatively high no matter in countryside or in city, while the academic qualification of countryside Science teachers is apparently lower.

3. Middle-aged teachers and the youth are the main part of primary school teachers' group and the average age of teachers in the west is apparently higher than that in the east and in the middle.

The present survey indicates that middle-aged teachers and the youth are the main part of primary school teachers' group for each subject, particularly for Chinese teachers, the percentage of teachers aged 40 or below is 76.40% out of total, higher than other three subjects by 12% around. From the perspective of region, the percentage of teachers aged 51 or above is fairly high, with more than 15% for each subject, higher than the average by 5–8% for each subject. The age difference between city and countryside teachers is not apparent (Fig. 1.7).

4. The opportunities for teachers to participate in training are few, with that for countryside are fewer than that for city.

The present survey has found that the average frequency for Grade 6 teachers of Chinese, Mathematics, Science and Morality and Society to participate in training is about once a year, among which, the opportunities for Morality and Society teachers to participate in training are the fewest. Opportunities for teachers of each subject in countryside schools are apparently fewer than that for city teachers, especially for Science and Morality and Society teachers, opportunities to participate in training are fewer than that for city teachers by about half (Fig. 1.8).

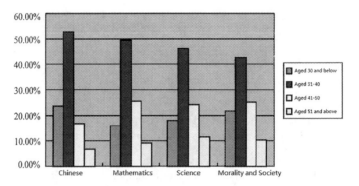

Fig. 1.7 Teachers' age distribution by subject

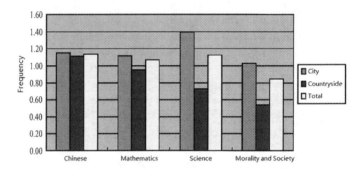

Fig. 1.8 Teachers' opportunities to participate in training by subject

5. The school running condition for schools in the east is apparently better than that in the middle and in the west.

The present survey has found that the school running condition for schools in the east is apparently better than that in the middle and in the west, which is mainly represented in the aspects as follows.

First, from the number of computers, among the 303 primary schools surveyed, every 11 students own 1 computer on average, in which, every 8 students own 1 computer in the east, 13.7 students in the middle and 15.8 students in the west; 10.8 students own 1 computer in city, while 11.9 students in countryside.

Then, from the number of computers for teachers to prepare classes, every 2.3 teachers own 1 computer for class preparing on average, in which, every 1.4 teachers own 1 computer for class preparing in the east, 3.8 teachers in the middle and 5 teachers in the west; 2.2 teachers own 1 computer for class preparing in city, while 2.8 teachers in countryside.

Third, from the area of functional classroom for each student, the total average size is 1.31 m^2, with the area of functional classroom for each student below 1.36 m^2 for 75% of schools. And the average area is 1.94 m^2 for the east, 0.89 m^2

1.7 Analysis of Factors Influencing Students' Academic Achievement

for the middle and 1.04 m² for the west; the average area is 1.35 m² for city, while 1.27 m² for countryside.

Fourth, from the number of books for each student, the total average number is 15.89 books, in which the average number is 21.03 books for the east, 11.32 books for the middle and 19.62 books for the west; the average number is 17.64 books for city, while 13.55 books for countryside.

Fifth, from the experimental equipment, experimental equipment in 46% of schools cannot satisfy the requirement for grouping experimental teaching regulated in textbooks, in which, the percentages of schools choosing "basically can satisfy" and above in the east and in the middle are about 70%, while the percentage reaches 75% in the west. It needs to find out the reason that the school running condition has been improved a lot with the strong support of the nation or the similarity is caused by the west teachers' misunderstanding of the grouping experimental teaching requirements regulated in the textbooks or their standard is fairly low. The percentage of schools in the city choosing "basically and fully can satisfy teaching requirements" is about 7% higher than that in the countryside (Table 1.28).

6. The school and district teaching research activities are comparatively fewer, research activities on teaching in school in the east and in the middle are more than that in the west and research activities on teaching in school in city are more than that in countryside.

In the 303 schools surveyed in the present research, the average duration of new curriculum implementation is 6.38 years. All schools can participate in or organize types of teaching research activities, in which, the subject groups in 52.98% of schools organize teaching research activities at least once a week, and the grade groups in 42.23% of schools organize teaching research activities at least once a week. However, the frequency for entire school teachers' teaching research activities or district teaching research activities is fairly low. 43.79% of schools organize entire school teachers' teaching research activities two to three times every semester and 62.25% of schools participate activities at district level or above two to three times every semester. The frequency for the teaching research activities of schools in the east, in the middle and in the west goes lower and lower. And the percentages of schools with subject groups organizing teaching research activities at least once a week in the east and in the middle are higher than that in the west by 30 and 20%. Regarding the participation in district activities, the percentages of schools choosing once a month both in the east and in the middle reach 30% above, while

Table 1.28 Whether experimental equipment can satisfy the requirements of grouping experimental teaching regulated in the textbooks (%)

	Total	City	Countryside	East	Middle	West
Fully cannot satisfy	20.62	16.87	25.00	7.62	30.26	17.65
Basically cannot satisfy	25.43	25.90	25.00	21.90	32.24	5.88
Basically can satisfy	41.58	44.58	37.90	52.38	31.58	52.94
Fully can satisfy	12.37	12.65	12.10	18.10	5.92	23.53

the percentage is only 8% in the west. The frequency for city schools' teaching research activities is apparently higher than that of countryside schools, and the percentage difference is 10% for the subject groups' teaching research activities at least once a week, and the percentage difference is 24% for that of grade groups. And for the participation in teaching research activities at district level or above one to two times every month, the percentage is higher for city schools than for countryside schools by 10% (Table 1.29).

Table 1.29 Complexion of research activities on teaching in school (%)

		Total	Region			School location	
			East	Middle	West	City	Countryside
Subject groups' teaching research activities	At least once a week	52.98	63.06	50.97	30.56	56.74	47.15
	One to two times every month	38.08	34.23	34.84	63.89	37.64	39.02
	Two to three times every semester	8.94	2.70	14.19	5.56	5.62	13.82
	Never	0.00	0.00	0.00	0.00	0.00	0.00
Grade groups' teaching research activities	At least once a week	42.23	55.56	35.48	30.30	51.98	27.12
	One to two times every month	35.14	37.04	36.77	21.21	35.03	35.59
	Two to three times every semester	16.89	5.56	21.29	33.33	10.17	27.12
	Never	5.74	1.85	6.45	15.15	2.82	10.17
Entire school teachers' teaching research activities	At least once a week	15.69	13.51	18.35	10.81	17.98	11.81
	One to two times every month	39.87	43.24	33.54	56.76	38.76	41.73
	Two to three times every semester	43.79	42.34	47.47	32.43	42.13	46.46
	Never	0.65	0.90	0.63	0.00	1.12	0.00
Participation in district teaching research activities	At least once a week	4.64	6.48	4.43	0.00	6.21	2.42
	One to two times every month	30.79	38.89	30.38	8.33	35.03	25.00
	Two to three times every semester	62.25	54.63	63.92	77.78	55.93	70.97
	Never	2.32	0.00	1.27	13.89	2.82	1.61

1.7.2 Multilevel Model Analysis of Factors Influencing Students' Academic Achievement

With the employment of multivariate regression analysis, the present survey has tested factors influencing students' academic achievement. The academic achievement sum of the four subjects is treated as dependent variable, with the four groups of variables including students' family, students' learning, teaching in school and school management, etc., introduced to generate five models (Specific results of each model could be seen in the questionnaire survey report).

Based on the prior four models, the complete model makes significant variables from the four groups of variables, including students' family, students' learning, teaching in school and school management, added together into the model to participate in the calculation. The results show that the interclass correlation at student individual level is 43.27%, the interclass correlation at school level is 36.40% and the interclass correlation at regional level is 20.33%. This indicates that the difference of students' academic achievement is mainly caused by the difference of the aspects including individuals and family. The percentages of variances explained at individual level, school level and regional level are 22.67, 33.24 and 32.93% and the percentage of total variance explained is 28.98%.

The specific analysis of the influence on students' academic achievement by factors of the four aspects including students' family, students' learning, teaching in school, and school management is done as follows.

1.7.2.1 Students' Family Factor

The present survey shows that in the aspect of student family, factors which produce significant influence on students' academic achievement mainly include family materialistic and cultural situation, parents' educational background, distance between home and school, parent–child interaction, etc. Whether students are left-behind children by their parents or go to the city with their parents and study there and the influence of variables of city or countryside and region are explained by the effects of other factors.

1. The better the students' family materialistic and cultural situation is, the higher the students' academic achievement is.

In the aspect of family materialistic and cultural situation, the results show that although there is no significant difference on the academic achievement between students with fewer than 10 books in their family and those with from 11 to 25 books, students' academic achievement level gradually rises when there are more books in students' family and the difference reaches significant level. Specifically, with other background variables controlled the same, the academic achievement of students with from 26 to 100 books, from 101 to 200 books, and more than 200 books in family is higher than that of students with fewer than 10 books in family by 0.17 marks, 0.22 marks, and 0.41 marks, respectively. And other family materialistic conditions, such as particular learning space, computer, types of books, etc., also make significant influence on students' academic achievement. Every 1 mark increases for the variable of student family, 0.07 marks is raised for students' academic achievement.

2. The higher parents' education degree is, the higher students' academic achievement is.

The present survey indicates that parents' educational background is another important factor influencing students' academic achievement. Taking parents' education degree at junior high school level as reference, the higher the parents' education degree is, the higher the students' academic achievement is. Specifically, with other background variables controlled the same, the academic achievement of students whose parents' education degree at junior college level or vocational technical college, at undergraduate level and at postgraduate level is higher than that of students whose parents' education degree at junior high school level by 0.26 marks, 0.54 marks, and 0.64 marks, respectively.

3. The more time students spend on the way to school, the lower their academic achievement.

The present survey indicates that family-home distance is a significant variable influencing students' academic achievement. The more time students spend on the way to school, the lower their academic achievement. Specifically, with other background variables controlled the same, the academic achievement of students who spend from 30 min to 1 h and more than 1 h on the way to school is lower than that of students who spend less than 30 min by 0.12 marks and 0.52 marks, respectively.

4. The higher the frequency of parent–child interaction is, the higher the students' academic achievement is.

The present survey indicates that parent–child interaction is one of the variables influencing students' academic achievement. Equal parent–child communication can positively affect students' academic achievement. With other background variables controlled the same, the academic achievement of students who can "often" talk with their parents about what takes place in school is higher than that of students who "never" "seldom" or "sometimes" talk with their parents by 0.35 marks, 0.10 marks and 0.12 marks, respectively; the academic achievement of students who can "often" talk with their parents about the national and international social affairs is higher than that of students who "never", "seldom", or "sometimes" talk with their parents by 0.19 marks, 0.03 marks, and 0.01 marks, respectively. However, family support in lack of interaction, such as "family encourages me to behave myself in school", does not have significant influence on students' academic achievement; and the academic achievement of students whose family help with their homework at high frequency is significantly lower than that of students whose family help with their homework at low frequency, which might be in that students whose academic achievement is fairly weak need help. This is also represented in the posterior relationship between students' learning independence and their academic achievement, showing that the stronger the students' learning independence is, the higher their academic achievement is.

1.7.2.2 Students' Learning

The present survey indicates that in the aspect of students' learning, factors which produce significant influence on students' academic achievement mainly include learning efficacy and learning load. Students' learning autonomy has no significant influence on their academic achievement, which needs to be further researched.

1. The stronger the students' learning efficacy is, the higher the students' academic achievement level is.

The present survey indicates that students' efficacy for Mathematics and Science learning has a significant correlation with their academic achievement. The stronger the students' efficacy for Mathematics and Science learning is, the higher the students' academic achievement level is. Specifically, with the condition that other background variables are the same, every 1 factorial mark increased to students' efficacy for Mathematics and Science learning, 0.23 and 0.03 standard scores, respectively, are raised to students' academic achievement.

2. The heavier the students' learning load is, the lower the students' academic achievement level is.

The present survey indicates that students' time allocation, including sleep, reading extracurricular books, extracurricular reviewing participation, sports, entertainment, etc., has significant influence on students' academic achievement. The heavier the students' learning load is, the lower the students' academic achievement level is.

First, the less the students' sleeping time is, the lower the students' academic achievement level is. With other background variables controlled the same, the academic achievement of students who sleep less than 6 h is lower than that of students whose time of sleep is 9 h or more by 0.66 standard scores.

Second, the academic achievement of students who do not participate in extracurricular reviewing is not necessarily lower than that of students who participate in extracurricular reviewing. Specifically, the academic achievement of students who do not participate in extracurricular reviewing on Mathematics is significantly higher than that of students who participate for less than 1 h by 0.37 standard scores, and has no significant difference with that of those who participate for 1–2 h and for 2–4 h, but is lower than that of students who participate for more than 4 h by 0.29 standard scores. The academic achievement level of students who do not participate in extracurricular reviewing on Chinese is significantly higher than that of students who participate for different lengths of time. There is no significant difference between the academic achievement level of students who do not participate in extracurricular reviewing on Science and that of those who participate in reviewing. Besides, the academic achievement level of students who do not participate in other extracurricular reviewing is higher than that of students who participate for 1–2 h by 0.17 standard scores and has no significant difference with that of those who participate in other reviewing for different lengths of time.

Third, there is no significant correlation between students' daily time length for school assignment and their academic achievement, i.e., long time students spend on school assignment every day does not necessarily result in high academic achievement level.

Fourth, the academic achievement level of students who read extracurricular books every day is significantly higher than that of those who do not read extracurricular books. Specifically, with the condition that other background variables are controlled the same, the academic achievement level of students who read extracurricular books for less than 1 h, for 1–2 h, for 2–4 h, and for more than 4 h, respectively, is higher than that of students who do not read extracurricular books by 0.30, 0.38, 042, and 0.37 standard scores.

Fifth, there is no significant difference between the academic achievement level of students who surf on the Internet for less than 2 h every day and that of those who do not surf on the Internet. However, the academic achievement level of students who surf on the Internet for more than 2 h every day is significantly lower than that of those who do not surf the Internet. Specifically, with the condition that other background variables are the same, the academic achievement level of students who surf on the Internet for 2–4 h and for more than 4 h every day, respectively, is lower than that of students who do not surf on the Internet by 0.26 and 0.55 standard scores.

Sixth, there is no significant difference between the academic achievement level of students who do sports within 1 h and that of those who do not do sports. However, the academic achievement level of students who do sports for a long time is significantly lower than that of those who do not do sports. Specifically, with the condition that other background variables are the same, the academic achievement level of students who do sports for 1–2 h, for 2–4 h and for more than 4 h every day, respectively, is lower than that of students who do not do sports by 0.18, 0.43 and 0.80 standard scores.

Seventh, there is no significant difference between the academic achievement level of students who do housework for less than 2 h and that of those who do not do housework. However, the academic achievement level of students who do housework for 2–4 h and for more than 4 h is significantly lower than that of those who do not do housework by 0.35 and 0.48 standard scores.

From the analysis above, it could be seen that it is an important precondition to elevate students' academic achievement level by improving class efficiency, reducing students' learning load and reasonably assign students' learning, entertainment, and rest time.

1.7 Analysis of Factors Influencing Students' Academic Achievement

3. The stronger the students' learning independence is, the higher the students' academic achievement level is.

The present survey indicates that there is a significant correlation between students' learning independence and their academic achievement. The stronger the students' learning independence is, the higher the students' academic achievement level is. Specifically, with the condition that other background variables are controlled the same, the academic achievement level of students who can "often" independently finish their assignment, respectively, is higher than that of students who "never", "seldom", or "sometimes" independently finish their assignment by 0.39, 0.49, and 0.34 standard scores.

1.7.2.3 Factors of Teaching in School

The present survey indicates that in the aspect of teaching in school, factors which produce significant influence on students' academic achievement mainly are teaching methods and arrangement of class hours.

1. The higher the support degree of teachers' teaching for students' self-access learning is, the higher students' academic achievement level is.

The present survey indicates that the higher the support degree of teachers' teaching for students' self-access learning is, the higher students' academic achievement level is. Specifically, with the condition that other background variables are controlled the same, every 1 unit increased to the support of Mathematics teaching for students' self-access learning, 0.03 standard scores is raised to students' academic achievement; every 1 unit increased to the support of Reading teaching for students' self-access learning, 0.02 standard scores is raised to students' academic achievement.

2. The academic achievement level of students whose school carries out teaching seriously according to class hours is apparently higher than that of those whose school increases or reduces class hours.

The present survey indicates that prolonging teaching class hours cannot bring the elevation of academic achievement and the academic achievement level of students whose school carries out teaching seriously according to class hours is the highest. Specifically, with the condition that other background variables are the same, there is no significant difference between the academic achievement level of students whose school increases class hours on Mathematics teaching and that of those whose school follows class hours, but the academic achievement level of students whose school reduces class hours is significantly lower than that of those whose school follows class hours by 0.50 standard scores; the academic achievement level of students whose school increases or reduces class hours on Science teaching is significantly lower than that of those whose school follows class hours by 0.33 and 0.50 standard scores; and the academic achievement level of students whose school increases class hours on Morality and Society teaching is significantly lower than that of those whose school follows class hours by 0.50 standard scores. It could be seen that long teaching time does not mean good academic achievement and apparently deficient teaching time necessarily influences students' basic learning. Therefore, it is a basic condition to improve students' academic achievement by following class hour rules to guarantee students' basic learning time for each subject.

1.7.2.4 Factor of School Management

The present survey indicates that in the aspect of school management, factors which produce significant influence on students' academic achievement mainly are principals' professional duration and teaching and research activities. The influence of school running condition, teachers' academic qualification, age and professional title, etc., is not significant to students' academic achievement.

1. The correlation between principals' professional duration and students' academic achievement level is positive.

The present survey indicates that principals' professional duration in the present school has significant influence on students' academic achievement. Regarding the principals' professional duration, every 1 year higher than the average length, 0.09 standard scores is higher to students' academic achievement.

2. The correlation between the frequency of teaching and research activities and students' academic achievement level is positive.

The present survey indicates that teaching and research activities, especially school-wide teaching and research activities, as an important approach to improve teachers' professional capability and teaching quality, has significant influence on students' academic achievement. Specifically, the academic achievement level of students whose school carries out school-wide teaching and research activities at least once every week is higher than that of those whose school carries out school-wide teaching and research activities once or twice every month and two or three times every semester by 0.75 and 1.22 standard scores, respectively (Table 1.30).

1.8 Research Conclusions

Through the present survey on primary school Grade 6 students' academic achievement and its influencing factors, a fairly thorough and clear complexion of the basic situation of primary school Grade 6 students' academic achievement and the main influencing factors has been gained. The basic conclusions of the present research are as follows.

1.8 Research Conclusions

Table 1.30 Multilevel model analysis of factors influencing students' academic achievement

	Null model		Model 2: family background		Model 3: individual learning		Model 4: school education and management		Complete model	
	Coefficient	Standard error	Coefficient	Standard error	Coefficient	Standard error	Coefficient	Standard error	Coefficient	Standard error
Fixed part	3.40	0.33	3.52	0.30	3.85	0.31	4.61	0.46	4.38	0.43
Constant term			−0.12	0.03						
Age										
Number of books in family (0–10 books as the reference)			−0.03	0.07					−0.02	0.08
11–25 books			0.22	0.08					0.17	0.08
26–100 books			0.36	0.09					0.22	0.09
101–200 books			0.45	0.10					0.41	0.10
More than 200 books			0.08	0.01					0.07	0.01
Family socioeconomic support										
Parents' education degree (Junior high school level as the reference)			−0.63	0.20					−0.30	0.21
Primary school level or below			−0.25	0.08					−0.10	0.09
Primary school level			0.06	0.05					0.11	0.05
Senior high school level or technical secondary school level			0.37	0.08					0.26	0.08
Junior college level or vocational technical college			0.64	0.08					0.54	0.08
Undergraduate level			0.72	0.13					0.64	0.13
Postgraduate level										
Home–school distance (less than 30 min as the reference)			−0.05	0.08					−0.12	0.08

(continued)

Table 1.30 (continued)

	Null model		Model 2: family background		Model 3: individual learning		Model 4: school education and management		Complete model	
	Coefficient	Standard error	Coefficient	Standard error	Coefficient	Standard error	Coefficient	Standard error	Coefficient	Standard error
30 min–1 h			−0.59	0.19					−0.52	0.19
More than 1 h			0.29	0.07					0.17	0.07
My family or friends help me with my homework (often as the reference)										
Never			0.33	0.07					0.22	0.07
Seldom			0.15	0.07					0.07	0.07
Sometimes										
My family talks about the things happening in school with me (often as the reference)			−0.50	0.08					−0.35	0.08
Never			−0.32	0.06					−0.10	0.06
Seldom			−0.24	0.05					−0.12	0.05
Sometimes										
My family talks about the national and international social affairs with me (often as the reference)			−0.39	0.07					−0.19	0.07
Never			−0.06	0.06					0.03	0.06
Seldom			−0.06	0.06					−0.01	0.06
Sometimes										
Live with whom (parents as the reference)			0.22	0.07						

(continued)

1.8 Research Conclusions

Table 1.30 (continued)

	Null model		Model 2: family background		Model 3: individual learning		Model 4: school education and management		Complete model	
	Coefficient	Standard error	Coefficient	Standard error	Coefficient	Standard error	Coefficient	Standard error	Coefficient	Standard error
Mother			−0.18	0.15						
Father			−0.09	0.07						
Grandparents and others										
Time of sleep (9 h or more as the reference)										
Less than 6 h					−0.71	0.12			−0.66	0.14
7 h					−0.13	0.06			−0.08	0.07
8 h					0.08	0.04			0.06	0.04
Mathematics learning efficacy					0.25	0.01			0.23	0.01
Science learning efficacy					0.06	0.01			0.03	0.01
Independently finish homework (often as the reference)										
Never					−0.56	0.18			−0.39	0.23
Seldom					−0.71	0.11			−0.49	0.13
Sometimes					−0.40	0.06			−0.34	0.07
Extracurricular reviewing related to Mathematics (none as the reference)					−0.23	0.08			−0.37	0.08
Less than 1 h					0.13	0.09			−0.12	0.06
1–2 h					0.53	0.13			0.14	0.08
2–4 h					0.77	0.18			0.29	0.12

(continued)

Table 1.30 (continued)

	Null model		Model 2: family background		Model 3: individual learning		Model 4: school education and management		Complete model	
	Coefficient	Standard error	Coefficient	Standard error	Coefficient	Standard error	Coefficient	Standard error	Coefficient	Standard error
More than 4 h									−0.37	0.07
Extracurricular reviewing related to Chinese (none as the reference)										
Less than 1 h					0.10	0.09			−0.22	0.07
1–2 h					0.04	0.14			−0.34	0.09
2–4 h					0.04	0.20			−0.51	0.16
More than 4 h										
Other extracurricular reviewing (none as the reference)					0.04	0.07			−0.11	0.07
Less than 1 h					0.24	0.08			−0.17	0.06
1–2 h					0.66	0.11			0.09	0.07
2–4 h					0.81	0.15			0.09	0.09
More than 4 h										
Time of doing housework (none as the reference)					0.11	0.06			0.08	0.06
Less than 1 h					−0.01	0.06			0.02	0.07
1–2 h					−0.27	0.11			−0.35	0.13
2–4 h					−0.52	0.17			−0.48	0.20
More than 4 h										
Time of doing sports (none as the reference)					0.02	0.05			−0.09	0.06

(continued)

1.8 Research Conclusions

Table 1.30 (continued)

	Null model		Model 2: family background		Model 3: individual learning		Model 4: school education and management		Complete model	
	Coefficient	Standard error	Coefficient	Standard error	Coefficient	Standard error	Coefficient	Standard error	Coefficient	Standard error
Less than 1 h					−0.07	0.06			−0.18	0.07
1–2 h					−0.30	0.09			−0.43	0.10
2–4 h					−0.61	0.15			−0.80	0.18
More than 4 h										
Time of reading extracurricular books (none as the reference)					0.29	0.08			0.30	0.10
Less than 1 h					0.38	0.08			0.38	0.10
1–2 h					0.49	0.10			0.42	0.11
2–4 h					0.44	0.12			0.37	0.14
More than 4 h										
Time of surfing on the Internet (none as the reference)					0.01	0.05			−0.10	0.05
Less than 1 h					0.03	0.06			−0.10	0.07
1–2 h					−0.28	0.11			−0.26	0.12
2–4 h					−0.48	0.15			−0.55	0.17
More than 4 h										
Mathematics teaching and learning way							0.09	0.01	0.03	0.01
							0.04	0.01	0.02	0.01
Reading teaching and learning way							0.07	0.04	0.09	0.04
Years as headmaster in this school							0.05	0.02	0.04	0.02

(continued)

Table 1.30 (continued)

	Null model		Model 2: family background		Model 3: individual learning		Model 4: school education and management		Complete model	
	Coefficient	Standard error	Coefficient	Standard error	Coefficient	Standard error	Coefficient	Standard error	Coefficient	Standard error
Number of Science classes teachers listen to each semester										
Teaching and research activities of subject group (once per week as the reference)							0.23	0.31	0.28	0.28
Once to twice per month							1.36	0.56	1.40	0.51
Two to three times per semester									0.00	0.00
Never										
Teaching and research activities of whole school teachers (once per week as the reference)							−0.87	0.39	−0.75	0.36
Once to twice per month							−1.34	0.41	−1.22	0.38
Two to three times per semester							0.27	2.10	0.61	1.93
Never										
Actual classes compared with the classes planed in schedule (same as the reference)							−0.76	0.12	−0.50	0.12
Actual classes of Mathematics are fewer than the curriculum schedule							0.16	0.05	0.05	0.05
Actual classes of Mathematics are more than the curriculum schedule							−0.41	0.06	−0.33	0.06

(continued)

1.8 Research Conclusions

Table 1.30 (continued)

	Null model		Model 2: family background		Model 3: individual learning		Model 4: school education and management		Complete model	
	Coefficient	Standard error	Coefficient	Standard error	Coefficient	Standard error	Coefficient	Standard error	Coefficient	Standard error
Actual classes of Science are fewer than the curriculum schedule							−0.58	0.18	−0.50	0.18
Actual classes of Science are more than the curriculum schedule							−0.14	0.06	−0.06	0.06
Actual classes of Morality and Society are fewer than the curriculum schedule							−0.70	0.18	−0.50	0.18
Actual classes of Morality and Society are more than the curriculum schedule										
Random part										
Regional level	2.51	0.79	1.75	0.59	1.65	0.55	2.24	0.73	1.68	0.56
Constant term										
School level	4.51	0.40	3.89	0.36	3.73	0.34	3.56	0.36	3.01	0.30
Constant term										
Student level	4.63	0.05	4.23	0.06	3.82	0.05	4.24	0.06	3.58	0.05
Constant term										
Logistic likelihood function	66722.52		53206.98		57838.28		47965.10		42948.44	
Sample quantity: districts or counties	28		27		27		27		27	
Sample quantity: school	296		285		285		242		242	
Sample quantity: student	15,001		12,187		13,580		10,990		10,229	

1.8.1 Students' Academic Achievement

1. Students' learning of the four subjects including Chinese, Mathematics, Science and Morality and Society has basically reached the requirements of curriculum standards, among which, the percentage of students reaching basically qualified level or above on Mathematics is the highest, and then on Science and Morality and Society, and the percentage of students who reach basically qualified level or above on Chinese is comparatively low.
2. The academic achievement level of students in the east is apparently higher than that of students in the middle and in the west, and the academic achievement level of students in city is higher than that of students in countryside.
3. There is no apparent difference between the academic achievement level of male students and female students.
4. Students basically reach the requirements of content and competency in the curriculum standard of each subject, but are deficient in some aspects of knowledge and skills and the ability to comprehensively solve problems is to be improved.

1.8.2 Factors Influencing Students' Academic Achievement

1. The influence of student individual and family factor on students' academic achievement is higher than the influence of school.
2. The correlations between family materialistic and cultural condition, parents' education level, parent–child interaction, and students' academic achievement are significantly positive. The less the time spent on the way to school, the higher the students' academic achievement level.
3. The stronger the students' self-efficacy of learning and independence, the higher the students' academic achievement level. If students' learning load is too heavy, the correlation between the learning time and the academic achievement is not positive.
4. The correlation between the support degree of teachers' teaching for students' self-access learning and students' academic achievement level is significantly positive. The academic achievement level of students whose schools seriously follow class hours is apparently higher than that of those whose schools increase or reduce class hours.
5. The correlations between principals' profession duration the frequency of teaching in school and research activities and students' academic achievement level are positive.

1.9 Countermeasures and Suggestions

Based on the results of the present academic achievement survey, countermeasures and suggestions are proposed as follows.

1.9.1 Drawing Lessons from International Advanced Experience to Implement the Quality Monitoring of the National Education

Quality of basic education, as the decisive factor to improve national competitiveness, is an important signal for a country's comprehensive national strength. Since many countries and regions in the world have already carried out students' academic achievement assessment at national level, it is enforced to build the quality monitoring system of the basic education with Chinese characteristics based on the lessons drawn from international advanced experience. Through the quality monitoring of the national basic education, on the one hand, the present situation of the basic education quality could be accurately mastered and the existing questions in the process of education development could be scientifically analyzed to provide basis for exploring the law of talents development; on the other hand, accurate and effective evidence could be provided for education management and education policy-making, accelerating the balanced development of basic education with great efforts, to practically realize the scientificalness, democratization and professionalization of decision-making, and management of educational administration management departments, improving the efficacy of management.

1.9.2 To Build the Quality Monitoring System of the National Education to Carry Out Continuous Monitoring of the Quality of Education

Based on the national strategy of priority to education development, the national education has received unprecedented attention in the recent years, but has also endured huge pressure, with a series of questions to be answered, such as the present situation of the quality of basic education, the effects of new curriculum reform, the direction and way to the educational devotion and how to provide children of different socioeconomic background with fair education, etc. To scientifically give responses to these questions, it is necessary to carry out continuous monitoring of education quality nationally. Due to the reason that the scale of the national basic education is large, it is hard to realize the quality monitoring of basic education depending on one department. Thus, a four-level monitoring system of the nation, province, prefecture, and county should be constructed to form the layout that the nation provides monitoring standard and technology, the provinces and municipalities are responsible for the regional design, counties and districts are responsible for the monitoring implementation, in order to provide more efficient, scientific, and accurate evidence for the nation to make and adjust policies, to provide support for local education administration and education management.

1.9.3 To Further Transform Students' Learning Way to Improve Students' Ability to Comprehensively Solve Problems

The present survey has found that although students basically reach the requirements of content and competency regulated in the curriculum standard of each subject, the ability to solve the complicated problems in practical life by flexibly applying the knowledge and skills learned is comparatively quite weak. Students who have this ability to comprehensively solve problems in the four subjects are no more than one third. On the one hand, this might be caused by the unclear requirement in new curriculum standard, thus, the development of students' ability to comprehensively solve problems should be further paid attention to in the modification of new curriculum. On the other hand, this is related to the deficiency of students' self-access learning sense and ability. In the present survey, the percentages of students who often can "actively find examples or evidence of knowledge learned in daily life" and can "manipulate what teachers deliver in class at home" are only 43.70 and 35.0%. It could be seen that it is an important reason that students lack the sense to actively combine the knowledge learned and life and to apply the knowledge learned into life which results in the deficiency of the ability to practically solve problems. Therefore, it is a key issue at present to transform students' learning way and to strengthen the development of students' self-access learning sense and ability which should be particularly paid attention to.

1.9.4 To Improve Schools' Teaching Efficiency and to Reduce Students' Learning Load

The present survey has found that the correlation between students' learning time and their academic achievement is not positive. The heavier the students' learning load is, the lower their academic achievement level is. However, it generally exists that students' learning load is too heavy at present. About two-thirds of students do school assignment for more than 1 h every day and participate in various types of extracurricular reviewing and training classes. The time of sleep for more than half of students is less than 9 h and this phenomenon is particularly apparent in the middle and in the west. The percentage of students who do school assignment for more than 1 h every day is approaching three fourths and the percentage of students whose time of sleep is less than 9 h reaches 60%. This is an important reason resulting in that the academic achievement level of students in the middle and in the west is apparently lower than that of students in the east. Thus, it is an important present issue in the primary school education to be solved with an urge that to improve the efficiency of schools' classroom teaching, to reduce students' learning load and to reasonably arrange students' time on learning, entertainment and rest.

1.9.5 To Strengthen the Continuing Education Training of Teachers in the West and in the Countryside and to Improve Teachers' Professional Literacy

The present survey has found that the percentages of schools participating in training activities at district level or above once or twice per month in the east and in the middle both reach 30% above, while the percentage is only 8% in the west. The opportunities for participating in training for teachers in the countryside schools are apparently fewer than that for teachers in city. The frequency of participating training for countryside teachers of each subject is lower than that for teachers in city. Especially for the teachers of subjects of Science and Morality and Society, the opportunities for the teachers in countryside are fewer than that for teachers in city by a half. The percentage of schools participating in teaching and research activities at district level or above once or twice per month in countryside is lower than that of schools in city by 10%. As an important way to improve teachers' professional level, teachers' training and teaching and research activities at district level play a vital role in teachers' professional development. The deficiency of teachers' in-service training is a crucial reason resulting in the fairly low quality of teachers in the west and in countryside. Thus, it is an outstanding problem to strengthen the training of teachers in the west and in countryside and to improve their professional literacy, which should be urgently solved for teachers' professional development in the present situation of our country.

1.9.6 To Pay Attention to the Teaching of Science and Morality and Society and to Improve Teachers' Professional Literacy

The present survey indicates that students like Chinese and Mathematics more than Science and Morality and Society, and most teachers of the subjects students like are responsible for students' learning, can teach based on students' features, give interesting and vivid classes, pay attention to individuals' learning and give extra help to students when they need, etc. Apparently, teachers of Science and Morality and Society are not as good as teachers of Chinese and Mathematics on these aspects. This is reflected in the survey result that the support from the teaching of Chinese and Mathematics for students' self-access learning is apparently higher than that from Science and Morality and Society. Meanwhile, the present survey has found the phenomenon that the class hours of Science and Morality and Society are occupied with Chinese and Mathematics generally exists. Besides, from the perspective of teachers' quality, the academic qualification of Science teachers is apparently lower, especially in countryside, the academic qualification of Science and Morality and Society teachers is apparently lower than that of Chinese and Mathematics teachers. Therefore, it is a special issue to give emphasis to the teaching of Science and Morality and Society and to improve the teachers' professional literacy in the new curriculum reform.

Chapter 2
Chinese Reading Assessment Report

2.1 Research Background

At present, two important international assessment programs on students' academic achievement are, respectively, organized by IEA and OECD, which are particularly on Reading, Mathematics, and Science. The programs have wide influence in the world because of their assessment content, indices, scientific instrument, and standardized assessment procedures. Meanwhile, countries regularly organize surveys on students' academic achievement, to build national norm and to carry out the longitudinal and crosswise comparative studies. No matter the national studies or international programs, the methods employed are paper–pencil test and questionnaire research. Regarding the participant selection, the stratified sampling technique is usually used. And, norm reference and standard reference are the two main assessment approaches to analyze the survey results. Overall, the difficulty or problem in the international programs is the weak assessment on students' affect and attitude; in the national or regional programs, assessment on authenticity, performance, growing up portfolio, and team cooperation, which could fairly represent students autonomy and society development, has problems to solve the validity and reliability, and in large-scale surveys, it is hard to differentiate the students' potential, efficiency of education and teaching, and the influence of social environment.

The research on students' academic achievement in China mainland started in 1990s. Some research has been continuously carried out in many areas, which make some creative contribution on the aspects of referring international experience, developing assessment indices and instruments, extending assessment methods, data collection, and explaining assessment results. However, these researches lack follow-up extension, emphasize micro-aspects, or are not objective. At present, there is a long distance from the existing research to build the national norm and data bank of students' academic achievement in compulsory education. *The Research on Students' Academic Achievement in Primary and High Schools*, an important national project in "The 11th Five-Year Plan", is developed to respond the decision-making needs of basic education reform development, the accountability needs from citizens on education quality, and the needs to accelerate students' learning and to develop the assessment theory and practice in the country.

With the direction of *Basic Education Curriculum Reform Guideline (Pilot version)*, the present project does research on students' academic achievement based on *Full-time Compulsory Education Chinese Curriculum Standard (Experimental version)* (*Chinese Curriculum Standard* in abbreviation) published by Ministry of Education, referring the national- and international-related research results. Therefore, according to the research design, the Chinese branch project, based on *Chinese Curriculum Standard*, does research on students' reading academic achievement, i.e., competence in reading, referring international research results on reading academic achievement.

2.2 Theoretical Framework

At present, it is fairly recognized in the field of Chinese that reading competence is composed of multi-factors and multi-levels. Multi-factors contain a certain quantity of characters and words, reading skills, intellectual, nonintellectual psychological factors, etc. Multi-levels include the recognition competency (to recognize characters, words, and sentences), the comprehension competency (can accurately construe words and explain sentences; can accurately understand the relations between language factors and text structure; can categorize paragraphs, conclude the meanings of paragraphs and the main idea, analysis, conclusion, and deduction from the linguistic comprehension level to the content comprehension level; cannot only specifically construe the meanings of words and sentences through mind analysis, imagination, connection and deduction, but also can generally master the specific content through mind abstract, conclusion, comparison, and judgment to achieve the deep comprehension level), the comment and appreciation competency (to give positive or negative analysis and judgment on the meaning, emotion, and language expressed in the essay based on the recognition and comprehension, to represent individuals' cognition level and effect), application competency, etc.

Based on the recognition above, *Chinese Curriculum Standard* further underlines that the emphasis of reading teaching is to develop students' ability to feel, understand, appreciate, and evaluate; to gradually develop students' ability on exploratory reading and creative reading, advocating multi-perspective reading with creativity to extend the thinking space and to promote the reading quality by employing reading expectation, reading reflection, critical evaluation, etc.; and to further require that reading assessment should comprehensively assess students' feelings, experience, comprehension and values in reading process, should assess their reading interest, methods, habits, reading materials selection and reading quantity, and also require to pay attention to multi-perspective and creative reading assessment. Therefore, in the curriculum "overall goal", it has proposed that

2.2 Theoretical Framework

students should "have independent reading ability, lay emphasis on affect experience, have fairly abundant accumulation and shape quite good language sense, learn to apply some reading methods, can preliminarily understand and appreciate literature works, be edified by highly minded sentiments and taste, develop personalized characters and enrich personal spirit world, can read simple ancient classical Chinese with the help of reference books, and make the 9-year extracurricular reading quantity reach 4 million characters." In the "stage goals", *Chinese Curriculum Standard* proposes stage requirements. Besides, *Chinese Curriculum Standard* also puts forward the assessment suggestions. The related content in *Chinese Curriculum Standard* is as follows (Table 2.1).

Table 2.1 Primary school *Chinese Curriculum Standard* requirements for student reading competence

Content	Curriculum goals	
	3rd stage goals	Assessment suggestions
Reading aloud and Silent reading	Can accurately, fluently, and emotionally read texts in Mandarin Chinese Read silently at a certain speed, no less than 300 characters when reading in general	"Can accurately, fluently and emotionally read texts in Mandarin Chinese" is the overall requirement. Based on the stage goals, there could be different emphasis at different stages. Reading aloud can be assessed in the aspects of pronunciation, tones, emotion, etc., and students' comprehension of the content and literary styles should also be assessed Assessment on students' daily reading aloud should be underlined, by encouraging students to read aloud more, to increase accumulation in aloud reading practice, to develop language sense, and to deepen experience and comprehension Students' silent reading should be comprehensively assessed based on stage goals in the aspects of silent reading methods, speed, effects, habits, etc.
Intense reading	Can read with the help of dictionary, construe the appropriate meanings of words in language environment, and tell the word emotional coloring Correlate the context and personal accumulation to guess the related words' meanings and learn the expressing effects	Students' comprehensive comprehension ability should be emphasized in the assessment, with students' emotion experience and creative comprehension underlined. Based on the stage goals, students' performance on the aspects of word and sentence

(continued)

Table 2.1 (continued)

Content	Curriculum goals	
	3rd stage goals	Assessment suggestions
	Try to figure out the text expression sequence in reading, learn to know the author's mind and sentiments, and preliminarily understand the basic expression way in the text. Can bravely propose personal ideas and make judgments in communication and discussion Can grasp the main idea when reading expository texts and know the basic explanatory methods Can grasp the outline when reading narrative texts, briefly describe the situation, people, details which impress deepest, speak out the feelings of love, hatred, respect, expectation, sympathy, etc. Learn to know the different usages of dunhao (Chinese back-sloping comma) and comma, semicolon and full stop when reading sentences (texts)	construe, text comprehension, main idea conclusion, content exploration, works feelings, etc. should be specifically assessed
Skimming and scanning	Learn skimming, enlarge the scope of knowledge, and retrieve information based on needs Try to do exploratory reading by making use of library and network information ways. Extend the reading scope and make the extracurricular reading quantity no less than 1 million characters	The emphasis of skimming is to assess whether students grasp the main idea of reading materials, and the assessment on scanning ability underlines whether to find out the important information
Literature works reading	Generally, get the main idea of the poem when reading poems, imagine the situation described in the poems, and try to feel the poets' emotion. Be affected and encouraged by excellent works, expect and chase beautiful dreams	Due to the features of figurativeness and emotionality for literature works, students' feelings for figures and their emotional experience could be assessed as an emphasis. Students' special feelings and experience should be encouraged
Ancient poems and prose reading	Read excellent poems and prose to experience and understand the content and emotion by paying attention to the tones, rhythms, etc. Memorize and recite 60 excellent poems and prose	Students' ancient poems and prose reading should be assessed with the emphasis on their accumulation process of memorization and recitation. Their comprehension on the poems and prose should be assessed, rather than the mastery degree of word usages, sentence structures, and so on

2.2 Theoretical Framework

In PISA, reading competence is generalized into five proficiency levels. First, it is to get information, which requires students to find out related information in text, such as the main roles in the event, time, place and background the event took place, theme, and perspectives of the text. Second, it is to generate broad and holistic understanding, requiring students to form the holistic perception of the text and general understanding, such as to get the purpose, topic and explanation sequence of the text through its title, to know the coverage and functions of the data in the charts and tables, and to describe the main roles, background and situation of the story, etc. Third, it is to generate thorough explanation, which requires students to thoroughly read the text, linking the related information of each sector, and to understand the text logically. Students also need to compare or contrast the information in the text, charts, or tables, to infer the author's purpose by linking the related information, to list the related evidence and to make conclusion, etc. Fourth, it is to reflect and evaluate the text content, which requires students to extract their knowledge to construct the deep comprehension for the text, and to evaluate the perspective of the text with related evidence. Fifth, it is to reflect and evaluate the expression way of the text, which requires students to reflect and evaluate the format feature of the text, such as the structure, type, and linguistic features of the text, to evaluate the author's writing style and the nuance of the language use, such as the function for expressing effect resulting from the selection of an adjective.[1]

Obviously, no matter in the related rules in the curriculum standard or in PISA, reading is recognized as a mental activity with the goals of extracting information, understanding the content, experiencing the emotion, and evaluating. With the analysis above, recognition, understanding, and application competencies are considered the core of the reading competence (more information could be found in the two-dimensional table of the reading competence) which although contains various factors, and make the theoretical foundation for the reading academic achievement in the present research.

2.3 Research Method and Instrument

2.3.1 *The Bases of the Instrument Development*

Basis 1 is *Chinese Curriculum Standard*. With the direction of the basic belief that "to thoroughly raise students' Chinese literacy," it requires students, with the teachers' efficient teaching and the variety of activities, to acquire the Chinese literacy, which is comprehensively composed of the related knowledge and competencies, process and methods, affect, attitude, and values.

---

[1] Dong PF (2009) 2009 international student assessment on reading literacy. Global Education10:91.

Chinese literacy, represented in the specific academic achievement, include knowing and writing the characters, reading, writing, oral communicative competence, etc. And, the present project, which takes primary school students' reading academic achievement assessment as the important research topic, is first based on the importance of reading literacy in Chinese literacy. Among the so-called four kinds of abilities, which are listening, speaking, reading, and writing, listening and reading are information input, while speaking and writing are the output of information. There is no output without input, so it is clear for the importance of reading. As the mother tongue, spoken language has been developed to some extent for students, while it is just the beginning to systematically learn the written language, which makes the written language learning as the priority of priorities for the primary school students in their Chinese study. Thus, the importance and urgency of reading are quite obvious. Meanwhile, no matter from the perspective of information input, or from the perspective of urgency and importance to learn written language, reading is crucial, because reading is an important way for humans to get information and also a major approach to know the world. With the reading activities, students could gradually develop their reading abilities in recognition, understanding, and application. The present project is to comprehensively assess students' feelings, experience, comprehension and value tendency in reading process, to assess their reading ability in the aspects of recognition, understanding and application, and to pay attention to the multi-perspective and creative reading assessment, which is in accordance with the requirements on reading competence assessment in curriculum standard.

Basis 2 is SOLO taxonomy. According to the theory, with the analysis on students' cognitive development, students' performance on the questions are categorized into five structural levels, which are pre-structural level, uni-structural level, multi-structural level, relational level, and extended abstract level. The meanings of the five levels could be read in the general report.

2.3.2 The Procedures of the Instrument Development

The principles to be followed in the procedures of the instrument development have been introduced in the overall report. Regarding the item writing in the Chinese reading assessment, the following rules should be particularly emphasized.

1. Practicality

Reading ability is actually the transformation and application of reading practice and reading knowledge. It is hard to raise the reading ability without active reading experience but the reading knowledge. Therefore, the practicality should be underlined as more as possible.

2.3 Research Method and Instrument

Preparation period
It is to clarify research aim and research method, to learn SOLO taxonomy, to consult the research results of the related international and national programs, such as IEA, PISA, to analyze the belief of new curriculum reform and *Chinese Curriculum Standard*, and to make discussions and communication.

Construction period
Based on curriculum standard requirements and SOLO taxonomy, it is to construct the cognitive structural framework of the primary school Grade-6 student reading ability, including the related content domains, curriculum standard requirements, requirements on student ability, and the uni-structural, multi-structural and relational level items with certain proportions.

Modification period
With discussion and communication, including the direction of foreign experts, it is to adjust and modify the content in the cognitive structural framework and the predicted difficulty structure design. Regarding the fairly difficult items, it is to make modifications based on students' pilot test results, and to modify the sequence of items and the sequence of options in the items.

Pilot test period
It is to choose two schools in Chaoyang district in Beijing, including 120 students, to do the pilot test, of which the testing time is recorded and the results is analyzed.

Re-modification period
With the analysis results in the pilot test, it is to re-modify and to re-select the content in the cognitive structural framework and to make adjustment on item difficulty structural level and on the sequence of options in the items. The rating scales are modified at the same time.

Final draft period
It is to fix the final draft of the cognitive structural framework of the primary school Grade-6 student reading ability, test items, rating scales, to solve the problems in the layout design and printing in order to make ready for the formal test.

2. Conciseness

Item statement should be concise and accurate in order to make students at all levels understand item requirements. And, the options in the items should be correct with similar length of more or less numbers of characters.

3. Problem-solving characteristic

Students' true reading ability development should be assessed as much as possible, with the simple knowledge memorization avoided.

2.3.3 Construction of the Two-Dimensional Table of Specifications

To design the scientific and brief reading competence assessment framework is the base and precondition to construct the reading competence test instrument. The assessment framework in the present reading competence test project is based on *Chinese Curriculum Standard* and SOLO taxonomy, i.e., based on *Chinese Curriculum Standard*, some key content goals are selected in the aspects of accumulation and application, and reading comprehension, and then these are stated into general ability requirements and transformed into the predicted results of students' learning. After this, test items are employed to make learning results manipulative. Based on SOLO taxonomy, uni-structural (U), multi-structural (M), and relational-level (R) test items are designed with the proportion of 2:2:1, and the reading competence cognitive structure framework is formed as follows (Table 2.2).

Table 2.3 could be formed from the two-dimensional table of specifications.

2.3.4 The Test Item Writing

According to curriculum standard and SOLO taxonomy theory, the test paper is constructed based on the consensus achieved on the basic questions. Two types of items are included in the test paper, multiple-choice questions and open-ended questions. The examples provided below show the design process of the test items at U, M, and R structural levels in the two-dimensional table of specifications.

1. U structural level

Example: Multiple-choice item 2

Whom are the related historical people in the phrases "fu jing qing zui", "wo xin chang dan", "wen ji qi wu", and "ju gong jin cui" encountered in the reading?

2.3 Research Method and Instrument

Table 2.2 Primary school Grade 6 student reading competence cognitive structure framework

Content domains	Content standard	Ability requirement	Competency category	Item sequential number/key	Structural level	Percentage
Characters and words 4 (number means the number of items, below ditto)	Characters and words recognition	Can accurately tell the pronunciation of the polyphonic and polysemous characters in the context	Recognition	8/A	M	U:2 M:1 R:1
		Can accurately tell the pronunciation of the polyphonic and polysemous characters in the context	Recognition	9/B	R	
	Understanding words	Can accurately understand the definite meanings of words in the language environment	Understanding	1/D	U	
	Understanding words	Can accurately understand the particular meanings of idioms	Understanding	2/C	U	
Sentences and paragraphs 4	Application of punctuation	Can learn from experiencing the different usages of dunhao (Chinese back-sloping comma) and comma, semicolon and full stop, and appropriately apply them	Application	7/B	M	U:1 M:3 R:0
	Understanding sentences	Can accurately tell the sentence meaning	Understanding	6/D	M	
	Understanding the relation of sentences	Can accurately apply conjunctions	Application	4/C	U	
		Can put the sentences in order	Understanding	5/D	M	

(continued)

Table 2.2 (continued)

Content domains	Content standard	Ability requirement	Competency category	Item sequential number/key	Structural level	Percentage
Chapters 14	Memorizing and reciting excellent poems	Can accurately read and memorize ancient poems	Reading	3/A	U	U:6 M:5 R:3
	Extracting information based on needs	Can accurately extract related information from narrative texts	Understanding	10/B	U	
	Learning from experiencing the expressing effect	Can learn from experiencing the expressing effect and evaluate it in their own language	Application	11/D	R	
	Understanding the meanings of the words in the poem	Can accurately understand the meanings of the keywords in the poem	Understanding	12/C	U	
	Understanding the meanings of the lines in the poem	Can accurately understand the meanings of lines in the poem	Understanding	14/A	M	
	Understanding the main content in poems	Can accurately understand the main content of the poem	Understanding	13/C	U	

(continued)

2.3 Research Method and Instrument

Table 2.2 (continued)

Content domains	Content standard	Ability requirement	Competency category	Item sequential number/key	Structural level	Percentage
Chapters 14	Extracting information based on needs	Can accurately extract related information from narrative texts	Understanding	15/A	U	U:6 M:5 R:3
		Can accurately extract multiple information from narrative texts	Understanding	16/B	M	
		Can accurately extract and deal with related information from narrative texts	Understanding	17/D	M	
	Summarizing the main content of the narrative texts	Can accurately understand and use their own language to summarize the main content of the texts	Application	18/D	R	
	Learning from experiencing the expression way of the expository texts	Can tell the explaining methods used in the texts	Understanding	19/B	U	
	Understanding the main content of the expository texts	Can accurately extract and integrate related information from the expository texts	Understanding	20/D	M	
		Can grasp the explained key points	Understanding	21/B	M	
		Can accurately judge, infer, and express in their own language	Application	22/D	R	

Note Based on SOLO taxonomy, U represents uni-structural level, M represents multi-structural level, and R represents relational level

Table 2.3 Number of items distribution

	Number of items distribution	Percentage (%)	Total number
Content domains	Character and word domain: 4	18	22
	Sentence and paragraph domain: 4	18	
	Chapter domain: 14	64	
Reading competencies	Recognition competency: 3	14	
	Understanding competency: 14	64	
	Application competency: 5	22	
Performance level	Uni-structural level: 9	41	
	Multi-structural level: 9	41	
	Relational level: 4	18	

A. Jing Ke, Gou Jian, Zu Ti, Zhu Geliang.
B. Jing Ke, Lian Po, Gou Jian, Zhou Enlai.
C. Lian Po, Gou Jian, Zu Ti, Zhu Geliang.
D. Lian Po, Fu Chai, Zu Ti, Zhou Enlai.

This is a uni-structural level item, mainly assessing whether students can accurately remember the sources of the phrases, designed according to the reading ability requirement of "understanding and accumulating words" in the curriculum standard. Students who choose the key C own the reading ability at uni-structural level, while others' reading ability is at pre-structural level.

2. M structural level

Example: Multiple-choice item 21

What is the main cause for iron-deficiency anemia?

A. No regular physical practice participation.
B. Food preference and the lack of vegetables and fruits.
C. Too much intake of oil-fried food and alkaline beverage.
D. Unbalanced diet, the lack of iron and too much of lead.

This is a multi-structural-level item, mainly assessing students' ability to summarize the general idea of the text, designed according to the reading ability requirement of "can grasp the main idea of the texts" in the curriculum standard. Those students choose D means they own the multi-structural-level reading ability, while students who choose B or C at uni-structural level, and students who choose A at pre-structural level.

3. R structural level

Example: Open-ended item 22

Whether anemia influences students' learning achievement? And state the reasons.

2.3 Research Method and Instrument

A. It influences students' learning achievement. The reason is as follows:
B. It does not influence students' learning achievement. The reason is as follows:

This is a relational-level open-ended item, mainly assessing students' comprehensive ability to judge, infer and express, designed according to the reading ability requirement of "can grasp the main idea of the texts" in the curriculum standard. If students' statements are like "easy to get tired, reaction ability and memorization ability will decrease and the intelligence will be affected," their reading ability is at relational level; if the statements are like "reaction ability and memorization ability will decrease," their reading ability is at multi-structural level; if the statements are like "easy to get tired, and the intelligence will be affected," their reading ability is at uni-structural level; if the statements are like "it will not influence learning achievement," it means that their reading ability is at pre-structural level.

Usually, open-ended questions are relational-level test items, while multiple-choice questions including uni-structural-level, multi-structural-level, and relational-level test items.

2.3.5 Pilot Test and Modification

In the early April 2009, the pilot test was carried out in the Primary School Affiliated to Chaoyang Teachers College with the help of the overall project team. The analysis report of the pilot test showed that the reliability of the Chinese test items was 0.98. In general, the reliability of the academic achievement test paper should be over 0.90, and for the reliability coefficient, the nearer to approach 1, the more reliable. The reliability of the present test paper met the requirement. The analysis on the Chinese test items and the observation about the distribution chart of the item difficulty and student ability and chart of the model fit indices showed that the difficulty fit indices of the items in the Chinese test were in the acceptable coverage, which was $-3.21 \sim 4.75$. It could be seen from this that the item difficulty coverage was appropriate. Modification was done based on the problems reflected in the analysis report. At the end of April, the test instrument was fixed and printed. After the training in the early May, the sampling test was carried out in the country.

2.3.6 The Characteristic Parameter of the Test Instrument and Measurement Index of the Test Paper

1. Test Item Validity, Difficulty, Discrimination, and Fit Index

Based on the project research needs, 18,000 students from 600 schools of 30 counties participated in the formal test and 16,799 papers were valid. According to

Table 2.4 Reliability of test item

	Student test results	Item
Reliability	0.44	1.00
M	0.42	
SD	0.95	

the test results, Winsteps 2.0 was employed to analyze the validity and reliability of the test instrument and the item characteristic to attain the ability parameter of each student, with the results in the tables listed below.

It could be known from Table 2.4, the reliability of the test item is 1.00, and the holistic reliability of the test paper to the prediction of the student ability is 0.44. The reliability of the test paper is fairly satisfying. The test item parameters, including difficulty, discrimination, fit index and average response could be seen in Table 2.5.

It could be known from Table 2.6 that the minimum of the item difficulty is −3.47 and the maximum is 3.99. The mean of the difficulty is 0.00 and standard deviation is 2.38. The difficulty coverage is quite wide.

Table 2.5 Statistical results of test item difficulty, discrimination, fit index, etc.

Item	Difficulty	Discrimination (point biserial correlation)	Discrimination	Infit mean square	p-value
1	−2.91	0.25	1.06	0.92	0.95
2	−1.62	0.20	1.01	1.00	0.85
3	−3.47	0.20	1.04	0.95	0.97
4	−1.71	0.29	1.08	0.92	0.86
5	3.38	−0.07	0.89	1.07	0.07
6	1.44	0.00	0.69	1.12	0.30
7	2.80	−0.07	0.85	1.11	0.11
8	2.96	−0.15	0.80	1.14	0.10
9	−0.65	0.23	1.04	0.98	0.71
10	−0.39	0.29	1.19	0.92	0.67
11	3.93	0.04	0.99	1.00	0.04
12	−2.34	0.23	1.04	0.95	0.92
13	−0.52	0.25	1.09	0.96	0.69
14	−1.32	0.18	0.99	1.02	0.82
15	−1.20	0.25	1.06	0.96	0.80
16	−1.24	0.25	1.05	0.96	0.80
17	−1.55	0.16	0.97	1.03	0.84
18	3.65	0.15	1.06	0.94	0.05
19	−1.87	0.18	1.00	1.00	0.88
20	−1.00	0.25	1.06	0.96	0.77
21	−0.36	0.28	1.16	0.93	0.66
22	3.99	0.10	1.03	0.97	0.04

2.3 Research Method and Instrument

There are two types of discrimination in Table 2.6. One is the correlation between whether the item is passed or not and the total score, i.e., point biserial correlation, which is used to show the discrimination extent of items for student ability. From the table, it could be seen that the average discrimination of items in the present paper is 0.16, with the deviation 0.30, which is not so ideal.

The discrimination can also be given in Classical Test Theory (CTT in abbreviation) way. The hypothesis of Rasch model employed in Winsteps, the discrimination of all items is considered 1.00, which is the foundation to fit Rasch model. If the discrimination is 1.00, it is consistent with the prediction of item difficulty in Rasch model. If the discrimination is over or less than 1.00, it means that the practical item discrimination is inconsistent with the prediction of item difficulty in Rasch model. It could be seen from the table that the mean of the practical item discrimination is 1.00, consistent with the prediction of item difficulty in Rasch model.

Another statistical data in Table 2.6, which is explained the average response to item (the way to score students' responses with two or multiple values), is 0.59.

Regarding the validity of the test results, two methods were employed. One is the content structure validity of the test paper. From Table 2.6, the infit index coverage is from 0.92 to 1.14, with the mean 0.99 and standard deviation 0.07, which means the content structure validity of the test paper is high, in accordance with the hypothesis of unidimensionality. The other is the correlation between reading test results and the test results of three other subjects (which could be seen in Table 2.7) as the empirical validity index of test instrument, which could be called congruent validity, to show the consistency extent of the test results of the same ability assessed with different test instruments. It could be seen from Table 2.7 that the correlation between Reading ability and Mathematics is 0.503, 0.429 for the correlation with Science, and 0.473 for the correlation with Morality and Society, which shows that there is significant correlation between the test results of the reading ability and of the abilities in other subjects.

Table 2.6 Descriptive statistics

	N	Minimum	Maximum	Mean	Standard deviation
Difficulty	22	−3.47	3.99	0.00	2.38
Discrimination (point biserial correlation)	22	−0.15	0.29	0.16	0.13
Discrimination	22	0.69	1.19	1.00	0.11
Infit mean square	22	0.92	1.14	0.99	0.07
p-value	22	0.04	0.97	0.59	0.35

Table 2.7 Correlation analysis between reading ability and abilities in other subjects

		Reading	Mathematics	Science	Morality and society
Reading	Pearson correlation coefficient	1	0.503[a]	0.429[a]	0.473[a]
	Sig. (2-tailed)	–	0.000	0.000	0.000
	N	16,799	16,543	15,168	16,617
Mathematics	Pearson correlation coefficient	0.503[a]	1	0.601[a]	0.611[a]
	Sig. (2-tailed)	0.000	–	0.000	0.000
	N	16,543	17,898	16,253	17,832
Science	Pearson correlation coefficient	0.429[a]	0.601[a]	1	0.707[a]
	Sig. (2-tailed)	0.000	0.000	–	0.000
	N	15,168	16,253	16,378	17,832
Morality and society	Pearson correlation coefficient	0.473[a]	0.611[a]	0.707[a]	1
	Sig. (2-tailed)	0.000	0.000	0.000	–
	N	16,617	17,832	17,832	18,024

Note [a]Means reaching significance level of 0.01

2. Item Characteristic Curves

It could be known from Fig. 2.1 that there are 22 test items in total, but not every item characteristic curve in accordance with IRT model. The item difficulty covers from −3.47 to 3.99. Although the difficulty distribution area is quite large, the distribution is unbalanced, with the middle fault appearing in student ability.

2.4 Analysis and Discussion on the Reading Test Results

2.4.1 The Overall Complexion of Student Ability Distribution

From Table 2.8, it could be seen that the test results analysis of 16,799 students' reading ability has been obtained with the mean of the estimated value 0.42 and standard deviation 0.95.

The student performance in percentile could be seen in Table 2.9, with student ability value transformed with the formula T = 50 + 10 × original ability value.

It could be known from Table 2.9 that the lowest score of the 16,799 students' reading ability test results is about 0, and the highest score is around 93. The mean is about 54 and standard deviation is around 9.48.

2.4 Analysis and Discussion on the Reading Test Results

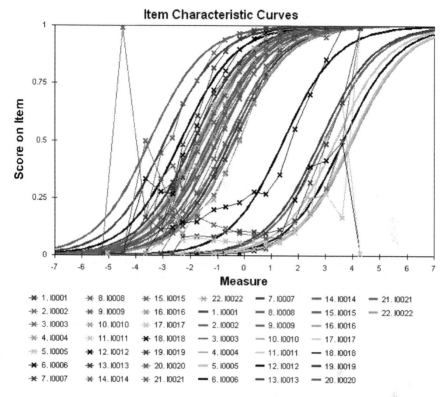

Fig. 2.1 Chinese item characteristic curves (Color figure online)

Table 2.8 Descriptive statistics

	N	Minimum	Maximum	Mean	SD
Estimated value	16,799	−5.25	4.27	0.42	0.95
Valid sampling	16,799				

Table 2.9 Descriptive statistics

	N	Minimum	Maximum	Mean	SD
Estimated value	16,799	−2.50	92.70	54.22	9.48
Valid sampling	16,799				

2.4.2 The Grouping Analysis on Student Ability Performance

Based on the 16,799 students' responses to items with different difficulties, students are divided into five ability groups from high (A) to low (E) with the mean of the estimated ability value as the midpoint and about 1 standard deviation as interval. The range of each group divided by the original ability value and by the transformed value could be seen in Table 2.10. The number of students in each ability group, the percentage of the students in each ability group out of the total, and the accumulative percentage could also be seen in Table 2.10.

From the bar chart of the student frequency distribution, it could be known that the student ability is almost in normal distribution (Fig. 2.2). The number of students in the highest ability group (A) is 346, 2.1% of the total students. There are 4214 students in Group B, with the ability lower than the highest ability group, but higher than the average ability group, which is 25.1% of the total students. The number of the students in the average ability group (C) is 5990, 35.7% of the total students. There are 4778 students in Group C, with the ability lower than the average ability group, but higher than the lowest ability group, which is 28.4% of the total students. And, the number of students in the lowest ability group (E) is

Table 2.10 Performance of students in each ability group

Groups	Original ability value grouping ability starting point-terminal point	Transformed ability value grouping ability starting point-terminal point	Number of students	Percentage of each group students out of the total (%)	Accumulative percentage (%)
Group of the highest ability (A)	1.898–Maximum	69–93	346	2.1	2.1
Group of the ability above average (B)	0.914–1.898	59–69	4214	25.1	27.1
Group of the average ability (C)	0.07–0.914	50–59	5990	35.7	62.8
Group of the ability below average (D)	−0.877 to 0.07	41–50	4778	28.4	91.2
Group of the lowest ability (E)	Minimum to −0.877	0–41	1471	8.8	100.0

Note Transformation formula is T = 50 + 10 × original ability value

2.4 Analysis and Discussion on the Reading Test Results

Fig. 2.2 Distribution of student frequency in five ability groups

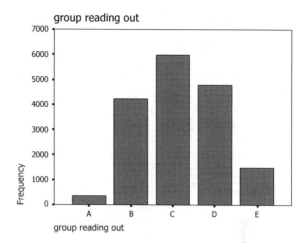

1471, 8.8% of the total students. The accumulative number of students in and above the average ability group is 10,550 (346 + 4214 + 5990), which is 62.9% (2.1% + 25.1% + 35.7%) of the total students, while the accumulative number of students below the average ability group is 6249 (4778 + 1471), which is 37.2% (28.4% + 8.8%) of the total students.

If the groups A, B, C, D, and E are corresponding to excellent, proficient, qualified, basically qualified, and unqualified, it could be obtained that out of the 16,799 participants, the performance of 2.1% of students is excellent, the performance of 25.1% of students is proficient, the performance of 35.7% of students is qualified, the performance of 28.4% of students is basically qualified, and the performance of 8.8% of students is fairly bad.

From the holistic test results of the 16,799 Grade 6 students' reading ability, over 60% of students meet the requirements of *Chinese Curriculum Standard*, with the basic reading ability, such as can understand the appropriate meanings of words in language environment and the particular meanings of idioms, can read and memorize the ancient poems, can apply conjunctions, can understand the meanings of keywords in poems, can accurately tell and understand sentence meaning, can accurately extract the related information from narrative texts, can tell the explaining methods used in texts, can extract and integrate the related information from expository texts, can grasp the key points, etc. However, near 40% of students have some difficulty to achieve the requirements of *Chinese Curriculum Standard*, with quite weak reading ability. There are even some students (8.8%) with fairly bad reading ability.

2.4.3 The Proportion of Students in Different Ability Groups and the Tasks That Can Be Accomplished

As Fig. 2.3 illustrates, the tasks that can be accomplished by students in different ability groups are categorized from high to low, i.e., A → E, among which, Group A is the group of students with excellent ability, who can accomplish all the tasks included in Group A, B, C, D, and E; Group B is the group of students with

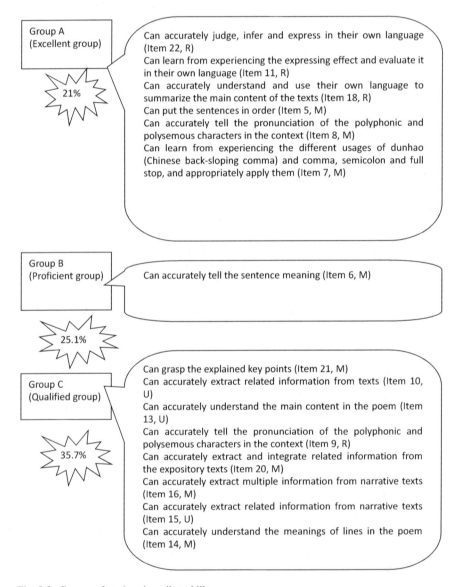

Fig. 2.3 Groups of students' reading ability

2.4 Analysis and Discussion on the Reading Test Results 81

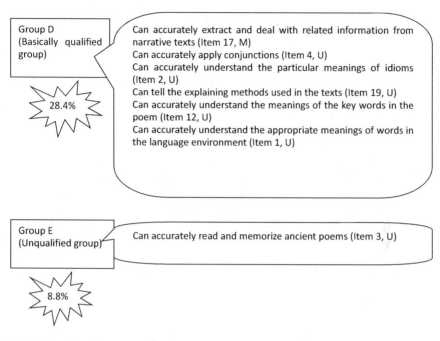

Fig. 2.3 (continued)

fairly good ability, who can accomplish all the tasks included in Group B, C, D, and E; Group C is the group of students with qualified ability, who can accomplish all the tasks included in Group C, D, and E; Group D is the group of students with basic ability, who can accomplish all the tasks included in Group D and E; and Group E is the group of students with unqualified ability, who can only accomplish the tasks included in Group E.

From the tasks which could be accomplished by students in different ability groups above, it could be seen that the five-level ability groups from the lowest ability group (Group E) to the highest ability group (Group A) do reflect the obvious difference.

1. From the developmental level of students' reading ability, the reading tasks that can be accomplished by students reflect the gradual process of their cognitive level and language ability from low to high. For example, Group E (the lowest ability group) reflects the ability to accurately read and memorize ancient poems, and the percentage of students at this ability level is 8.8%; Group D (the basically qualified group) mainly reflects the ability to understand and apply at the level of words and sentences and to retrieve information in the texts based on needs, and the percentage of students at this ability level is 28.4%; Group C (the qualified group) mainly reflects the ability to extract and integrate information in the text and to understand the main idea of the text, and the percentage of students at this ability level is 35.7%; Group B (the proficient group) hardly

reflects students' ability development change due to the lack of appropriate reading tasks; however, the test statistical data shows that the percentage of students at this ability level is 25.1%; Group A (excellent group) reflects the ability to understand and apply the text content, but the percentage of students at this ability level is only 2.1%, which means that students' ability is generally weak to holistically perceive, understand, learn from experience, evaluate, and apply at the level of text.
2. From the structural levels of SOLO taxonomy, the tasks that can be accomplished by students also reflect the gradual process of their cognitive level from uni-structural to relational. Group E (the lowest ability group) students can only read and memorize ancient poems, Group D (the basically qualified group) students are basically at U structural level, Group C (the qualified group) students are basically at the crossing period from U structural level to M structural level, while in Group B (proficient group) the related conclusions cannot be obtained since there are not enough reading tasks. And, Group A (excellent group) students own the ability to solve the fairly complicated problems, and can answer those reading tasks at R level which require to link several events.

2.4.4 The Corresponding Analysis of Students' Practical Ability Performance and Item Target Test Level

It could be found from Fig. 2.4, the distribution of the practical difficulty of the reading ability test items is fairly skewed, such as most of the test items are covered by the students with the reading ability in basically qualified group, qualified group and excellent group, which makes that there is only 1 item suitable for the ability of the students in proficient group and their percentage is 25.1%, while the percentage of students in excellent group is only 2.1% and there are 6 items suitable for them.

According to Fig. 2.4, the main reasons for the inconsistency of them are analyzed based on the corresponding relation for students' practical ability performance and item target test level (difficulty) to formulate Table 2.11.

From Table 2.11, some conclusions could be obtained as follows:

1. There are five items with the practical difficulty higher than target level, i.e., estimated difficulty, which account for 23% of the total items, and these items are items 5, 7, 8, 10, and 13. Among them, there are two items rising to be M level from U level, which are item 10, to extract related information from texts and item 13, to accurately understand the main content in the poem, which indicates that student ability to effectively tell from multiple interference information should be strengthened and students have certain difficulty to master the holistic content of poems and emotion. And, there are three items rising to be R level from M level, which are item 5, to put the sentences in order, item 7, whether can learn from experiencing the different usages of dunhao (Chinese

2.4 Analysis and Discussion on the Reading Test Results

Fig. 2.4 Item difficulty and student ability distribution

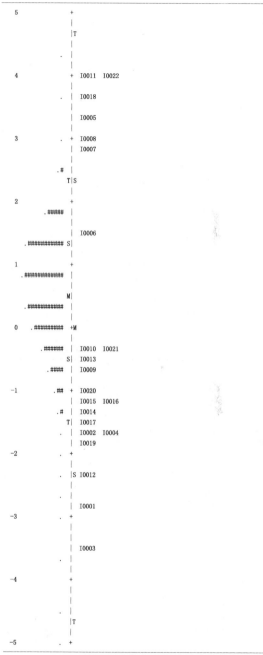

EACH '#' IS 244.

Table 2.11 Corresponding analysis of students' practical ability performance and item target test level

Item	Tested ability description (referring to the two-dimensional table of specifications)	Target test level	Difficulty value	Explanation
1	Can accurately understand the appropriate meanings of words in the language environment	U	−2.91	There are 95% of students achieving U level, with the average ability of 0.49. The practical difficulty and student ability accord with the target test level
2	Can accurately understand the particular meanings of idioms	U	−1.62	There are 85% of students achieving U level, with the average ability of 0.55. The practical difficulty and student ability accord with the target test level
3	Can accurately read and memorize ancient poems	U	−3.47	There are 97% of students achieving U level, with the average ability of 0.46. The practical difficulty and student ability accord with the target test level
4	Can accurately apply conjunctions	U	−1.71	There are 86% of students achieving U level, with the average ability of 0.57. The practical difficulty and student ability accord with the target test level
5	Can put the sentences in order	M	3.38	There are 7% of students achieving M level, with the average ability of 0.57, and there are 73% of students achieving U level. The practical difficulty is higher than the target test level, which means that the students are in chaos to understand the logical sequence between sentences
6	Can accurately tell the sentence meaning	M	1.44	There are 30% of students achieving M level, with the average ability of 0.72, and there are 40% of students achieving U level. The practical difficulty and student ability accord with the target test level

(continued)

2.4 Analysis and Discussion on the Reading Test Results

Table 2.11 (continued)

Item	Tested ability description (referring to the two-dimensional table of specifications)	Target test level	Difficulty value	Explanation
7	Can learn from experiencing the different usages of dunhao (Chinese back-sloping comma) and comma, semicolon and full stop, and appropriately apply them	M	2.80	There are 11% of students achieving M level, with the average ability of 0.62, and there are 36% of students achieving U level. The practical difficulty is higher than the target test level, which means that the students' ability to accurately use punctuation marks is weak
8	Can accurately tell the pronunciation of the polyphonic and polysemous characters in the context	M	2.96	There are 10% of students achieving M level, with the average ability of 0.36, and there are 73% of students achieving U level. The practical difficulty is higher than the target test level, which means that the students have difficulty to tell the pronunciation of the polyphonic and polysemous characters
9	Can accurately tell the pronunciation of the polyphonic and polysemous characters in the context	R	−0.65	There are 71% of students achieving R level, with the average ability of 0.66, and there are 25% of students achieving M level. The practical difficulty is lower than the target test level, which means that the student ability has been lowly predicted
10	Can accurately extract related information from texts	U	−0.39	There are 67% of students achieving U level, with the average ability of 0.74. The practical difficulty is higher than the target test level, which means that the student ability to effectively tell from multiple interference information should be strengthened
11	Can learn from experiencing the expressing effect and evaluate it in their own language	R	3.93	There are 4% of students achieving R level, with the average ability of 1.06. The practical difficulty and student ability accord with the target test level

(continued)

Table 2.11 (continued)

Item	Tested ability description (referring to the two-dimensional table of specifications)	Target test level	Difficulty value	Explanation
12	Can accurately understand the meanings of the keywords in the poem	U	−2.34	There are 92% of students achieving U level, with the average ability of 0.51. The practical difficulty and student ability accord with the target test level
13	Can accurately understand the main content in the poem	U	−0.52	There are 69% of students achieving U level, with the average ability of 0.69. The practical difficulty is higher than the target test level, which means that the students have certain difficulty to master the holistic content of poems and emotion
14	Can accurately understand the meanings of lines in the poem	M	−1.32	There are 82% of students achieving M level, with the average ability of 0.57, and there are 15% of students achieving U level. The practical difficulty is lower than the target test level, which means that the student ability to understand the meanings of the lines in the poem is strong
15	Can accurately extract related information from narrative texts	U	−1.20	There are 80% of students achieving U level, with the average ability of 0.61. The practical difficulty and student ability accord with the target test level
16	Can accurately extract multiple information from narrative texts	M	−1.24	There are 80% of students achieving M level, with the average ability of 0.60, and there are 19% of students achieving U level. The practical difficulty is lower than the target test level, which means that the student ability to extract information is fairly strong
17	Can accurately extract and deal with related	M	−1.55	There are 84% of students achieving M level, with the average ability of 0.54, and

(continued)

2.4 Analysis and Discussion on the Reading Test Results

Table 2.11 (continued)

Item	Tested ability description (referring to the two-dimensional table of specifications)	Target test level	Difficulty value	Explanation
	information from narrative texts			there are 15% of students achieving U level. The practical difficulty is lower than the target test level, which means that the student ability to extract and deal with related information is fairly strong
18	Can accurately understand and use their own language to summarize the main content of the texts	R	3.65	There are 5% of students achieving R level, with the average ability of 1.51. The practical difficulty and student ability accord with the target test level
19	Can tell the explaining methods used in the texts	U	−1.87	There are 88% of students achieving U level, with the average ability of 0.53. The practical difficulty and student ability accord with the target test level
20	Can accurately extract and integrate related information from the expository texts	M	−1.00	There are 77% of students achieving M level, with the average ability of 0.63, and there are 16% of students achieving U level. The practical difficulty and student ability accord with the target test level
21	Can grasp the explained key points	M	−0.36	There are 66% of students achieving M level, with the average ability of 0.73, and there are 28% of students achieving U level. The practical difficulty and student ability accord with the target test level
22	Can accurately judge, infer, and express in their own language	R	3.99	There are 4% of students achieving R level, with the average ability of 1.38. The practical difficulty and student ability accord with the target test level

back-sloping comma) and comma, semicolon and full stop, and appropriately apply them, and item 8, to accurately tell the pronunciation of the polyphonic and polysemous characters in the context, which indicates that students are still in chaos to understand the logical sequence between sentences, their ability to accurately use punctuation marks is weak, and they also have difficulty to tell the pronunciation of the polyphonic and polysemous characters.

2. There are four items with the practical difficulty lower than target level, i.e., estimated difficulty, which accounts for 18% of the total items, and these items are items 9, 14, 16, and 17. Among them, there are three items descending to be U level from M level, which are item 14 (whether can accurately understand the meanings of lines in the poem), item 16 (whether can accurately extract multiple information from narrative texts), and item 17 (whether can accurately extract and deal with related information from narrative texts). And, there is 1 item descending to be M level from R level, which is item 9 (whether can accurately tell the pronunciation of the polyphonic and polysemous characters in the context). This indicates that the student ability to understand the meanings of the lines in the poem, to extract and deal with related information and to tell the pronunciation of the polyphonic and polysemous characters in the context is stronger than predicted.

3. There are 13 items with the practical difficulty in accordance with the target level of student ability, which accounts for 59% of the total items. Among them, there are 7 items at U level, which are items 1, 2, 3, 4, 12, 15, and 19, indicating that students can understand the appropriate meanings of words in the language environment and the particular meanings of idioms, can read and memorize ancient poems, can apply conjunctions, can understand the meanings of the keywords in the poem, can accurately extract related information from narrative texts, can tell the explaining methods used in the texts, etc. There are three items at M level, which are items 6, 20 and 21, indicating that students can accurately tell the sentence meaning, can extract and integrate related information from the expository texts, and can grasp the explained key points. And there are three items at R level, which are items 11, 18, and 22, indicating that the practical difficulty accord with the student ability target test level, that is, to say student practical ability to learn from experiencing the expressing effect and to evaluate with their own language, to understand and summarize the main content of the texts, and to accurately judge, infer, and express are deficient.

2.5 The Main Findings

Based on the result analysis of this survey, the main findings are as follows.

2.5 The Main Findings

2.5.1 *The Overall Complexion*

From the results of the survey on the reading ability of 16,799 students in Grade 6, it could be seen that over 60% of students can basically achieve the requirements of the curriculum standard, owning the basic reading ability, such as can accurately understand the appropriate meanings of words in the language environment and the particular meanings of idioms, can accurately read and memorize ancient poems, can accurately apply conjunctions, can accurately understand the meanings of the keywords in the poem, can accurately understand the meanings of sentences, can accurately extract related information from narrative texts, can tell the explaining methods used in the texts, can accurately extract and integrate related information from the expository texts, can grasp the explained key points, and so on. However, near 40% of students have a certain extent of difficulty to achieve the requirements of the curriculum standard, with fairly weak reading ability, even a small percentage of students (8.8%) have quite bad reading ability, which could be specifically concluded into the aspects as follows.

1. The development of students' reading ability is unbalanced in different content domains

The analysis results show that students perform at a fairly low level in the following content domains: learning from experiencing the different usages of dunhao (Chinese back-sloping comma) and comma, semicolon and full stop, and appropriately applying them, putting the sentences in order, learning from experiencing the expressing effect and evaluating it in their own language, accurately understanding and using their own language to summarize the main content of the texts, accurately understanding the main content in the poem, and accurately judging, inferring, and using their own language to express. But students perform at a fairly high level in the following content domains: accurately understanding the appropriate meanings of words in the language environment, accurately understanding the particular meanings of idioms, accurately reading and memorizing ancient poems, accurately applying conjunctions, accurately extracting, even integrating and dealing with related information from narrative texts, accurately understanding the meanings of the keywords and lines in the poem, etc. It can be seen that the development of students' reading ability is unbalanced in different content domains.

2. Difference exists in students' reading ability at different performance levels

From the perspective of the structural levels of SOLO taxonomy, the reading tasks students can accomplish reflect the gradual tendency of their reading ability from uni-structural level to relational level: Group E (the lowest ability group) students can only read and memorize ancient poems, Group D (the basically qualified group) students basically are at U structural level, Group C (the qualified group) students basically are at the crossing period from U structural level to M structural level, the related conclusions cannot be obtained for Group B (proficient group) students since there are not enough reading tasks. And, Group A (excellent group) students own the ability to solve the fairly complicated problems and can answer those reading tasks at R level which require to link several events.

2.5.2 The Positive Aspects

First, according to the corresponding analysis results of students' practical ability performance and item target test level, two objective tendencies of student reading ability development could be basically reflected from the test paper, which are the tendency of the gradual decay of the ability from recognition to understanding, and then to application, and the tendency of the gradual decay of the reading ability from character and word level, to sentence and paragraph level, and then to text level. For example, the ability to read and memorize ancient poems is reflected in the lowest ability group, and the basically qualified group mainly reflects student ability to understand and apply at the word and sentence level, and to retrieve information in the texts based on the needs, while the ability to extract and integrate information in the text language environment and the ability to understand the main idea of the texts are reflected in the qualified group, and the excellent group reflects student ability to understand and apply at the content domain of chapter level. The quite good correspondence of students' practical ability performance and item target test level indicate that the test reliability of the reading ability is fairly high.

Second, from the perspective of the structural levels of SOLO taxonomy, the reading tasks students can accomplish reflect the gradual tendency of their reading ability from uni-structural level to relational level: Group E (the lowest ability group) students can only read and memorize ancient poems, Group D (the basically qualified group) students basically are at U structural level, Group C (the qualified group) students basically are at the crossing period from U structural level to M structural level, and the related conclusions cannot be obtained for Group B (proficient group) students since there are not enough reading tasks. And, Group A (excellent group) students own the ability to solve the fairly complicated problems, and can answer those reading tasks at R level which require to link several events. This, from another perspective, also indicates that the test reliability of the reading ability is fairly high.

Last, from the perspective of the ability achievement in different reading domains, most of the students own the basic ability to recognize and to understand, although there is a certain distance to the curriculum standard requirement for the application. For example, the ability to read and memorize ancient poems, to understand the appropriate meanings of words in the language environment and the particular meanings of idioms, to apply conjunctions, to understand the meanings of the keywords in the poem, to accurately tell the meanings of sentences, to extract related information from narrative texts, to tell the explaining methods used in the texts, to extract and integrate related information from the expository texts, to grasp the explained key points, etc. Over 60% of students almost own these reading comprehension abilities. Generally, comprehension ability is the core of reading

2.5 The Main Findings

ability, which makes it easy to transfer to the application ability, i.e., it makes the foundation to sustainably develop reading ability.

2.5.3 The Aspects Which Are Not so Satisfying

1. Students' overall reading ability is on the low side

If the percentile is employed to transform the score, the lowest score of the test results is about 0 and the highest score is about 93 (92.70), with the average around 54.22, which could be seen that the holistic test result is quite low. If student reading ability is divided into five levels, the result shows that out of the 16,799 participants, the performance of 2.1% of students is excellent, the performance of 25.1% of students is proficient, the performance of 35.7% of students is qualified, the performance of 28.4% of students is basically qualified, and the performance of 8.8% of students is fairly bad. That is to say, over 60% of students can achieve the requirement of the curriculum standard, owning the basic reading ability. However, near 40% of students have some extent of difficulty to reach the requirement of the curriculum standard, with quite weak reading ability.

2. Students lack the application ability in the aspects of learning from experiencing the expressing effect and evaluating with their own language, of understanding and summarizing the main content of the texts, and of accurately judging, inferring, and using their own language to express

From the structural levels of the SOLO taxonomy, 37.2% (8.8% of students from the lowest ability group +28.4% of students from the basically qualified group) of students are almost totally at uni-structural level; only 2.1% of students in the excellent group own the ability to solve the fairly complicated problems, at the transferring period from M structural level to R structural level. Even though it is like this, the ability consistency is not represented from their performance on the multiple-choice questions and on the open-ended questions, which represents that students lack the application ability in the aspects of learning from experiencing the expressing effect and evaluating it in their own language, of understanding and summarizing the main content of the texts, and of accurately judging, inferring, and using their own language to express. The main difference between students in the excellent group and in other groups is shown on the ability to understand and apply at the content domain of chapter level, but only 2.1% of students are at this ability level, indicating that student ability to holistically perceive, understand, learn from experiencing, evaluate, and apply is generally fairly bad.

2.6 Countermeasures and Suggestions

2.6.1 To Strengthen the Reading Ability Practice and to Optimize the Classroom Teaching Efficiency

Since students' overall reading ability is on the low side, the reading ability practice should be vigorously strengthened and the classroom teaching efficiency should also be optimized, to raise students' reading ability in the reading practice. Meanwhile, since students' reading ability is developed with unbalance in different content domains and differences exist at different performance levels, stratified reading teaching should be carried out based on students' practical needs. Students should be taught in accordance with their aptitude, aiming to make every student develop well.

2.6.2 To Develop Colorful Extracurricular Reading Activities and to Actively Build Schools with Book Fragrance

To optimize the classroom teaching efficiency is only one of the important methods to promote students' reading ability. Colorful extracurricular reading activities can also be developed in schools and schools are built with book fragrance to motivate students' interest in reading, accelerating to promote students' reading ability.

2.6.3 To Strive to Form Family Reading Atmosphere and to Build Parent–Offspring Reading Space

Parents are children's good teachers and helpful friends. If parents love reading, children, influenced by them, must love reading when they are young and shape good habits to read regularly. With accumulation day by day and month by month, the children's reading ability will be promoted a lot. If parents can interact with children, sharing and instructing reading, children's reading ability may also own the capability to develop sustainably. Therefore, parents should try to form healthy family reading atmosphere.

2.6.4 To Vigorously Advocate the National Reading to Comply with the Needs of the Information Age

Situated in the information age, people are required to largely elevate the ability to collect and deal with the information, and to actively acquire the new knowledge, which make it need to raise the national reading literacy. Thus, if the national reading could be vigorously advocated to comply with the needs of the information age, the social atmosphere, to some extent, will affect children's reading ability to develop.

Chapter 3
Mathematics Assessment Report

3.1 Research Background

Students' academic achievement is the developmental level in the aspects of knowledge, skills, and affect & attitude achieved by students through learning activities with teachers' instruction. It is the core indicator of education quality and an important method to monitor the national education quality. It is necessary and urgent to carry out large-scale surveys on students' academic achievement in order to know the holistic situation of students' learning nationally, to find problems and to provide solutions. At present, the function of mathematics is more and more important in people's daily life and industry, and also for the development of human beings. Therefore, in the curriculum system of basic education in every country, mathematics plays a crucial role. To know students' academic achievement on mathematics, the internationally influential academic achievement surveys are carried out on students' academic achievement on mathematics, such as IEA/TIMSS, OECD/PISA and NAEP in the USA. With this background, the monitoring of education quality in our country should also pay particular attention to students' academic achievement on mathematics.

3.2 Theoretical Framework

3.2.1 Definition of Subject Competence

3.2.1.1 Problem-Solving in the Subject of Mathematics in Primary School

Problem-solving is the action slogan of mathematics education proposed by international mathematics education during the process from "New Math" to "Back to Basics" in the late twentieth century. Meanwhile, it is also an important aspect to

© Springer-Verlag GmbH Germany and Educational Science Publishing House 2019
H. Tian and Z. Sun, *Assessment Report on Chinese Primary School Students' Academic Achievement*, https://doi.org/10.1007/978-3-662-57530-7_3

which the international mathematics education development of the new century pays close attention. The problem-solving in mathematics takes the mathematical problem as research target, which could develop students' creative mind, promote students' intention to apply mathematics, and is one of the foci in the present mathematics education reform and research. Many famous educationists and mathematics educationists, such as Dewey, Celestin, Klix, Webster, Doerner, Polya, Ausubel, etc., from different perspectives, have made arguments on the situations, categories, and features of problem-solving in mathematics education. The scholars in our country have also proposed their own opinions, such as Prof. Gao Wen, who integrates the various ideas on problem-solving process and concludes problem-solving into five steps, i.e., problem recognizing and problem defining, problem representation, strategy selection and application, resources allocation, monitoring, and assessment.[1]

Internationally, no matter in PISA 2000 or in PISA 2003 mathematics tests, particular attention was paid to the assessment on how students solve various types of problems with mathematical knowledge, especially the problems in the practical world. With mathematics as research emphasis, "problem-solving skill" was added in PISA 2003, besides assessment on literacies of reading and writing, mathematics and science. In recent years, problem-solving has also been given special attention in national mathematics teaching and research in primary schools. And there are quite clear statements on the definition, nature, and process of problem-solving in primary school mathematics.

3.2.1.2 Definition of Problem-Solving in Primary School Mathematics

In the primary school mathematics teaching and learning, problem-solving is the psychological activity in which individuals, with the related knowledge acquired, employ new strategies to seek the solutions to the problems in new situations.[2]

3.2.1.3 Nature of Problem-Solving in Primary School Mathematics

- The problems are those new ones students encounter the first time, rather than the common exercises in their daily life.
- The methods and approaches in problem-solving are new, with which students need to make use of the recombination of acquired knowledge, skills, and methods, at least students need to do the fairly complicated process for the

---

[1]Xu YB (2001) Mathematics education outlook. East China Normal University Press, Shanghai.
[2]Zhou YR (1999) Primary school math pedagogy. China Renmin University Press Co. LTD, Beijing.

acquired knowledge, skills, and methods. Problem-solving is an exploring activity for students to overcome kinds of difficulties.
- The methods and approaches in problem-solving could include implicit mind activities and explicit manipulation activities.
- Once the problem has been solved, the new method, approach, and strategy acquired in the problem-solving process could be a part of cognitive structure, and become the already-known methods and approaches to solve other problems. That is to say, it is no longer problem-solving to solve other problems with these methods and approaches.

3.2.1.4 Process of Problem-Solving in Primary School Mathematics

- Understanding the problem

Understanding the problem means that students have holistic understanding of the given conditions and of the original situation of the target, and keep clear impression of them to make ready to find the solution to the problem with already-known knowledge and strategy, in which the given conditions are the given information in the test item, including data, relation, and reasons. It is extremely important for understanding the problem whether there is a fixation point in the students' original cognitive structure to unite the new knowledge.

- Seeking the solution

With the understanding of the given conditions and of the relation between conditions and target, it needs to seek the breakthrough in the gap between the conditions and target. Whether and how to fill in the gap between the conditions and target is the key issue in the process of problem-solving. With the conditions of the problem and the original situation of the target, students need to link their acquired knowledge and judge whether it is a transformation of any of the problems they have met. If not, students need to judge whether it can apply some of the regular patterns. When the content stated in the test item is abstract, the aids, such as figures of line segment, tables, and conditions extracting, could be used to make the hidden numerical relationship obvious. If the successive thought encounters obstacles when analyzing the numerical relationship, reverse thought could be tried and the both-side squeezing method of looking for key sentences could also be applied to approach the target. If the gap between the conditions and target is fairly large, in other words, it is not easy to seek the solution due to several existing unknown transitive questions, information processing should be done for the numerical relationship per se, through transforming the conditions or the way of the statement of the problem target, to reduce the difficulty of problem-solving. When it is hard to build the direct relationship between the problem and the original cognitive structure, students should use types of effective strategies, with analysis and synthesis, to propose hypotheses and finally decide the plan to solve the problem.

- Solving the problem

Based on the thinking process, students devise the problem-solving plan, lay it out step by step and solve the problem finally. In the process, students' reckoning, equation calculation, or graph drawing in every step should be accurate, and they can use clear language to clarify their reason, proving the accuracy of every step.

- Reviewing and evaluating

Reviewing is mainly to verify the answer, while evaluating requires students to analyze whether their problem-solving method is brief, whether reasoning is rigorous, and to inquire further whether the method could be applied to other problems.

3.2.2 The Present Research Complexion of the Subject Competence Assessment

In the year 2001, Ministry of Education published *Basic Education Curriculum Reform Guideline (Pilot version)*, Compulsory Education Curriculum Design Plan and curriculum standard of every subject, based on which, a series of research projects on assessment and testing reform have been carried out by the Department for Basic Education and National Center for School Curriculum and Textbook Development. And certain of fruits have been achieved within the 5 years, which made effective attempts in the aspects of scientificalness, feasibility, and manipulability to build the national analysis and direction system on primary and secondary school students' academic achievement. Since 2003, under the guidelines from the National Center for School Curriculum and Textbook Development, Ministry of Education, the project team of "To Build National Analysis and Direction System on Primary and Secondary School Students' Academic Achievement" has been established. On November 4, 2005, with the cooperation between the project team and the Education Bureau of Liaoning province, a provincial-level sampling test on Grade 3 students' Chinese and Mathematics and on Grade 8 students' Chinese, Mathematics, English, and Science was carried out in Liaoning province. The definition of mathematics academic achievement quality in the project is "During the compulsory education period, students' mathematics academic achievement quality, with the mathematical literacy as the core, is shown on the abilities that students master the basics of mathematical knowledge and skills, own mathematical thinking and mathematical intention, can logically communicate with others with mathematical language and symbols, can explore some basic mathematical phenomena and problems, and solve some simple problems in the practical life and other subject fields with mathematical methods."

In this test, "solving problem" is quite similar to the "problem-solving" in the present project (In the modification of curriculum standard, the original "solving problem" has been modified into "problem-solving".), which requires students to analyze the mathematical relation from the given information, and to solve it

3.2 Theoretical Framework

through constructing mathematical models. Students should have the ability to make reasonable hypothesis, effective assumptions and inferences from the given information, to analyze the possible existing rules of numbers in the problem situation with the employment of data information or data results, to decompose simple geometric shapes (solids) in order to simplify the problem, to solve unregular problems with some mathematical models, and to discuss and evaluate the mathematical thinking and methods used in the process of solving problems and generalize them.

There is some research on assessing primary school students' ability of problem-solving in the Ministry of Education key project "Research on Primary School Students' Academic Achievement Assessment Reform" in National Education Sciences "10th 5-year" Planning, which could also provide some valuable reference, although it is not particularly for mathematics subject. The indicator system to assess primary school students' ability of problem-solving has been decomposed in the research, in which problem discovering, problem analyzing, and problem-solving are treated as the first-level indices to assess the ability of problem-solving. Problem discovering means to produce new problems through exploring the problematic situation, which also includes posing new problems during the problem-solving process. Problem analyzing is to confirm the problem-solving way, based on the understanding of the relationship between components, to analyze and select a strategy, and to hypothesize the results. Problem-solving is to achieve the target of problem-solving with the employment of the methods including logic reasoning, manipulative experiments, etc., to state and reflect the results. In the research, the second-level indicator of problem discovering is the quantity and quality of the problem discovered, and the second-level indicator of problem analyzing is to understand the problem, to confirm the thinking, to select the strategy, and to hypothesize the supposition, while the second-level indicator of problem-solving includes reasoning and argument, results expression, reflection and adjustment, etc.

The testing content of the internationally influential PISA is not to simply repeat the acquired knowledge, but to see whether students can actively associate and think. The test items are based on children's life experience, extracted from the real situation and mostly focus on the link between the questions and practical life. The content assessed includes the acquired knowledge and structure needed by students in every domain and the application of knowledge and skills, in which calculation and mathematical thinking are included in the assessment on mathematical competence. The mathematical literacy test items no matter in PISA 2000 or in PISA 2003 emphasized to assess how students solve various types of problems, especially the problems in the practical world.

The test form of PISA is paper-and-pencil test, in which a questionnaire on individuals' background and learning situation is required to be filled in. Most of the test items are multiple choice, closed-ended questions and open-ended questions. The test items are based on children's life experience, extracted from the real situation and mostly focus on the link between the questions and practical life, in which calculation and mathematical thinking are included in the assessment on mathematical competence.

About the assessment structure of mathematical literacy, PISA test items pay attention to four aspects, which are mathematical content, mathematical process, mathematical situation, and item type. Among them, mathematical process is related to the process of "mathematisation", in which the competencies, such as thinking and reasoning, argumentation, communication, modeling, problem posing and solving, representation, using symbolic, formal, or technical language and operations, and use of aids and tools, are made use of. Among these competencies, many are overlapping, and when using mathematics, it is usually necessary to draw simultaneously on many of these abilities. Thus, three competency clusters are given by PISA as follows. The first is the reproduction cluster, essentially involving reproduction of some practiced knowledge, such as simple computations or very familiar definitions. The second is the connections cluster, based on the reproduction cluster, related to the abilities required to solve the problems in situations that are not simply routine but still familiar or fairly familiar settings, in which integration and connection of material and linking in the problem need to be considered. The third is reflection cluster, based on the connections cluster, related to some opinions, reflection, and creativity, such as mathematical thinking, reasoning, induction, etc., produced in the process of confirming some related mathematical knowledge and connecting related knowledge to seek a solution to the problem, requiring students to participate in explaining and defining the mathematical factors in the given situation, and then to make argument. Specifically, the following content is mainly included: ① recognizing the interdisciplinary problem, ② recognizing the information and conditions of related subjects, ③ proposing possible solutions and plans, ④ selecting the strategies for the solutions and plans, ⑤ solving the problem, ⑥ reviewing and reflecting, and ⑦ communicating the solution results.

In the assessment program, analytical reasoning is the core content in the assessment of solving problem skill. In the first test in the year 2003, 19 questions were designed, mainly around three levels which are ubiquitous and widely used in life. The assessment results are recorded at three levels.

Level 1: basic problem solver. They can understand the nature of the problem, seek the information related to the main features of the problem, and transform the information of the problem and represent it in a different form, such as to transform the information in the table into a diagram or curve. However, they can only solve the problem from one resource, rather than the problem from over one resources or the problem requiring students to reason with the provided information, i.e., students cannot fluently deal with the multifaceted problems.

Level 2: reasoning and decision-making problem solver. They can integrate information from various resources, apply all types of reasoning, such as induction and deduction reasoning, causal-relational reasoning or the integration of various reasonings, fairly systematically confirm the all possible changes in the situation and definitely make decisions based on the requirements. Meanwhile, they can integrate the introduction in different forms, such as written language, numerical information, diagrammatic information, etc., deal with unfamiliar introduction, such

3.2 Theoretical Framework

as the statement on design language, the flowchart related to machine, and so on, and can make inference based on two or more information resources.

Level 3: reflective and communicative problem solver. They can systematically approach the problem, not only analyze the conditions given in the situation and make reasonable decisions, but also consider the potential factors and the relationship between them and the solution plan, build their own expression method to facilitate them to solve problems and justify whether their solution could satisfy all the requirements, and can accurately state in the written way or other expression methods to communicate their solutions with others. They can consider and deal with many conditions, such as to control variables, explain the restrictions at that time or other limitations, form their special solution method, and successfully solve the problem.

For those below Level 1, it indicates that they can only deal with the easily understandable problems which seldom or never require reasoning, and have big difficulties in the aspects of making decisions, analyzing, or evaluating methods and solving problems.

In the 2003 assessment, the following six manipulative levels were used to indicate students' mathematical literacy.

Level 1: Students can respond to the problems with a familiar situation and all related information clearly given, can confirm the information according to the direct instruction and accomplish fixed steps, and can accomplish apparent tasks.

Level 2: Students can explain and recognize the problem situation which only requires direct reasoning, can find related information from given conditions and representative models, can apply basic algebra, equation, and steps, and can directly reason and literally explain the results.

Level 3: Students can clearly execute described steps, can select and apply simple problem-solving strategy, can explain and apply different given conditions and directly achieve inference, and can briefly report their explanation, results, and inference.

Level 4: Students can effectively apply models in the complicated situation related to constraint conditions or requiring making hypothesis, can select and integrate different expression ways, can do outstanding thinking and flexible reasoning, and can communicate and explain the results.

Level 5: Students can form and apply models in the complicated situation and confirm constraints and hypothesis, can select, compare, and evaluate corresponding problem-solving strategies, can strategically do outstanding thinking and reasoning and appropriately link the situational expression, symbols, and features, and can reflect their behavior, form, and communicate their explanation and inference.

Level 6: Students can model and induce the complicated situational problems based on surveys, can connect different information resources, can do deep mathematical thinking and reasoning, can apply symbols, calculation, and their relations to form new methods and strategy in new situation, can clearly express and accurately communicate, and can reflect their findings, explanation, argument, and the adaptability of the results.

The problem situation of PISA items could be divided into the following types: the personal situation directly link with students' daily activity, the educational and occupational situation related to students' school life and working environment, the public situation requiring students to observe some aspects of wider context, and the abstract scientific and intra-mathematical situation related to some technique process, theoretical context, or some definite mathematical problems.

Four item types are included in the PISA test, which are standardized multiple choice items, closed constructed-response items, open constructed-response items, and simple-response items. Different item types link different abilities. For example, multiple choice items are related to the abilities of low-cognitive-level skills, such as representation and connection, while open constructed-response items are often related to fairly high-cognitive-level activities.

During the period from 1990 to 1991, China mainland participated in the research activity organized by the International Assessment of Educational Progress (IAEP) during the second time, in which 20 countries and regions were involved. The IAEP test items were two-dimensional oriented, content and process, with 75 questions in total. Regarding the content dimension, it included 27 items of "numbers and calculation", 13 items of "measurement", 11 items of "geometry", 9 items of "data analysis, probability and statistics", and 15 items of "algebra and functions". The process included conceptual understanding, procedural knowledge, and problem-solving. And the problem-solving means the ability with which students apply their mathematical knowledge in the new problem situation. It requires the students to recognize the problems they encounter, to judge whether the conditions of the problems are complete, and to form and select an appropriate strategy based on the given conditions, integrate the acquired knowledge to solve the problems. It reflects students' ability to apply their acquired knowledge in the new problem situation.

The research of Richard E. Mayer is enlightening for the test item design. He proposed a cognitive analytical model to study and solve mathematical word problems. His model is based on such a hypothesis that there are two main steps to solve problems, which are to represent and to seek a method to solve the problem. To represent the problem, students have to own the ability to transform every sentence in the word problem into the form of internal representation, such as an equation, and can integrate each part of the problem into a fluent entirety. In order to find the solution to the problem, students also have to plan and find a sufficiently effective algorithm, and then accurately execute the algorithm. In Mayer's model, the four cognitive components related to solving mathematical word problems were categorized and analyzed as the following steps: transformation, which means that students transform a sentence into their psychological representation; integration, which means that students integrate the selected information to represent the whole problem; plan, meaning that students decompose the problem into small problems

3.2 Theoretical Framework

and some related steps; and execution, in which students specifically carry out their plan, with the execution process emphasized.

The cognitive level of TIMMS 2003 mathematics test has similarity to the present project. It assesses students' ability from four different cognitive levels of knowing facts and procedures, using concepts, solving routine problems, and reasoning, with specific requirements as follows.

Knowing Facts and Procedures

Facts encompass the factual knowledge that provides the basic language of mathematics, and the essential mathematical facts and properties that form the foundation for mathematical thought. Procedures form a bridge between more basic knowledge and the use of mathematics for solving routine problems, especially those encountered by many people in their daily lives. In essence, a fluent use of procedures entails recall of sets of actions and how to carry them out. Students need to be efficient and accurate in using a variety of computational procedures and tools. They need to see that particular procedures can be used to solve entire classes of problems, not just individual problems. The test items at this cognitive level mainly assess students' abilities as follows: ① whether they can recall definitions, vocabulary, units, number facts, etc.; ② whether they can recognize/identify mathematical entities that are mathematically equivalent; ③ whether they know algorithmic procedures for $+$, $-$, $\times$, $\div$, or a combination of these procedures for approximating numbers, estimating measures, solving equations, evaluating expressions and formulas, dividing a quantity in a given ration, increasing or decreasing a quantity by a given percent, simplifying, factoring, expanding algebraic and numerical expressions, and collecting like terms; ④ whether they can use mathematics and measuring instruments, read scales, draw lines, angles, or shapes to given specifications, use straightedge and compass to construct the perpendicular bisector of a line, angle bisector, triangles, and quadrilaterals, given necessary measures.

Using Concepts

Using concepts is shown to know, classify, represent, formulate, and distinguish the concepts, which could be explained as follows. To know means knowing that length, area, and volume are conserved under certain conditions, and having an appreciation of concepts such as inclusion and exclusion, generality, equal likelihood, representation, proof, cardinality and ordinality, mathematical relationships, place value. To classify means classifying/grouping objects, shapes, numbers, expressions, and ideas according to common properties, making correct decisions about class membership, and ordering numbers and objects by attributes. To represent means representing numbers using models, displaying mathematical information or data in diagrams, tables, charts, graph, and generating an equivalent representation for a given mathematical entity or relationship, such as generating ordered pairs that describe the function from given a function rule. To formulate means formulating problems or situations that could be modeled by given equations or expressions. To distinguish means distinguishing questions that can be addressed by given information, such as a data set, from those that cannot.

Solving Routine Problems

The routine problems will have been standard in classroom exercises designed to provide practice in particular methods or techniques. Each of these types of problems is expected to be sufficiently familiar to students that they will essentially involve selecting and applying learned procedures, including to select/use an efficient method or strategy for solving problems where there is a known algorithm or method of solution; to generate an appropriate model, such as an equation or diagram, for solving a routine problem; to interpret given mathematical models (equations, diagrams, etc.) and to accomplish a task by following and executing a set of mathematical instructions; to apply knowledge of facts, procedures, and concepts to solve routine mathematical (including real-life) problems, i.e., problems similar to those target students are likely to have encountered in class; and to verify/check the correctness of the solution to a problem and to evaluate the reasonableness of the solution to a problem.

Reasoning

Reasoning mathematically involves the capacity for logical, systematic thinking. It includes intuitive and inductive reasoning based on patterns and regularities that can be used to arrive at solutions to nonroutine problems. Nonroutine problems are problems that are very likely to be unfamiliar to students.

The specific skills are included: ① to hypothesize, conjecture, and predict. Make suitable conjectures while investigating patterns, discussing ideas, proposing models, examining data sets; specify an outcome (number, pattern, amount, transformation, etc.) that will result from some operation or experiment before it is performed.

② to analyze. Determine and describe or use relationships between variables and objects in mathematical situations; analyze univariate statistical data; decompose geometric figures to simplify solving a problem; draw the net of a given unfamiliar solid; make valid inferences from given information.

③ to evaluate. Discuss and critically evaluate a mathematical idea, conjecture, problem-solving strategy, method, proof, etc.

④ to generalize. Extend the domain to which the result of mathematical thinking and problem-solving is applicable by restating results in more general and more widely applicable terms.

⑤ to connect. Connect new knowledge to existing knowledge; male connections between different elements of knowledge and related representations; make linkages between related mathematical ideas or objects.

⑥ to synthesize or integrate. Combine disparate mathematical procedures to establish results; combine results to produce a further result.

⑦ to solve nonroutine problems. Solve problems set in mathematical or real-life contexts where target students are very unlikely to have encountered closely similar items; apply mathematical procedures in unfamiliar contexts.

⑧ to justify and prove. Provide evidence for the validity of an action or the truth of a statement by reference to mathematical results or properties; develop mathematical arguments to prove or disprove statements, given relevant information.

The four proficiency levels are gradually rising, which are also the ability requirements for students in countries' mathematical curriculum standards or mathematical teaching guidelines. For students in different grades, the requirements correspondingly vary, which represents not only in the different requirements within a content, but also in the different proportions of knowledge contents, which are similar to the contents regulated in the Content Standards in the national curriculum standards.

At present, the mathematical teaching reform requires the focus of the mathematical cognitive analysis transferred to the cognition of the information processing or to the attention to quantity, i.e., the models of strategy and representation for problem-solving, etc. During recent years, the progress on the assessment technique for the mathematical performance shows the feasibility and importance to assess students' mathematical thinking in the cognitive aspect with open-ended questions. Through the analysis on a series of open-ended mathematical problems and students' solutions to the problems, it has been found that it is feasible to assess students' mathematical thinking through appropriate mathematical problems. And for the quantitative analysis on the solution to each problem, the emphasis is on important cognitive aspects, such as problem-solving strategy, mathematical mistakes, mathematical representation, etc., which are considered crucial in problem-solving in the field of cognitive psychology. The application of proper strategy in the problem-solving reflects students' proficiency in mathematics. The inspection of the strategies students use and whether these strategies are successful could provide the information on the aspects of students' mathematical thinking and reasoning. The problem representation reflects the processes of students to solve problems and to communicate mathematical thought and thinking. And the study on mathematical mistakes provides the information on features of mistakes, solutions and how students correct their mistakes. Based on these cognitive aspects, problem-solving strategy, mathematical mistakes and mathematical representation to each problem could be inspected with a specific quantitative coding schema. Such cognitive analysis has been proved to be highly reliable in the prior researches, which could also provide important information about students' thinking and reasoning.

3.2.3 The Requirement of the New Curriculum Reform for the Subject Competence Assessment

It is explicitly pointed out in the Basic Beliefs in the *Full-time Compulsory Education Mathematics Curriculum Standard (Experimental version)* (*Mathematics Curriculum Standard* in abbreviation) that "the main aim of the assessment is to thoroughly know the students' mathematics learning process, to motivate students' learning and to improve teachers' teaching. The assessment system with multiple assessment goals and various assessment methods should be constructed. Regarding the mathematics learning assessment, students learning results should be cared and their learning process should be paid more attention to; students' mathematics learning proficiency should be taken into consideration, and their affect and attitude represented during the mathematics activities should be emphasized more to help students know themselves and build their confidence." This is the general description of the new curriculum assessment. In the Execution Suggestions, specific assessment suggestions for each learning stage are proposed, which specifically represents the assessment belief in each learning stage. To creatively understand the assessment beliefs and carry them out in the practical teaching process is an important step to guarantee that the new curriculum is effectively executed. The assessment on basic knowledge and basic skills should follow the basic beliefs in *Mathematics Curriculum Standard*, which assesses students' understanding and mastery degree of basic knowledge and basic skills based on the knowledge and skill goals in each learning stage. At the first learning stage, students often need to make use of concrete things or physical models to achieve learning tasks. Therefore, when students are assessed, the students' comprehension for the practical meaning of the content learned with concrete materials should be assessed as an emphasis. At the second and the third learning stages, assessment should be combined with practical background and the problem-solving process, and the understanding for the meaning of the content per se and the application based on the understanding should be paid more attention to in the assessment on concepts, formulas, and rules.

The previous test for mathematical knowledge mainly collectively assessed whether students can memorize the definition of a concept, by asking students to give or to choose, from some options, an accurate example related to the concept, or to differentiate a concept from others in accordance with conditions. However, it should be much more than that for the concept understanding. The real understanding for a concept implies that students can give certain of positive examples and negative examples related to the concept; can compare the similarities and differences between concepts and realize the different interpretations corresponding to different concepts; can transfer concepts from the literal statement into symbolic, photographic, or oral statement. All of these abilities related to concepts are very important to induce by applying concepts and to solve problems.

What the mathematics students learn in schools includes the feature of skills, and the traditional teaching, learning, and test also concentrate on this aspect, which seldom assesses whether students understand the relationships among concepts that implicitly exist in the skill application, let alone the invisible application of the problem-solving strategies during the mathematical thinking process. The new curriculums stress that the assessment on skills should not only assess students' mastery degree of the skills, but also assess students' understanding and mastery of the related concepts and the application of various problem-solving strategies. Thus, the assessment on skills assesses the complexion how students apply these skills in practice, and also assesses whether students can accurately judge which rule should be applied in the situation. For example, estimation is an important skill related to calculation. Students have to know the various estimation methods and know when estimation should be used and why estimation can solve problems.

To assess the abilities to discover problems and to solve problems actually lays stress on the assessment of mathematics learning process and methods. Students' mathematics should not just master some concepts and skills, but experience the process of exploration, guess and induction, etc., to solve the related problems. *Mathematics Curriculum Standard* explicitly takes "to formulate some basic strategies to solve problems" as a crucial curriculum goal, which makes it necessary to assess the complexion how students master these strategies.

It could be concluded that problem-solving is a comprehensive ability in mathematics learning. Students with strong problem-solving ability can extract the key features of problems, the relations and correlations included in the problems, can flexibly apply acquired knowledge, appropriate skills and accurate solving strategies to solve problems and express, and do necessary reflection and adjustment. Problem-solving of primary school mathematics is of the essence in primary school mathematics education. The ability of mathematical problem-solving students acquire in mathematics learning meanwhile can also accelerate them to learn mathematics better. Therefore, primary school students' mathematics learning could be assessed through the test on their mathematical problem-solving ability.

3.3 Research Method and Instrument

3.3.1 The Instrument Development and Its Reliability and Validity

3.3.1.1 The Bases of the Instrument Development

Mathematics Curriculum Standard

As a survey on academic achievement, the premise is the curriculum standard published by the country. Regarding the development of the present test instrument, the stage goals in the aspects of knowledge and skills, mathematical thinking, solving problem, affect and attitude, etc., at the second learning stage (Grades 4–6) are taken as the main foundation, with the test items thoroughly covering the content standard, and the difficulty based on the corresponding regulations in the curriculum standard.

SOLO Taxonomy

SOLO taxonomy is employed to analyze students' cognitive development, with students' performance on the questions categorized into five structural levels, which are pre-structural level, uni-structural level, multi-structural level, relational level, and extended abstract level. The meanings of the five levels could be read in the general report.

3.3.1.2 The Procedures of the Instrument Development

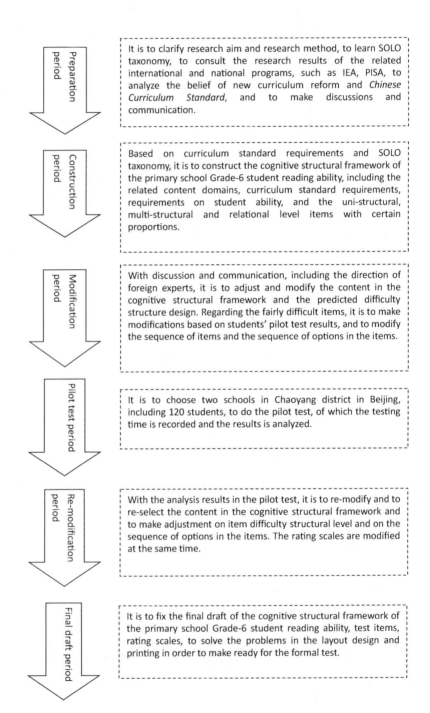

3.3 Research Method and Instrument   109

3.3.1.3 Construction of the Two-Dimensional Table of Specifications

To design the scientific and brief assessment framework is the base and precondition to construct the test instrument. The assessment framework in the present test project is based on the *Mathematics Curriculum Standard* and SOLO taxonomy, i.e., based on *Mathematics Curriculum Standard*, some key content goals are selected in the aspects of number and algebra, space and shape, statistics and probability, and comprehensive application, and then these are stated into general ability requirements and transformed into the predicted results of students' learning. After this, test items are employed to make learning results manipulative. Based on SOLO taxonomy, uni-structural (U), multi-structural (M), and relational (R) level test items are designed with the proportion of 2:2:1, and the cognitive structure framework is formed. The final proportion of the practical items is 14:17:6, and the testing time is 60 min, with 70 min as the pilot testing time, and the quantity of the pilot test items 1.33 times as many as that of the formal test.

Based on the analysis and study of the overall goals of the curriculum standard, the stage goals and the content domains, the content that could be assessed is selected as the content to be tested, and the statement of the curriculum standard is transferred into the specific skill requirements. For example, the requirement of "In specific situations, students can make conversion between graphic distance and practical distance with the given proportion; can fix the location based on the direction and distance" in the curriculum standard is transferred into "Mark a road in accordance with the conditions in the graph" as the skill requirement in the present test. The two-dimensional table of specifications for the test of Grade 6 in primary school is formed as follows (Table 3.1).

3.3.1.4 The Test Item Writing

Example 1: Item 28

Known that the Electricity Company is located 200 m south of Heping Square, and the Jiankang road is about 120 m the north of Heping square and parallel with Heping road, which figure below is accurate? Note: the dotted line represents Jiankang road.

Table 3.1 Primary school Grade-6 student mathematical competence cognitive structure framework

Content standard in the mathematics curriculum		Ability requirement (Students can)	Competency category	Structural level	Item sequential number	Proportion
Content domains	Content standard					
Numbers and algebra	Numeric recognition	Recognize, read, and write the numbers within 100 million, and know decimal system	Write the integer not smaller than 10 given conditions	Knowledge and skill	U	1	U:12 M:6 R:2
			Write the decimal given conditions	Knowledge and skill	U	3	
		Can use "wan" (10 thousand) or "yi" (100 million), as unit, to represent big numbers	Transform into the numbers with "yi" (100 million) as unit by omitting mantissa	Knowledge and skill	U	2	
		Can find common multiples and the least common multiple of two natural numbers within 10, and can find common factors and the biggest common factor of two natural numbers	Use the numeric concept to judge	Mathematical thinking	M	15	
		Know integers, odd integers, even integers, prime numbers, and composite numbers	Use the numeric concept to infer	Mathematical thinking	M	16	
		Feel the meaning of big numbers in a real-life situation and can make an estimation	Estimate the quantity related to areas in life	Mathematical thinking	U	5	
			Estimate the fairly big numbers in life	Mathematical thinking	U	6	
		Further know decimal and fraction, and know percent	Use fraction to describe the change of numbers after the decimal point is moved	Knowledge and skill	U	8	
		Can solve the simple practical problems related to decimal, fraction and percent	Solve the practical problems related to the fraction	Mathematical thinking	M	23	
			Judge the situation students meet the basic requirements in the test with the full score unequal to 100	Knowledge and skill	M	24	
		Explore the relationship between decimal, fraction and percent, and can make the transference	Judge whether a fraction could be transferred into finite decimals	Knowledge and skill	U	7	
		In the familiar real-life context, know the meaning of negative numbers, and can use negative numbers to express some problems in daily life	Express the going direction with a positive number or negative number and the final result of distance in a specific situation	Knowledge and skill	U	4	

(continued)

3.3 Research Method and Instrument 111

Table 3.1 (continued)

Content standard in the mathematics curriculum		Ability requirement (Students can)	Competency category	Structural level	Item sequential number	Proportion
Content domains	Content standard					
	Direct proportion, inverse proportion	In a practical situation, understand what the distribution based on proportion is, and can solve simple problems	Mathematical thinking	U	10	
		Apply the relationship of proportion to solve the practical problems in need of calculation	Knowledge and skill	U	11	
		Transfer the quantity in the representation of fraction into proportion				
	Numeric operation	Can calculate in writing the multiplication of three-digital number multiplied by two-digital number and the division of three-digital number divided by two-digital number	Knowledge and skill	U	9	
		Calculate the division of three-digital number divided by two-digital number	Mathematical thinking	M	18	
		In the process to solve concrete problems, can choose an appropriate estimation method and keep the estimation habit				
		Use estimation to solve problems based on specific real-life context	Mathematical thinking	M	22	
		Solve simple practical problems	Apply the four arithmetic operation to solve practical problems			
	Expression and equation	In a specific situation, can use letters to express numbers; can use the equation to express the equivalent relationship in simple contexts; understand the property of equations and can use the properties to solve simple equation	Knowledge and skill	U	12	
		Obtain the unknown number based on the equivalent relationship	Knowledge and skill	R	33	
		Display the equation to obtain the unknown number				
	Exploring rules	Explore the implicit rules or change tendency of the given things	Make inference based on the found rules	Mathematical thinking	R	35	
Space and shape	Shape and change	Emphasize the methods of observation, manipulation, and inference to make students gradually know the shapes, size, location and change of simple geometry and plane figures	Judge the shape of an object seen from the front, the above and the left	Knowledge and skill	M	29	U:1 M:3 R:1
	Shape and location	In specific situations, can make a conversion of the map distance and practical distance; can fix the location of the object based on direction and distance	Mark the road in accordance with conditions in the map	Knowledge and skill	M	28	
	Measurement	Explore and master the circumference formula of rectangle and square	Calculate the circumference of a half circle	Knowledge and skill	R	34	
		Explore and master the area formula of rectangle and square					
		Explore and master the circumference and area formulae of circle					
		With the combination of specific situation, explore and master the calculation methods of the volume and surface area of a rectangular solid, cube and circular cylinder, and of the volume of cone	Calculate the surface area of a bucket without lid	Knowledge and skill	U	13	
			Calculate the volume of a bucket and the mass of the water it could contain	Knowledge and skill	M	14	

(continued)

Table 3.1 (continued)

Content standard in the mathematics curriculum			Ability requirement (Students can)	Competency category	Structural level	Item sequential number	Proportion
Content domains		Content standard					
Statistics and probability	Statistics	Can read simple statistical figures; can answer questions based on statistical figures; can explain statistical results and make a simple judgment, prediction, and communication based on the results	Make calculation based on the numerical relationship in the statistical figures	Knowledge and skill	R	37	U:0 M:2 R:1
		Can obtain the mean, median and mode	Calculate the difference between median and mode	Knowledge and skill	M	27	
	Probability	Can get the possibility of simple events	Get the possibility of a simple event	Mathematical thinking	M	17	
Comprehensive application		Obtain the activity experience and methods through solving simple practical problems by comprehensively applying the knowledge learned	Obtain the information related to time from the time–distance figure	Knowledge and skill	U	30	U:1 M:6 R:2
			Indirectly obtain the information related to speed from the time–distance figure	Knowledge and skill	M	31	
			Obtain the accurate implicit information from the time–distance figure	Mathematical thinking	R	32	
			Solve the two-step inverse multiple application problem	Mathematical thinking	R	36	
			Calculate the area of compound shapes	Knowledge and skill	M	25	
			Solve the practical problem of weighted mean	Mathematical thinking	M	19	
			Calculate the increased quantity	Knowledge and skill	M	20	
			Use the comparison of the fraction to make inference	Mathematical thinking	M	21	
			Use the distribution based on proportion to calculate the problem of shapes	Mathematical thinking	M	26	

Note The holistic proportion—U:14 M:17 R:6, 70 min for pilot testing time, 60 min for formal testing time (Numbers and algebra: space and shape: statistics and probability: comprehensive application = 20:5:3:9 (37 items in total)

3.3 Research Method and Instrument

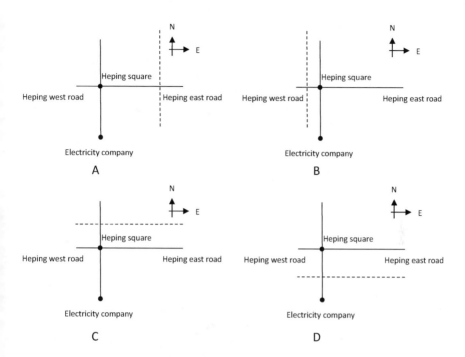

This is an item at the multi-structural level. Distance, going direction, and location are needed to be considered at the same time. The key is C. If D is chosen, it means only distance and going direction have been paid attention to, belonging to uni-structural level.

Example 2: Item 4

Starting from Mingming's home, it is positive to go east and negative to go west. If Mingming goes +30 m from his home, and then −30 m, where he is now?

A. At the place 30 m away east from his home.
B. At the place 30 m away west from his home.
C. At a place 60 m away from his home.
D. At his home.

This is an item at uni-structural level. It only needs to make clear the relationship between direction and positive and negative. The key is D.

Example 3: Item 15

For the two numbers "a × b" and "b × c", what is their least common multiple?

A. a × b × b × c
B. b
C. a × b × c
D. 1

This is an item at the multi-structural level. First students need to understand what the common multiple is and can use symbol to represent, and then the least common multiple. The key is C, if A is chosen, it means that students know the product of two numbers is their common multiple, which is at uni-structural level.

Example 4: Item 35

Based on the sequence rules of the following shapes, what are the two shapes followed?

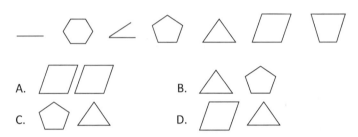

This is an item at the relational level, implicitly including two groups of rules, which requires students to discover and their relationship. The key is B. If C is chosen, it means that students can discover the two groups of rules, but cannot accurately apply them, which is at multi-structural level. If D is chosen, it means that students just discover part of the rules, at uni-structural level.

3.3.1.5 Pilot Test and Modification

The sample of the pilot test is 187 students. The analysis report of the pilot test shows that the reliability of the Mathematics test items is 0.98 and the reliability of the testees is 0.84. In general, the reliability of the academic achievement test paper should be over 0.90. The reliability of the present test paper met the requirement.

The analysis on the Mathematics test items and the observation about the distribution chart of the item difficulty and student ability and chart of the model fit indices show that the difficulty fit indices of the items in the Mathematics test are in the acceptable coverage, which is −2.22–1.83 (4.05 logit values). It could be seen from this that the item difficulty coverage was appropriate.

Further analysis on item difficulty, discrimination, and model fit index show that the item discrimination of each item is fairly good.

3.3.1.6 The Characteristic Parameter of the Test Instrument and Measurement Index of the Test Paper

The item parameters and the validity and reliability of test paper are analyzed with Winstep3.63, based on which, each student ability parameter is attained.

3.3 Research Method and Instrument

The item discrimination in the table is given in two types. One is the correlation between whether the item is passed or not and the total score, i.e., point biserial correlation, which is used to show the discrimination extent of items for student ability, with the value range 0–1.00. If the value is negative, it indicates that the relationship is opposite between the reaction to the item and the responding results to the whole test paper, showing that the item is problematic or a different dimensional ability is assessed. Generally, it is acceptable when the item discrimination is above 0.20, and if it is over 0.40, it is very ideal.

The other way is discrimination. The hypothesis of the Rasch model employed in Winsteps, the discrimination of all items is considered 1.00, which is the foundation to fit the Rasch model. But the CTT item discrimination never equal incidentally, thus, the post hoc test result (a type of fit statistical variable) of the item discrimination is reported by Winsteps, to show the difference between the practical discrimination and 1.00, which is taken as an index for the fit extent of the items and Rasch model. If the discrimination is 1.00, it is consistent with the prediction of item difficulty in the Rasch model. If the discrimination is over or less than 1.00, it means that the practical item discrimination is inconsistent with the prediction of item difficulty in the Rasch model. It indicates over-discrimination with the value over 1.00 and under-discrimination with the value less than 1.00.

In the test item analysis, the most important frequently reported is the average response, which is used to show the sample percentage consistent with the items in the dichotomy marking way, and is explained the average response to items (in dichotomy or multistep marking way).

1. Test Item Difficulty, Discrimination, and Fit Index

In the present research, 18,600 students from 31 counties participated in the formal test, with 96.3% as the collection rate and 17,898 papers were valid. According to the test results, Winsteps 2.0 was employed to analyze the test instrument and the item characteristics, with the results listed in Tables 3.2, 3.3, and 3.4.

The item reliability is 1.00. The minimum of the item difficulty is -1.94 and the maximum is 1.74. The mean of the difficulty is 0.00, and the standard deviation is 1.07. The difficulty coverage is quite narrow.

The reliability of the test paper for students ability estimate is 0.80. Regarding the validity of the test results, two methods have been employed. One is the content structure validity of the test paper. From the Table 3.4, the mean of the fit index is 0.99 and the standard deviation is 0.07, which means the content structure validity of the test paper is high, in accordance with the unidimensionality hypothesis of the Rasch model. The other is the correlation between Mathematics test results and the test results of three other subjects (which could be seen in Table 3.5) as the empirical validity index of test instrument, which could be called congruent validity, to show the consistency extent of the test results of the same ability assessed with different test instruments.

Table 3.2 Statistical results of test item difficulty, discrimination, fit index, etc.

Item	Difficulty	Discrimination	Discrimination	Infit index	P-value
1	−1.83	0.24	1.01	0.97	0.95
2	−0.84	0.26	0.91	1.07	0.88
3	−0.08	0.39	0.99	1.01	0.80
4	−1.46	0.26	0.99	1.00	0.93
5	−1.94	0.20	0.98	1.01	0.95
6	−0.02	0.35	0.89	1.07	0.79
7	0.71	0.39	0.80	1.10	0.68
8	−0.65	0.34	1.00	1.00	0.86
9	−1.75	0.26	1.02	0.96	0.94
10	−1.18	0.36	1.09	0.89	0.91
11	−1.12	0.40	1.12	0.85	0.91
12	−1.73	0.31	1.07	0.90	0.94
13	−0.60	0.31	0.95	1.02	0.86
14	1.01	0.41	0.76	1.10	0.63
15	0.71	0.47	1.06	0.98	0.68
16	−0.21	0.49	1.20	0.84	0.82
17	−0.14	0.38	0.99	1.01	0.81
18	−0.65	0.36	1.03	0.96	0.87
19	−0.54	0.42	1.10	0.90	0.85
20	1.12	0.49	1.04	0.98	0.61
21	1.67	0.45	0.80	1.07	0.51
22	−0.12	0.32	0.86	1.10	0.81
23	−0.83	0.46	0.99	1.00	0.66
24	−0.26	0.47	1.17	0.86	0.82
25	0.15	0.46	1.10	0.93	0.77
26	−0.51	0.39	1.06	0.93	0.85
27	0.45	0.41	0.94	1.04	0.72
28	−0.59	0.39	1.06	0.95	0.86
29	−0.51	0.35	1.00	1.00	0.85
30	0.32	0.41	0.96	1.03	0.74
31	1.71	0.52	1.07	0.96	0.50
32	1.74	0.46	0.83	1.06	0.49
33	1.12	0.49	1.05	0.98	0.61
34	1.37	0.50	1.04	0.98	0.56
35	1.02	0.44	0.88	1.05	0.63
36	1.07	0.48	1.01	1.00	0.62
37	1.73	0.46	0.81	1.07	0.50
Mean	0.00			0.99	
SD	1.07			0.07	

Note Item reliability = 1.00

3.3 Research Method and Instrument

Table 3.3 Students test results

Reliability	Mean	Standard deviation
0.80	1.61	1.20

Table 3.4 Statistical characteristic parameters

	N	Minimum	Maximum	Mean	Standard deviation
Difficulty	37	−1.94	1.74	0.00	1.07
Discrimination (point biserial correlation)	37	0.20	0.52	0.39	0.08
Discrimination	37	0.76	1.20	0.99	0.10
Infit mean square	37	0.84	1.10	0.99	0.07
P-value	37	0.49	0.95	0.76	0.14

Table 3.5 Correlation analysis between mathematics ability and abilities in other subjects

		Reading	Mathematics	Science	Morality and Society
Reading	Pearson correlation coefficient	1	0.503[a]	0.429[a]	0.473[a]
	Sig. (2-tailed)	–	0.000	0.000	0.000
	N	16,799	16,543	15,168	16,617
Mathematics	Pearson correlation coefficient	0.503[a]	1	0.601[a]	0.611[a]
	Sig. (2-tailed)	0.000	–	0.000	0.000
	N	16,543	17,898	16,253	17,832
Science	Pearson correlation coefficient	0.429[a]	0.601[a]	1	0.707[a]
	Sig. (2-tailed)	0.000	0.000	–	0.000
	N	15,168	16,253	16,378	17,832
Morality and Society	Pearson correlation coefficient	0.473[a]	0.611[a]	0.707[a]	1
	Sig. (2-tailed)	0.000	0.000	0.000	–
	N	16,617	17,832	16,315	18,024

Note [a] means reaching significance level of 0.01

2. Item Characteristic Curves

It could be known from Fig. 3.1 that there are 37 test items in total, and most of the items, except some items, are in accordance with the IRT model. The possibility for students with a higher ability is larger to respond to the more difficult items and get a higher score. The item difficulty covers from −2.4 to 1.9 and the coverage is quite narrow.

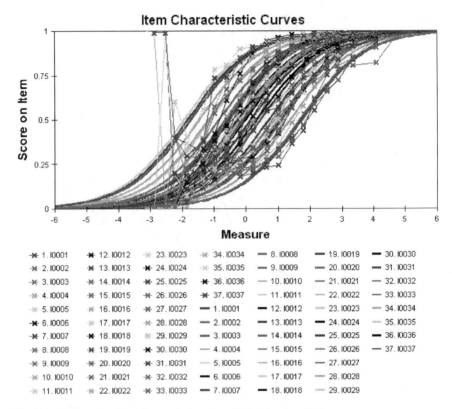

Fig. 3.1 Mathematics item characteristic curves (Color figure online)

3.3.2 The Testing Time

The primary school mathematics testing time is 60 min.

3.4 Analysis and Discussion on the Test Results

3.4.1 The Overall Complexion of Student Ability Distribution

From Table 3.3, it could be seen that the test results analysis of students' ability has been obtained with the mean of the estimated value 1.61 and standard deviation 1.20.

The student ability distribution could be seen in Table 3.6.

3.4 Analysis and Discussion on the Test Results

Table 3.6 Overall complexion of the student ability distribution

	N	Minimum	Maximum	Mean	SD
Transferred mathematical ability	17,898	−2.87	4.80	1.7400	1.33655
Valid sample	17,898	–	–	–	–

3.4.2 The Grouping Analysis of Student Ability Performance

With the mean of the estimated ability value (1.74) as the midpoint and about 1 standard deviation as interval, students are divided into 5 ability groups from high (A) to low (E). The range of each group divided by the original ability value and by the transformed value, the number of students in each ability group, the percentage of the students in each ability group out of the total, and the accumulative percentage could be seen in Table 3.7.

Combined with the bar chart of the student frequency distribution, it could be analyzed that the student ability is almost in the normal distribution. The number of students in the Excellent group is 1695, 9.5% of the total students participating in the test. There are 3478 students in the Proficient group, which is 28.9% of the total students. The number of students in the Qualified group is 8850, 49.4% of the total students. There are 3434 students in the Basically qualified group, which is 19.2%

Table 3.7 Number, percentage and accumulative percentage of students in each ability group

Groups	Original ability value Grouping ability Starting point-terminal point	Transformed ability value Grouping ability Starting point-terminal point	Number of students	Percentage of each group students out of the total (%)	Accumulative percentage (%)
Excellent group (A)	3.745–Maximum	87–98	1695	9.5	9.5
Proficient group (B)	2.408–3.745	74–87	3478	19.4	25.9
Qualified group (C)	0.668–2.408	57–74	8850	49.4	78.3
Basically qualified group (D)	−0.669 to 0.668	43–57	3434	19.2	97.5
Unqualified group (E)	Minimum to −0.669	0–43	441	2.5	100.0

Note Transformation formula is T = 50 + 10 X original ability value

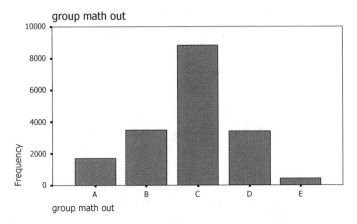

Fig. 3.2 Distribution of student frequency in five ability groups

of the total students. And the number of students in the Unqualified group is 441, 2.5% of the total students. The accumulative number of students in and above Qualified group is 14,023, which is 78.3% of the total students, while the accumulative number of students in the Basically qualified group and Unqualified group is 3875, which is 21.7% of the total students (Fig. 3.2).

3.4.3 The Tasks That Can Be Accomplished by Students in Different Ability Groups

See Fig. 3.3.

3.4.4 The Corresponding Analysis of Students' Practical Ability Performance and Item Target Test Level

It could be found that from Fig. 3.4, the distribution of the practical difficulty of test items is normal, and the performance of students in different ability groups is approaching normal distribution. Overall, the test items seem a little bit easy. It will be more ideal if there are more items with the difficulty value above 2.0.

According to Fig. 3.4, the main reasons for the inconsistency of them are analyzed based on the corresponding relation for students' practical ability performance and item target test level (difficulty) to formulate Table 3.8.

3.4 Analysis and Discussion on the Test Results

Unqualified group: Students can use fraction to describe the change of numbers after the decimal point moves; use estimation to solve problems based on specific real-life context; transform into the numbers with "yi" (100 million) as unit by omitting mantissa; apply the relationship of proportion to solve the practical problems in need of calculation; transfer the quantity in the representation of fraction into proportion; express the going direction with positive number or negative number and the final result of distance in specific situation; calculate the division of three-digital number divided by two-digital number; obtain the unknown number based on the equivalent relationship; write the integer not smaller than 10 given conditions; and estimate the quantity related to areas in life.

Basically qualified group: Besides the tasks which could be accomplished by students in Unqualified group, students in this group can judge whether a fraction could be transferred into finite decimals; use the numeric concept to judge; calculate the difference between median and mode; obtain the information related to time from the time-distance figure; calculate the area of compound shapes; estimate the fairly big numbers in life; write the decimal given conditions; get the possibility of a simple event; apply the four arithmetic operation to solve practical problems; use the numeric concept to infer; judge the situation students meet the basic requirements in the test with the full score unequal to 100; calculate the surface area of a bucket without lid; solve the practical problem of weighted mean; use the distribution based on proportion to calculate the problem of shapes; mark the road in accordance with conditions in the map; and judge the shape of an object seen from the front, above and left.

Qualified group: Besides the tasks which could be accomplished by students in Unqualified group and Basically qualified group, students in this group can calculate the circumference of a half circle; calculate the increased quantity; display the equation to obtain the unknown number; solve the two-step inverse multiple application problem; calculate the volume of a bucket and the mass of the water it could contain; make inference based on the found rules; and solve the practical problems related to fraction.

Fig. 3.3 Tasks and groups of students' ability

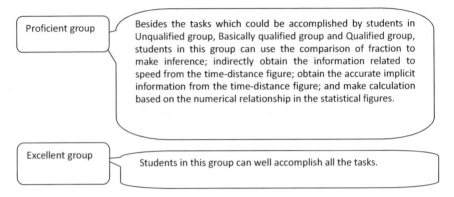

Fig. 3.3 (continued)

From the analysis of students' responses to each item, some conclusions could be further obtained as follows.

1. The students in Unqualified group perform fairly well in the following aspects: ① Know decimal, fraction, and percent; ② In the process to solve concrete problems, can choose the appropriate estimation method and keep the estimation habit; ③ In practical situation, understand what the distribution based on proportion is, and can solve simple problems; ④ Can use "wan" (10 thousand) or "yi" (100 million), as unit, to represent big numbers; ⑤ In the familiar real-life context, know the meaning of negative numbers, and can use negative numbers to express some problems in daily life; and ⑥ Can calculate in writing the multiplication of three-digital number multiplied by two-digital number and the division of three-digital number divided by two-digital number, etc.

In the aspect of "In specific situation, can use letters to express numbers; can use equation to express the equivalent relationship in simple contexts; understand the property of equations and can use the properties to solve simple equation," the students of this ability group although can accomplish item 12, but cannot achieve to finish item 33, which means that students only own the ability to use the equivalent relationship to get the unknown number, but cannot flexibly apply it in a new situation.

In the aspect of "Recognize, read and write the numbers within 100 million, and know decimal system," the students of this ability group although can accomplish item 1, but cannot achieve to finish item 3, which means that students master fairly well to read and write multi-digit integers, but have difficulty to read and write decimals.

3.4 Analysis and Discussion on the Test Results

```
Math Test                                            math out Oct 9  3:40 2009
INPUT: 17898 STDNTS, 37 TMS  MEASURED: 17898 STDNTS, 37 TMS, 2 CATS      3.35
-------------------------------------------------------------------------------
        STDNTS MAP OF TMS
                              <more>|<rare>
                          5   #######  +
                                       |
                                       |
                                       |
                                       |
                                       |
                            . ######### |
                          4              T+
                                       |
                                       |
                                       |
                                       |
                            . ########## |
                          3              +
                            . ############ S|
                                       |
                            . ############ |
                                       |
                            . ############ |
                                       |T
                          2 . ############ +
                                       |
                            . ##########  |   I0021  I0031  I0032  I0037
                            . ##########  M|
                            . #########   |   I0034
                            . #########   |
                            . ########    |S  I0020  I0033
                          1              +   I0014  I0035  I0036
                            . ########    |   I0023
                            . #######     |   I0007  I0015
                            . ######      |
                            . #####     S |   I0027
                            . #####       |   I0030
                            . ####        |   I0025
                          0   . #######   +M  I0006
                             . ##         |   I0003  I0016  I0017  I0022
                             . ##         |   I0024
                             . #          |
                             . #          |   I0013  I0019  I0026  I0028  I0029
                             . #          |   I0008  I0018
                             . #        T |   I0002
                         -1   .          +
                                         |S  I0010  I0011
                              .          |
                                         |   I0004
                              .          |
                                         |   I0009  I0012
                              .          |   I0001
                         -2   .          +   I0005
                                         |T
                              .          |
                                         |
                              .          |
                                         |
                              .          |
                         -3              +
                              <less>|<frequ>
-------------------------------------------------------------------------------
EACH '#' IS 94.
```

Fig. 3.4 Item difficulty and student ability distribution

Table 3.8 Item analysis of the primary school mathematics test for Grade-6 students

Item	Tested ability description	Target test level	Difficulty value	Explanation
1	Write the integer not smaller than 10 given conditions	U	−1.83	There are 95% of students achieving U level, with the average ability 1.82. The practical difficulty and student ability accord with the target test level
2	Transform into the numbers with "yi" (100 million) as unit by omitting mantissa	U	−0.84	There are 88% of students achieving U level, with the average ability 1.86. The practical difficulty and student ability accord with the target test level
3	Write the decimal given conditions	U	−0.08	There are 80% of students achieving U level, with the average ability 2.00. The practical difficulty and student ability accord with the target test level
4	Express the going direction with a positive number or negative number and the final result of distance in a specific situation	U	−1.46	There are 93% of students achieving U level, with the average ability 1.83. The practical difficulty and student ability accord with the target test level
5	Estimate the quantity related to areas in life	U	−1.94	There are 95% of students achieving U level, with the average ability 1.80. The practical difficulty and student ability accord with the target test level
6	Estimate the fairly big numbers in life	U	−0.02	There are 79% of students achieving U level, with the average ability 1.98. The practical difficulty and student ability accord with the target test level
7	Judge whether a fraction could be transferred into finite decimals	U	0.71	There are 68% of students achieving U level, with the average ability 2.09. And 30% of students cannot well judge whether a fraction could be transferred into finite decimals. The reason might be that the content is fairly abstract and boring to be understood for primary school students, and it is also possible that students have

(continued)

3.4 Analysis and Discussion on the Test Results 125

Table 3.8 (continued)

Item	Tested ability description	Target test level	Difficulty value	Explanation
				not well mastered the knowledge of decomposition of the quality factor
8	Use fraction to describe the change of numbers after the decimal point moves	U	−0.65	There are 86% of students achieving U level, with the average ability 1.92 The practical difficulty and student ability to accord with the target test level
9	Calculate the division of three-digital number divided by two-digital number	U	−1.75	There are 94% of students achieving U level, with the average ability 1.82 The practical difficulty and student ability to accord with the target test level
10	Apply the relationship of proportion to solve the practical problems in need of calculation	U	−1.18	There are 91% of students achieving U level, with the average ability 1.89 The practical difficulty and student ability to accord with the target test level
11	Transfer the quantity in the representation of fraction into proportion	U	−1.12	There are 91% of students achieving U level, with the average ability 1.91 The practical difficulty and student ability to accord with the target test level
12	Obtain the unknown number based on the equivalent relationship	U	−1.73	There are 94% of students achieving U level, with the average ability 1.84 The practical difficulty and student ability to accord with the target test level
13	Calculate the surface area of a bucket without a lid	U	−0.60	There are 86% of students achieving U level, with the average ability 1.91 The practical difficulty and student ability to accord with the target test level
14	Calculate the volume of a bucket and the mass of the water it could contain	M	1.01	There are 63% of students achieving M level, with the average ability 2.61, and there are 15% of students achieving U level, with the average ability 1.81 The practical difficulty and student ability to accord with the target test level

(continued)

Table 3.8 (continued)

Item	Tested ability description	Target test level	Difficulty value	Explanation
15	Use the numeric concept to judge	M	0.71	There are 68% of students achieving M level, with the average ability 2.17, and there are 7% of students achieving U level, with the average ability 1.04 The practical difficulty and student ability to accord with the target test level
16	Use the numeric concept to infer	M	−0.21	There are 82% of students achieving M level, with the average ability 2.05, and there are 9% of students achieving U level, with the average ability 0.36 The practical difficulty and student ability to accord with the target test level
17	Get the possibility of a simple event	M	−0.14	There are 81% of students achieving M level, with the average ability 1.99, and there are 18% of students achieving U level, with the average ability 0.67 and 0.78, respectively, for the two answers at U level The practical difficulty and student ability to accord with the target test level
18	Use estimation to solve problems based on specific real-life context	M	−0.65	There are 87% of students achieving M level, with the average ability 1.93, and there are 11% of students achieving U level, with the average ability 0.73 and 0.49, respectively, for the two answers at U level The practical difficulty and student ability to accord with the target test level
19	Solve the practical problem of weighted mean	M	−0.54	There are 85% of students achieving M level, with the average ability 1.97, and there are 8% of students achieving U level, with the average ability 0.12 and

(continued)

3.4 Analysis and Discussion on the Test Results

Table 3.8 (continued)

Item	Tested ability description	Target test level	Difficulty value	Explanation
				0.24, respectively, for the two answers at U level. The practical difficulty and student ability to accord with the target test level
20	Calculate the increased quantity	M	1.12	There are 61% of students achieving M level, with the average ability 2.27, and there are 28% of students achieving U level, with the average ability 1.10. The practical difficulty and student ability to accord with the target test level
21	Use the comparison of the fraction to make an inference	M	1.67	There are 51% of students achieving M level, with the average ability 2.33, and there are 20% of students achieving U level, with the average ability 1.07. The practical difficulty and student ability to accord with the target test level
22	Apply the four arithmetic operation to solve practical problems	M	−0.12	There are 81% of students achieving M level, with the average ability 1.95, and there are 17% of students achieving U level, with the average ability 1.11 and 0.10, respectively, for the two answers at U level. The practical difficulty and student ability to accord with the target test level
23	Solve the practical problems related to fraction	M	0.83	There are 66% of students achieving M level, with the average ability 2.18, and there are 23% of students achieving U level, with the average ability 1.10. The practical difficulty and student ability to accord with the target test level
24	Judge the situation students meet the basic requirements in the test with the full score unequal to 100	M	−0.26	There are 82% of students achieving M level, with the average ability 2.03, and there are 5% of students

(continued)

Table 3.8 (continued)

Item	Tested ability description	Target test level	Difficulty value	Explanation
				achieving U level, with the average ability 0.39 The practical difficulty and student ability to accord with the target test level
25	Calculate the area of compound shapes	M	0.15	There are 77% of students achieving M level, with the average ability 2.08, and there are 8% of students achieving U level, with the average ability 0.96 The practical difficulty and student ability to accord with the target test level
26	Use the distribution based on proportion to calculate the problem of shapes	M	−0.51	There are 89% of students achieving M level, with the average ability 0.98 The practical difficulty and student ability to accord with the target test level
27	Calculate the difference between median and mode	M	0.45	There are 52% of students achieving M level, with the average ability 1.25, and there are 15% of students achieving U level, with the average ability 0.81 The practical difficulty and student ability to accord with the target test level
28	Mark the road in accordance with conditions in the map	M	−0.59	There are 86% of students achieving M level, with the average ability 1.95, and there are 5% of students achieving U level, with the average ability 0.72 The practical difficulty and student ability to accord with the target test level
29	Judge the shape of an object seen from the front, above, and left	M	−0.51	There are 85% of students achieving M level, with the average ability 1.94, and there are 4% of students achieving U level, with the average ability 0.72 The practical difficulty and student ability to accord with the target test level

(continued)

3.4 Analysis and Discussion on the Test Results

Table 3.8 (continued)

Item	Tested ability description	Target test level	Difficulty value	Explanation
30	Obtain the information related to time from the time–distance figure	U	0.32	There are 74% of students achieving U level, with the average ability 2.06 The practical difficulty and student ability to accord with the target test level
31	Indirectly obtain the information related to speed from the time–distance figure	M	1.71	There are 50% of students achieving M level, with the average ability 2.44, and there are 16% of students achieving U level, with the average ability 1.11 The practical difficulty and student ability to accord with the target test level
32	Obtain the accurate implicit information from the time–distance figure	R	1.74	There are 49% of students achieving R level, with the average ability 2.36; 12% of students achieving M level, with the average ability 1.38, and there are 22% of students achieving U level, with the average ability 1.05 The practical difficulty and student ability to accord with the target test level
33	Display the equation to obtain the unknown number	R	1.12	There are 61% of students achieving R level, with the average ability 2.27; 4% of students achieving M level, with the average ability 0.71, and there are 18% of students achieving U level, with the average ability 1.22 The practical difficulty and student ability to accord with the target test level
34	Calculate the circumference of a half circle	R	1.37	There are 56% of students achieving R level, with the average ability 2.33; 9% of students achieving M level, with the average ability 0.94, and there are 26% of students achieving U level, with the average ability 1.07 The practical difficulty and student ability to accord with the target test level

(continued)

Table 3.8 (continued)

Item	Tested ability description	Target test level	Difficulty value	Explanation
35	Make inference based on the found rules	R	1.02	There are 63% of students achieving R level, with the average ability 2.20; 23% of students achieving M level, with the average ability 1.10, and there are 11% of students achieving U level, with the average ability 0.84 The practical difficulty and student ability to accord with the target test level
36	Solve the two-step inverse multiple application problem	R	1.07	There are 62% of students achieving R level, with the average ability 2.24; 11% of students achieving M level, with the average ability 1.07, and there are 25% of students achieving U level, with the average ability 0.91 The practical difficulty and student ability to accord with the target test level
37	Make calculation based on the numerical relationship in the statistical figures	R	1.73	There are 50% of students achieving R level, with the average ability 2.35; 3% of students achieving M level, with the average ability 0.61, and there are 36% of students achieving U level, with the average ability 1.23 The practical difficulty and student ability to accord with the target test level

In the aspect of "Feel the meaning of big numbers in real-life situation and can make estimation," the students of this ability group although can accomplish item 5, but cannot achieve to finish item 6, which means that students have some ability to estimate, but are quite weak in numeric sense, and cannot experience and feel big numbers.

Since students of this ability group cannot accomplish items 15, 16, 23, 24, 7, 22, 35, 29, 28, 34, 13, 14, 37, 27, and 17, it means that students have not achieved the requirements of curriculum standard in the aspects of "Can find common multiples and the least common multiple of two natural numbers within 10, and can find common factors and the biggest common factor of two natural numbers," "Know integers, odd integers, even integers, prime numbers and composite numbers," "Can solve the simple practical problems related to decimal, fraction and percent," "Explore the relationship between decimal, fraction and percent, and can make transference," "Solve simple practical problems" (numeric operation), "Explore the implicit rules or change tendency of the given things," "Emphasize the methods of observation, manipulation and inference to make students gradually know the shapes, size, location and change of simple geometry and plane figures," "In specific situations, can make conversion of the map distance and practical distance; can fix the location of the object based on direction and distance," "Explore and master the circumference and area formulae of circle," "With the combination of specific situation, explore and master the calculation methods of the volume and surface area of rectangular solid, cube and circular cylinder, and of the volume of cone," "Can read simple statistical figures," "Can answer questions based on statistical figures," "Can explain statistical results and make simple judgment, prediction, and communication based on the results," "Can obtain the mean, median and mode," "Can get the possibility of simple events," etc.

In addition, students cannot accomplish any item among items 30, 31, 32, 36, 25, 19, 20, 21, and 20, which indicates that students don't have the ability to solve practical problems by comprehensively applying the knowledge learned.

2. Besides the content mastered by the students in Unqualified group, the students in Basically qualified group also perform fairly well in the following aspects: ① Explore the relationship between decimal, fraction, and percent, and can make transference; ② Can find common multiples and the least common multiple of two natural numbers within 10, and can find common factors and the biggest common factor of two natural numbers; ③ Can obtain the mean, median, and mode; ④ Obtain the activity experience and methods through solving simple practical problems by comprehensively applying the knowledge learned; ⑤ Feel the meaning of big numbers in real-life situation and can make estimation; ⑥ Recognize, read, and write the numbers within 100 million, and know decimal system; ⑦ Can get the possibility of simple events; ⑧ Know integers, odd integers, even integers, prime numbers, and composite numbers; ⑨ In specific situations, can make conversion of the map distance and practical distance; can fix the location of the object based on direction and distance; ⑩ Emphasize the methods of observation, manipulation and inference to make students gradually know the shapes, size, location and change of simple geometry and plane figures, etc.

In the aspect of "Can solve the simple practical problems related to decimal, fraction and percent," the students of this ability group although can accomplish item 24, but cannot achieve to finish item 23, which means that students still have difficulty to solve real-life practical problems.

In the aspect of "With the combination of specific situation, explore and master the calculation methods of the volume and surface area of rectangular solid, cube and circular cylinder, and of the volume of cone," the students of this ability group although can accomplish item 13 (uni-structural level), but cannot achieve to finish item 14 (multi-structural level), which means that students have not fully mastered the knowledge of this content.

In the aspect of "In specific situation, can use letters to express numbers; can use equation to express the equivalent relationship in simple contexts; understand the property of equations and can use the properties to solve simple equation," the students of this ability group although can accomplish item 12, but cannot achieve to finish item 33, which means that students only own the ability to use the equivalent relationship to get the unknown number, but cannot flexibly apply it in a new situation.

In the aspect of "Obtain the activity experience and methods through solving simple practical problems by comprehensively applying the knowledge learned," the students of this ability group although can accomplish item 19 (uni-structural level) and item 26 (uni-structural level), but cannot achieve to finish item 30, item 31 or item 32 (gradual questions proposed based on time–distance figure, which, respectively, are at uni-structural level, multi-structural level and relational level), item 36 (relational level), item 25 (multi-structural level), item 20 (multi-structural level), and item 21 (multi-structural level), which means that students must have the preliminary ability to solve practical problems by comprehensively applying the knowledge learned.

Since students cannot achieve to finish item 35, item 34, or item 37, it means that students have not achieved the requirements of curriculum standard in the aspects of "Explore the implicit rules or change tendency of the given things," "Explore and master the circumference and area formulae of circle," "Can read simple statistical figures," "Can answer questions based on statistical figures," and "Can explain statistical results and make simple judgment, prediction, and communication based on the results," etc.

3. Besides the content mastered by the students in Unqualified group and in Basically qualified group, students in Qualified group also perform fairly well in the following aspects: ① Explore and master the circumference and area formulae of circle; ② In a specific situation, can use letters to express numbers; can use equation to express the equivalent relationship in simple contexts; understand the property of equations and can use the properties to solve simple equation; ③ With the combination of specific situation, explore and master the calculation methods of the volume and surface area of rectangular solid, cube, and circular cylinder, and of the volume of cone; ④ Explore the implicit rules or change tendency of the given things; and ⑤ Can solve the simple practical problems related to decimal, fraction, percent, etc.

Since students cannot achieve to finish item 21, item 31, item 32, or item 37, it means that students have not achieved the requirements of curriculum standard in the aspects of "Can read simple statistical figures; can answer questions based on statistical figures; can explain statistical results and make simple judgment, prediction, and communication based on the results," and still have difficulty to solve practical problems by comprehensively applying the knowledge learned.

4. Besides the content mastered by the students in Unqualified group, in Basically qualified group and in Qualified group, students in Proficient group also perform fairly well in the following aspects: "Can read simple statistical figures; can answer

questions based on statistical figures; can explain statistical results and make simple judgment, prediction, and communication based on the results" and "Obtain the activity experience and methods through solving simple practical problems by comprehensively applying the knowledge learned," etc.

5. Students in Excellent group have fully achieved the requirements included in the curriculum standard and well show their ability to solve practical problems.

3.5 The Main Findings

1. There are 78.3% of students who achieve at the qualified level or above in the mathematics subject learning and 97.5% of students achieve at the basically qualified level or above, while the percentage for the students at the unqualified level is only 2.5%. This indicates that students in Grade 6, primary school, almost achieve the requirements of *Mathematics Curriculum Standard*. The main problems for the students at the unqualified level are as follows: ① Cannot understand well and master the basic knowledge and basic skills (such as numeric recognition). These students cannot find common factors and the biggest common factor of two natural numbers, cannot make transference between decimal, fraction, and percent, and vaguely know integers, odd integers, even integers, prime numbers, and composite numbers; ② Cannot fairly well apply knowledge to solve problems. For example, they although achieve the requirement on operation, cannot solve simple practical problems; although can obtain unknown number based one equivalent relationship, cannot apply equation to solve problems, and none of the items which need to be answered by comprehensively apply the knowledge has been accurately responded; ③ The numeric sense is quite weak. Students can make an estimation for small numbers but cannot well experience and feel the big numbers; ④ The spatial conception has not well built. Students cannot judge the shape of an object seen from the front, above and left, cannot accurately judge the shapes, size, or location relationship of simple geometry and plane figures, and cannot mark the road in accordance with conditions in the map; ⑤ The practical learning level for "statistics and probability" is far from the requirements of the curriculum standard. Students cannot make a calculation based on the numerical relationship in the statistical figures, cannot calculate the difference between median and mode; and cannot get the possibility of a simple event; ⑥ The mathematical thinking is obviously weak. Students cannot find rules out of the given things and in turn, make an inference.
2. Students perform better in "Numbers and algebra" than in "Statistics and probability" or "Space and shape". The ability to read figures and get the information in need is still weak. For example, students in Unqualified group can basically accomplish the tasks of "Use fraction to describe the change of numbers after the decimal point moves," "Use estimation to solve problems

based on specific real-life context," "Transform into the numbers with 'yi' (100 million) as unit by omitting mantissa," "Apply the relationship of proportion to solve the practical problems in need of calculation," "Transfer the quantity in the representation of fraction into proportion," "Express the going direction with positive number or negative number and the final result of distance in specific situation," "Calculate the division of three-digital number divided by two-digital number," "Obtain the unknown number based on the equivalent relationship," and "Write the integer not smaller than 10 given conditions," etc. However, the tasks of "Indirectly obtain the information related to speed from the time–distance figure," "Obtain the accurate implicit information from the time–distance figure," "Make calculation based on the numerical relationship in the statistical figures," etc., can only be accomplished by students in Proficient group and Excellent group. And the task, such as "Calculate the circumference of a half circle," can only be accomplished by students in Qualified group, Proficient group, and Excellent group.
3. Students' performance on "mathematical thinking" is not as good as that on "Knowledge and skill". The ability to find rules and make inferences still needs to be improved. For example, "Make inference based on the found rules" cannot be accomplished until Qualified group, by some students. And the students of this group can basically accomplish the content in the domain of knowledge and skills included in *Mathematics Curriculum Standard*. And the task, such as "Use the comparison of fraction to make inference," cannot be accomplished until Proficient group, by some students.
4. The development of numeric sense should be emphasized, and the ability to make estimation linking with the practical life is weak, such as item 6, to which 21% of students cannot estimate the times of heartbeats per day.
5. The teaching about the concepts of fraction and decimal still needs to be improved, particularly to help students understand the knowledge. There are 20% of students who cannot write the decimal given conditions, and the percentage is obviously higher than that for the corresponding item on integers. There are 30% of students who cannot judge whether a fraction could be transferred into finite decimals, and the reason might be that the content is fairly abstract and boring to be understood for primary school students, and it is also possible that students have not well mastered the knowledge of decomposition of the quality factor. The percentage of students who can use the fraction to describe the change of numbers after the decimal point moves is also not high.
6. There are 92% of students who can obtain the unknown number based on the equivalent relationship, but only 61% of students can apply the equation to solve problems. There are 82% of students who can judge "the situation students meet the basic requirements in the test with the full score unequal to 100," but only 66% of students can solve the practical problems related to the fraction. Among the 9 items on solving problems by comprehensively applying the knowledge, there are 1 item, 6 items, and 2 items, respectively, at uni-structural level, multi-structural level, and relational level. The difficulty is not very high, but students in Unqualified group cannot accomplish any of them, and students in

3.5 The Main Findings

Basically qualified group only can accomplish two multi-structural level items, while there are 3 items which cannot be accomplished by students in Qualified group.
7. The application items on fraction and percent are still the difficult part of teaching, and it is not easy for students to get clear multiple. For example, 28% of students cannot accomplish item 20.

3.6 Countermeasures and Suggestions

3.6.1 To Improve Mathematics Curriculum Standard

Statistical conception, spatial conception, and the ability to get statistical information are the content particularly emphasized in *Mathematics Curriculum Standard*. However, students' performance on these aspects is fairly weak, which indicates that further researches on how to teach and how to learn this part should be carried out. Meanwhile, we could look back at the *Mathematics Curriculum Standard*. The description statements of this part are unclear sometimes, which to some extent influences the teaching, learning, and assessment. The content and requirements of *Mathematics Curriculum Standard* need to be further clarified and to solve the problem of "what to be taught."

Compared with the prior teaching and learning guidelines, *Mathematics Curriculum Standard* gets rid of the wording of "application item", and proposes "mathematical thinking" and "solving problem" in the overall goal, which is the transcendence and extension of the traditional "application item", represents the high-degree emphasis on solving problem and makes the mathematical subject feature outstanding. Since it exists in the overall goal, it is also stated in the stage goal, but in a general way, which is still at the theoretical layer and lacks manipulation methods, resulting in difficulties in teaching and learning. To guarantee students' mastery of basic knowledge and basic skills, it is unmanageable for teachers to merge "mathematical thinking" and "problem-solving" into the teaching of all the knowledge and skills in classroom, which inevitably makes the phenomenon "favour one more than another" appear. Thus, the requirements of this aspect should be refined further in the *Mathematics Curriculum Standard*. "Performance standard" should be particularly considered to be added, to practically develop "mathematical thinking" and "problem-solving".

3.6.2 To Further Transform Students' Learning Approach

Students' mastery of "problem-solving", "mathematical thinking", and some other knowledge content is not strong, which is inseparable from their learning approach.

The present curriculum reform makes great efforts in the aspect of transforming students' learning approach, and the effects are prominent. However, it should be seen that the tendency of formalization, shallowness, and absolutization still exits during the process of carrying out the curriculum reform beliefs. It is a must-do to further stress the teaching research and teacher training and to improve the teaching materials writing, aiming to make students can really bring their autonomy, activeness, and exploratory spirits into play.

3.6.3 To Emphasize and Strengthen the Teaching on Mathematical Thinking Methods

Besides to improve the teaching materials writing, to strengthen the teaching on mathematical thinking method also is an important way to ameliorate the weak part of students' mathematics learning. This also gains the attention in the present curriculum reform, but not enough in the teaching materials writing and classroom teaching, for which there are various reasons. Lack of specialized research is a crucial factor, which results in that the teaching materials writers and teachers have no chapter to follow. A piece of specific mathematical knowledge in the teaching material can always represent a variety of mathematical thinking methods. And for a concrete mathematical thinking method, it could be designed with the three steps of many-time gestation, initial formation, application, and development. During the process of teaching materials writing, attention should be paid to occasionally dig the various mathematical thinking methods contained in the teaching content and to particularly give direction, to strengthen primary school students' experience and feeling for mathematical thinking methods.

Chapter 4
Science Assessment Report

4.1 Research Background

As the international competition becomes fierce and compulsory, education reform goes further, every country in the world pays more and more attention to the improvement of educational competitiveness. And the educational competitiveness is represented in various aspects, one of which is learners' academic achievement. The academic achievement survey of primary school and secondary school students is an activity, based on some standards, to collect the data about learners' academic development level and to judge values. With the background that every country in the world generally emphasizes the quality of education and carries out students' academic achievement assessment, it is significant, in the aspects of theoretical meaning and practical value, to realize "2-Bases", to thoroughly develop quality education, to deepen curriculum reform, and to particularly carry out the academic assessment survey on primary school Science, a subject in *the Research on Students' Academic Achievement in Primary and High Schools*, an important national project in "The 11th five-year plan", with the premise that Science curriculum has been executed since Grade 3 in primary school. There is fairly much progress with the related research on the assessment of Science academic achievement, which is enlightening and has a reference value for the present programme.

4.1.1 The Development of International Science Academic Achievement Assessment Research

4.1.1.1 IEA Assessment Program

IEA, International Association for the Evaluation of Educational Achievement, is the earliest and most influential international institute on educational achievement assessment in the world. Till now, IEA has developed 23 international researches, including TIMSS, Progress in International Reading Literacy Study (PIRLS), Second Information Technology in Education Study (SITES), International Civic and Citizenship Study The Civic Education Study (CIVED and ICCS), Preprimary Project (PPP), etc. From 1994 to 1995, the Third International Mathematics and Science Study was carried out, in which 500,000 students from 45 countries participated. After that, IEA does the research every four years and has modified the name into Trends in International Mathematics and Science Study (TIMSS in abbreviation). And the assessment related to Science was done from 1970 to 1971, from 1983 to 1984, in 1995, in 2003 and in 2007.

The research value of TIMSS is to help the countries to monitor and assess the cross-year and cross-grade teaching and learning of mathematics and science. The participating countries can get comprehensive and international reference data on the aspects of the mathematical and scientific concepts, process and attitude developed by students in Grade 4 and in Grade 8; the development of mathematics and science learning of students in Grade 4 and in Grade 8 from international perspective; help countries with the international comparison on the key factors related to high-level students' academic achievement, such as the comparison on curriculum policy, teaching and learning, and resources, to explain the problems of national policy, etc.[1]

The assessment framework of early TIMSS consists of three dimensions, content, performance expectation, and attitude. With the progress in each test, in the TIMSS 2007 Science assessment, the structural content of the assessment framework showed new change.[2]

First, the assessment framework is composed of two dimensions. TIMSS 2007 Science assessment framework includes content dimension and cognitive dimension. In content dimension, the domains and topics related to Science assessment are described in detail, and cognitive dimension describes the series of behavior expected to be performed by students when learning Science content. The content of content dimension and cognitive dimension (in Table 4.1) is the Grade 4 and Grade 8 assessment foundation for TIMSS 2007.

Second change is the presentation of domains and topics. Each content domain of the TIMSS 2007 Science assessment framework contains some main topics, each of which, as a goal, is included in most of the Science curriculum standards of participant countries, and a set of assessment objectives is provided around the topic. These objectives are the items described based on the possible behavior of students, which shows the expectation for students' understanding and ability. Topics included in each Science content domain for Grade 4 are shown in Table 4.2.

---

[1] Su YM (2008) Look into the primary school science learning in Hong Kong from TIMSS. Asia-Pacific Forum on Science Learning and Teaching 6:16.
[2] Hu J (2008) How to assess students' science learning achievement—enlightenment from TIMSS science assessment framework. Science Lesson 6:26.

4.1 Research Background

Table 4.1 TIMSS 2007 science assessment framework

Dimensions	Domains		Percentage (%)
Content	Grade 4	Life science	45
		Physical science	35
		Earth science	20
	Grade 8	Biology	35
		Chemistry	20
		Physics	25
		Earth science	20
Cognitive	Grade 4	Knowing	40
		Applying	35
		Reasoning	25
	Grade 8	Knowing	30
		Applying	35
		Reasoning	35

Table 4.2 Grade 4 content domains and the topics included

Content domains	Topics included
Life science	Characteristics and life processes of living things
	Life cycle, reproduction, and heredity
	Interaction with the environment
	Ecosystem
	Human health
Physics science	Classification and properties of matter
	State of matter and changes in matter
	Energy, heat, and temperature
	Light and sound
	Electricity and magnetism
	Force and motion
Earth science	Earth's structure, physical characteristics, and resources
	Earth's movement, periodic variation, and history
	Earth in the solar system

In the assessment framework, it also provides a set of assessment objectives around each topic, such as in the content domain of Life Science, the assessment objectives around the topic of interaction with the environment includes associating physical features of plants and animals with the environments in which they live, identifying or providing examples of certain physical or behavioral characteristics of plans and animals that make them better suited for survival in particular environments and explaining why; and describing bodily actions in response to outside conditions (e.g., heat, cold, danger) and activities.

Third, the domains and topics are well selected. With the foundation of comprehensive analysis and discussion on the curriculum standards of TIMSS countries, the related team reviewed and modified the domains and objectives to ensure that the content of the framework, to the most extent, is the significant education areas and objectives accepted in common by many TIMSS countries, and to make them more appropriate and feasible in the context of a large-scale international assessment.

Fourth, the content domains and topics are separately described for the two Grades. TIMSS 2007 separately describes the mathematics and science content domains for Grade 4 and Grade 8, which more clearly reflects the different content domains for the two Grades and the topics and objectives contained in each domain.

The content domains included for the two Grades are different. The content domains in TIMSS 2007 Science assessment framework are different for Grade 4 and Grade 8. Life Science is more emphasized for Grade 4, while Grade 8 starts from Biology, and Physics and Chemistry are assessed as two separate parts which is different from the composite of Physical Science in Grade 4. Not like TIMSS 2003, Environmental Science is not listed together with Life Science, etc., but merged into Life Science, Physical Science, and Earth Science.

Fifth, the cognitive dimension includes three domains, each of which contains the expectation description of different abilities. The cognitive dimension is divided into three domains based on what students have to know and do when confronting the various items developed for the TIMSS 2007 assessment. The first domain, *Knowing*, covers facts, procedures, and concepts students need to know, while the second domain, *Applying*, focuses on the ability of the student to apply knowledge and conceptual understanding in a problem situation. The third domain, *Reasoning*, goes beyond the solution of routine problems to encompass unfamiliar situations, complex contexts, and multi-step problems. Specifically, Knowing includes to recall/recognize, to define, to describe, to demonstrate, and to use tools and procedures. While Applying contains the abilities to compare/contrast/classify, to use models, to relate, to interpret information, to find solutions and to explain, and Reasoning consists of the abilities to analyze/solve problems, to integrate/synthesize, to hypothesize/predict, to design/plan, to draw conclusions, to generalize, to evaluate, and to justify. Moreover, the corresponding concrete skills are outlined for abilities.

Sixth, change is its penetration of the scientific inquiry. Scientific inquiry is treated as an overarching assessment strand. It overlaps all of the domains of science and has both content-based and skill-based components. Assessment of scientific inquiry includes items and tasks requiring students to demonstrate knowledge of the tools, methods, and procedures necessary to do science, to apply this knowledge to engage in scientific investigations, and to use scientific understanding to propose explanations based on evidence. These processes of scientific inquiry promote a broader understanding of scientific concepts as well as reasoning and problem-solving skills. It is expected that students at both grade levels will possess some general knowledge of the nature of science and scientific inquiry, including the fact that scientific knowledge is subject to change, the importance of using different types of scientific investigations in verifying scientific knowledge, the use of basic "scientific methods", communication of results, and the interaction of science, mathematics, and technology. In addition to this general knowledge, students are expected to demonstrate the skills and abilities involved in five major aspects of the scientific inquiry process: formulating questions and hypotheses, designing investigations, representing data, analyzing and interpreting data, drawing conclusions and developing explanations.

Compared with OECD/PISA, TIMESS assessment framework relies on curriculum standards more and pays more attention to the assessment on students' learning outcomes of the related curriculum.

4.1.1.2 OECD Assessment Program

Programme for International Student Assessment (PISA in abbreviation) is an assessment program launched and carried out by OECD for countries to monitor their educational effects. With the application of modern testing theory, PISA assesses the developmental level in Reading, Mathematics, and Science of students at the end of compulsory schooling (around age 15), along with the questionnaire survey to evaluate the participating country's educational effects and to make international comparison, overcoming the limitation of the traditional test, which is one of the fairly influential international educational assessment programs.

In the first test in 2000, 32 countries participated in PISA, and after that, with 3 years as a cycle, there is a field emphasized in each cycle, which takes two-thirds of the testing time. Every three years, the program makes an analysis on the change tendency of a field, and every nine years, it can thoroughly evaluate students' mastery of every field. In 2000, the major focus is on students' reading literacy. In the second cycle in 2003, there were 41 participating countries and economies with students' mathematical literacy as the major focus. And in the third cycle in 2006, there were 56 participating countries and economies with students' scientific literacy as the major focus.[3]

PISA 2006 uses the term of "scientific literacy" rather than "science", which is different from the traditional learning focusing on simple repetition of scientific knowledge, paying more attention to the importance of applying scientific knowledge into the practical life context. Knowledge use needs to apply scientific method and ability (scientific inquiry) and depends on individuals' affection, interest, value, and action to science-related issues. Students' scientific competence includes two aspects. One aspect is that students own certain scientific knowledge,

---

[3]Yang BS (2008) The execution of science academic achievement survey. Asia-Pacific Forum on Science Learning and Teaching 6:1.

the other aspect means students' understanding of the characteristic features of science as a form of human knowledge and enquiry. Meanwhile, it is acknowledged that the performance of scientific competence depends on individuals' attitude to science and willingness to engage in science-related issues. However, the noncognitive aspect, such as motivation, is also considered competency. The definition of PISA 2006 scientific literacy relates the fours aspects as follows:

1. Situations and Context Realize the situations and context in life are related to science and arts, including health, natural resources, environment, crisis, technological frontier, etc.
2. Scientific Knowledge Based on scientific knowledge including natural science and science-related knowledge to understand the natural world.
3. Scientific Competencies Demonstrate some abilities including identifying questions, explaining scientific phenomena, and drawing evidence-based conclusions about science-related issues.
4. Attitudes towards Science show interest in science, support science research, and actively take the responsibilities, such as responsibilities for natural resources and environment.

Based on this, Scientific Literacy Assessment Framework for PISA 2006 has been formed (Fig. 4.1).[4]

In scientific literacy, it is very important for individuals to own certain scientific competencies. Scientific literacy assessment framework for PISA 2006 makes scientific competencies clear, which mainly mean identifying scientific issues, explaining phenomena scientifically, and using scientific evidence.

Identifying scientific issues includes the following:

(1) recognizing issues that are possible to investigate scientifically;
(2) identifying keywords to search for scientific information; and
(3) recognizing the key features of a scientific investigation.

Explaining phenomena scientifically covers the following:

(1) applying knowledge of science in a given situation;
(2) describing or interpreting phenomena scientifically and predicting changes; and
(3) identifying appropriate descriptions, explanations, and predictions.

Using scientific evidence includes the following:

(1) interpreting scientific evidence and making and communicating conclusions;
(2) identifying the assumptions, evidence, and reasoning behind conclusions; and
(3) reflecting on the societal implications of science and technological developments.

In the aspect of content, the framework shows the new characteristics as follows.

---

[4]Assessing scientific, reading and mathematical literacy: a framework for PISA 2006. http://www.pisa.oecd.org. Accessed 24 May 2012.

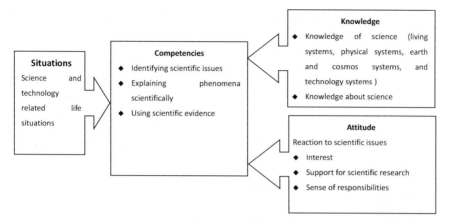

Fig. 4.1 Scientific literacy assessment framework for PISA 2006

First, the characteristic of scientific method. It includes methods to recognize scientific issues and evidence, to draw and express conclusions, and to verify the known scientific concepts.

Second, the characteristic of scientific concepts. Regarding scientific themes, it makes prominent in the aspects of structures and properties of matter, force and motion, form and function, ecosystem, energy transformation, etc. In the domain of application, it emphasizes science in life and health, science in Earth and environment, and science in technology.

Third, the characteristic of situations. In scientific literacy assessment framework for PISA 2006, the aspects of individual, community and globe and history make the situational characteristic outstanding.

From the perspective of the orientation of students' academic achievement survey, IEA comparatively emphasizes students' academic achievement based on schooling education, while OECD fairly focuses students' life ability as adults after they leave school. From the perspective of the content of students' academic achievement survey, both concentrate on the core subjects of reading, mathematics, science, etc. From the perspective of the result of students' academic achievement survey, most of the participating countries, based on the international sequence of students' academic achievement, reflect the various factors influencing students' academic achievement, such as curriculum teaching, educational system, social culture, home environment, etc.

4.1.1.3 The Execution of Science Academic Achievement Assessment in Other Countries

1. National Assessment of Educational Progress (NAEP)

At present, NAEP is the only nationally representative assessment of students' academic achievement in America, which lasts several decades. In 1963, since

America lacked the information related to students' academic achievement, Francis Keppel, US Commissioner of Education, called for a national assessment system of students' academic achievement, and invited Ralph Tyler, well-known psychologist, and educator, to participate the preparation work together. Because it was a creatively new assessment to reflect students' achievement proficiency in various subjects at different ages, the development of the assessment took an unexpectedly longer time. Till 1969, the whole programme was renamed National Assessment of Educational Progress (NAEP).

Since the 1960s, the assessments have been given in reading, mathematics, science and writing, history, civics, geography, and arts periodically. The assessment target is the nationally representative students at Grades 4, 8, and 12. Till 1969, the assessment system was totally set, including national NAEP, state NAEP, NAEP trial urban district assessment, and long-term trend NAEP.[5]

The design approach of the standard-oriented NAEP is to accelerate students' learning, emphasizing reversed design, forehand rules (assessment design is prior to teaching implementation), and the combination of assessment and teaching. Items are written based on students' performance expected, and it is to assess and explain what students know and can do through students' response to items (Fig. 4.2).[6]

2. British Assessment Performance Unit (APU)

APU started in 1975. The survey mainly assesses students' academic achievement in three fields, including language, mathematics, and science, with the purpose to accelerate the development of measurement method, to monitor school children's achievement, and to identify the situation of low academic achievement. Based on these, APU has four main functions.[7]

First, to identify and evaluate the existing assessment methods and tools, in order to achieve the goals above;

Second, to support the development of new assessment tools and technology, meanwhile considering statistical and sampling methods;

Third, to accelerate the cooperation between regional bureaus of education and teachers, to carry out assessment;

Fourth, to identify the significant difference of students' academic achievement in different learning environments, including the low achievement and publicizing the assessment results to educational departments and to the people responsible for resources distribution within schools.

---

[5]Wu HL, Yang YY, Zheng MH (2008) Science assessment in American national assessment of educational progress, Asia-Pacific Forum on Science Learning and Teaching 6:23.

[6]Cui YH, Wang SF, Xia XM (2007) Standards-based assessments of students' academic achievement. East China Normal University Press, Shanghai.

[7]Li YJ (2008) British students' science achievement assessment. Asia-Pacific Forum on Science Learning and Teaching 6:30.

4.1 Research Background

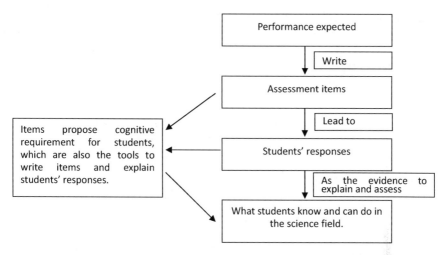

Fig. 4.2 Assessment mode of standard-based NAEP

4.1.2 The Development of National Science Academic Achievement Assessment Research

Due to various reasons, China mainland does not holistically take direct participation in the international students' academic achievement assessment such as IEA or OECD. However, Hong Kong and Taiwan participated several times. For example, Hong Kong participated in SISS 1983–1984, TIMSS-1995, TIMSS-2003 and TIMSS-2007. Since the late 1970s, from the aspects of cognition, skills, affects, students' morality, etc., the national theoretical field has introduced, absorbed and localized the educational taxonomy framework such as Bloom taxonomy. Since 1990s, various explorations and practice have been carried out in the aspects of students' academic achievement survey and the influencing factor analysis.

4.1.2.1 District Level

At the district level, during the period of the "10th five-year plan", there are some influential projects, such as "Research on Primary School Academic Achievement Assessment Reform" by Beijing Academy of Educational Sciences, "Academic Management and Assessment Research in the Execution of Primary and Secondary School Quality Education", and the later academic achievement measurement and assessment for Grades 5 and 8 students by the Beijing Compulsory Education Academic Achievement Assessment Team since 2007. Some assessment believes and manipulation methods in the researches mentioned above provide some reference for the present survey on science academic achievement.

Table 4.3 Beijing science/biology assessment framework (part)

Dimensions	Domains
Content	Structure of organism
	Life activities of organism
	Continuity of life
	Biology and environment
	Biological technology
Competency	Manipulation skill
	Inquiry skill
	Comprehensive skill

For example, some meaningful exploration has been done on the academic management and assessment research of none-tested subjects' teaching goals, of meeting students' difference, of students' autonomy development, etc., in the exploration of Academic Management and Assessment Research by the educational bureau in Huangpu district, Shanghai.

Another example, through the research during the period of "10th five-year plan", Beijing Academy of Educational Sciences initially constructed primary school academic achievement index system including the representative competencies of application of knowledge and skills, information, communication, problem-solving, etc., and the key factors of learning attitude, interest, will, value and affect, etc. Since 2007, based on the *Full-time Compulsory Education Science Curriculum Standard (Experimental version)* (*Science Curriculum Standard* in abbreviation), Beijing Compulsory Education Academic Achievement Assessment Team assessed the science academic achievement of 6546 students at Grades 5 and 8 in the downtown and suburb areas.[8] This assessment included content domains and competency domains, which could be seen in Table 4.3.

The results show that there is increasing tendency of the score difference for student groups of downtown and suburb, which, to some extent, represents the real situation of the science curriculum execution in some areas in our country.

4.1.2.2 National Level

At national level, during the period of the "10th five-year plan", there are some influential projects, such as "8-provincial sampling survey", "East Asia-Pacific students' academic achievement assessment research", carried out by the original National Education Commission Basic Education Department, United Nations International Children's Emergency Fund, and United Nations Educational, Scientific and Cultural Organization was the first macro-monitoring for primary school students' academic achievement in our country, with the sample of 24,000

---

[8]Wang YC, Hao Y, Hu J (2009) Assessment results analysis on Beijing 2007 compulsory education period academic achievement. Educational Science Research 9:43.

4.1 Research Background

primary school students at Grades 4 and 6 in near 1300 primary schools and over 6000 teachers. The survey employed internationally normative design, including multi-stratified random sampling, and the definition of "basic learning needs" of "Education for All" for education quality. Besides test, a large quantity of data related to students, family, teachers, and schools were also collected. Some assessment believes and manipulation strategies in the researches mentioned above provide a fairly valuable reference for the present survey on science academic achievement.

Since the new curriculum was carried out, the Ministry of Education authorized some universities to build project teams to do researches related to assessment. Regarding junior middle school period, "Ministry of Education Junior Middle School Graduation Academic Achievement Assessment" Science team carried out practical exploration on item writing and development of junior middle school graduation test. For the holistic theoretical framework, there was no obvious direction, but for the assessment on science knowledge, science inquiry, affect and attitude, etc., the research provided some constructive item-writing principles and requirements. Regarding senior middle school period, "Senior Middle School Students' Academic Achievement Assessment with New Curriculum Background" project team began to do theoretical research and practical exploration on students' academic achievement assessment since 2003. The project research could be divided into two periods. The first period was from 2003 to 2005, during which the basic believes and framework of senior middle school students' academic achievement assessment, the orientation, and design of module summative test, believes and methods of formative assessment and the development of open-ended items were discussed and explored. The second period is since 2005, during which academic achievement assessment on senior middle school compulsory curriculum has been explored, and the researches on item writing and test have been carried out.

Besides, PISA China project hosted by National Education Examinations Authority was officially launched in October 2006. The project team sampled more than 5000 students from 150 sampling schools and realized to assess reading literacy, mathematical literacy and scientific literacy of 160,000 students aged 15 from near 1200 schools in the pilot districts. In the assessment of scientific literacy, the programme mainly built based on the competency domain of "Identifying scientific issues", "Explaining phenomena scientifically" and "Using scientific evidence" and attitude domain of "Interest in science" and "Support for scientific research".[9] Beijing Normal University "Accelerating Teachers' Development and Students' Growth Assessment Research" project team has carried out years' exploration on assessment methods since 2002. They tried to build an electronic development assessment system, aiming to improve assessment efficiency and to provide individual feedback and instruction. National Basic Education Quality

---

[9]Wang L (2007) New Exploration on Educational Assessment. Xi'an Jiaotong University Press, Xi'an.

Monitoring and Assessment Center set in Beijing and Shanghai also, respectively, carried out a survey on primary and middle school students' academic achievement.

The researches mentioned above have done exploration and practice in the aspects of international experience reference, construction of assessment index and assessment tool, extension of assessment methods, collection of related data and inference of assessment results, which provide constructive opinions and suggestions for the present research. From the perspective of the assessment manipulation of the national student science academic achievement, the test item development is mostly based on experience, lack of theoretical direction, the assessment approach and method are still fairly sole, and the use of assessment results is not regulatory. Therefore, it urgently needs to explore fairly good assessment tool representing the situation of local students' development, to carry out the survey on national basic education period students' science academic achievement, to analyze the factors influencing students' science academic achievement, and to provide appropriate and reliable evidence for educational decision-making. The present survey on science academic achievement carried out in the 31 districts or counties is developed based on the considerations above.

4.2 Theoretical Bases and Main Analysis of the Research

4.2.1 The Theoretical Bases

Based on the background and the practical situation, the present research proposed that this survey, with *Basic Education Curriculum Reform Guideline (Pilot version)* as direction, *Science Curriculum Standard* and SOLO taxonomy as the bases, Item Response Theory (IRT) and Rasch model as the main measurement theoretical foundation, and related national and international research results as the main reference, creatively developed assessment framework and instruments.

4.2.1.1 Basic Education Curriculum Reform Guideline (Pilot Version) (Guideline in Abbreviation Below) as the Direction

With the collection of the essence in the areas of education and teaching and curriculum research for years, *Guideline* represents the requirements of the Party and Nation for the development of basic education, of which the basic believes, basic principles and execution strategies could be the basic value orientation of the present research. *Guideline* requires building the assessment system to accelerate students' all-round development. Not only paying attention to students' academic achievement, but assessment also should find and develop students' potentials in various aspects, know students' needs in their development, help students' know themselves, and build their confidence. The educational function of the assessment should be developed to accelerate students' development based on their original level.

4.2 Theoretical Bases and Main Analysis of the Research 149

4.2.1.2 *Science Curriculum Standard* as the Survey Basic Basis

Primary School Science Curriculum is science enlightenment curriculum with the orientation of developing scientific literacy.[10] The science curriculum learning within primary school period is good for students to develop scientific cognitive method and scientific view of nature, to enrich their childhood life, to develop their characters and to develop their potentials for creation. The new basic believes emphasizes that science curriculum should face all students, with openness and content satisfying the needs of both society and students; students are the main body of science learning; and the science learning should make inquiry as core, with assessment to accelerate the development of scientific literacy. The development of instrument will make the content and requirements of *Science Curriculum Standard* as the foundation, including the content of Life World, Physical World, and Earth-Cosmos World.

4.2.1.3 Item Response Theory (IRT) and Rasch Model as the Foundation

IRT could be interpreted as a probability method to explore the relationship between the testee' response to item and the potential feature. Rasch model could also be called uni-parameter logical model, i.e., the objective equal-interval scales are obtained through the testees' responses. No matter the validity analysis, reliability analysis, norm analysis, fit analysis, standard-reference test and norm-reference test, Rasch model or IRT reveals their advantages.

4.2.1.4 SOLO Taxonomy as Marking Method

The nature of SOLO taxonomy describes the levels of learners' learning quality, which is a marking method based on the level description. Students' learning results, from low to high, are divided into five different levels, which are pre-structural level, uni-structural level, multi-structural level, relational level, and extended abstract level.

The five SOLO levels represent students' mastery level of specific knowledge. From the students' responses to an item, teachers could refer to the standard mentioned above and make judgment for students' mastery of knowledge. It could be seen that SOLO taxonomy could be used in formative students' academic assessment. And in assessment, if different level scores are given to the five levels above, the quality of students' responses to items could be quantified, and the

---

[10]Ministry of Education of the People's Republic of China (2001) Full-time compulsory education science (grades 3–6) curriculum standard (experimental version). Beijing Normal University Publishing Group, Beijing.

quantified scores could be the basis for summative assessment. There is a natural difference between the multiple-choice items constructed based on SOLO taxonomy and the general ones. For the general multiple-choice items, there is only one option as the key, which could get marks, while other options are wrong and cannot get marks. However, the multiple-choice items constructed based on SOLO taxonomy includes this uni-option multiple-choice type and the multi-option multiple-choice type, which means that the key is not only one option or some options are meaningful, reflecting the different developmental levels of students' mind. Different marks could be given to different options to finally know students' development situation and to take corresponding teaching and learning strategies.

4.2.2 Definition of Basic Concepts

4.2.2.1 Students' Academic Achievement

Students' academic achievement is the developmental level achieved by students through learning activities, based on their prior experience, in aspects of knowledge, skills, affect and attitude, etc., with teachers' teaching. Students' academic achievement in the present project means students' developmental level in primary school science subject learning.

4.2.2.2 Science Subject Competence

Science subject competence is the developmental level achieved by students through learning activities, based on their prior experience, in aspects of knowledge, skills, affect and attitude, etc., with teachers' teaching or self-access learning. Science subject competence in the present projects means the developmental level of students' ability in primary school science subject learning, which meanwhile relates students' basic abilities in comprehensive practical activities and related learning areas.

4.2.2.3 Science Subject Competence Test

Science subject competence test is the measurement on the knowledge and skills mastered by students, and on their development situation of affect and attitude in a learning task and the process to make valuable judgment. Science subject competence is influenced by many factors in and out of schools, thus, related influencing factors should be surveyed with the measurement.

4.2.3 Reference for Research on Science Subject Competence Assessment

In the international researches on Science subject competence assessment, the researches on assessment framework own important values. For example, TIMSS Science assessment framework is composed of two parts: content dimension and cognitive dimension. In the content dimension, the related domains or topics include life, physics, earth and cosmos world, etc.; in the cognitive dimension, it describes the series of behaviors expectedly performed by students when learning science content, including knowing, applying, reasoning, etc., each of which contains the ability requirement of different levels. Scientific inquiry ability, as the main assessment index, exists through the content and process of the holistic assessment from the beginning to the end.

The assessment framework of PISA Science subject competence is based on lifelong-learning dynamic model. Its basic believes have the basis of two layers. First, students' school learning is the basis for the knowledge and skills required in the future; second, the function of schools is oriented in making students own lifelong-learning ability. In assessment, the application of students' basic knowledge, skills, attitude, affect, etc., in Science, in the real context is assessed as an emphasis. Scientific literacy is the focus of the assessment.

Besides, NAEP Science assessment framework regulates the academic achievement assessment levels of students in Grades 4, 8, and 12. The assessment framework includes two parts of scientific fields and cognitive element. Scientific fields relate Earth science, Physical science, and Life science, among which, Physical science includes Physics and Chemistry; Cognitive element includes conceptual understanding, scientific investigation, and practical reasoning.

In the national research and practice of our country, the related assessment of Science subject competence more particularly refers to the assessment of scientific literacy. During the period of recent years, our country also has done various discussions and practices on the scientific literacy assessment framework. Especially after the new curriculum was executed, scientific literacy has become the primary goal in our country's science curriculum education. In the assessment of Science subject academic achievement, scientific literacy, based on Science assessment framework with three dimensions of scientific knowledge and skills, process and method, and affect, attitude, and values, is more prominently assessed.

From the present situation of our country's assessment of students' Science subject competence, it could be seen that the content requiring memorization and remembering has not obviously reduced. Although opportunities for students to explore and to manipulate with hands increase, there is quite distance to achieve the requirement of curriculum standard. Regarding the manipulation of Science academic achievement assessment, influenced by the examination-oriented education and utilitarianism, the phenomena of "learning for examination, teaching for examination" still exists. The construction of testing items is only based on experience, fairly lack of theory and regulation. We have seen that after the new curriculum was carried out, the belief of the new curriculum has been gradually accepted by people. Science curriculum faces all the students, with an inquiry as for the core in science learning, and assessment accelerates the formation and development of scientific literacy.

4.2.4 New Requirements for Science Subject Competence Assessment from Our Country's Educational Reform

From the long-term goal of our country's educational reform, new requirements for primary school Science subject competence assessment have been proposed. With the orientation to develop primary school students' scientific literacy, it actively advocates to let students experience learning activities with exploration as the main part, to develop their curiosity and desire for exploring, and to develop their understanding for the nature of science, aiming to make them learn the strategies to explore and solve problems, and to make foundation for their lifelong learning and life.

At present, in the aspects of assessment goals, content, method, etc., the practical situation of our country's educational reform development has proposed some new requirements for the assessment of primary school Science subject competence. For example, regarding the assessment of Science subject competence, it should fully make assessment goals clear, accurately master assessment content, and flexibly apply assessment method. Meanwhile, in the assessment of Science curriculum learning, it should emphasize to pay attention to the pluralism of assessment main body, to the thoroughness of assessment content, to the diversity of assessment method, and to the feature of assessment opportunities through the whole learning process. Assessment should reflect the three dimensions of scientific inquiry, affect, attitude, and values and scientific knowledge, with the basis of real daily leaning, and should fully apply all the learning activities in and out of the classroom, thoroughly reflecting the situation of students' learning and development.

4.2.5 Specific Requirements for Science Subject Competence Assessment from Our Country's New Curriculum

New curriculum proposes specific requirements for Science subject competence assessment in the aspects of goal, content, method, etc., which are represented in the three aspects: to fully make assessment goals clear, to accurately master assessment content, and to flexibly apply assessment method.[11]

---

[11]Ministry of Education of the People's Republic of China (2001) Full-time compulsory education science (grades 3–6) curriculum standard (experimental version). Beijing Normal University Publishing Group, Beijing.

4.2.5.1 To Fully Make Assessment Goals Clear

For the assessment of Science curriculum learning, the main aim is to know the situation of students' practical learning and development, to finally raise students' scientific literacy, which is the main goal. Thus, new curriculum underlines that in the assessment of Science curriculum learning, it should pay attention to the pluralism of assessment main body, to the thoroughness of assessment content, to the diversity of assessment method, and to the feature of assessment opportunities through the whole learning process.

4.2.5.2 To Accurately Master Assessment Content

Science curriculum learning assessment mainly includes the three aspects of scientific inquiry, affect, attitude, and value and scientific knowledge. In the Science curriculum learning assessment, the three aspects above collectively reflect the practical level students' scientific literacy should achieve at the end of Grade 6.

First, scientific inquiry. The assessment on scientific inquiry ability in new curriculum mainly assesses students' interest, skills, thinking level, and ability in "doing" science with a brain. For example, whether students are active, persistent and seeking truth from facts when participating activities; whether students' observation is thorough, questions proposed are appropriate, measurement is accurate, design is reasonable, expression is clear, and communication is bidirectional or multidirectional; how students' ability to collect information, to deal with information and to make reasonable explanations is, etc.

Second, affect, attitude, and value. The assessment on affect, attitude and value in new curriculum mainly assesses students' attitude to science learning. For example, whether students have strong interest in learning science; whether students not only respect facts and evidence but also are brave to imagine and to create; and whether students are happy to cooperate, to communicate, to accept others' suggestions, to improve their own learning or study, etc.

Third, scientific knowledge. The assessment on scientific knowledge in new curriculum mainly assesses students' understanding process and application of the basic concepts and skills in the aspects of Life Science, Physical Science, and Earth and Cosmos Science, rather than how much information students memorize. Compared with that of the past, this part mainly employs the methods of classroom observation, assignments analysis, necessary test, theme check, etc.

4.2.5.3 To Flexibly Apply Assessment Method

Science curriculum learning assessment, mainly taking the real daily learning as the basis, fully applies all the learning activities in and out of class to thoroughly reflect the situation of students' learning and development. In science curriculum learning assessment, the main methods include teachers' observation, talk with students, records of outstanding performance, test and examination, analysis of activity results, students' growth records, assessment scales, assignments, discussion, appraisal, etc.

4.2.6 Basic Views

First, science subject competence is one piece of the core content of students' academic achievement. The development of Science subject competence relies on school curriculum learning. It could be described in the two dimensions of structure and process. Structure reflects its thoroughness and integrity, while process reflects its extent of activeness and development situation. The former emphasizes the subject content and the latter underlines the presentation form and process. Affect and attitude, represented in structure and reflected in form and process, is the main power for science subject competence to be improved.

Second, there are various factors influencing science subject competence, which mainly exist in four levels of student individuals, school, family, and socioeconomic political-cultural environment. Factors at the level of student individuals include sex, social background, self-consciousness (self-efficacy, self-concept), motivation (learning interest, participation extent, confidence), educational expectation, etc.; factors at the level of school include school type, school structure, school resources (quality of humanity, educational, and materialistic resources; teachers and usability of computers), school atmosphere (students' and teachers' behavior and morality), school management and classroom practice (activity, student assessment, teaching and learning time, teachers' monitoring), etc.,[12] in which factors at teaching and learning level include teaching and learning strategies, the class atmosphere students perceive, class size, teachers' support, use of teaching materials, school organization and structure, etc.

Third, the improvement of students' academic achievement needs both the deep feedback provided by macro-monitoring and class assessment approach with continuous improvement. The two aspects, with their own advantage, compensate each other and complement each other. And the study of the latter is carried out mainly through cases. Case study should equally emphasize concluding the old experience and creating new experience and pay attention to theoretical promotion.

Fourth, district difference and individual difference widely exist in students' academic achievement in our country. It is the mission for education to protect difference and to improve quality. Seeking the factors which result in the unfavorable difference to give proper invention and compensation is the original intention of the present research, which is also to realize the real educational equality and equity.

---

[12]Wang L, Jiao LY (2006) Brief introduction to PISA and re-assessing Hong Kong PISA 2003 assessment report. China Examination 9:10.

4.3 Research Aims and Methods

The present survey is curriculum-based students' academic achievement assessment, which aims to satisfy the requirement of public accountability outside and to meet the requirement of improving student learning inside. The realization of the two aims cannot be separated from curriculum standard. Curriculum standard is the effective bedrock of students' academic achievement assessment, which bears the function and responsibility of students' academic achievement assessment standard.

4.3.1 Development of Assessment Framework and Test Instrument

4.3.1.1 Assessment Framework

Based on the national and international assessment framework of students' academic achievement and the features of our country's curriculum reform, the assessment framework has been developed, mainly including three dimensions (shown in Fig. 4.3), i.e., content domains, scientific competencies, and performance levels. The survey on students' attitude, affect, and value to science is conducted through questionnaires.

- Content dimension

Content dimension is mainly based on the three content domains of Life World, Physical World, and Earth and Cosmos World in *Science Curriculum Standard*. Each content domain includes several topics and each topic contains several concrete content standards. In Life World, through the initial understanding about life phenomena, it is to develop students' love for life world, care for ecological sustainable development, good personal sanitation habits, and healthy life. In Physical World, students need to know the nature and change process of the common material, such as water, metal, etc. "Motion and force" makes students start getting to know the concepts of position and motion, know the relationship of force and motion change and know common simple mechanics; "presentation form of power" includes the physical phenomena of sound, heat, light, electricity, and magnetism and makes students know they are different presentation forms of power and power could be transferred. In Earth and Cosmos World, it makes primary school students get to have a more thorough impression about the earth, including the complexion of the earth, component materials and the various changes caused by earth movement.[13]

---

[13]Ministry of Education of the People's Republic of China (2001) Full-time compulsory education science (grades 3–6) curriculum standard (experimental version). Beijing Normal University Publishing Group, Beijing.

Fig. 4.3 Dimensions of the assessment framework

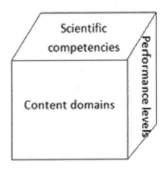

- Scientific competency

There are many connotations and classifications for scientific competency. Mainly based on the related ability requirements in curriculum standard and the classification further classified, with the consideration of scientific competence development condition and nature of physical and mental development of Grade–6 students in primary school, the present survey lays particular emphasis on scientific practice and stresses the assessment on the three aspects of students' scientific presentation, scientific application, and scientific inquiry, each of which includes various concrete abilities or the main tasks to be accomplished. For example, scientific application includes applying scientific knowledge to explain common phenomena in daily life, to identify or distinguish scientific concepts and application of principles, to analyze the internal links between objects and to solve problems with knowledge and skills acquired. Similarly, scientific presentation includes the abilities to state content, to use and construct models and to further present and explain. And scientific inquiry includes the abilities to observe phenomena, to analyze materials and to carry out experiments, etc. This classification is oriented at not only knowing what students know through science curriculum learning, but also exploring what they can do. The scientific competency is refined as in Table 4.4.

- Performance level

According to SOLO taxonomy, it is to analyze students' ability development and divide students' responses to questions into five levels or five structures,[14] which are pre-structural level, uni-structural level, multi-structural level, relational level and extended abstract level.

---

[14]Cai YH (2006) SOLO taxonomy theory and its application in teaching. Teacher Education Research 1: 34.

4.3 Research Aims and Methods

Table 4.4 Scientific competency and its specific descriptions

Scientific competency	Concrete abilities (can-do tasks)
Scientific presentation (P)	Stating content (P1): to define, list, state, describe, illustrate, identify
	Constructing models (P2): diagrammatic presentation, object modeling, mathematical modeling
Scientific application (A)	Explaining phenomena (A1): to identify, distinguish, build relations, explain (causal relationship), judge/evaluate
	Solving problems (A2): to identify problems, seek methods, list alternatives, confirm solution, execute solution, evaluate (results)
Scientific inquiry (I)	Observing phenomena (I1): to propose questions, observe, measure, record, classify, compare/contrast, get conclusions
	Analyzing materials (I2): to confirm topics, search information, survey/interview, read text materials, read diagrams, identify facts and ideas, analyze/infer/generalize, testify, argue, judge/evaluate
	Doing experiments (I3): to predict (propose questions), confirm variables, propose hypothesis, list experimental steps, select materials, and tools, manipulate experiments, deal with data with diagrams, get conclusions, discuss, judge/evaluate

Table 4.5 Relationship among the three dimensions

Scientific competency	Content domains		
	Life world	Physical world	Earth and cosmos world
Presentation	Ability performance expectation	Ability performance expectation	Ability performance expectation
Application	Ability performance expectation	Ability performance expectation	Ability performance expectation
Inquiry	Ability performance expectation	Ability performance expectation	Ability performance expectation

The scientific content students master and the scientific competencies they possess cannot be solely assessed, because it is impossible for students to have no performance in front of the assessment content, neither that students have visible performance without content orientation. The intersection of the two aspects could be expressed that students' "performance expectation" or "ability requirement" in different content domains (shown in Table 4.5), which is taken as the basis to write items. To judge the performance level (uni-structural level, multi-structural level, and relational level) of students' various abilities through their responses to items is just the internal relationship among the three dimensions.

Table 4.6 Two-dimensional table of specifications for primary school Grade 6 Science test

Science curriculum content standard			Performance expectation (ability requirement) (students can)	Competency classification	Performance level	Item No./key	Proportion
Content domains	Topic	Content standard					
Life world 11 (Number indicates quantity of items, the same below)	A variety of organism	Know fungus is a kind of organism which does not belong to plant or animal	Distinguish the organism which does not belong to plant or animal	P1 distinguish	M	1/C	U:6 M:4 R:1
	Common features of organisms	Know that life processes of different organisms are different	Observe and analyze the main difference of the life processes of cabbage butterfly and grasshopper	I1 observe	U	4/C	
		Can recognize the six organs of plant	Recognize the edible part of common vegetables is which organ	A1 explain	U	3/A	
		Know many features of organisms are heritable	Identify the feature inherited from parents among some features	A1 identify	M	8/C	
	Organism and environment	Observe the physical appearance of plants and link the observed results with their living environment	Explain the relationship between the features of cactus' physical appearance and its living environment	A1 explain	U	2/B	
		Understand the meaning of food chain	Analyze and infer the relation between two members in the food chain	I2 analyze, infer	U	41/B	
			Analyze and infer the relation between three or more members in the food chain	I2 analyze, infer	R	42/A	
	Healthy life	Know the breathing process of human's body, the generation, and prevention of common diseases of respiratory system	Distinguish the main functions of lung	P1 Distinguish	M	5/B	
		Know the generation and prevention of common diseases of respiratory system	Identify which disease is easily caused by smoking	A1 identify	U	6/C	
		Pay attention to the application of science and technology	Analyze which method of giving up smoking is based on technology	A2 solve	M	7/D	
		Know various factors influencing health	Identify the possible diseases caused by drinking polluted water	A1 identify	U	11/B	
Physical world 19	Object and substance	*Features of object* Know heating or cooling can make shapes or sizes of objects change, and list common phenomena of expansion caused by heat and contraction caused by cold	Analyze and explain the reasons for deflated table tennis get inflated after it is heated	I2 analyze, infer	M	23/C	U:5 M:9 R:5
	Motion and force	*Change of substance* Know there are three types of state for substance: solid, liquid and gas; know that the change of temperature can make the state of substance change	Analyze line chart and read to get the temperature for a metal to change into liquid from solid	I2 read diagrams	M	29/B	
			Analyze line chart and read to get the time for a metal to change into gas from liquid	I2 read diagrams	R	30/A	
			Explain the reasons of the less possibilities to see fog in desert than at seaside	A1 explain	M	28/D	

(continued)

4.3 Research Aims and Methods 159

Table 4.6 (continued)

Science curriculum content standard			Performance expectation (ability requirement) (students can)	Competency classification	Performance level	Item No./key	Proportion
Content domains	Topic	Content standard					
		Position and motion Can confirmatively describe the position of an object and understand that the position of an object needs to be comparatively confirmed by the position of another object	Read diagrams, select different references and describe the position relationship of three objects	I2 read diagrams	R	38/C	
		Common forces Know the common forces in daily life, such as wind force, water force, gravity, elastic force, buoyancy force, frictional force, etc.	Calculate the weight of the apparatus in weightlessness on the moon	A2 calculate	M	20/D	
			Identify which force the pole brings to sportsman	A1 identify	U	21/B	
			Find the methods to reduce friction in daily life	A2 solve	M	27/B	
		Simple mechanics Know making use of mechanics can promote working effectiveness, and know the use of simple mechanics, such as inclined plane, lever, gear, pulley, etc.	Analyze common tools and identify which applies the lever principle	A1 explain	U	34/B	
			Distinguish the simple mechanics and complex mechanics (robot)	P1 distinguish	U	39/C	
	Presentation forms of energy	*Heat phenomenon* Know temperature indicates the extent of hot or cold of objects, know the unit of temperature, and know how to use thermometer	Select the thermometer most appropriate to measure the temperature of warm water	I3 Select tools	M	25/D	
			Accurately use thermometer to measure the temperature of objects	I3 use tools	M	35/D	
			Accurately read the display of thermometer and order the temperatures with the sequence from low to high	I2 read, infer	R	40/B	
		Know heat always transmits from high-temperature object to low-temperature object till the objects are at the same temperature Know the common methods for heat transmission and insulation	Apply the knowledge that hot air rises while cold air falls to analyze cases and find the method to quickly cool soda water	A2 solve	M	22/D	
			Analyze data and infer the effects of their function to keep warm based on the materials' effects of heat insulation	I2 read, infer	R	24/A	
			Analyze cases and recognize which item is designed and made based on the principle that hot air rises	A1 explain	U	26/C	
			Analyze the results measured and judge which is accurate from the results gained	I3 get conclusions	M	36/C	
			Analyze the results measured and judge which is inaccurate from the results gained	I3 get conclusions	R	37/D	
		Simple electric circuit Know some materials are easy to conduct electricity while some others not	Select the materials with weak function of electric conduction	A2 solve	U	32/D	

(continued)

Table 4.6 (continued)

Science curriculum content standard			Performance expectation (ability requirement) (students can)	Competency classification	Performance level	Item No./key	Proportion
Content domains	Topic	Content standard					
Earth and Cosmos World 12	Complexion of the earth and substance of the earth	Know the earth is composed of small-proportion land and large-proportion water area	Describe the distribution of the composition of land and water area at the earth surface	P1 describe	U	16/B	U: 5 M: 5 R: 2
		Design the experiment on the effects of different types of soil for plant growth	Design the inquiry experiment, with controlled variable, that "The growth of green plants needs the soil with sand contained"	I3 confirm variable	M	19/D	
		Know the composition of soil	Describe that soil is mainly composed of what substances	P1 describe	M	12/D	
			Infer their capacity of water retention based on the water infiltration of different types of soil	I2 read, infer	R	18/A	
		Realize the close relationship between human being's existence and land materials and the importance to protect land materials	Explain the main aim of forest tree planting	A1 explain	U	14/C	
		Know the danger of water area pollution and the main reasons	Infer the main functions of impounding reservoirs	I2 read, analyze	U	9/C	
			Infer the function of Chlorine addition during the process of water purification	I2 read, analyze	R	10/A	
		Can use some methods to confirm the existence of air; Know the human beings' use about air features	Predict the experiment result and judge the candle in which bottle goes out first	I1 observe, analyze	M	33.C	
	Earth movement and changes caused	Know the earth rotates with nonstop, and the rotation period is a day which needs 24 h	Describe the time needed for the earth rotation	P1 describe	U	31/A	
		Know the function of every kind of power of nature for earth surface to change	Recognize cobblestones are formed with the function of what power of nature	A1 explain	M	13/B	
		Know the weather can be described in measurable scales	Identify the symbols of sand storm	P2 recognize symbols	U	15/B	
	Planets in the space	Know the representative constellations of four seasons	Observe and analyze diagrams to identify Charles's Wain in which star map	P2 recognize	M	17/D	

4.3 Research Aims and Methods

4.3.1.2 Construction of the Two-Dimensional Table of Specifications

Based on assessment framework, important content goals are selected from the three content domains of life world, physical world, and earth and cosmos world, and then are transferred into the performance expectations of students' learning (ability requirements). With ability classification marked and learning results are made manipulative with test items, test items, at uni-structural level, multi-structural level and relational level with the proportion of 2:2:1, are designed based on SOLO taxonomy. And the two-dimensional table of specifications is constructed, which could be seen in Table 4.6.

The distribution of item quantity could be gained from the two-dimensional table of specifications and shown in Table 4.7.

Table 4.7 Distribution of item quantity

		Distribution of item quantity	Total quantity
Content domains		Life domain: 11 items, about 26% of the total quantity of items	42 items
		Physical domain: 19 items, about 45% of the total quantity of items	
		Earth domain: 12 items, about 29% of the total quantity of items	
Scientific competencies		Scientific presentation: 8 items, about 19% of the total quantity of items	
		Scientific application: 16 items, about 38% of the total quantity of items	
		Scientific inquiry: 18 items, about 43% of the total quantity of items	
Performance levels		Uni-structural level (U): 16 items, about 38% of the total quantity of items	
		Multi-structural level (M): 18 items, about 42% of the total quantity of items	
		Relational level (R): 8 items, about 20% of the total quantity of items	

4.3.1.3 Development Procedures of the Test Instrument

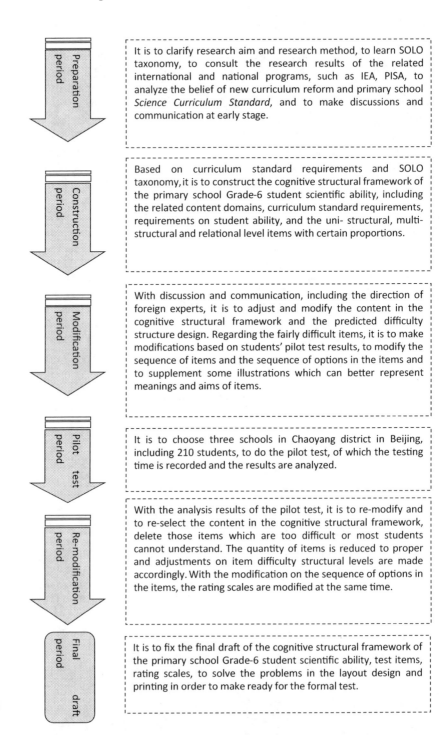

4.3 Research Aims and Methods

The principles to be followed in the procedures of the instrument development are as follows:

1. Students' cognitive pattern and age features should be followed.
2. The content of every domain in *Science Curriculum Standard* should be thoroughly considered and requirements of key points in each domain should be chosen.
3. Manipulative and assessable verbs are used to describe the requirements on students' ability.
4. Item stem language should be brief, with clear illustrations, to make students at all levels understand the item requirement. And the words in options in similar length are properly used.
5. The structural level, proportion, quantity, timing, rating scales of items are well designed.

Meanwhile, regarding item writing, the following rules should be particularly emphasized.

1. Practicality. Scientific ability is actually the transformation and application of practice and knowledge. It is hard to really apply knowledge into life to solve practical problems without active experience, self-willing practice, and hands-on manipulation but the knowledge. Therefore, the manipulation and practicality should be underlined as more as possible in design.
2. Interesting characteristic. Boring text description should be avoided. Situations which can give rise to students' interest and connect their practical life are created and vivid diagram presentations are employed as more as possible.
3. Problem-solving characteristic. Students' ability to analyze and to solve social phenomena and life problems and the true developmental level performed should be assessed as much as possible, with the simple knowledge memorization avoided.

4.3.1.4 Test Item Writing

Based on the two-dimensional table of specifications, important content goals in the three domains of Life world, Physical world, Earth and Cosmos world in *Science Curriculum Standard* have been selected, stated into generalized ability requirements and transferred into the expected outcomes of students' learning. According to SOLO taxonomy, test items, at uni-structural level (U), multi-structural level (M) and relational level (R) with the proportion of 2:2:1, are designed. Based on the analysis results of pilot test, modifications are done to stem, option, illustration, and key. The structural level and capacity of the whole test paper are then adjusted to guarantee the test could be finished within the time given. Example items at each level are provided as follows:

1. Item at uni-structural level

Item 15: Which of the following weather symbols represents sand storm? ( )

This item belongs to the content of Earth and Cosmos world in *Science Curriculum Standard*. With the requirement of "*Know the weather can be described in measurable scales*" in *Science Curriculum Standard*, the item is designed to encourage students to pay attention to weather, develop students' ability and habit to observe and record the weather change with the use of symbols and words. To recognize and identify the weather symbols is the basis. Based on the SOLO taxonomy, this item is at uni-structural level. With the already-acquired knowledge and experience (maybe the information gained from class or television programme, such as weather forecast), students directly identify the only symbol representing sand storm (B) or rule out the other three fairly familiar symbols with exclusive methods. If students chose other options, they could be treated at pre-structural level, because they do not own the simple knowledge and ability related to the item.

2. Item at multi-structural level

Item 8: Among the following options, ( ) can be inherited from parents.

A. Height and weight.
B. Hobby and hairline.
C. Skin color and hair color.
D. Saprodontia.

This item belongs to the content of Life world in *Science Curriculum Standard*. With the requirement of "*Know many features of organisms are heritable*" in *Science Curriculum Standard*, the item is designed to ask students to identify the feature inherited from parents among some features. Based on the SOLO taxonomy, this item is at multi-structural level. With the already-acquired knowledge and experience, students find the accurate related features as many as possible and link multi isolated events to answer the question. Among the options, Skin color, hair color and hairline are the main features which could be inherited from parents. Therefore, it is multi-structural level to choose the key C, while it is uni-structural level to choose B. And it is pre-structural level to choose A or D since neither of them contains the simple knowledge or ability related to the item.

4.3 Research Aims and Methods

3. Item at multi-structural level

Item 23. A deflated table tennis will get inflated when put into the hot water. The main reason is that ( ).

A. The surface of the table tennis expands in volume when heated.
B. It is affected by the air pressure.
C. The air inside of the table tennis expands in volume when heated.
D. The hot water flows into the table tennis to make it expand in volume.

This item belongs to the content of Physical world in *Science Curriculum Standard*. With the requirement of *"Know heating or cooling can make shapes or sizes of objects change, and list common phenomena of expansion caused by heat and contraction caused by cold"* in *Science Curriculum Standard*, the item is designed to ask students to explain the problems encountered in life with knowledge acquired. Based on the SOLO taxonomy, this item is at multi-structural level. With the already-acquired knowledge and experience, students analyze and explain the reasons for deflated table tennis get inflated after it is heated, which is related to solid (shell of the table tennis), gas (air in the table tennis) and liquid with the feature of *expansion caused by heat and contraction caused by cold*. It is multi-structural level if students can consider every factor and can compare that the feature of expansion caused by heat and contraction caused by cold is more obvious for gas than for solid, which is the main reason for the table tennis to get inflated and choose the key C. And it is uni-structural level to choose option A, which means that only the feature expansion caused by heat and contraction caused by cold is considered.

4. Item at relational level

Item 24. In order to reach the same effect of heat insulation, materials below are required to be as thick as

Air	8mm
Feather	8.5mm
Rabbit fur	9mm
Wool	12mm

Different materials have different heat insulation effect. Based on the information above, these four materials could be rearranged according to their heat preservation from strong to weak as ( ).

A. Air–feather–rabbit fur–wool.
B. Wool–rabbit fur–feather–air.

C. Feather–rabbit fur–wool–air.
D. Rabbit fur–wool–air–feather.

This item belongs to the content of Physical world in *Science Curriculum Standard*. With the requirement of *"Know the features of some materials (such as electricity conduction, dissolution, heat transmission and the feature of floating and sinking) and categorize the materials based on them"* in *Science Curriculum Standard*, the item is designed to ask students to analyze data and infer the effects of their function to keep warm based on the materials' effects of heat insulation. Based on the SOLO taxonomy, this item is at relational level. With the table given in the item, students first need to be clear that to achieve the same effects of heat insulation, the sequence of the materials thickness is from little to much, and then analyze that in the condition of the same the effects of heat insulation, the thickness is less, the effect of heat preservation is better. Thus, the sequence of the feature of heat preservation from strong to weak is the sequence of material need from little to much, i.e. from thin to thick (Key A). This item is related to the relations of multiple events, which requires students to infer the fairly complicated question of different materials' heat preservation capacity from their capacity of heat insulation, so it is at relational level. And it is multi-structural level to choose option B, implying that students infer the result that to reach the same heat insulation effect, the sequence of materials required is from thick to thin. It is uni-structural level if students choose option C or D, which means that students only can judge the single event, rather than find the accurate relations of multiple events.

5. Item at relational level

Item 42. Here is a food chain composed by four types of creatures.

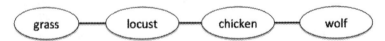

42. In this food chain, if a large number of wolves die, then the number of grass will ( ).

A. Greatly increase.
B. Greatly reduce.
C. Not change obviously.
D. Be hard to judge.

This item belongs to the content of Life world in *Science Curriculum Standard*. With the requirement of *"Understand the meaning of food chain"* in *Science Curriculum Standard*, the item is designed to ask students to analyze and infer the relation between three or more members in the food chain. Based on the SOLO taxonomy, this item is at relational level. With the food chain given in the item, students firstly need to be clear with the "eat or be eaten" relation of the members in the food chain, and then analyze that if a large number of wolves die, the number of the chicken will increase, which will make the number of locust decrease and results in the number of grass greatly increase (Key A). This item is related to the relations of multiple events, which requires students to analyze their mutual relationship of number change and then answer the fairly complicated question, so it is at relational level. And it is multi-structural level to choose option B, implying that students can analyze and infer the relation between two members in the food chain, but not more. It is uni-structural level if students choose option C, which means that students only can judge the single event, rather than find the accurate relations of two or more events.

This item was an open-ended question, related to the relationship change of three members, requiring students to analyze the situation that with the number of one member decreases, the numbers of other members will increase or decrease, and explain reasons. With the analysis result of the pilot test, it could be found that the cognitive process of reasons explained by the students who answered accurately is consistent with the analysis process above, without other explanations. Therefore, it could be modified into the form of multiple choice, giving the possible options and judging students' cognitive process and ability level through the option they choose.

4.3.1.5 Pilot Test and Modification

The pilot test was carried out in Beijing. In Anhuali No. 2 Primary School, Hepingjie Central Primary School and Huixinli Primary School, 210 test papers were distributed with 207 back. The recovery reached 98.6%. Analysis report of the results shows that the reliability of the Science test items is 0.98 and the reliability of the testees is 0.80. In general, the reliability of the academic achievement test paper should be over 0.90. The reliability of the present test paper meets the requirement. The analysis on the Science test items and the observation about the distribution chart of the item difficulty and student ability and chart of the model fit indices show that the difficulty fit indices of the items in the Science test are within the acceptable coverage, which is -1.83 to 3.08 (4.91 logit values). It could be seen from the information above that the item difficulty coverage is appropriate. Further analysis on item difficulty, discrimination, and model fit index was done and the result showed that discrimination of the original items 13 and 22 is below 0.05, which is quite low. Based on the requirement of the project team and the test situation, the items with low discrimination index were modified and the open-ended items were deleted. And the number of items is 42 in the final test paper.

In the present survey, pencil–paper test was carried out with questionnaire. The pencil–paper was used to survey students' academic achievement, while the questionnaire was used to analyze the influencing factors for students' academic achievement.

4.3.2 The Characteristic Parameter of the Test Instrument and Measurement Index of the Test Paper

4.3.2.1 Item Difficulty, Discrimination and Fit Index

The formal test was carried out with 18,600 primary school students in Grade 6 in 31 counties national wide (Sampling method could be found in general report). The valid test paper is 16,378, and the recovery is 88.1%. The item parameters and the validity and reliability of test paper are analyzed with Winstep3.63. The results could be seen as follows (Table 4.8).

Table 4.8 Statistical results of test item difficulty, discrimination, fit index, etc.

Item	Difficulty	Discrimination (point biserial correlation)	Discrimination	Infit mean square	p-value
1	0.46	0.42	1.12	0.97	0.58
2	−1.81	0.21	0.99	0.99	0.91
3	0.57	0.28	0.58	1.11	0.56
4	−1.27	0.29	1.02	0.98	0.86
5	1.84	0.32	0.85	1.06	0.3
6	−1.09	0.35	1.07	0.94	0.84
7	0.54	0.38	0.95	1.02	0.56
8	−0.40	0.35	1.03	0.99	0.74
9	0.40	0.42	1.14	0.96	0.59
10	1.22	0.34	0.81	1.06	0.42
11	−.90	0.34	1.05	0.97	0.82
12	0.24	0.31	0.79	1.06	0.62
13	0.59	0.33	0.77	1.06	0.55
14	−0.89	0.36	1.07	0.94	0.82
15	−2.73	0.20	1.03	0.96	0.96
16	−1.06	0.40	1.13	0.89	0.84
17	0.20	0.31	0.8	1.06	0.63
18	0.71	0.47	1.29	0.92	0.53
19	−0.31	0.32	0.96	1.02	0.73
20	0.01	0.38	1.05	0.98	0.67
21	−0.83	0.27	0.96	1.02	0.81
22	0.80	0.27	0.52	1.13	0.51
23	−0.16	0.38	1.05	0.98	0.7
24	1.50	0.39	0.96	1.01	0.37
25	1.49	0.17	0.39	1.24	0.37
26	−1.51	0.32	1.06	0.94	0.89
27	0.74	0.40	1.02	1.00	0.52

(continued)

4.3 Research Aims and Methods

Table 4.8 (continued)

Item	Difficulty	Discrimination (point biserial correlation)	Discrimination	Infit mean square	p-value
28	−0.10	0.37	1.04	0.98	0.69
29	0.57	0.41	1.07	0.98	0.56
30	1.70	0.48	1.18	0.91	0.33
31	0.35	0.47	1.3	0.91	0.6
32	0.11	0.40	1.08	0.97	0.65
33	−0.54	0.39	1.11	0.94	0.77
34	−0.65	0.28	0.94	1.03	0.78
35	−0.43	0.40	1.11	0.94	0.75
36	−0.42	0.38	1.09	0.95	0.75
37	0.77	0.34	0.81	1.05	0.52
38	−0.04	0.42	1.15	0.94	0.68
39	−1.05	0.34	1.07	0.95	0.84
40	1.60	0.42	1.04	0.97	0.35
41	−1.05	0.35	1.07	0.94	0.84
42	0.80	0.31	0.66	1.09	0.51

Note Test item reliability is 1.00

Table 4.9 could be attained with further calculation of the data in columns 2–6 of Table 4.8.

In Table 4.9, the first row is the data descriptors, with the item difficulty (threshold) estimated through Rasch model in row 2, and the third row contains item discrimination, presented in point biserial correlation between the pass of each item and of total items, which indicates the item feature to discriminate students' ability. Row 4 is another way to present item discrimination, and row 5 includes fit index, which is an indicator of the fit degree for the item and Rasch model. The sixth row includes the average response, which explained the average response to items (dichotomous or multi-categorical rating ways).

Table 4.9 Statistical characteristic parameters

	Minimum	Maximum	Mean	Standard deviation
Difficulty	−2.73	1.84	0.00	1.01
Discrimination (point biserial correlation)	0.17	0.48	0.35	0.07
Discrimination	0.39	1.30	0.98	0.19
Infit mean square	0.89	1.24	1.00	0.07
p-value	0.30	0.96	0.65	0.17

From Tables 4.8 to 4.9, the conclusions could be gained as follows:

A. High item reliability. The item reliability is 1.00, indicating high reliability.
B. Good item difficulty coverage. The minimum of the item difficulty is −2.73 and the maximum is 1.84. The mean of the difficulty is 0.00, and standard deviation is 1.01. The difficulty coverage is quite appropriate.
C. Good item discrimination. The minimum of the first item discrimination (point biserial correlation) is 0.17 and the maximum is 0.48. The mean of the difficulty is 0.35, and standard deviation is 0.07. The minimum of the second item discrimination is 0.39 and the maximum is 1.30. The mean of the difficulty is 0.98, and standard deviation is approaching 1.00. These indicate item discrimination is quite appropriate, consistent with the Rasch model estimation for item difficulty.
D. High test validity. The reliability of the test paper for students' ability estimate is 0.83. Regarding the validity of the test results, two methods have been employed. One is the content structure validity of the test paper. From Table 4.9, the mean of the fit index (infit mean square) is 1.00 and the standard deviation is 0.07. And each item in Table 4.10 shows high infit index, which means the content structure validity of the test paper is high, in accordance with the unidimensionality hypothesis of the Rasch model. The other is the correlation between Science test results and the test results of three other subjects (Chinese, Mathematics, and Society) as the empirical validity index of test instrument, which could be called congruent validity, to show the consistency extent of the test results of the same ability assessed with different test instruments. Table 4.11 shows the correlations between Science and Chinese, Mathematics and Society, respectively, are 0.429, 0.601, and 0.707, indicating fairly high correlation with Mathematics and Society and fairly high test validity.

4.3.2.2 Item Characteristic Curves

It could be known from Fig. 4.4 that there are 42 test items in total, and most of the items, are in accordance with Item Response Theory (IRT) model. The possibility for students with higher ability is larger to respond to the more difficult items and get higher score. The item difficulty covers from −3.1 to 4.8 with fairly wide coverage, which could be good to assess students' real ability level.

4.3.3 The Testing Time

The primary school science testing time is 50 min.

4.3 Research Aims and Methods 171

Table 4.10 Item infit

```
INFIT
MNSQ         .63        .71        .83       1.00       1.20       1.40       1.60
      ---------+----------+----------+----------+----------+----------+----------+
   1 item 1                          .          * |          .
   2 item 2                          .           *           .
   3 item 3                          .          |    *       .
   4 item 4                          .         *|           .
   5 item 5                          .          |  *         .
   6 item 6                          .        * |           .
   7 item 7                          .          |*          .
   8 item 8                          .         *|           .
   9 item 9                          .        * |           .
  10 item 10                         .          |  *         .
  11 item 11                         .        * |           .
  12 item 12                         .          |  *         .
  13 item 13                         .          |  *         .
  14 item 14                         .       *  |           .
  15 item 15                         .        * |           .
  16 item 16                         .     *    |           .
  17 item 17                         .          | *          .
  18 item 18                         .      *   |           .
  19 item 19                         .          |*           .
  20 item 20                         .         *|           .
  21 item 21                         .          |*           .
  22 item 22                         .          |      *     .
  23 item 23                         .         *|           .
  24 item 24                         .          |*           .
  25 item 25                         .          |        *   .
  26 item 26                         .        * |           .
  27 item 27                         .          *           .
  28 item 28                         .         *|           .
  29 item 29                         .         *|           .
  30 item 30                         .    *     |           .
  31 item 31                         .    *     |           .
  32 item 32                         .         *|           .
  33 item 33                         .       *  |           .
  34 item 34                         .          |  *         .
  35 item 35                         .       *  |           .
  36 item 36                         .       *  |           .
  37 item 37                         .          | *          .
  38 item 38                         .       *  |           .
  39 item 39                         .       *  |           .
  40 item 40                         .         *|           .
  41 item 41                         .       *  |           .
  42 item 42                         .          |    *       .
==================================================================
```

Table 4.11 Correlation analysis between mathematics ability and abilities in other subjects

		Chinese	Mathematics	Science	Morality and society
Chinese	Pearson correlation coefficient	1	0.503**	0.429**	0.473**
	Sig. (2-tailed)	–	0.000	0.000	0.000
	N	16,799	16,543	15,168	16,617
Mathematics	Pearson correlation coefficient	0.503**	1	0.601**	0.611**
	Sig. (2-tailed)	0.000	–	0.000	0.000
	N	16,543	17,898	16,253	17,832
Science	Pearson correlation coefficient	0.429**	0.601**	1	0.707**
	Sig. (2-tailed)	0.000	0.000	–	0.000
	N	15,168	16,253	16,378	17,832
Morality and society	Pearson correlation coefficient	0.473**	0.611**	0.707**	1
	Sig. (2-tailed)	0.000	0.000	0.000	–
	N	16,617	17,832	16,315	18,024

**Correlation is significant at the 0.01 level (2-tailed)
Note The table shows the correlations between Science and Chinese, Mathematics and Society respectively are 0.429, 0.601 and 0.707, indicating fairly high correlation with Mathematics and Social Science

4.4 Analysis and Discussion on the Test Results

4.4.1 The Overall Complexion of Student Ability Distribution

Through the test results analysis of 16,378 students' scientific ability, it has been obtained that the mean of the estimated value of student ability is 0.87, with standard deviation 0.98, and the student ability estimate coverage is from −4.9 to 4.9 (Table 4.12).

4.4.2 Distribution of Student Scientific Ability Performance

In the present research, with the mean of student ability as the basis point, half standard deviation plus and minus the basis point, i.e., 0.87 ± 0.98/2, as the average ability coverage (0.375–1.359); with the average ability group as baseline and 1 standard deviation as interval, the average ability above group coverage (1.359–2.341) and average ability below group coverage (−0.607 to 0.375) are, respectively, attained with 1 standard deviation plus and minus. And so on, the

4.4 Analysis and Discussion on the Test Results

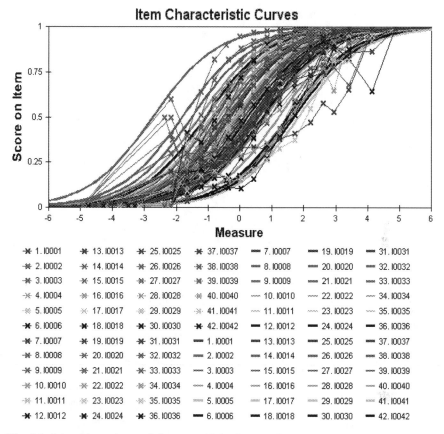

Fig. 4.4 Science item characteristic curves (Color figure online)

Table 4.12 Overall complexion of student ability distribution

	N	Minimum	Maximum	Mean	SD
Transferred scientific ability	16,378	−4.9	4.9	0.867	0.9821

highest ability group coverage (2.341–maximum) could be gained with 1 standard deviation plus average ability above group, and the lowest ability group coverage (minimum to −0.607) could be gained with 1 standard deviation minus average ability below group. The division of the five ability groups, percentage of the students in each ability group out of the total and the accumulative percentage could be seen in Table 4.13.

Combined with the bar Fig. 4.5, it could be analyzed that the student ability is almost in normal distribution. The number of students in the highest ability group (A) is 1093, 6.7% of the total students participating in the test. There are 3632

Table 4.13 Distribution of student scientific ability

Groups	Ability groups Ability value Starting point-terminal point	Number of students	Percentage of each group students out of the total (%)	Accumulative percentage (%)
Highest ability group (A)	2.341–maximum	1093	6.7	6.7
Average ability above group (B)	1.359–2.341	3632	22.2	28.9
Average ability group (C)	0.375–1.359	6902	42.1	71.0
Average ability below group (D)	−0.607 to 0.375	4037	24.6	95.6
Lowest ability group (E)	Minimum to −0.607	714	4.4	100

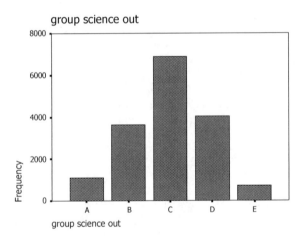

Fig. 4.5 Distribution of student frequency in 5 ability groups

students in average ability above group (B), which is 22.2% of the total students. The number of students in average ability group (C) is 6902, 42.1% of the total students. There are 4037 students in average ability below group (D), which is 24.6% of the total students. And the number of students in the lowest ability group (E) is 714, 4.4% of the total students. The accumulative number of students in and above average ability group is 11,627 (6902 + 3632 + 1093), which is 71% (42.1% + 22.2% + 6.7%) of the total students, while the accumulative number of students below the average ability group is 4751 (4037 + 714), which is 29% (24.6% + 4.4%) of the total students.

4.4 Analysis and Discussion on the Test Results

If the groups A, B, C, D, and E above are corresponding to excellent, proficient, qualified, basically qualified, and unqualified, it could be obtained that out of the 16,378 participants, the performance of 6.7% of students is excellent, the performance of 22.2% of students is proficient, the performance of 42.1% of students is qualified, the performance of 24.6% of students is basically qualified, and the performance of 4.4% of students is unqualified. From the holistic test results, 71% of students are qualified, with 95.6% of students are basically qualified and above, while 4.4% of students are unqualified. That is to say, with the background of new curriculum reform, since Science curriculum was carried out in Grade 3 primary school in Year 2001, about 70% (71%) of students meet the requirements of main contents in *Science Curriculum Standard*, owning the basic scientific knowledge and competencies, and can express and identify scientific concepts and principles, can apply scientific knowledge and principles to explain the common phenomena and to solve problems in life, and can do simple scientific inquiry and technology design. The other 30% (29%) of students obtain certain of basic knowledge and competencies, but have difficulties in realizing the content standards and requirements of curriculum standard and the ability to apply scientific principles and to do scientific inquiry is quite weak. Among these, 4.4% of students do not obtain the basic scientific knowledge and competencies which are assumed to be obtained by Grade 6 students, and they only can recognize simple and scientific concepts and principles, and their ability to apply scientific principles and to do scientific inquiry is very little.

4.4.3 The Proportion of Students in Different Ability Groups and the Tasks That Can Be Accomplished

Based on the analysis results and two-dimensional table of specifications, main tasks that can be accomplished by students of different ability groups could be attained.

From the tasks which could be accomplished by students in different ability groups above, some conclusions could be achieved as follows.

1. With the ability group from low to high, the level of students' responses to tasks goes from low to high.
   From Fig. 4.6, most of the tasks (83%) that could be accomplished by unqualified group (Group E) students are at uni-structural level, while qualified group (Group C) students not only can accomplish uni-structural level items, but also some items at multi-structural level and at relational level. And most of the tasks (almost 70%) that could be accomplished by proficient group (Group B) students are at relational level. That is to say, students with higher ability have higher level response to items and can accomplish tasks and solve problems with more difficulty.

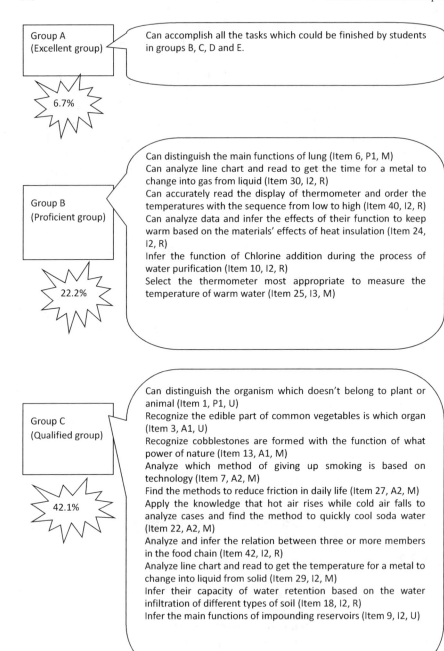

Fig. 4.6 Proportion of students in different ability groups and the tasks that can be accomplished

4.4 Analysis and Discussion on the Test Results

Group D (Basically qualified group)

24.6%

- Can describe that soil is mainly composed of what substances (Item 12, P1, M)
- Describe the time needed for the earth rotation (Item 31, P1, U)
- Observe and analyze diagrams to identify Charles's Wain in which star map (Item 17, P2, M)
- Identify the feature inherited from parents among some features (Item 8, A1, M)
- Explain the reasons of the less possibilities to see fog in desert than at seaside (Item 28, A1, M)
- Calculate the weight of the apparatus in weightlessness on the moon (Item 20, A2, M)
- Select the materials with weak function of electric conduction (Item 32, A2, U)
- Predict the experiment result and judge the candle in which bottle goes out first (Item 33, I1, M)
- Analyze and explain the reasons for deflated table tennis get inflated after it is heated (Item 23, I2, U)
- Read diagrams, select different references and describe the position relationship of three objects (Item 38, I2, R)
- Analyze the results measured and judge which is accurate from the results gained (Item 36, I3, M)
- Design the inquiry experiment, with controlled variable, that "The growth of green plants needs the soil with sand contained" (Item 19, I3, M)
- Accurately use thermometer to measure the temperature of objects (Item 35, I3, M)

Group E (Unqualified group)

4.4%

- Can distinguish the simple mechanics and complex mechanics (robot) (Item 39, P1, U)
- Describe the distribution of the composition of land and water area at the earth surface (Item 16, P1, U)
- Identify the symbols of sand storm (Item 15, P2, U)
- Explain the relationship between the features of cactus' physical appearance and its living environment (Item 2, A1, U)
- Identify which disease is easily caused by smoking (Item 6, A1, U)
- Identify the possible diseases caused by drinking polluted water (Item 11, A1, U)
- Identify which force the pole brings to sportsman (Item 21, A1, U)
- Analyze common tools and identify which applies the lever principle (Item 34, A1, U)
- Analyze cases and recognize which item is designed and made based on the principle that hot air rises (Item 26, A1, U)
- Explain the main aim of forest tree planting (Item 14, A1, U)
- Observe and analyze the main difference of the life processes of cabbage butterfly and grasshopper (Item 4, I1, U)
- Analyze and infer the relation between two members in the food chain (Item 41, I2, U)

Fig. 4.6 (continued)

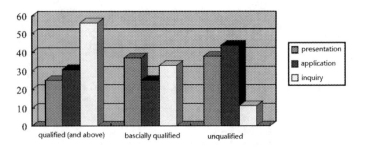

Fig. 4.7 Distribution illustration of different abilities

2. With the ability group from low to high, students' scientific inquiry ability gradually increases.

   The content domains related to the present survey are the three domains of life world, physical world, and Earth and Cosmos World, based on primary school *Science Curriculum Standard*, and the scientific competencies mainly include scientific presentation, scientific application, and scientific inquiry. The information on students' specific abilities of each competency could be seen in Fig. 4.7.

   Students of each ability group perform different proportions of competencies when accomplishing tasks (items). For examples, among the 12 items which can be accomplished by students of unqualified group, there are 3 items related to presentation competency, 7 items related to application competency and 2 items related to inquiry competency, which are, respectively, 38, 44, and 11% of the total items in each aspect (8, 16, and 18 items).

   Through the analysis of Fig. 4.7 and of the competency classification (table) of assessment framework, it could be attained that 70% of the total students perform comparatively outstanding in scientific inquiry competency, i.e., students not only possess a certain of abilities on scientific presentation and application but also have quite strong scientific inquiry ability. Students perform quite strong abilities to identify, distinguish, and describe scientific concepts and principles, to apply scientific knowledge and principles to explain phenomena, to do scientific observation and analysis, to comprehensively make use of calculation, analysis and induction to solve fairly complicated problems, to appropriately use equipment, tools to do experiments, control variables, use data to explain experiments and infer complicated conclusions, and to carry out scientific inquiry. However, compared with students in qualified group, 4.4% of the total students in unqualified group have comparatively outstanding abilities on scientific presentation and application among the three competencies but are very weak on scientific inquiry competency. That is to say, students can identify and distinguish simple scientific concepts and principles, find the differences through observing illustrations, analyze simple data and diagrams, make use of acquired scientific knowledge and principles to explain simple phenomena, solve simple problems and infer simple conclusions, reaching the abilities which should be owned by students in Grade 4 or 5, rather than by students in Grade 6. The concrete abilities owned by students in basically qualified group are between students in qualified group and in unqualified group, and have roughly equivalent proportions.

4.4.4 The Corresponding Analysis of Students' Practical Ability Performance and Item Target Test Level

It could be found that from Fig. 4.8, the distribution of the practical difficulty of the scientific competence test items is normal, and the performance of students in different ability groups is in normal distribution. Overall, the test items are designed fairly proper. However, it will be more ideal if there are more items with the difficulty value above 2.0.

According to Fig. 4.8, the main reasons for the inconsistency of them are analyzed based on the corresponding relation for students' practical ability performance and item target test level (difficulty) to formulate Table 4.14.

From the analysis of students' responses to 42 items, some conclusions could be further obtained as follows:

1. Students' real ability performance to 6 items (items 3, 5, 9, 25, 31 and 32) is lower than the target test level (difficulty);
2. Students' real ability performance to 1 items (item 38) is higher than the target test level (difficulty);
3. Students' real ability performance to other 35 items approximately accord with the target test level (difficulty).

The reasons analyzed could be seen in "Analysis and Explanation" in Table 4.14.

4.5 The Main Findings

Since the new curriculum reform started in Year 2001, with the background that curriculum, teaching materials, teaching approach, and learning method change, the main findings have been attained as follows, based on the result analysis of Science academic achievement survey for students in Grade 6, primary school.

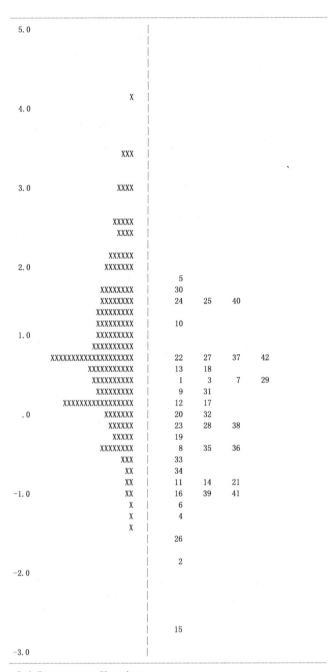

Fig. 4.8 Item difficulty and student ability distribution

4.5 The Main Findings

Table 4.14 Item analysis and explanation

Item	Target test level	Difficulty value	Analysis and explanation
1	M	0.46	• There are 58% of students achieving M level, with the average ability 1.22, and there are 19% of students achieving U level, with the average ability 0.55 • The practical difficulty and student ability accord with the target test level, indicating that 40% of students do not have enough ability to distinguish the feature of plant, animal, and fungus, not reaching the requirements of *Science Curriculum Standard*
2	U	−1.81	• There are 91% of students achieving U level, with the average ability 0.93 • The practical difficulty and student ability accord with the target test level, indicating that students have fairly strong ability to recognize the function of an organism with specialization
3	U	0.57	• There are only 56% of students achieving U level, with the average ability 1.11 • The practical difficulty is higher than the target test level, indicating that students only can recognize the six organs of plant demonstrated in class, but are weak at linking the practical life to recognize the edible part of carrot is root
4	U	−1.27	• There are 86% of students achieving U level, with the average ability 0.98 • The practical difficulty and student ability accord with the target test level, indicating that most students have fairly strong ability to observe and find the differences
5	M	1.84	• There are 30% of students achieving M level, with the average ability 1.35, and there are 30% of students achieving U level, with the average ability 0.73 • The practical difficulty is higher than the target test level, indicating that 70% of students cannot distinguish the main functions of lung
6	U	−1.09	• There are 84% of students achieving U level, with the average ability 1.02 • The practical difficulty and student ability accord with the target test level, indicating that most students have fairly strong ability to identify which disease is easily caused by smoking
7	M	0.54	• There are 56% of students achieving M level, with the average ability 1.19, and there are 30% of students achieving U level, with the average ability 0.48 • The practical difficulty and student ability accord with the target test level, indicating that almost 60% of students can analyze which method to solve problem is based on technology

(continued)

Table 4.14 (continued)

Item	Target test level	Difficulty value	Analysis and explanation
8	M	−0.40	• There are 74% of students achieving M level, with the average ability 1.07, and there are 8% of students achieving U level, with the average ability 0.16 • The practical difficulty and student ability accord with the target test level, indicating that almost 80% of students have fairly strong ability to identify the feature inherited
9	U	0.40	• There are 59% of students achieving U level, with the average ability 1.21 • The practical difficulty is higher than the target test level, indicating that 40% of students do not master enough knowledge of water purification process and the technology needed, do not pay enough attention to the application of science and technology and have weak ability to explain technological process. It might be that the polluted water purification process is strange for students in advanced regions or hard to be understood by students in Grade 6
10	R	1.22	• There are 42% of students achieving R level, with the average ability 1.26; 26% of students achieving M level, with the average ability 0.75, and there are 3% of students achieving U level, with the average ability 0.12 • The practical difficulty is higher than the target test level, indicating that almost 60% of students do not master enough knowledge of water purification process and the technology needed, do not pay enough attention to the application of science and technology and have weak ability to explain technological process. It might be that the polluted water purification process is strange for students in advanced regions or hard to be understood by students in Grade 6
11	U	−0.90	• There are 82% of students achieving U level, with the average ability 1.02 • The practical difficulty and student ability accord with the target test level, indicating that most students have fairly strong ability to identify the possible diseases caused by drinking polluted water
12	M	0.24	• There are 62% of students achieving M level, with the average ability 1.10, and there are 20% of students achieving U level, with the average ability 0.64 • The practical difficulty and student ability accord with the target test level, indicating that most students have fairly strong ability to describe that soil is mainly composed of what substances
13	M	0.59	• There are 55% of students achieving M level, with the average ability 1.16, and there are 13% of students achieving U level, with the average ability 0.38

(continued)

4.5 The Main Findings

Table 4.14 (continued)

Item	Target test level	Difficulty value	Analysis and explanation
			• The practical difficulty and student ability approximately accord with the target test level, indicating that almost 60% of students have fairly strong ability to analyze the function of power of nature
14	U	−0.89	• There are 82% of students achieving U level, with the average ability 1.03 • The practical difficulty and student ability accord with the target test level, indicating that most students understand the main aim of forest tree planting and have fairly strong sense for environment protection
15	U	−2.73	• There are 96% of students achieving U level, with the average ability 0.91 • The practical difficulty and student ability accord with the target test level, indicating that almost all students have fairly strong ability to identify the symbols of weather
16	U	−1.06	• There are 84% of students achieving U level, with the average ability 1.04 • The practical difficulty and student ability accord with the target test level, indicating that most students have fairly strong ability to describe the composition of the earth surface
17	M	0.20	• There are 63% of students achieving M level, with the average ability 1.10, and there are 21% of students achieving U level, with the average ability 0.65 • The practical difficulty and student ability accord with the target test level, indicating that 60% of students have fairly strong ability to observe star map
18	R	0.71	• There are 53% of students achieving R level, with the average ability 1.31; 37% of students achieving M level, with the average ability 0.44, and there are 6% of students achieving U level, with the average ability 0.15 • The practical difficulty and student ability accord with the target test level, indicating that over 40% of students have fairly weak ability to infer conclusions through observing experiment results
19	M	−0.31	• There are 73% of students achieving M level, with the average ability 1.06, and there are 7% of students achieving U level, with the average ability 0.26 • The practical difficulty and student ability accord with the target test level, indicating that 70% of students have fairly strong ability to control and compare variables in experiments
20	M	0.01	• There are 67% of students achieving M level, with the average ability 1.13, and there are 24% of students achieving U level, with the average ability 0.43

(continued)

Table 4.14 (continued)

Item	Target test level	Difficulty value	Analysis and explanation
			• The practical difficulty and student ability accord with the target test level, indicating that almost 70% of students have fairly strong ability to calculate the weight in weightlessness
21	U	−0.83	• There are 81% of students achieving U level, with the average ability 1.00 • The practical difficulty and student ability accord with the target test level, indicating that most students have fairly strong ability to identify the force application
22	M	0.80	• There are 51% of students achieving M level, with the average ability 1.13, and there are 34% of students achieving U level, with the average ability 0.71 • The practical difficulty and student ability accord with the target test level, indicating that half of students have fairly strong ability to solve practical problems in life
23	M	−0.16	• There are 70% of students achieving M level, with the average ability 1.11, and there are 17% of students achieving U level, with the average ability 0.38 • The practical difficulty and student ability accord with the target test level, indicating that 70% of students have fairly strong ability to explain the principle application of expansion caused by heat and contraction caused by cold
24	R	1.50	• There are 37% of students achieving R level, with the average ability 1.37; 54% of students achieving M level, with the average ability 0.64, and there are 4% of students achieving U level, with the average ability 0.15 • The practical difficulty and student ability accord with the target test level, indicating that over 60% of students have fairly weak ability to infer conclusions through observing experiment results
25	M	1.49	• There are 37% of students achieving M level, with the average ability 1.08, and there are 22% of students achieving U level, with the average ability 0.96 • The practical difficulty is higher than the target test level, indicating that students have fairly weak application ability to select the most appropriate measurement tool
26	U	−1.51	• There are 89% of students achieving U level, with the average ability 0.98 • The practical difficulty and student ability accord with the target test level, indicating that most students have fairly strong ability to explain the principle use of hot air
27	M	0.74	• There are 52% of students achieving M level, with the average ability 1.25, and there are 15% of students achieving U level, with the average ability 0.50 • The practical difficulty and student ability accord with the target test level, indicating that only half of students have the ability to identify and reduce friction in practical application in daily life

(continued)

4.5 The Main Findings

Table 4.14 (continued)

Item	Target test level	Difficulty value	Analysis and explanation
28	M	−0.10	• There are 69% of students achieving M level, with the average ability 1.11, and there are 14% of students achieving U level, with the average ability 0.37 • The practical difficulty and student ability accord with the target test level, indicating that 70% of students have the fairly strong ability to explain the weather change
29	M	0.57	• There are 56% of students achieving M level, with the average ability 1.23, and there are 19% of students achieving U level, with the average ability 0.40 • The practical difficulty and student ability accord with the target test level, indicating that almost 60% of students have the fairly strong ability to read and analyze experimental data diagrams to answer simple questions
30	R	1.70	• There are 33% of students achieving R level, with the average ability 1.54; 40% of students achieving M level, with the average ability 0.59, and there are 14% of students achieving U level, with the average ability 0.58 • The practical difficulty and student ability accord with the target test level, indicating that almost 60% of students have the fairly weak ability to read diagrams to answer complicated questions
31	U	0.35	• There are 60% of students achieving U level, with the average ability 1.25 • The practical difficulty is higher than the target test level, about 40% of students are not clear the time needed for the earth rotation, and student ability is slightly lower than the target test level, indicating that students have difficulty to master the spatial sense of earth and space and the basic knowledge, not reaching the requirements of *Science Curriculum Standard*. It certainly cannot eliminate the reason that the requirement is too high, and in the situation that they do not have spatial sense of space, primary school students cannot understand or develop firm scientific concepts with simple memorization
32	U	0.11	• There are 65% of students achieving U level, with the average ability 1.15 • The practical difficulty is higher than the target test level, students should have mastered the ability to judge that metal conducts electricity and common plastic does not conduct electricity. However, 34% of students choose metal to use as the material for the power switch box, reflecting that students' ability to solve problems linking the life is weak, which cannot eliminate the reason that students have not read the item clearly. The item requires students to choose appropriate material for power switch box not for power switch

(continued)

Table 4.14 (continued)

Item	Target test level	Difficulty value	Analysis and explanation
33	M	−0.54	• There are 77% of students achieving M level, with the average ability 1.08, and there are 9% of students achieving U level, with the average ability 0.21 • The practical difficulty and student ability accord with the target test level, indicating that students have a fairly strong ability to predict experiment results through observation and analysis. Most students can judge that the air in the small-volume and airproofing bottle is little and candle goes out first
34	U	−0.65	• There are 78% of students achieving U level, with the average ability 1.01 • The practical difficulty and student ability accord with the target test level, indicating that most students have the fairly strong ability to analyze common tools, explain and identify the principles applied
35	M	−0.43	• There are 75% of students achieving M level, with the average ability 1.09, and there are 14% of students achieving U level, with the average ability 0.24 • The practical difficulty and student ability accord with the target test level, indicating that most students have the experimental ability to accurately use thermometer to measure and read numbers
36	M	−0.42	• There are 75% of students achieving M level, with the average ability 1.09, and there are 11% of students achieving U level, with the average ability 0.28 • The practical difficulty and student ability accord with the target test level, indicating that most students have a fairly strong ability to analyze the experimental data and get simple conclusions
37	R	0.77	• There are 52% of students achieving R level, with the average ability 1.20; 19% of students achieving M level, with the average ability 0.49, and there are 17% of students achieving U level, with the average ability 0.64 • The practical difficulty and student ability accord with the target test level, indicating that almost half of students have the fairly weak ability to analyze the experimental data and make complicated inferences.
38	R	−0.04	• There are 68% of students achieving R level, with the average ability 1.15; 8% of students achieving M level, with the average ability 0.33, and there are 9% of students achieving U level, with the average ability 0.20 • The practical difficulty is lower than the target test level, and student ability is higher than the target test level, almost 70% of students have the fairly weak ability to judge positions. It does not eliminate the limitation of SOLO taxonomy, and the position relationship related to three objects is at relational level

(continued)

4.5 The Main Findings

Table 4.14 (continued)

Item	Target test level	Difficulty value	Analysis and explanation
39	U	−1.05	• There are 84% of students achieving U level, with the average ability 1.02 • The practical difficulty and student ability accord with the target test level, indicating that most students have the fairly strong ability to distinguish the features of robots
40	R	1.60	• There are 35% of students achieving R level, with the average ability 1.44; 33% of students achieving M level, with the average ability 0.70, and there are 24% of students achieving U level, with the average ability 0.46 • The practical difficulty and student ability accord with the target test level, indicating that only 35% of students have the fairly strong ability to accurately read the display of thermometer and order the temperatures in sequence. Other students' ability to accurately read the display of thermometer below zero degrees and to compare the temperature above zero degrees is fairly weak
41	U	−1.05	• There are 84% of students achieving U level, with the average ability 1.02 • The practical difficulty and student ability accord with the target test level, indicating that most students have the fairly weak ability to analyze the number change relation between two members in the food chain
42	R	0.80	• There are 51% of students achieving R level, with the average ability 1.16; 17% of students achieving M level, with the average ability 0.63, and there are 7% of students achieving U level, with the average ability 0.56 • The practical difficulty and student ability accord with the target test level, indicating that almost half of students have the fairly weak ability to analyze the number change relation between three or more members in the food chain

4.5.1 Overall Complexion

1. About 70% (71%) of students meet the requirements of main contents in *Science Curriculum Standard*.

    About 70% (71%) of students meet the requirements of main contents in *Science Curriculum Standard*, owning the basic scientific knowledge and competencies, and can express and identify scientific concepts and principles, can apply scientific knowledge and principles to explain the phenomena and to solve problems, and can do simple scientific inquiry and technology design. The other 30% (29%) of students obtain certain of basic knowledge and competencies but have difficulties in realizing the content standards and requirements of *Science Curriculum Standard* and the ability to apply scientific principles and to do scientific inquiry is quite weak. Among these, 4.4% of students do not obtain the basic scientific knowledge and competencies which are assumed to be obtained by Grade 6 students, and they only can recognize simple and scientific concepts and principles, and their ability to apply scientific principles and to do scientific inquiry is very little.

2. With students' scientific ability level goes up, the level of students' response to tasks goes from uni-structural to relational.

   With SOLO taxonomy to analyze students' cognitive development, the level of students' responses to tasks could be divided into five layers, i.e., pre-structural level, uni-structural level, multi-structural level, relational level, and extended abstract level. From Fig. 4.6, most of the tasks (83%) that could be accomplished by unqualified group (Group E) students are at uni-structural level, while qualified group (Group C) students not only can accomplish uni-structural level items but also some items at multi-structural level and at relational level. And most of the tasks (almost 70%) that could be accomplished by proficient group (Group B) students are at relational level. That is to say, students with higher ability have higher level response to items and can accomplish tasks and solve problems with more difficulty.

3. There is no significant disparity of students' ability performance in the three domains of Life World, Physical World and Earth and Cosmos World, which is fairly equivalent.

   Students' real ability performance to 2 items in the domain of Life World is lower than the target test level, to 3 items in the domain of Physical World is lower than the target test level, and to 1 item in the domain of Earth and Cosmos World is lower than the target test level.

4. With students' scientific ability level goes up, students' scientific inquiry ability gradually increases.

   Regarding the three abilities of scientific presentation, application and inquiry mainly surveyed, students in excellent and proficient groups have stronger scientific application ability and inquiry ability when owning fairly strong scientific presentation ability, while students in qualified and basically qualified groups perform fairly strong scientific presentation ability, and good scientific application ability and inquiry ability. And students in unqualified group only perform good scientific presentation ability and application ability, while their scientific inquiry ability is very weak.

4.5.2 Aspects Improved

1. Students' observation ability and imaginary thinking ability have been improved.

   From students' responses to some items, it could be found that students' ability to observe with the help of illustrations and to identify features has been improved. For example, 86% of students can find the main differences between organisms in complete metamorphosis and in incomplete metamorphosis through illustration observation, 70% of students can observe map and judge the position relationship of three objects, and almost all students can recognize the weather symbol representing sand storm. It could be said that this is related to vivid illustrated new curriculum Science experimental textbook which is helpful for Science learning. And this is also the fruit, since the new curriculum was carried out, it emphasizes to develop students' ability and habit of observation and recording, and experiencing scientific activities.

2. Students' ability to read diagrams and do experimental analysis has been thoroughly improved.

   From students' responses to some items, it could be found that students' ability to read every type of diagrams, to analyze simple data, to get conclusions, to accurately use measurement tool and to control experimental variable has been thoroughly improved. Near 60% of students can read line chart and find the relation between time and temperature for metal to change into liquid from solid, 75% of students can accurately use thermometer to measure and read its display, and 73% of students can accurately control the variable in comparative experiment. This is highly related to that since new curriculum, it has advocated and as many as possible provided opportunities for students to actively participate in activities, has enhanced using hands to do experiment and inquiry, and has paid much attention to developing students' ability to analyze data, to explain with experimental facts and to make conclusions.

3. It is fairly satisfying regarding students' attention to life health and mastery of sanitation general knowledge.

   Over 80% of students can identify that smoking a lot is most likely to enhance the risk of suffering from bronchitis, 70% of students can realize that it is most likely to cause diarrhea by drinking polluted water, and more than 70% of students can accurately identify the feature inherited from parents. It could be seen that through Science education, it is beneficial for children, from childhood, to develop good sanitation and living habits, to pay attention to healthy life, to respect life and love life, accordingly to realize people's comprehensive development.

4.5.3 Aspects to Be Emphasized

1. Students' mastery of basic knowledge, basic common sense and basic ability is not enough.

   From students' responses to some items, it could be found that some students' understanding and mastery of some basic scientific concepts do not reach the designated level and they lack some scientific general knowledge which should be acquired and cannot accurately describe or express. For example, 40% of students cannot identify that mushroom is a kind of organism which does not belong to plant or animal, 70% of students cannot accurately recognize the main functions of lung, and about 40% of students cannot accurately answer the time needed for Earth to turn on its axis once, and 28% of students think it takes 1 year for Earth to turn on its axis once, which cannot reach the curriculum standard requirement of "knowing Earth is self-rotating nonstop, and it takes 1 day to turn on its axis once, which is 24 h." In the situation that primary school students almost do not understand the movements of stars in space, and only simple memorization cannot develop accurate and firm scientific concepts. To find its cause, there are two reasons. One aspect is that students' recognition, memorization, and understanding level is fairly low, and they cannot well master some basic scientific concepts. The other aspect is that it cannot eliminate the reason that the requirement of *Science Curriculum Standard* on trial is too high, and it brings difficulty for students to build and develop firm scientific concepts based on understanding. This deserves attention in the curriculum standard revision.

2. Students' ability to apply knowledge acquired, linking with life, to analyze and explain practical problems and phenomena is fairly weak.

   From students' responses to some items, it could be found that problems will come out in students' practical application once the knowledge and skills which seem to have been mastered in class link with life. For example, when recognizing the edible part of which common vegetable is root, only 56% of students answer accurately (carrot), with the average ability 1.11, and the real difficulty exceeds the target test level, while 24% of students choose potato. Students possibly can only identify the features and functions of the six organs of typical plants demonstrated in class, but cannot fully make use of the relationship feature of root and stalk to identify in practice when linking with life. Only half of students can find the most efficient method to cool soda water, and near half of the students cannot find the methods to help reduce friction in daily life, to which near 20% of students mistakenly think that it is to reduce friction when turning with dry cloth on the soft drink bottle. And there are 34% of students choose metal rather than plastic for the material of power switch box, indicating that they cannot choose accurate option by making use of the knowledge acquired that metal is appropriate for electricity conduction material, while plastic, etc., nonmetal materials are appropriate for insulating materials. Thus, it is necessary to develop students' ability, through Science curriculum teaching and learning, to apply knowledge acquired, linking with life, to analyze and explain practical problems and phenomena, which is also the premise and basis to develop talents with creativity.

3. Students' ability to comprehensively apply multiple skills (abilities) to solve complicated problems needs to be enhanced.

From students' responses to some items, it could be found that students have fairly large difficulty when comprehensively apply the ability to describe, to state, to read diagrams, to analyze materials and data, to experiment and to make conclusions to deal with fairly complicated problems. For example, only 35% of students accurately read the display of thermometer and order the temperatures of the four types of liquid with the sequence from low to high, and most students' ability to accurately read the display of thermometer below zero degrees and to compare the temperature above zero degrees is fairly weak. Near half of students' ability to analyze experimental data of groups and to make fairly complicated inferences is quite weak. And almost half of students have fairly weak ability to analyze the relation between three or more members in the food chain. In addition, some students are weak, regarding the knowledge and skills related to technology, especially when analyzing the aims and functions of main steps in technology process (such as polluted water treatment), they have difficulty.

4.6 Countermeasures and Suggestions

4.6.1 To Pay Attention to Science Education in Compulsory Education from the Perspective of "Developing the Country Through Science and Education" Strategy

Although it is explicit that Science curriculum starts from Grade 3, primary school, in the new curriculum reform, it has been found through a survey that some districts and schools cannot normally provide Science curriculum. No matter in mind or in action, the importance of Science enlightenment education for students from childhood is not fully recognized, and the important position of Science education in our country's modernization construction is ignored, let alone to well understand the national strategy of "Developing the Country through Science and Education". Therefore, today, with the rapid development of science and technology, the first problem to be solved is to elevate the position of Science education in compulsory education, to strengthen the research on Science education, to pay attention to the training for Science educators, to advance Science curriculum reform, in order to develop students' scientific literacy, to accelerate students' thorough development and to improve our country's core competencies.

4.6.2 To Enhance Students' Practice and Mastery of Scientific Basic Knowledge and of Basic Abilities

The experience of international and national Science education reform and assessment tells us that no matter how to change, learning and construction of scientific basic knowledge, basic principles, and basic abilities is the firm cornerstone of Science education. It is the responsibility and duty for every Science educator to make use of students' acquired knowledge and experience, linking with life, to improve teaching approach and learning method, at different students' development steps, to help students learn and construct basic scientific concepts and principles, practice and master basic scientific abilities, based on their physical and mental development features, which is the premise to develop students' scientific literacy and to realize Science education goals.

4.6.3 To Develop Students' Ability to Comprehensively Apply Multiple Skills and to Solve Complicated Problems, and to Thoroughly Improve Students' Comprehensive Quality

The development of future society needs talents with comprehensive quality. Science educators should look at Science education from the multiple and comprehensive perspective. It is the orientation and goal for every science educator to pay attention to the combination of science with philosophy, humanities and arts, to inter-disciplinarily develop students' ability to comprehensively apply multiple skills and to solve complicated problems, to fully make use of resources in and out of school aiming at that students have more opportunities to participate in and devote in scientific and technological activities closely related to life, love science, use science and respect science, to integrate science and technology education to further develop and improve students practice ability and creativity, and to thoroughly improve students' comprehensive quality.

Chapter 5
Morality and Society Assessment Report

5.1 Research Background

To face the requirements of times with rapid development and various challenges from society and economy, how to improve the quality of basic education will be treated as the common vision and goal of the countries' educational reform in the world. To carry out the monitoring of basic education quality based on the survey and assessment of students' academic achievement at the national macro-level is undoubtedly the foundation programme for every country to improve the quality of education. Through this assessment and monitoring, it can help, to some extent, to master the quality complexion of basic education, to scientifically diagnose the problems and reasons existing in basic education, to provide scientific evidence for the governmental educational policy and to make clear the development direction for educational and teaching practice, which is finally beneficial for the improvement of basic education quality.

At present, with the further development and continuous advance of the new curriculum reform in our country, the issue of how to effectively assess curriculum gets much attention from many people. The reform of curriculum assessment has been explicitly set as one of the goals in curriculum reform in *Basic Education Curriculum Reform Guideline (Pilot version)*. And students' academic achievement assessment is the core content of curriculum assessment. The practice has indicated that curriculum assessment is not only the important content of curriculum reform, but also the crucial system guarantee to move new curriculum forward. Therefore, it is doubtless an urgent critical issue, related to whether the curriculum reform can develop positively, that how to build and refine, as soon as possible, curriculum assessment system matching new curriculum, including the design and construction of students' academic achievement framework and standards based on curriculum standard of each subject, to scientifically and objectively assess students' academic achievement since the national new curriculum was carried out, to guide the curriculum implementation, and to improve education and teaching.

Morality and Society is a comprehensive subject provided in middle and high grades in primary school, meanwhile, it is also a new curriculum in this curriculum reform. Compared with curriculum such as Chinese, Mathematics, etc., its history is quite short. Thus, it is more necessary to know and master the effectiveness achieved by students through the curriculum learning. The national *Full-time Compulsory Education Morality and Society Curriculum Standard (Experimental version)* (in the abbreviation of *Morality and Society Curriculum Standard* below) is the basis for teaching materials writing, teaching and learning, assessment and test item writing, and is the foundation for the nation to administrate and assess curriculum, representing the country's basic requirements for the primary school students as qualified citizens in the future in the aspects of knowledge and skills, process and method, and affect, attitude, and values, etc. The survey and assessment of students' Morality and Society subject academic achievement just aims at combining these requirements with the educational and teaching practice, transforming curriculum standard into explicit and manipulative assessment goals and assessment content, and judging whether students achieve curriculum goals and the degree of the achievement with the help of appropriate assessment approach. This will assist us to fairly thoroughly and truly master and judge the complexion of the aspects of primary school students' basic citizen literacy, including development of morality and social development. At the same time, it assists us to understand and analyze the related factors influencing students' academic achievement, such as the curriculum execution situation, the situation of curriculum goals achievement and the situation of students' learning and teachers' teaching, to look for the policy suggestions and corresponding approaches to improve students' academic achievement, in order to improve Morality and Society curriculum teaching and better accelerate students' thorough development.

5.2 Theoretical Framework on Students' Social Development Assessment

Although the present research is evidence research with the main assessment methods of questionnaire and test paper, it also needs deep theoretical research as its support and foundation, needs to know the already research fruits in the academic field, needs to actually master the situation of the subject assessment research, and needs more to make clear the conceptions of the core competencies to be assessed, the internal structural and content dimensions and representation features, etc. Based on these basic researches, it is possible to create the basic index system of assessment.

5.2.1 Taking Students' Social Development as the Basic Assessment Scope and Competence of Morality and Society Subject

Morality and Society is a "comprehensive curriculum, with children's social life as basis, to accelerate students' development of good morality and social development". The curriculum design is oriented at "establishing foundations for students to be qualified citizens of socialism".[1] Based on the national regulations for the curriculum nature, it is not hard to infer that the situation of students' morality development and social development reflects the level of their citizen literacy to some extent, which could be taken as the two main indicators to assess the development and progress students make after they finish learning the curriculum.

All the time, that how to assess morality curriculum schools provide oriented to develop students moral affect, attitude, and values is a problem obsessing morality researchers and school practice. No matter national or international, the evidence research appropriate to be used for students' assessment is not much, which is farther less active than other subjects. With the consideration of the complication of morality measurement and assessment, of the fact that the present morality measurement and assessment methods still has problems of validity, reliability, predictability, feasibility, etc.,[2] and plus the reason that there are various ways and factors influencing students' morality development, which has attributional complexity and it is difficult to effectively measure and assess the curriculum influence for students' morality development with the present morality measurement and assessment method, "limited research" is chosen, which fairly emphasizes the assessment of students' social development. With the content requirements of *Morality and Society Curriculum Standard* as the basic foundation, the performance standards and assessment framework reflecting students' social development will be researched, and then appropriate assessment methods will be adopted to test and assess students.

There are critical theoretical value and practical meaning to assess students' social development. Through this kind of assessment research, it can help to judge the situation of students' social development at the national macro-level, to unveil the law of students' social development, and to analyze the factors influencing students' social development. Meanwhile, to some extent, it can help with the situation of Morality and Society execution and of teachers' teaching and students' learning, and with the existing problems, which is beneficial for the country to effectively regulated and control and intervene, to together accelerate students' social development in a healthy way.

---

[1]Ministry of Education of the People's Republic of China (2001) Full-time compulsory education morality and society curriculum standard (experimental version). Beijing Normal University Publishing Group, Beijing.

[2]Lin CD (2002) Education and development. Beijing Normal University Publishing Group, Beijing.

5.2.2 Conception Definition and Content Structure of Curriculum Standard-Based Social Development

Through the literature review and analysis, it could be seen that researchers' studies on human being's social development mainly focus on the fields of Anthropology, Psychology, and Sociology. However, the present assessment is a criterion-referenced assessment, i.e., the manipulative assessment goals and assessment content are development based on the corresponding national curriculum standard to assess whether students acquire the basic knowledge and skills which should be acquired, to assess whether students' affect and values develop and advance and the degree. Thus, although the conception of "social development" is used in *Morality and Society Curriculum Standard*, the meaning of its nature and its content structure are quite different from that in the field of Psychology. But how the difference is embodied in this curriculum, specific explanation and clarifications are not given in curriculum standard. Therefore, before the assessment research is carried out, the research on it in the fields of Psychology and Sociology should be mastered, and it needs more to redefine its conception and collate and stipulate its basic content structure, based on *Morality and Society Curriculum Standard* and other curriculum standards related, for the sake of increasing the "curriculum feature" and adaptability of social development assessment.

5.2.2.1 Conception Definition of Social Development

Human being's social development and socialization are the common projects paid attention to in the fields of Anthropology, Sociology, and Psychology, but with different perspectives and theoretical basis. Anthropology fairly emphasizes the cultural heritage in the process of socialization. For example, the anthropologist T. Husen pointed that "Socialization is the process how human beings' adopt the values, customs and perspectives of the surrounding culture or subcultures."[3] While Sociology fairly emphasizes to be from the interactive relationship between human beings and society to assess human beings' social development and socialization, and believes individuals' socialization is "the process of individuals' social development through learning the culture and learning to take social roles."[4] Developmental psychologist Mussen, etc., think that socialization is the process for adolescents to learn the norms and actions appropriate to individuals as members of their particular culture and society.[5]

Therefore, it could be seen that social development and socialization are two closely related but different conceptions. Social development is the comprehensive

---

[3] Husen T (1991) International encyclopedia of education, volume 8 (trans: Ding TS et al). Guizhou Education Publishing House, Guiyang.
[4] Wu ZJ et al (1997) Modern sociology. Shanghai People's Publishing House, Shanghai.
[5] Huang XT (1988) Personality psychology. Tung Hua Book Company Limited, Taipei.

5.2 Theoretical Framework on Students' Social Development Assessment

social features in the aspects of emotions, thinking ways, cognition, abilities, and behaviors developed and reflected in the process that individuals actively interact with others and society. While socialization is the process to make individuals have social development by giving social influence. Individuals' social development is created and developed in the socialization process.

To sum up, there are researchers generalizing the meaning of social development, believing that individuals' social development is mainly the process in which individuals, in the interaction with society, through learning and internalize social culture, gradually develop their behavioral way to be accustomed with society, behave their roles expected by society, and develop their own sociality, which is a process for individuals to transform from natural person into qualified social members in accordance with the requirements of society.[6]

At different stages of life, there are different content and tasks for social development. Regarding primary school period, from the perspective of goal requirements and content scope of *Morality and Society Curriculum Standard*, we think that students' social development is the dynamic development process in which students, as social members, in interaction with society, initially understand and master social regulations, recognize social relationship and social environment, get to know social living way, gradually acquire basic social life skills, own the ability to effectively participate in society, and make their personal behaviors in accordance with society.

5.2.2.2 Structure and Meaning of Social Development

Regarding the structure of social development, Chinese and foreign researchers have done outstanding researches from different perspectives. The fairly representative idea is developmental psychologist Mussen's "interdependence", which believes that social development includes social emotion, attachment to parents, temperament, moral values, moral conventions, self-consciousness, sexual roles, prosocial behavior, self-control and control of aggressiveness, peer relationship, etc. Our country's researchers have proposed views including the "three-dimensional structure" composed of interpersonal relationship, social regulations, and self-development, the "five domains" made up of social cognition, social emotions, social behaviors, self-generative mechanism, and generative mechanism of sociality,[7] and the "seven dimensions" proposed by Chen Huichang, which divides children's social development into seven main dimensions, i.e., social skills,

---

[6]Ministry of Education of the People's Republic of China (2001) Full-time compulsory education morality and society curriculum standard (experimental version). Beijing Normal University Publishing Group, Beijing.

[7]Zhang WX (1999) Children's social development. Beijing Normal University Publishing Group, Beijing.

self-concept, moral character, will character, social cognition, social adaptability, and social emotions.[8]

These structural divisions provide us with positive enlightenment and reference. As stated above, based on the conception and meaning of social development, from the perspective of goal requirements and content scope of *Morality and Society Curriculum Standard*, we think that students' social development in the content structure mainly includes the five dimensions of social cognition, social skills, social abilities, social affect and attitude, social behavior, etc. To further describe, students' social development in each structural dimension could be specifically presented in the aspects as follows.

1. To have basic social cognition and to understand basic social conventions

The cognitive understanding of society and its conventions is the foundation for thinking and behavior. Curriculum requires the cognitive understanding of the knowledge in the aspects of basic history, geography, labor, society, etc., of the interdependent relationship between people and nature or environment, of the common problems faced by human beings, and of the historical events in and out of China. Students also need to have the cognitive understanding of the social conventions of political system, law, customs and habits, conduct of life, and religions, etc., through which, students can only understand their own social roles, related rights, and duties.

2. To acquire basic social skills

To acquire basic social skills is to have certain of basic skills adapting modern society, including the basic skills in the aspects that students need to smoothly adapt family life, school life, social life, etc., such as the social skills to guarantee life health and safety, and the social skills to look after themselves or to live on their own.

3. To have the abilities to analyze and think social phenomena, to participate in social life, and to solve social problems

As valid social members, students should have the basic social abilities including the ability to learn and to inquire, the ability to democratically and effectively participate in society, the ability to make social judgment and inference, and the ability to acquire information and to use resources. And they also should learn the methods to analyze, to think, and to solve social problems with connectivity, integration, and feasibility.

4. To develop the affect, attitude, and values caring society

This is the dynamic mechanism for social behaviors to come into being, including the sense of national identity, the sense of social responsibility, the international sense, and the sense of environmental protection. It also includes that in the

---

[8]Chen HC (1994) Construction of children's social development scale and norm design. Psychological Development and Education 4: 62.

complicated and changeable social environment, students can distinguish between truth and falsehood, can make right value judgment, and have the consciousness of democracy, of rule of law and of rules.

5. Behavior to participate in social life

It means the behavior to care society, to participate in social practice and all the actions good for society and others in the social interactions, such as being modest, helping each other, cooperating and sharing, etc.

To conclude, a student with positive social development should have basic social cognition and social understanding, acquire basic social skills, initially own the abilities to judge and think social phenomena and to solve social problems, develop the attitude to care society, and behave actively to participate in social life.

5.2.3 Visualization on Students' Social Development

5.2.3.1 Meaning of Students' Social Development

Assessment of students' social development is the important composite of students' academic achievement assessment, which is the value judgment process with goals and plans to assess students' social development based on the goals of social development established in *Morality and Society Curriculum Standard*, with the employment of education assessment theory and methods. The assessment scope could be the whole complexion of students' holistic social development or a side of students' social development.

5.2.3.2 Main Content Framework of Students' Social Development

The assessment content of students' social development is very abundant. The present assessment is a fairly large-scale academic achievement activity with the national sample of 18,000 participants. With the consideration of assessment execution feasibility, brief and manipulation, and the requirement of assessment methods, two aspects of social development assessment content are emphasized. One is the core content domains reflecting students' social development in *Morality and Society Curriculum Standard*, and the other is the aspects, which could be assessed through questionnaire and test paper, collated and stipulated from assessment dimension, such as social cognition, social skills and abilities, social affect and values, etc. Based on the considerations above, the assessment framework is finally developed, including three dimensions of content domains, competencies and affect and attitude, which could be seen in Fig. 5.1.

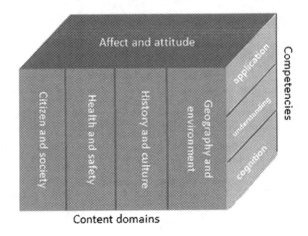

Fig. 5.1 Three-dimensional chart of social development assessment framework

1. Content domains

The dimension of content domains herein is equivalent with social cognition (social knowledge) in social development, mainly regulating what students should know and should do. The most general and basic aspects, which set foundation for students to enter social life in the future and are highly related to students' life, from *Morality and Society Curriculum Standard* are selected for content domains to be assessed and tested. Content dimension is divided into four domains, each of which has its concrete topics and goals.

Citizen and society include the national sense, globalization sense, consciousness of social rules, and sense of democracy participation qualified citizens should have. It also requires students to know related knowledge of law and social subjects and phenomena, and to make integrative and connective thinking and judgment of social subjects, phenomena or problems with the help of related information.

Health and safety require students to basically master the knowledge and to have the basic skills to keep their own health and safety.

History and culture require students to initially know the representative world historical culture, to know basic historical knowledge, important historical events and their influence, and to initially analyze and judge historical subjects with the help of related materials and information.

Geography and environment require students to have basic geographic knowledge and skills, such as Earth, measurement scale, landform, climate, reading map, recognizing directions, etc., and to analyze geographical subjects and phenomena with application of related geographic knowledge and skills; to know some basic geographic complexion about China and the world and to initially understand the relationship between natural environment and people's life; to know some environmental and resource problems human beings face; and to initially have the sense of environmental protection and perform in daily life behaviors.

2. Competencies

The dimension of competencies herein is equivalent with social cognition, social skills, and abilities in social development, which is mainly used to clearly explain the level of social understanding students should have when achieving the content dimension. Competency dimension includes three levels, which are cognition, understanding, and application. Competency at different levels is usually described with different explicit action verbs.

"Cognition" is mainly in the performance of knowing and of re-recognizing some factual knowledge such as basic social knowledge, geographical and historical knowledge and conceptions. It is usually expressed with the action verbs of know, recognize, distinguish, describe, example, confirm, etc.

"Understanding" is mainly reflected that students can explain, illustrate, judge, identify, compare, and categorize the related social information and materials, core conceptions, and social principles and phenomena.

"Application" is mainly reflected that students can flexibly and comprehensively apply the acquired knowledge, conceptions and principles in the problematic context and extract valid information, and can build the relation between social subjects and phenomena, induce the natural features of subjects from concrete events, judge, predict, and infer the development of subjects, etc.

3. Affect, attitude and values

Affect, attitude, and values herein include two parts. One is the social attitude and value content in social development, such as the sense of national identity, the sense of social responsibility, the international sense, and the sense of environmental protection. It also includes that in the complicated and changeable social environment, students can distinguish between truth and falsehood, can make right value judgment, and have the consciousness of democracy, of rule of law and of rules, care society, and love environment. The other part includes students' attitude, interest, and so on, when learning Morality and Society curriculum.

5.2.3.3 Definition of Students' Social Development

Based on students' performance in the three dimensions above of content domains, competencies, affect, and attitude, students' social development could be divided into three levels of "qualified", "proficient" and "excellent", with specific literal descriptions to differentiate the performance of each level, which could reflect to some extent students' academic achievement level at the subject of Morality and Society. Table 5.1 provides concrete information.

Table 5.1 Level descriptions of primary school students' social development

Level	Specific descriptions of social development
Qualified level	Initially have the national sense, globalization sense, consciousness of social rules, and sense of democracy participation; know related knowledge of law; and make initial analysis, thinking and judgment of social subjects, phenomena or problems with the help of related information
	Basically master the knowledge and to have the basic skills to keep their own health and safety
	Initially know the representative world historical culture; know basic historical knowledge, important historical events, and their influence; and initially analyze and judge historical subjects with the help of related materials and information
	Know basic geographic knowledge and skills, such as Earth, measurement scale, landform, climate, reading map, recognizing directions, etc., and can analyze geographical subjects and phenomena with application of related geographic knowledge and skills; know some basic geographic complexion about China and the world and initially understand the relationship between natural environment and people's life; know some environmental and resource problems human beings face; and initially have the sense of environmental protection and perform in daily life behaviors
Proficient level	Have certain of the national sense, globalization sense, consciousness of social rules, and sense of democracy participation; fairly know related knowledge of law; and make integrative, connective and practical analysis, thinking and judgment of social subjects, phenomena, or problems with the help of related information
	Master the knowledge to keep their own health and safety, and can use fairly proper and accurate approaches and methods to solve the safety problems when encountering and to protect their own health in a fairly reasonable way
	Can know the representative world historical culture; initially understand basic historical knowledge and know important historical events and their influence; and can fairly accurately analyze and judge historical subjects with the help of related materials and information
	Master basic geographic knowledge and skills, such as Earth, measurement scale, landform, climate, reading map, recognizing directions, etc., and can analyze geographical subjects and phenomena with application of related geographic knowledge and skills to initially solve some problems in life; initially understand some basic geographic complexion about China and the world and the relationship between natural environment and people's life; can understand some environmental and resource problems human beings face and the importance of sustainable development; and have certain of the sense of environmental protection and perform basic behaviors to care and protect environment
Excellent level	Have the national sense, globalization sense, consciousness of social rules, and sense of democracy participation qualified citizens should have; clearly know related knowledge of law; and make integrative, connective and practical analysis and thinking of social subjects, phenomena or problems with the help of related information, based which judgment, inference, and prediction are made

(continued)

5.2 Theoretical Framework on Students' Social Development Assessment

Table 5.1 (continued)

Level	Specific descriptions of social development
	Master the knowledge to keep their own health and safety, and can use proper and accurate approaches and methods to solve the safety problems when encountering and to protect their own health in reasonable way
	Can clearly know the representative world historical culture; understand basic historical knowledge, know and understand important historical events and their influence; and can accurately analyze and judge historical subjects with the help of related materials and information
	Accurately master basic geographic knowledge and skills, such as Earth, measurement scale, landform, climate, reading map, recognizing directions, etc., and can analyze geographical subjects and phenomena with flexible application of related geographic knowledge and skills to initially solve some problems in life; initially understand some basic geographic complexion about China and the world and the relationship between natural environment and people's life; can understand some environmental and resource problems human beings face and the importance of sustainable development; and have fairly strong sense of environmental protection and perform basic behaviors to care and protect environment

5.2.3.4 Assessment Methods of Students' Social Development

Assessment for students' social development related to various aspects. For different assessment content, appropriate corresponding assessment methods need to be employed. For example, it is appropriate to carry out performance assessment and formative assessment to assess students' "social affect and attitude and social behaviors" through the methods of long-term and short-term orientation observation (daily context and class teaching), interview, works presentation, etc. It is appropriate to create specific situations to do performance assessment for some social skills assessment. Regarding the related content scope stated above of the present survey and assessment and the national large-scale sampling situation, the assessment approach employed is the standardized paper test and questionnaire survey.

5.3 Development of Test Instrument and Test

With the foundation of the social development assessment framework developed based on the goals and content requirements of *Morality and Society Curriculum Standard*, the theory and method of SOLO taxonomy are employed as the basic technology of the assessment, to develop the corresponding assessment index system and test items reflecting students' social development level.

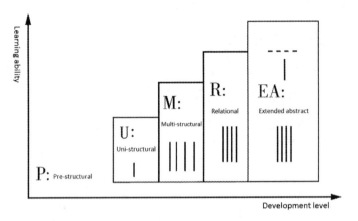

Fig. 5.2 Structure of the observed learning outcome

5.3.1 The Theory and Method of SOLO Taxonomy

"Structure of the Observed Learning Outcome" (SOLO taxonomy in abbreviation) is the thinking structure performed by a person when answering a specific question, proposed by Biggs, Australian educational psychologist and professor on educational psychology in the University of Hong Kong, and his colleague after long-term research. SOLO taxonomy is the inheritance and development of Piaget's theory of cognitive development, which tries to reflect the level of students' cognitive development through their explicit and observable learning outcomes. This theory assumes that there is a general increasing sequence of the structural complexity in student's understanding of learning many conceptions and skills, and this sequence can lead teachers to adjust specific teaching goals or to assess concrete learning outcomes. This theory divides students' learning outcomes (or responses to questions) into five levels or called five structural levels, i.e., pre-structural level, uni-structural level, multi-structural level, relational level, and extended abstract level. These five structural levels closely link, with the sequence of increasing complexity, which could be seen in Fig. 5.2.

The cognitive structure of students in primary school period is mainly reflected in the three structural levels of uni-structural level, multi-structural level, and relational level. Thus, through designing and developing the test items reflecting the three structural levels to assess students' learning outcomes, every subject can gain the result which, to some extent, reflects students' cognitive developmental level and the situation of students' academic achievement.

5.3.2 Development Procedures of the Test Instrument

Preparation period: It is to clarify research aim and research method, to consult the research results of the international and national programs related to social development, to analyze the belief of new curriculum reform and primary school *Morality and Society Curriculum Standard*, to learn SOLO taxonomy, and to make discussions and communication at early stage.

Construction period: Based on curriculum standard requirements and SOLO taxonomy, it is to construct the cognitive structural framework of the primary school Grade-6 student social development assessment, including the related content domains and topics, curriculum standard requirements, requirements on student ability, and the uni-structural, multi-structural and relational level items with certain proportions.

Modification period: With discussion and communication, including the direction of national and foreign experts, it is to adjust and modify the content in the cognitive structural framework and the predicted difficulty structure design. Regarding the fairly difficult items, it is to make modifications based on students' pilot test results, to modify the sequence of items and the sequence of options in the items and to supplement some illustrations which can better represent meanings and aims of items.

Pilot test period: It is to choose 3 schools in Chaoyang district in Beijing, including 195 students, to do the pilot test, of which the testing time is recorded and the results are analyzed.

Re-modification period: With the analysis results of the pilot test, it is to re-modify and to re-select the content in the cognitive structural framework, delete those items which are ambiguous or cannot elicit satisfying responses (such as open-ended items). The quantity of items is reduced to proper from 1.3 times of actual quantity required and adjustments on item difficulty structural levels are made accordingly. With the modification on the sequence of options in the items, the rating scales are modified at the same time.

Final draft period: It is to fix the final draft of the cognitive structural framework of the primary school Grade-6 student scientific ability, test items, rating scales, to solve the problems in the layout design and printing in order to make ready for the formal test.

5.3.3 Construction of the Two-Dimensional Table of Specifications

To design scientific and clear assessment framework is the premise and foundation for test item writing. The design basis of social development assessment framework is *Morality and Society Curriculum Standard* and SOLO taxonomy. According to the content of *Morality and Society Curriculum Standard*, core content is selected and divided into four content domains of citizen and society, health and safety, history and culture, and geography and environment. The content goals are stated into generalized ability requirements, and then transformed into the expected outcomes of students' learning, which are in manipulation of test items. With the proportion of 2:2:1, test items are to be designed at the uni-structural, multi-structural, and relational levels and the following cognitive structural framework is developed (Tables 5.2 and 5.3).

5.3.4 Test Item Writing and Examples

According to curriculum standard and SOLO taxonomy, the pilot test paper was tried to be developed based on the consensus on some basic issues through the repeated discussion and wide communication with related experts. The pilot test

Table 5.2 Item quantity distribution in content domains, competencies, and SOLO levels

		Item quantity distribution	Total items
Content domains		Citizen and society: 10 items, which is about 24% of the total items	42
		Health and safety, 9 items, which is about 18% of the total items	
		History and culture, 7 items, which is about 21% of the total items	
		Geography and environment: 16 items, which is about 38% of the total items	
Competencies		Cognition competency: 12 items, which is about 29% of the total items	
		Understanding competency: 21 items, which is about 50% of the total items	
		Application competency: 9 items, which is about 21% of the total items	
Structural levels		Uni-structural level: 16 items, which is about 38% of the total items	
		Multi-structural level: 18 items, which is about 43% of the total items	
		Relational level: 8 items, which is about 19% of the total items	

5.3 Development of Test Instrument and Test

Table 5.3 Cognitive structural framework of social development for primary school

Content domains	First-layer index (content standard)	Second-layer index (ability requirement)	Item number	Competencies	Structural level	Composition proportion
Citizen and society	Know some international organizations and their functions	Recognize the symbol of United Nations	1	Cognition	U	U:3 M:3 R:4
	Know the common knowledge of laws related to adolescents, and learn to self-protect with the law	Know the related content of *Compulsory Education Law of the People's Republic of China* and *Law of the People's Republic of China on Protection of Minors*	7	Cognition	U	
	Know the function of rules in collective life, and initially develop the consciousness of rules	Understand the rules of cleaning classroom sanitation	21	Understanding	M	
	Understand the realistic significance of equality and democracy in social life	Clearly know and experience the democracy in class life	20	Understanding	R	
	Initially understand that rapid increase in the population is one of the common problems the world faces	Can make a judgment related to population problem based on dialogue information	15	Understanding	R	
	Know some feature of economic activities	Understand that the price change of live chickens is influenced by supply–demand relationship	42	Understanding	R	
	Can apply related information to analyze the social subjects and phenomena	Acquire information related to telephone development from the telephone statistical chart	19	Applying	M	
		Predict the future situation of population receiving education from the table information	30	Applying	R	
	Know the achievements our country has gained since Reform and Openness	Clearly know the change since Reform and Openness through the use of various tickets and certificates	23	Cognition	U	
	Experience the world economic development and link and the influence they bring for peoples' life	Understand the influence of globalization through the goods used in daily life	17	Understanding	M	

(continued)

Table 5.3 (continued)

Content domains	First-layer index (content standard)	Second-layer index (ability requirement)	Item number	Competencies	Structural level	Composition proportion
Health and safety	Know common knowledge related to safety and initially have safety sense and the self-saving and self-protection ability	Confirm the age regulation for bike riding	2	Cognition	U	U:3 M:4 R:2
		Master the self-saving and self-protection method in fire accidents	3	Understanding	U	
		Can accurately deal with the scald/empyrosis in daily life	6	Understanding	M	
		Judge the truth or falseness of events and not readily believe others	9	Understanding	M	
	Learn the self-protection and mutual-help methods in front of natural disasters and develop corresponding ability	Identify the accurate self-protection methods in thunderstorm weather	4	Understanding	U	
		Understand the best escaping method in earthquake	14	Understanding	M	
	Learn the initial knowledge of shopping, and have the initial sense of consumer protection	Gain the information about quality guarantee period from the food packing bag	10	Applying	R	
	Know the risks of unhealthy living habits, care personal health and love life	Infer the damage degree of smoking for health	13	Applying	R	

(continued)

5.3 Development of Test Instrument and Test

Table 5.3 (continued)

Content domains	First-layer index (content standard)	Second-layer index (ability requirement)	Item number	Competencies	Structural level	Composition proportion
History and culture	Know that our country is a civilized ancient country with the history of thousands of years	Can understand the conceptual meaning of "B.C. and A.D."	18	Understanding	R	U:3 M:3 R:1
		Infer the living situation of Peking Man based on archaeological materials	38	Applying	M	
	Feel the huge contribution of Chinese nation for the world civilization	Know our country's Four Great Inventions	28	Cognition	U	
	Treasure the country's tradition of historical culture	Confirm our country's important festivals and the representative diets	29	Cognition	M	
	Know some human being's heritage of civilization	Identifying the world-famous historical and cultural buildings	12	Cognition	U	
	Know the humiliation and harm to Chinese people brought with great powers' aggression against China in modern history	Clearly know the historical event of Burning of Opium Stocks in Humen	5	Cognition	U	
		Clearly know the historical event of Burning Old Summer Palace	39	Cognition	M	
Geography and environment	Initially know the world distribution of sea and land and the basic knowledge of main landforms	Confirm the climate difference at the southern and northern earth at Christmas	25	Understanding	M	U:7 M:8 R:1
		Distinguish the information presented in school plan based on the position of the Sun	27	Applying	M	
		Identify the river's trend according to the direction in the illustration of Happy Island	31	Applying	U	
		Confirm the city according to the real distance of two places in Happy Island	32	Applying	U	
		Judge the city situation based on the basic information presented in the plan of Happy Island	33	Applying	M	
		Clearly know the relationship between altitude and temperature	35	Understanding	U	

(continued)

Table 5.3 (continued)

Content domains	First-layer index (content standard)	Second-layer index (ability requirement)	Item number	Competencies	Structural level	Composition proportion
	Know the differences of different areas in our country, and explore the influence of these differences to people's production and life	Make clear the relationship between the climate features in the south and north of our country and agricultural production	16		M	
		Clearly know the natural situation of our country's Tibet autonomous region	34	Cognition	U	
	Know the our country's territorial size, etc.	Confirm the size of the land area in our country	37	Cognition	U	
	Know the living habits and customs of different nationalities	Identify the clothing feature of Chaoxian nationality	8	Cognition	U	
	Understand that human beings and nature should harmoniously coexist	Know that human beings are a part of nature	22	Understanding	M	
		Understand different natural environments influence people's living ways	36	Understanding	M	
	Know some problems of ecological environment, and develop the consciousness of environmental protection and the sense of social responsibility	Know the different sorting ways of garbage	26	Understanding	M	
		Clearly know the conflict between economic development and environmental protection	40	Understanding	M	
	Initially know that environment deteriorates and lack of resources are the common problems in the present world	Clearly know that global warming causes the reduction of snow cover	24	Understanding	U	
		Clearly know the main factors causing greenhouse effect and global warming	41	Understanding	R	

5.3 Development of Test Instrument and Test

paper includes two types of items, multiple-choice and open-ended question. Some examples are provided as follows, from which the thinking line of item writing could be seen.

5.3.4.1 Multiple-Choice Items

Example 1 (U level)

Thunderstorm happens frequently in our daily life. When lightning flashes and thunder rumbles, we are supposed to ( ).

A. Get the clothes hung on the iron wire back.
B. Go near to the door or the window if we are at home.
C. Hide under a big tree for shelter if we are in an open area.
D. Crouch down in a low-lying place if we are in an open area.

Key: D

Explanation: This item belongs to the domain of health and safety, with low difficulty at the uni-structural level, i.e., only D is the accurate answer. The intention of this item is to assess whether students know the safety knowledge related to thunder and lightning protection, owning the basic self-protection ability, such as knowing that iron wire conducts electricity, knowing to be far away from doors or windows to prevent thunder and lightning hit indoors, and knowing to stay away from big trees since it is easy for them to firstly get the electricity in the air and clouds.

Example 2 (M level)

The main crop in the north of our country is wheat, while it is rice in the south. The reason causing the difference mainly is ( ).

A. The tradition of farming.
B. The landform factor.
C. The climate factor.
D. People's dietary habit.

Key: C

Explanation: Social problems and phenomena often have complexity and multi-dimensional feature, requiring students to extend in the width and depth of their thought. However, students usually see the surface and seldom have an insight into the nature of subjects to get the internal relationship between them. This item belongs to the domain of geography and environment at the multi-structural level, mainly assessing students' knowledge and understanding of the internal logical relationship between climate and crop. The four options respectively represent the different cognitive levels of this question. Option C is the key, while options A and

D at pre-structural level, implying students only see the superficial relation of subjects. Students choosing option B have considered one of the factors influencing the types of crops planting, reaching uni-structural level.

Example 3 (R level)

Archaeologists discovered thick ash and burned animal bones in the caves where Peking Man lived. The discovery indicates that (   ).

A. The body of Peking Man is short.
B. Peking Man lived upon the meet of animal.
C. The living ability of Peking Man has been improved.
D. Peking Man understood how to use fire.

Key: C

Explanation: This item related to the social and historical knowledge, with difficulty at relational level, mainly assessing students' ability to analyze, reasonably infer and judge the nature of social subjects penetrating the surface of subjects. The expression of option A is unrelated to the topic, which is at pre-structural level, while option B is only part of the nature, which is basically describing the fact, with cognitive ability at uni-structural level. Option D infers "Peking Man understood how to use fire". The implication of "use" is not only for roasting food, but also for getting warmth with fire, which obviously reaches multi-structural level. Based on option D, the meaning of "understanding how to use fire" has been elevated, including that cooked food and getting warmth with fire can make people strengthen their body, prevent diseases, reduce death and improve life quality; fire can disperse the threat of other animals and guarantee the life safety; and fire can give the light, providing the convenience for people, etc. To sum up, "the living ability of Peking Man has been improved". If students can realize this, their cognitive development reaches the relational level.

5.3.4.2 Open-Ended Questions

To effectively assess students' real comprehensive ability including the ability to understand, to analyze illustrations, to express in writing, to logically think and the ability of divergent thinking and its creativity when they face realistic problems, open-ended questions, which are usually relational level, are particularly designed to for students to freely respond.

Example 4 (R level)

The theme poster of the World Environment Day 1989 is "Earth sweats". Do you know why Earth "sweats"?

5.3 Development of Test Instrument and Test

Please list the reasons as many as possible based on the illustration below presents and your knowledge.

Reasons:

_____
_____
_____
_____
_____
_____

Explanation: This is an item related to environmental protection. Students nowadays often think everything they enjoy is oriented for them, taking everything granted, without knowing activities of human beings, including their own actions, often cause different degrees of influence to the environment. This item, through the reading and explanation of the illustration, is trying to attract students' attention to the environmental problems around to reflect their behavior and to increase the consciousness of the urgent environmental protection. The difficulty of this item reaches relational level. It is designed to be open-ended, with the orientation to better present the perspective of students' thinking and the degree difference of their cognitive development levels. The three levels are respectively as follows:

Uni-structural level: This level can list many phenomena, such as the quantity of waste gas gets rising because of cars, aviation, factory' producing, generating electricity with fire and the needs of people's life (such as air conditioner, fridge, etc.) or the human being's behavior such as cutting lots of forest and trees, etc.

Multi-structural level: This level can explain that human being's behaviors, increasing a large quantity of resources consumption of coal, oil, gas, etc., cause the carbon dioxide emitted into the air rises rapidly and the greenhouse effects come out, which results in that Earth "has a heat" or "sweats"; or that the rapid reduction of forest size in the world makes the trees' ability to absorb carbon dioxide decrease, which is another important reason for Earth to sweat.

Relational level: This level can analyze with the integration of these two aspects.

5.3.5 Pilot Test and Modifications

In April 2009, students (195 in total) from schools with fairly high, intermediate and fairly low teaching quality participated in the pilot test. Based on the results analysis, test items were dealt with in three ways. Items with fairly good validity, reliability, difficulty, and discrimination were preserved, such as Examples 1 and 2; items with unsatisfying infit, too high or low difficulty, or too low discrimination were deleted; and items with quite good content and structure but still with limitations were modified, such as Example 3 and open-ended question mentioned above.

In Example 3, the four options, written according to SOLO taxonomy, should fairly clearly reflect the four structural levels theoretically. However, the test result is out of expectation. 34% of students with the highest ability chose option D (not the predicted C) and 21% of students with fairly high ability chose option B, while only 35% of students with fairly weak ability chose the predicted accurate option C, which indicates that there is divergence between the prediction based on SOLO taxonomy and students' real thinking. And the real difficulty of the item only reached multi-structural level. With careful analysis, it is thought that option C might go beyond primary school students' present cognitive development level, reaching extended abstract level, which cannot be achieved with students' present ability. Regarding those students with fairly weak ability but accurately answering the question, it is possible the result of guessing, which cannot reflect their real ability level. Thus, it could be said that this option is invalid, and it is fairly ideal to design the item at multi-structural level. So, the item has been modified into multi-structural level, and the modified item is as follows:

38. Archaeologists discovered thick ash and burned animal bones in the caves where Peking Man lived. The discovery indicates that ( ).

A. the body of Peking Man is short.
B. Peking Man lived upon the meet of animal.
C. the main diet of Peking Man is cooked food.
D. Peking Man understood how to use fire.

Option D is accurate option (multi-structural level), option B or C is at uni-structural level.

It is also discovered that in pilot test, near 90% of students did not answer open-ended questions, which might be caused by time limitation, or by laziness. To avoid the invalidity, open-ended questions were tried to be transformed into multiple choice at relational level in the formal test, such as Example 4.

41. The picture on the right reflects the theme of World Environment Day in 1989: Earth sweats. The most directly related factor causing this phenomenon is ( ).

5.3 Development of Test Instrument and Test

A. that carbon dioxide in the air sharply increases.
B. that ecological environment is polluted increasingly.
C. the reduction of forest size with high speed.
D. the increase of world population with high speed.

5.3.6 The Characteristic Parameter of the Test Instrument and Measurement Index of the Test Paper

5.3.6.1 Item Reliability, Difficulty, Discrimination, and Fit Index

Based on the needs of project research, the formal test was carried out with 18,024 primary school students in 30 counties national wide, and the number of valid test papers is 18,024. The item parameters and the validity and reliability of test paper are analyzed with Winsteps 3.63. Based on this, the ability parameter of each student is acquired, with the results seen in Table 5.4.

From Table 5.4, it could be found that the reliability of test item is 1.00, and the holistic reliability for students' ability estimate is 0.80. Reliability of the test paper is quite satisfying. The test item parameters, including difficulty, discrimination, fit index and average response could be seen in Table 5.5.

From Table 5.6, it could be known that the smallest item difficulty is −2.2, while the biggest is 2.69, with the mean 0.00 and standard deviation 1.03. The difficulty coverage is quite wide and fairly satisfying.

Item discrimination in the table is provided in two ways. One is the correlation between the pass of each item and of total items, i.e., point biserial correlation, to show the item discrimination for students' ability. From the table, it could be seen

Table 5.4 Statistical results of test item reliability

	Students' test result	Test item
Reliability	0.80	1.00
Mean	0.68	
Standard deviation	0.87	

Table 5.5 Statistical table on parameter results of test item difficulty, discrimination, and fit index, item characteristic, etc

	Item difficulty	Discrimination (point biserial correlation)	Infit mean square	Discrimination	p-value
1	−2.2	0.23	0.96	1.04	0.93
2	−0.15	0.32	0.97	1.1	0.67
3	−0.57	0.34	0.94	1.11	0.75
4	0.09	0.26	1.02	0.96	0.62
5	−0.62	0.33	0.95	1.1	0.76
6	0.73	0.22	1.06	0.76	0.49
7	−1.46	0.19	1	0.99	0.87
8	−0.8	0.21	1.03	0.96	0.78
9	−0.38	0.08	1.14	0.67	0.71
10	−1.51	0.12	1.04	0.94	0.87
11	0.9	0.22	1.07	0.72	0.45
12	−0.05	0.3	0.99	1.05	0.65
13	−0.39	0.31	0.97	1.07	0.72
14	0.51	0.18	1.09	0.64	0.53
15	0.49	0.28	1.01	0.97	0.54
16	−0.25	0.34	0.95	1.13	0.69
17	0.35	0.27	1.02	0.94	0.57
18	1.78	0.34	0.93	1.11	0.28
19	−0.87	0.29	0.96	1.05	0.79
20	−0.27	0.27	1.01	0.99	0.69
21	−1.52	0.24	0.97	1.03	0.88
22	0.52	0.31	0.98	1.07	0.53
23	−0.54	0.33	0.95	1.11	0.74
24	−0.92	0.39	0.9	1.15	0.8
25	−0.2	0.4	0.91	1.24	0.68
26	0.17	0.14	1.12	0.58	0.6
27	1.57	0.22	1.05	0.89	0.31
28	−1.25	0.33	0.93	1.09	0.84
29	0.19	0.39	0.92	1.27	0.6
30	1.88	0.15	1.07	0.84	0.26
31	−0.3	0.35	0.94	1.14	0.7
32	1.04	0.23	1.04	0.83	0.42
33	0.12	0.33	0.97	1.12	0.62
34	0.25	0.37	0.94	1.24	0.59
35	−0.37	0.34	0.95	1.13	0.71
36	1.61	0.23	1.05	0.89	0.31
37	−1.5	0.23	0.97	1.02	0.87
38	0.27	0.31	0.98	1.06	0.59

(continued)

5.3 Development of Test Instrument and Test

Table 5.5 (continued)

	Item difficulty	Discrimination (point biserial correlation)	Infit mean square	Discrimination	p-value
39	−0.92	0.37	0.91	1.14	0.8
40	0.59	0.22	1.06	0.74	0.52
41	1.27	0.17	1.1	0.7	0.37
42	2.69	0.06	1.1	0.86	0.15

Table 5.6 Descriptive statistics

	N	Minimum	Maximum	Mean	Standard deviation
Difficulty	42	−2.2	2.69	0.00	1.03
Discrimination (point biserial correlation)	42	0.06	0.40	0.27	0.09
Infit mean square	42	0.90	1.14	1.00	0.06
Discrimination	42	0.58	1.27	0.99	0.17
p-value	42	0.15	0.93	0.63	0.19

that the discrimination mean of test paper items is 0.27, approaching to 0.30, which is quite satisfying.

Discrimination can be presented in another way. Winsteps software employs Rasch model prediction that all the items' discrimination is the same, equivalent with 1.00, based on which Rasch model is fitted. However, the empirical items' discrimination never coincidentally equals each other, thus, Winsteps reports the post hoc test result (a kind of fit statistical variant) of discrimination to indicate the difference between the real discrimination and 1.00, which is treated as an indicator of the fit degree between the item and Rasch model. Items with discrimination 1.00 correspond to Rasch model, while items with discrimination more or less than 1 is not in accordance with Rasch model regarding the discrimination prediction of items with this difficulty. From the table, it could be seen that the discrimination mean of items is 0.99, approaching 1.

Another important statistical variant, the average response, is often used to express the sample proportion consistent with items in dichotomous rating way. In Winsteps, it is explained the average response to items (dichotomous or multi-categorical rating ways). From the table, it could be seen that the mean of the average responses to items is 0.63.

Regarding the validity of test results, two methods are employed to test it. The first one is the validity of content structure. From Table 5.7, it could be seen that the fit indices of all items are between 0.90 and 1.14, with the average 1.00 and standard deviation 0.06, which indicates that the validity of content structure is very high, in accordance with Rasch model uni-dimensional prediction.

Table 5.7 Item infit

```
INFIT
MNSQ         .63        .71       .83      1.00      1.20      1.40      1.60
        ----------------+---------+---------+---------+---------+---------+
       1 item 1          .                   *  |
       2 item 2          .                   *  |
       3 item 3          .                   *  |
       4 item 4          .                      |*
       5 item 5          .                   *  |
       6 item 6          .                      |   *
       7 item 7          .                    *
       8 item 8          .                      |*
       9 item 9          .                      |      *
      10 item 10         .                      | *
      11 item 11         .                      | *
      12 item 12         .                  *|
      13 item 13         .                  *  |
      14 item 14         .                      |     *
      15 item 15         .                     *
      16 item 16         .                  *  |
      17 item 17         .                      |*
      18 item 18         .               *     |
      19 item 19         .                 *   |
      20 item 20         .                    *
      21 item 21         .                 *|
      22 item 22         .                 *|
      23 item 23         .                *   |
      24 item 24         .           *        |
      25 item 25         .            *       |
      26 item 26         .                      |    *
      27 item 27         .                      | *
      28 item 28         .              *      |
      29 item 29         .              *      |
      30 item 30         .                      |   *
      31 item 31         .                *    |
      32 item 32         .                      | *
      33 item 33         .               *|
      34 item 34         .               *|
      35 item 35         .               *|
      36 item 36         .                      | *
      37 item 37         .                *|
      38 item 38         .                *|
      39 item 39         .            *   |
      40 item 40         .                      |  *
      41 item 41         .                      |    *
      42 item 42         .                      |  *
```

5.3 Development of Test Instrument and Test

Table 5.8 Correlation analysis between society and other subjects

		Reading	Mathematics	Science	Morality and Society
Reading	Pearson correlation coefficient	1	0.503[a]	0.429[a]	0.473[a]
	Sig. (2-tailed)	–	0.000	0.000	0.000
	N	16,799	16,543	15,168	16,617
Mathematics	Pearson correlation coefficient	0.503[a]	1	0.601[a]	0.611[a]
	Sig. (2-tailed)	0.000	–	0.000	0.000
	N	16,543	17,898	16,253	17,832
Science	Pearson correlation coefficient	0.429[a]	0.601[a]	1	0.707[a]
	Sig. (2-tailed)	0.000	0.000	–	0.000
	N	15,168	16,253	16,378	17,832
Morality and Society	Pearson correlation coefficient	0.473[a]	0.611[a]	0.707[a]	1
	Sig. (2-tailed)	0.000	0.000	0.000	–
	N	16,617	17,832	16,315	18,024

[a]Correlation is significant at the 0.01 level (2-tailed)

The second one is the correlations between Society test result and test results of other three subjects (see Table 5.8), treated as the empirical validity index of test paper, which could be called congruent validity, indicating the consistence degree of the same ability tested with different instruments. From Table 5.8, it could be seen that the correlations between Society ability and abilities in other subjects are general and significant. The correlation is 0.707 with Science, 0.611 with Mathematics and 0.473 with Reading. This indicates that the result of Society subject has fairly high correlation with that of other subjects.

5.3.6.2 Analysis of Item Characteristic Curves

From Fig. 5.3, it could be attained that there are 42 test items in total, and almost all item characteristic curves correspond to IRT model, in the performance that students with higher ability can more answer items with larger difficulty (the probability to answer items with large difficulty is higher) and get higher scores. The scope of item difficulty is about between −3.0 and 4.2, with wide distribution, which is beneficial to better assess students' real ability.

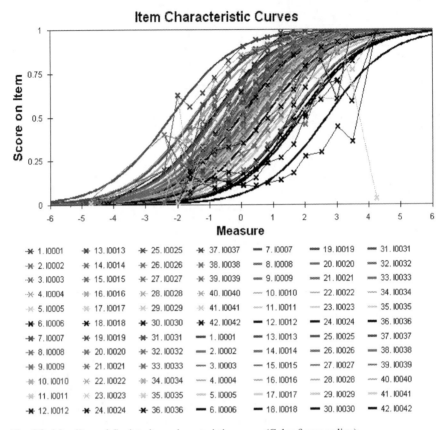

Fig. 5.3 Morality and Society item characteristic curves (Color figure online)

5.3.7 Analysis of Students' Responses to Typical Items

Typical item 1

Thunderstorm happens frequently in our daily life. When lightning flashes and thunder rumbles, we are supposed to ( ).

A. Get the clothes hung on the iron wire back.
B. Go near to the door or the window if we are at home.
C. Hide under a big tree for shelter if we are in an open area.
D. Crouch down in a low-lying place if we are in an open area.

Domain assessed: Health and safety

Ability assessed: Predicted level is uni-structural level, with multi-structural level as the real difficulty

Key: D

5.3 Development of Test Instrument and Test

Table 5.9 Statistical table of students' responses to typical item 1

Item number	Option analysis			
Item 4	Option	Number of students	Percentage (%)	Average ability
	C	137	0.80	−0.30
	B	826	4.68	0.17
	0	137	0.80	0.22
	A	5695	31.50	0.34
	D	11,229	63.30	0.91

Note "0" indicates no response

Analysis: From students' responses participating in the test, although 62% of students chose the accurate answer, more than 30% of students chose the wrong option "A get the clothes hung on the iron wire back". This indicates that these students have not really built the relationship between the phenomenon of thunder and storm and the material conducting electricity, which accordingly increases the item difficulty (Table 5.9).

Typical item 2

Liu Chang passed by a store yesterday after school, finding that the biscuit he always bought was 2 RMB cheaper than normal. He then saw the package printed "Produced on Nov. 10, 2008; Quality guarantee period: 6 months". Should he buy the biscuit? ( )

A. Yes. The biscuit is still within its quality guarantee period, and it is cheap. So he can buy and eat it.
B. No. The biscuit has already passed its quality guarantee period.
C. Yes. The biscuit has just passed its quality guarantee period but it is cheap. So he can buy and eat it.
D. No. He should also suggest the shopping assistant not to sell it anymore.

Domain assessed: Health and safety

Ability assessed: Predicted level is relational level, with uni-structural level as the real difficulty

Key: D

Analysis: Based on SOLO taxonomy, this item relates to various factors of the conceptual understanding of quality guarantee period, time calculation, goods price, self-protection consciousness as consumers, etc., which is set relational level. In reality, students know quite well the knowledge of goods quality guarantee period and have fairly strong self-protection consciousness, with 87% of students choosing the accurate answer, which makes the real item difficulty decrease to uni-structural level (Table 5.10).

Table 5.10 Statistical table of students' responses to typical item 2

Item number	Option analysis			
Item 10	Option	Number of students	Percentage (%)	Average ability
	C	73	0.40	−0.57
	A	328	1.80	−0.07
	0	72	0.40	0.01
	B	1788	9.90	0.42
	D	15,763	87.50	0.73

Note "0" indicates no response

Typical item 3

Based on the figure below, it could be inferred the change tendency of the phone number in the Year 2003 might be that ( ).

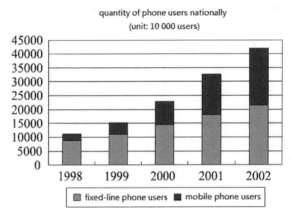

A. Quantity of fixed-line phones stays unchangeable, but the quantity of mobile phones increases.
B. Quantity of fixed-line phones increases more rapidly than that of mobile phones.
C. Quantity of mobile phones increases more rapidly than that of fixed-line phones.
D. Quantity of mobile phones increases at the same speed as that of fixed-line phones.

Domain assessed: Citizen and society

Ability assessed: Predicted level is multi-structural level, with uni-structural level as the real difficulty

5.3 Development of Test Instrument and Test

Table 5.11 Statistical table of students' responses to typical item 3

Item number	Option analysis			
Item 19	Option	Number of students	Percentage (%)	Average ability
	A	583	3.20	−0.16
	B	1206	6.70	0.09
	D	1736	9.60	0.17
	0	176	0.90	0.52
	C	14,323	79.60	0.83

Note "0" indicates no response

Key: C

Analysis: Based on SOLO taxonomy, this item is set multi-structural level. Actually, the number of students choosing the accurate answer reaches 79%, indicating that students' ability to analyze problems based on statistical charts is fairly strong, which accordingly makes the real difficulty of the item decrease to uni-structural level (Table 5.11).

Typical item 4

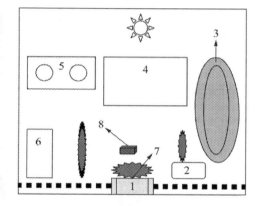

1. The school gate
2. The reception office
3. The sports ground
4. The teaching building
5. The basketball playground
6. The dining hall
7. The flowerbed
8. The flag-raising place

Answer the following questions based on the plan of Guangming Primary School.

The sun shown in the picture represents the location of sunrise in the morning. If Xiao Ming, on the basketball playground now, is going to answer a phone call in the reception office, how can he get there in the shortest way? (　)

A. Go southwards directly to the dining hall first, and then go eastwards along the flowerbed.
B. Go westwards directly to the dining hall first, and then go southwards along the flowerbed.
C. Go southeastwards passing by the flag-raising place.

D. Go southwestwards passing by the flag-raising place.

Domain assessed: Geography and environment

Ability assessed: Predicted level is multi-structural level, with relational level as the real difficulty

Key: D

Analysis: Based on SOLO taxonomy, since two factors of identifying directions and walking distance should be considered, this item is set multi-structural level. However, only 31% of students chose the accurate answer, while 49% of students could not identify the direction with the help of Sun's position in the illustration, and 11% of students did not consider the walking distance although choosing the accurate direction. Near 70% of students in total cannot accurately answer the question, which makes the item difficulty level increase to relational level (Table 5.12).

Typical item 5

Answer the question according to the map of Happy Island on the right.

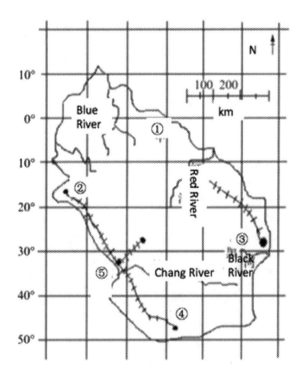

5.3 Development of Test Instrument and Test

Table 5.12 Statistical table of students' responses to typical item 4

Item number	Option analysis			
Item 27	Option	Number of students	Percentage (%)	Average ability
	A	1582	8.80	0.13
	0	88	0.50	0.23
	B	1916	10.60	0.38
	C	8785	48.70	0.59
	D	5653	34.40	1.07

Note "0" indicates no response

Somebody is leaving the second city to the next for travel. It is known that these two cities are 750 km away from each other. Based on the map scale, the city should be ( ).

    A. ①   B. ③   C. ④   D. ⑤

Domain assessed: Geography and environment

Ability assessed: Predicted level is uni-structural level, with relational level as the real difficulty

Key: B

Analysis: This item is to measure the distance between two cities according to the scale illustrated in the map, which is at uni-structural level. But only 42% of students chose the accurate answer, making the item difficulty increase, reaching the relational level. This might be because that students lack the ability to calculate the practical distance based on scale, or that it is not related in teaching or teaching materials, which makes the difficulty rise, and that students did not use rule to measure (Table 5.13).

Typical item 6

Answer the question below according to the map of Happy Island above.

Table 5.13 Statistical table of students' responses to typical item 5

Item number	Option analysis			
Item 32	Option	Number of students	Percentage (%)	Average ability
	0	216	1.20	0.10
	A	1443	8.00	0.29
	C	3731	20.70	0.44
	D	5055	28.00	0.51
	B	7579	42.10	1.00

Note "0" indicates no response

Table 5.14 Statistical table of students' responses to typical item 6

Item number	Option analysis			
Item 33	Option	Number of students	Percentage (%)	Average ability
	0	114	0.60	−0.07
	C	1431	7.90	0.02
	A	1578	8.80	0.09
	D	3802	21.10	0.41
	B	11,099	61.60	0.95

Note "0" indicates no response

The busiest port city is ( ).

  A. ④ B. ⑤ C. ① D. ③

Domain assessed: Geography and environment

Ability assessed: Predicted level is multi-structural level, with multi-structural level as the real difficulty

Key: B

Analysis: This item mainly assesses students' ability to acquire the information in the illustration and make comprehensive use of the information to solve problems. From the test result, 62% of students can thoroughly make use of the information on railways, rivers given by the illustration to confirm the busiest city and 21% of students can use partial information, with the predicted difficulty level in accordance with the real difficulty level (Table 5.14).

Typical item 7

There is such a paragraph "There are high mountains aloft and it is freezing and desolate. Trees and plants almost cannot be seen. A kind of cow with long hair is the important transportation tool for the residents, which is heavily depended on to transport and exchange goods with outside …… ". The natural situation of which province is described? ( )

A. Tibet autonomous region.
B. Inner Mongolia autonomous region.
C. Ningxia Hui autonomous region
D. Guangxi Zhuang autonomous region.

Domain assessed: Geography and environment

Ability assessed: Predicted level is uni-structural level, with multi-structural level as the real difficulty

Key: A

Analysis: From students' responses, although this is an item at uni-structural level, students' performance is unsatisfying. Only 59% of students chose the accurate

5.3 Development of Test Instrument and Test

Table 5.15 Statistical table of students' responses to typical item 7

Item number	Option analysis			
Item 33	Option	Number of students	Percentage (%)	Average ability
	0	126	0.70	−0.03
	D	1814	10.00	0.22
	C	1967	10.90	0.23
	B	3519	19.60	0.25
	A	10,598	58.80	0.99

Note "0" indicates no response

answer and those students who responded inaccurately were influenced by options B, C, and D. This indicates that over 40% of students lack accurate knowledge regarding the typical natural situation of Tibet region, which causes them to choose the wrong option and makes the item difficulty rise to multi-structural level (Table 5.15).

5.4 Analysis and Discussion on the Test Results

5.4.1 The Overall Complexion of Students' Social Development

The present survey assessed 18,024 students' social development, with the test results shown in Table 5.16.

From Table 5.16, it could be obtained the test results of 18,024 students' social development that the mean of the estimated value of student ability is 0.68, with standard deviation of 0.87.

5.4.2 Grouping Analysis of Students' Social Development Performance

Based on 18,024 students' responses to items with different difficulty, with the mean of the estimated ability value (0.68) as the midpoint and 1 standard deviation as interval, students are divided into 5 ability groups from high (A) to low (E), and

Table 5.16 Descriptive statistics

	N	Minimum	Maximum	Mean	SD
Transferred ability	18,024	−4.88	4.25	0.6780	0.87013
Valid sample	18,024				

Table 5.17 Number and percentage of students in each ability group

Groups	Original ability value Group ability value Starting point–terminal point	Number of students	Percentage of each group students out of the total (%)	Accumulative percentage (%)
Highest ability group (A)	1.983–Maximum	1182	6.6	6.6
Average ability above group (B)	1.113–1.983	3570	19.8	26.4
Average ability group (C)	0.243–1.113	7371	40.9	67.3
Average ability below group (D)	−0.622 to 0.243	5040	28.0	95.2
Lowest ability group (E)	Minimum to −0.622	861	4.8	100.0

the group interval coverage is divided by the original ability value. The number of students, the percentage of the students in each ability group out of the total, and the accumulative percentage could be seen in Table 5.17.

Combined with the bar chart of student frequency distribution in 5 ability group (Fig. 5.4), it could be analyzed that the student ability is basically in normal distribution. The number of students in the highest ability group (A) is 1182, 6.6% of the total students participating in the test. There are 3570 students in the group lower than the highest ability but higher than the average ability (B), which is 19.8% of the total students. The number of the students in average ability group (C) is 7371, 40.9% of the total students. There are 5040 students in the group lower

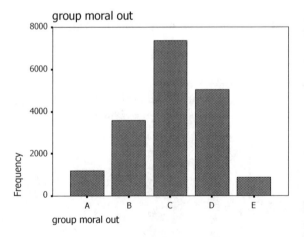

Fig. 5.4 Bar chart of student frequency distribution in five ability groups

5.4 Analysis and Discussion on the Test Results

than the average ability but higher than the lowest ability (D), which is 28.0% of the total students. And the number of students in the lowest ability group (E) is 861, 4.8% of the total students. The accumulative number of students in and above average ability group is 12,123 (7371 + 3570 + 1182), which is about 67% (40.9% + 19.8% + 6.6%) of the total students, while the accumulative number of students below the average ability group is 5901 (5040 + 861), which is about 33% (28.0% + 4.8%) of the total students.

If the groups A, B, C, D, and E stated above are respectively corresponding to excellent, proficient, qualified, basically qualified, and unqualified, it could be obtained that out of the 18,024 students, the performance of 6.6% of students is excellent, the performance of 19.8% of students is proficient, the performance of 40.9% of students is qualified, the performance of 28% of students is basically qualified, and the performance of 4.8% of students is unqualified.

To sum up, in the survey on the social ability of 18,024 students in Grade 6 primary school based on new curriculum standard, from the holistic results analysis, nearly 70% (67%) of students can fully meet the requirements of contents and abilities in curriculum standard, owning the basic social knowledge and skills, have certain of social abilities to analyze, to think and to judge, and have initially developed national sense, globalization sense, consciousness of social rules, and sense of democracy participation. Around 30% (28%) of students can basically meet the requirements of contents and abilities in curriculum standard, but they have deficiency in the mastery of social knowledge and social skills. And there is a small proportion (4.8%) of students, with fairly weak social abilities, who have not met the standards yet.

5.4.3 The Proportion of Students in Different Ability Groups and the Level Description of Their Academic Achievement

To make a direct and vivid description of students' academic achievement performance levels, tasks which can be accomplished by students in different ability groups from high to low (A → E) are grouped. Different groups represent the different academic achievement levels students can reach. Group A is excellent ability group, and students can accomplish all the tasks included in groups A, B, C, D, and E; Group B is proficient ability group, and students can accomplish all the tasks included in groups B, C, D, and E; Group C is qualified ability group, and students can accomplish all the tasks included in groups C, D, and E; Group D is basically qualified ability group, and students can accomplish all the tasks included in groups D and E; and Group E is unqualified ability group, and students can only accomplish the tasks included in this group. Specific information is shown in Fig. 5.5.

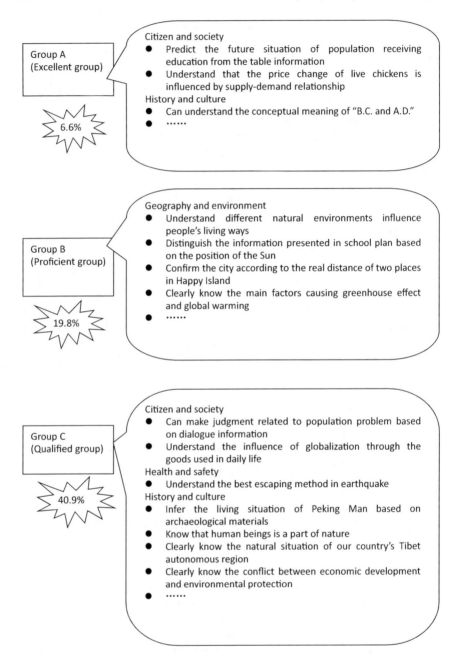

Fig. 5.5 The proportion of students in different ability groups and the tasks that can be accomplished

5.4 Analysis and Discussion on the Test Results

Group D (Basically qualified group)

28.0%

Citizen and society
- Clearly know the change since Reform and Openness through the use of various tickets and certificates
- Clearly know and experience the democracy in class life

Health and safety
- Infer the damage degree of smoking for health
- Judge the truth or falseness of events and not readily believe others
- Identify the accurate self-protection methods in thunderstorm weather
- Master the self-saving and self-protection method in fire accidents
- Confirm the age regulation for bike riding

History and culture
- Identifying the world famous historical and cultural buildings
- Confirm our country's important festivals and the representative diets

Geography and environment
- Clearly know the relationship between altitude and temperature
- Judge the city situation based on the basic information presented in the plan of Happy Island
- Identify the river's trend according to the direction in the illustration of Happy Island
- Know the different sorting ways of rubbish
- Confirm the climate difference at the southern and northern earth at Christmas
- Make clear the relationship between the climate features in the south and north of our country and agricultural production
- ……

Fig. 5.5 (continued)

From the tasks which could be accomplished by students in different ability groups above, the 5-level groups from the lowest ability group (Group E) to the highest ability group (Group A) do reflect the significant change of students' ability and represent students' different academic achievement levels.

1. The gradual change of students' cognitive level could be reflected from the application of action verbs describing the degree of achievement. Group E (the lowest ability group) presents more action verbs reflecting the general knowing and cognition of subjects, such as "re-recognize, identify, confirm", etc.; while Group C (qualified group) presents more action verbs reflecting the general understanding of subjects, such as "know, initially analyze, judge", etc.; and Group A (the highest ability group) presents more action verbs reflecting deep understanding of subjects, cognition of the internal relationship between

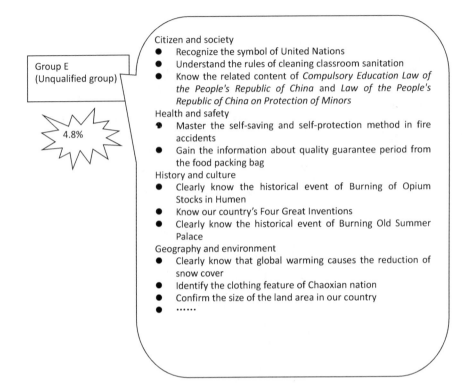

Fig. 5.5 (continued)

subjects and prediction for the future, such as "clearly know", "really understand", "predict", "infer", "judge", etc.
2. From the level of SOLO taxonomy achieved, tasks that could be accomplished by different groups of students show the gradual change tendency from uni-structural level to relational level of students' cognitive ability. Most of the tasks that could be accomplished by Group E (the lowest ability group) students are items only requiring memorization and simple recognition of singular subject at uni-structural level (11 items at uni-structural level and 1 item at multi-structural level), and most tasks Group C (qualified group) students, who do not own the ability to organically integrate, can accomplish are items requiring to link two or more events to analyze and judge problems at multi-structural level (16 items at uni-structural level and 19 item at multi-structural level), while Group B (the highest ability group) students have the ability to clearly know fairly complicated specific problems and to answer those items, requiring students to imagine and link multiple related events, at relational level (19 items at multi-structural level and 7 item at relational level).
3. From the proportions of students in different ability groups, students' holistic social development level shows the normal distribution. It could be seen from

5.4 Analysis and Discussion on the Test Results 233

Fig. 5.5 that out of the 18,024 students participating in the test, the performance of 6.6% of students is excellent, the performance of 19.8% of students is proficient, the performance of 40.9% of students is qualified, the performance of 28% of students is basically qualified, and the performance of 4.8% of students is unqualified, showing the normal distribution that the ability level is high, students at low levels are few and the number of students at intermediate level is outstanding, with the statistical significance in accordance with the situation of students' ability distribution in reality.

5.4.4 The Corresponding Analysis of Students' Practical Ability Performance and Item Target Test Level

From Fig. 5.6, it could be found that the real difficulty of Morality and Society test items is in normal distribution, and students' abilities are in normal distribution in item difficulty performance, with fairly wide difficulty interval. It indicates that from the holistic perspective, the design of test item difficulty is quite scientific and reasonable.

According to Fig. 5.6, the corresponding relation between students' practical ability performance and item target test level (difficulty) and the main reasons for the inconsistency are analyzed and listed in the column of "Analysis and Explanation" to formulate Table 5.18.

From the analysis of Table 5.18, some conclusions could be further obtained as follows:

1. There are 7 items in total with real difficulty higher than the predicted difficulty. Among them, there are 4 items from uni-structural level raised to be multi-structural level, which are item 2 about confirming the age regulation for bike riding, item 4 about identifying the accurate self-protection methods in thunderstorm weather, item 12 about identifying the world famous buildings and item 34 about confirming the natural situation of Tibet autonomous region, which indicates that students are limited with the prior experiential influence, lacking some basic education of common sense, and there is deficiency in their knowledge and view. There is 1 item that raised from uni-structural level to relational level, i.e., item 32 about the application of scale. Students' performance is out of expectation, which might be related to that students are lack of measurement tool which makes them guess. And there are 2 items that raised from multi-structural level to relational level, which are item 27 about distinguishing the direction and position based on graphic expression and plan, and item 36 about understanding the relationship between the living environment and living way. The two items are both in the domain of "geography and environment", indicating that students have a deficiency in flexibly applying knowledge and in recognition of the natural relationship between social phenomena.

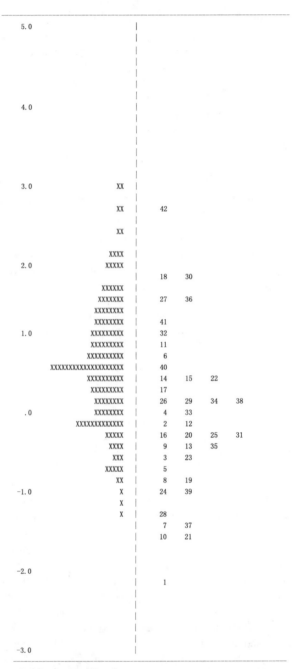

Each X represents 112 students

Fig. 5.6 Item difficulty and student ability distribution

5.4 Analysis and Discussion on the Test Results

Table 5.18 Corresponding analysis of students' practical ability and item target test level

Item number	Description of the ability to be assessed	Target test level	Real difficulty value	Analysis and explanation
1	Recognize the symbol of United Nations	U	−2.2	Students reaching uni-structural level are 93% and the average ability is 0.74 Real difficulty and students' ability are in accordance with item target test level
2	Confirm the age regulation for bike riding	U	−0.15	Students reaching uni-structural level are 67% and the average ability is 0.91 It might be that the riding situation in real-life influences students' accurate cognition of some regulations, which increases the real difficulty
3	Master the self-saving and self-protection method in fire accidents	U	−0.57	Students reaching uni-structural level are 75% and the average ability is 0.87 Real difficulty and students' ability are in accordance with item target test level
4	Identify the accurate self-protection methods in thunderstorm weather	U	0.09	Students reaching uni-structural level are 62% and the average ability is 0.91 Around 30% of students who might be misled by life experience choose wrong options, which increases the real difficulty
5	Clearly know the historical event of Burning of Opium Stocks in Humen	U	−0.62	Students reaching uni-structural level are 76% and the average ability is 0.86 Real difficulty and students' ability are in accordance with item target test level
6	Can accurately deal with the scald/empyrosis in daily life	M	0.73	Students reaching multi-structural level are 49% and the average ability is 0.95 Real difficulty and students' ability are in accordance with item target test level

(continued)

Table 5.18 (continued)

Item number	Description of the ability to be assessed	Target test level	Real difficulty value	Analysis and explanation
7	Know the related content of *Compulsory Education Law of the People's Republic of China* and *Law of the People's Republic of China on Protection of Minors*	U	−1.46	Students reaching uni-structural level are 87% and the average ability is 0.76. Real difficulty and students' ability are in accordance with item target test level
8	Identify the clothing feature of Chaoxian nationality	U	−0.8	Students reaching uni-structural level are 78% and the average ability is 0.80. Real difficulty and students' ability are in accordance with item target test level
9	Judge the truth or falseness of events and not readily believe others	M	−0.38	Students reaching multi-structural level are 71% and the average ability is 0.76. Students reaching uni-structural level are 24% and the average ability is 0.53. Real difficulty and students' ability are in accordance with item target test level
10	Gain the information about quality guarantee period from the food packing bag	R	−1.51	Students reaching relational level are 87% and the average ability is 0.73. Students reaching multi-structural level are 10% and the average ability is 0.42. According to SOLO taxonomy, the item is set at relational level. Actually, students have quite good knowledge of food quality protection period
11	How to self-save and save others in front of dangerous situation	M	0.9	Students reaching multi-structural level are 45% and the average ability is 0.95. Students reaching uni-structural level are 44% and the average ability is 0.53. Real difficulty and students' ability are in accordance with item target test level

5.4 Analysis and Discussion on the Test Results

Table 5.18 (continued)

Item number	Description of the ability to be assessed	Target test level	Real difficulty value	Analysis and explanation
12	Identifying the world-famous historical and cultural buildings	U	−0.05	Students reaching uni-structural level are only 65% and the average ability is 0.91 Around 30% of students lack the accurate cognition of world-famous historical and cultural buildings and choose the wrong options, which increases the real difficulty
13	Infer the damage degree of smoking for health	R	−0.39	Students reaching relational level are 72% and the average ability is 0.88 Students reaching multi-structural level are 20% and the average ability is 0.32 According to SOLO taxonomy, the item is set at relational level. Actually, students' ability to extract related information and to analyze based on diagram is fairly strong
14	Understand the best escaping method in earthquake	M	0.51	Students reaching multi-structural level are 53% and the average ability is 0.89 Students reaching uni-structural level are 39% and the average ability is 0.48 Real difficulty and students' ability are in accordance with item target test level
15	Can make judgment related to population problem based on dialogue information	R	0.49	Students reaching relational level are 54% and the average ability is 0.96 Students reaching multi-structural level are 23% and the average ability is 0.46 According to SOLO taxonomy, the item is set at relational level. Actually, students' ability to analyze problem based on item information is fairly strong

(continued)

Table 5.18 (continued)

Item number	Description of the ability to be assessed	Target test level	Real difficulty value	Analysis and explanation
16	Make clear the relationship between the climate features in the south and north of our country and agricultural production	M	−0.25	Students reaching multi-structural level are 69% and the average ability is 0.91 Students reaching uni-structural level are 11% and the average ability is 0.28 Real difficulty and students' ability are in accordance with item target test level
17	Understand the influence of globalization through the goods used in daily life	M	0.35	Students reaching multi-structural level are 57% and the average ability is 0.94 Students reaching uni-structural level are 22% and the average ability is 0.60 Real difficulty and students' ability are in accordance with item target test level
18	Can understand the conceptual meaning of "B.C. and A.D."	R	1.78	Students reaching relational level are 28% and the average ability is 1.26 Students reaching multi-structural level are 14% and the average ability is 0.74 Students reaching uni-structural level are 27% and the average ability is 0.44 Real difficulty and students' ability are in accordance with item target test level
19	Acquire information related to telephone development from the telephone statistical chart	M	−0.87	Students reaching multi-structural level are 79% and the average ability is 0.83 Students reaching uni-structural level are 1% and the average ability is 0.52 According to SOLO taxonomy, the item is set at multi-structural level. Actually, students' ability to analyze problem based on statistical chart is fairly strong

5.4 Analysis and Discussion on the Test Results

Table 5.18 (continued)

Item number	Description of the ability to be assessed	Target test level	Real difficulty value	Analysis and explanation
20	Clearly know and experience the democracy in class life	R	−0.27	Students reaching relational level are 69% and the average ability is 0.87 Students reaching multi-structural level are 7% and the average ability is 0.34 Students reaching uni-structural level are 13% and the average ability is 0.29 According to SOLO taxonomy, the item is set at relational level. Actually, students have fairly high ability to comprehensively analyze problem
21	Understand the rules of cleaning classroom sanitation	M	−1.52	Students reaching multi-structural level are 88% and the average ability is 0.77 Students reaching uni-structural level are 2% and the average ability is 0.04 According to SOLO taxonomy, the item is set at multi-structural level. Actually, students have fairly strong autonomous consciousness and ability
22	Know that human beings are a part of nature	M	0.52	Students reaching multi-structural level are 53% and the average ability is 0.99 Students reaching uni-structural level are 22% and the average ability is 0.51 Real difficulty and students' ability are in accordance with item target test level
23	Clearly know the change since Reform and Openness through the use of various tickets and certificates	U	−0.54	Students reaching uni-structural level are 74% and the average ability is 0.87 Real difficulty and students' ability are in accordance with item target test level

(continued)

Table 5.18 (continued)

Item number	Description of the ability to be assessed	Target test level	Real difficulty value	Analysis and explanation
24	Clearly know that global warming causes the reduction of snow cover	U	−0.92	Students reaching uni-structural level are 80% and the average ability is 0.86
				Real difficulty and students' ability are in accordance with item target test level
25	Confirm the climate difference at the southern and northern earth at Christmas	M	−0.20	Students reaching multi-structural level are 68% and the average ability is 0.94
				Students reaching uni-structural level are 11% and the average ability is 0.14
				Real difficulty and students' ability are in accordance with item target test level
26	Know the different sorting ways of rubbish	M	0.17	Students reaching multi-structural level are 60% and the average ability is 0.83
				Students reaching uni-structural level are 17% and the average ability is 0.60
				Real difficulty and students' ability are in accordance with item target test level
27	Distinguish the information presented in school plan based on the position of the Sun	M	1.57	Students reaching multi-structural level are only 31% and the average ability is 1.07
				Students reaching uni-structural level are 49% and the average ability is 0.59
				This indicates that students are deficient in the master of distinguishing geographical position and its plan, which accordingly increases the real difficulty of the item

(continued)

5.4 Analysis and Discussion on the Test Results

Table 5.18 (continued)

Item number	Description of the ability to be assessed	Target test level	Real difficulty value	Analysis and explanation
28	Know our country's Four Great Inventions	U	−1.25	Students reaching uni-structural level are 84% and the average ability is 0.81 Real difficulty and students' ability are in accordance with item target test level
29	Confirm our country's important festivals and the representative diets	M	0.19	Students reaching multi-structural level are 60% and the average ability is 0.99 Students reaching uni-structural level are 4% and the average ability is 0.25 Real difficulty and students' ability are in accordance with item target test level
30	Predict the future situation of population receiving education from the table information	R	1.88	Students reaching relational level are 26% and the average ability is 1.04 Students reaching multi-structural level are 38% and the average ability is 0.63 Students reaching uni-structural level are 17% and the average ability is 0.48 Real difficulty and students' ability are in accordance with item target test level
31	Identify the river's trend according to the direction in the illustration of Happy Island	U	−0.30	Students reaching uni-structural level are 70% and the average ability is 0.91 Real difficulty and students' ability are in accordance with item target test level

(continued)

Table 5.18 (continued)

Item number	Description of the ability to be assessed	Target test level	Real difficulty value	Analysis and explanation
32	Confirm the city according to the real distance of two places in Happy Island	U	1.04	Students reaching uni-structural level are only 42% and the average ability is 1.00 This indicates that students lack the ability to calculate the practical distance based on scale, or that it is not related in teaching or teaching materials, which increases the difficulty
33	Judge the city situation based on the basic information presented in the plan of Happy Island	M	0.12	Students reaching multi-structural level are 62% and the average ability is 0.95 Students reaching uni-structural level are 21% and the average ability is 0.41 Real difficulty and students' ability are in accordance with item target test level
34	Clearly know the natural situation of our country's Tibet autonomous region	U	0.25	Students reaching uni-structural level are only 59% and the average ability is 0.99 This indicates that students know little of the natural situation of our country's other areas, which increases the real difficulty
35	Clearly know the relationship between altitude and temperature	U	−0.37	Students reaching uni-structural level are 71% and the average ability is 0.90 Real difficulty and students' ability are in accordance with item target test level
36	Understand different natural environments influence people's living ways	M	1.61	Students reaching multi-structural level are 31% and the average ability is 1.07 Students reaching uni-structural level are 21% and the average ability is 0.79

(continued)

5.4 Analysis and Discussion on the Test Results

Table 5.18 (continued)

Item number	Description of the ability to be assessed	Target test level	Real difficulty value	Analysis and explanation
				This indicates that students lack deep understanding of the relationship between environment and people's life, which increases the real difficulty
37	Confirm the size of the land area in our country	U	−1.50	Students reaching uni-structural level are 87% and the average ability is 0.77
				Real difficulty and students' ability are in accordance with item target test level
38	Infer the living situation of Peking Man based on archaeological materials	M	0.27	Students reaching multi-structural level are 59% and the average ability is 0.95
				Students reaching uni-structural level are 25% and the average ability is 0.38
				Real difficulty and students' ability are in accordance with item target test level
39	Clearly know the historical event of Burning Old Summer Palace	M	−0.92	Students reaching uni-structural level are 80% and the average ability is 0.85
				This indicates that students know the historical event quite well, and their ability has been fairly lowly predicted
40	Clearly know the conflict between economic development and environmental protection	M	0.59	Students reaching multi-structural level are 52% and the average ability is 0.93
				Students reaching uni-structural level are 43% and the average ability is 0.48
				Real difficulty and students' ability are in accordance with item target test level

(continued)

Table 5.18 (continued)

Item number	Description of the ability to be assessed	Target test level	Real difficulty value	Analysis and explanation
41	Clearly know the main factors causing greenhouse effect and global warming	R	1.27	Students reaching relational level are 37% and the average ability is 0.96 Students reaching multi-structural level are 38% and the average ability is 0.68 Students reaching uni-structural level are 9% and the average ability is 0.29 Real difficulty and students' ability are in accordance with item target test level
42	Understand that the price change of live chickens is influenced by supply–demand relationship	R	2.69	Students reaching relational level are 15% and the average ability is 0.96 Students reaching multi-structural level are 70% and the average ability is 0.68 Students reaching uni-structural level are 7% and the average ability is 0.44 Real difficulty and students' ability are in accordance with item target test level

2. There are six items in total with real difficulty lower than the predicted difficulty. Among them, there are two items that lowered from multi-structural level to uni-structural level, which are item 21 about mastering the class and item 19 about acquiring information related to telephone development from the statistical chart; there are three items lowered from relational level to multi-structural level, which are item 13 about acquiring information related to relationship between smoking and health from the statistical chart, item 15 about making judgment related to population problem based on dialogue information, and item 20 about the sense of democracy in class life; and there is one item lowered from relational level to uni-structural level, which assesses the quality protection period. These changes indicate that first, the better integration of SOLO taxonomy and students' ability performance in specific subjects needs further practical exploration; second, from the perspective of information presentation, students can fairly effectively read and explain the information delivered by diagram per se, and organically link the question with the diagrammatic information to do further thinking and analysis, owning fairly strong diagrammatic analysis ability; and from the question orientation analysis, students perform fairly strong ability to solve problems, regarding those questions related to students' life. This might be closely related to that the teaching materials' presentation way is more vivid and multi-perspective since new curriculum reform started , to that the content is closer to life, and to that practice, inquiry and the link with life are more emphasized in teachers' teaching and students' learning ways.

From the analysis above, although there is some gap between the predicted difficulty of some items and the real difficulty, it does not influence the holistic analysis of item difficulty.

5.5 The Main Findings

Based on the result analysis of this survey, the main findings have been attained are as follows.

5.5.1 *Students' Social Development Level Almost Reaches the Requirements of Morality and Society Curriculum Standard, but Students' Holistic Social Ability Is Slightly Low*

In the present survey on the social ability of 18,024 students in Grade 6 primary school based on new curriculum standard, from the holistic results analysis, nearly 70% (67%) of students can fully meet the requirements of contents and abilities in curriculum standard, owning the basic social knowledge and skills, have certain of social abilities to analyze, to think and to judge, and have initially developed national sense, globalization sense, consciousness of social rules, and sense of democracy participation. Around 30% (28%) of students can basically meet the requirements of contents and abilities in curriculum standard, but they have a deficiency in the mastery of social knowledge and social skills. And there is a small proportion (4.8%) of students, with fairly weak social abilities, who have not met the standards yet. Meanwhile, it has been found that students' holistic ability performed slightly low in social science test, with only 67.8% of students who have completely qualified and above, while near one in third of students whose social development is basically qualified, with a deficiency in the mastery of social knowledge and social skills. This situation will fairly heavily influence students' existence in realistic society and sustainable development in future, to which enough attention should be paid.

5.5.2 Students' Mastery of Each Content Domain Is Fairly Balanced, with the Weakness in the Domain of Geography and Environment

In the four domains of citizen and society, health and safety, history and culture, and geography and environment, students' ability shows the situation as follows (Table 5.19).

From the perspective of content domains, the average score in the four domains are all less than 70%, indicating that students' holistic academic performance is slightly low. The average scores in the three domains of citizen and society (64%), health and safety (65%), history and culture (65%) are fairly close, which indicates that students perform quite well in the content as follows and there is a balance, such as national sense, globalization sense, consciousness of social rules, and sense of democracy participation, clearly knowing the related knowledge of law, mastering the knowledge to keep health and safety, knowing representative world historical culture, understanding historical knowledge, knowing and understanding important historical events and their influence, and accurately making analysis and judgment historical subjects and events. Among the four domains, the achievement

Table 5.19 Scoring of social development in each domain

Domains	Scoring			
	Minimum	Maximum	Mean	Standard deviation
Citizen and society	0	1	0.64	0.16
Health and safety	0	1	0.65	0.19
History and culture	0	1	0.65	0.23
Geography and environment	0	1	0.59	0.18

5.5 The Main Findings

in the domain of geography and environment is the lowest (59%), indicating that students' performance in the content learning below is comparatively weak, such as mastering some basic geographic knowledge and skills, understanding some basic geographic complexion about China and the world and the relationship between natural environment and people's life, and understanding some environmental and resource problems human beings face.

5.5.3 Students' Mastery of Basic Knowledge and Basic Skills of Society Is Fairly Satisfying, While the Ability to Solve Problems by Comprehensively Applying Acquired Knowledge Is to Be Improved

From the competency domains, students scoring percentage (76%) in recognition is obviously higher than in understanding and application, and the difference reaches the level of high significance (Table 5.20).

The data above indicates that, regarding recognition, most students' knowledge and mastery of basic social knowledge and basic skills, such as international knowledge, knowledge of law, historical knowledge, common knowledge of geography, and life skills, etc., are quite satisfying. While the scoring percentages in the abilities of understanding (57%) and application (59%) are comparatively low, which do not reach 60%, indicating that the performance of the two abilities is fairly comparatively weak and balanced. In the items of these two sections, it has found that students generally get higher response accuracy rate (over 60%) for the items closed to their life experience (such as the rules of democracy in class, issue of quality protection period, safety skills and results of global warming), for the items with fairly direct and singular relationship between subjects (such as the relationship between attitude and temperature, and the relationship between climate and crops, etc.) and for items with the representation of illustrations and diagrams, such as item 19 about acquiring information related to telephone development from the statistical chart and item 13 about acquiring information related to the relationship between smoking and health from the statistical chart, the real difficulty values of which are lower than that in prediction. It has also been found that students

Table 5.20 Scoring of social ability performance

Domains	Scoring			
	Minimum	Maximum	Mean	Standard deviation
Recognition	0	1	0.76	0.18
Understanding	0	1	0.57	0.16
Application	0	1	0.59	0.19

generally get lower response accuracy rate (less than 60%) for the items which slightly surpass their realistic life and present experience (such as earthquake and escaping method, relationship between living way and environment), for items whose the internal logic relationship within subjects is complicated, multiple, and abstract (such as the understanding conceptual meaning of "B.C. and A.D.", relationship between human being and nature, relationship between the price change and supply–demand and relationship between climate and human being activities) and for the items requiring students to solve problems by flexibly and comprehensively applying various types of knowledge and various abilities (such as the position identifying in combination with realistic situation, choice of self-protection in dilemma and extracting effective information to do future prediction, etc.). This indicates that students have the ability to do initial analysis and thinking of subjects and phenomena by making use of life experience and with the help of diagrammatic information. However, the width and depth of thinking need to be improved and the ability and sense to flexibly apply knowledge acquired and to comprehensively solve problems are to be strengthened.

5.5.4 The Social Development Test Paper Has Fairly High Stability and Is Quite Scientific

The statistical results of both test paper and students' performance show that the present test paper has fairly high validity and reliability, difficulty coverage is quite wide, item discrimination is fairly reasonable, and fit index is pretty satisfying. Item characteristic curve shape is in accordance with IRT model and the correlation coefficients with other subjects also reach a very significant level. The quality of test items is fairly stable, which to the most extent guarantees the scientificalness and effectiveness of this large-scale test, in the aspect of assessment instrument.

5.6 Countermeasures and Suggestions

Based on the test results of Morality and Society curriculum teaching and learning quality monitoring and students' developmental level with the main line of students' social development, with the combination of related causal factor analysis, the countermeasures and suggestions below are proposed to improve the Morality and Society curriculum teaching and learning quality and to accelerate students' social development.

5.6 Countermeasures and Suggestions

5.6.1 To Emphasize and Strengthen Morality and Society Curriculum, and Its Teaching and Learning, to Effectively Guarantee the Subject Position

The present test result holistically shows that students' ability in social development is slightly low, with only 70% (67%) of students who have completely achieve the requirements of content and ability in curriculum standard. This result and situation are directly related to the subject position in which Morality and Society locates and its existing situation. At present, many educational institutions and schools do not recognize the importance of the curriculum and do not pay enough attention, resulting in that the curriculum position cannot be guaranteed and stays in embarrassing situation due to the frequent marginalization. Because of this, various problems derive, such as that the teachers' team is not stable, their professional degree is low, the teaching level and quality are worrying, the curriculum time is randomly taken by other subjects and the assessment and monitoring are not enough, etc. The present survey further indicates that the phenomenon of taking Morality and Society curriculum time for other use generally exists, with 42% of schools showing that the reduction of curriculum time exists.

Morality and Society is a "comprehensive curriculum, with children's social life as basis, to accelerate students' development of good morality and social development". The curriculum design is oriented at "assisting students to participate in society and learn how to a human being" and further "establishing foundations for students to be qualified citizens of socialism", which is crucial for individuals' morality growth, personality construction, and social adaptability development. To improve the situation of Morality and Society curriculum and to elevate students' academic achievement level, educational institutions at each level and schools should be first required to pay attention to this curriculum, to strengthen the curriculum construction, to persist executing the national unified curriculum standard and teaching plan, to guarantee the curriculum provision, to give enough curriculum time, and to complete the teaching task to really carry out the curriculum teaching and learning.

5.6.2 To Build Fairly Stable Teachers' Team and to Improve Their Professional Development

The present survey shows the age distribution of Morality and Society teachers that there are 21% of students aged 30 below and teachers aged from 31 to 40 are 42%, with 37% of teachers aged 41 above. Compared with Chinese and Mathematics, the percentage of teachers at the intermediate age period is about 10% less, and the percentages of new teachers and aged teachers are quite high. Most teachers hold a concurrent post in other curriculum teaching or management work, and they devote much more energy to the "main subjects" they teach. Compared with the other three subjects, the opportunities for Morality and Society teachers to participate in training are the fewest, especially for the teachers in countryside schools whose opportunities are about half fewer than that in city. In addition, according to a survey in Beijing, in 2008, "the background knowledge and related educational and psychological knowledge of teachers giving classes are fairly deficient, and they need further understanding of the curriculum teaching goals and requirements."

These results indicate that Morality and Society teachers' team both has the internal deficiency and is limited by the external objective environment, which makes teachers' professional development face extremely serious obstacles and challenges. To completely change the situation that the professional development level of teachers' team is not high and to improve teachers' professional development, it is suggested that the nation further guarantees the profession of teachers' team, such as building teachers' team with full-time teachers as core (Each central primary school in towns is equipped with at least 1 or 2 Morality and Society full-time teachers and each complete primary school in counties, districts, and cities is equipped with at least 2 Morality and Society full-time teachers) and guarantees that Morality and Society teachers have equivalent rights and duties with other subject teachers in the aspects of professional title evaluation, promotion, prizes, training, material benefits, etc. Only with the specialization of teachers' team, it can gradually guarantee teachers to chase for the profession without distractions, to study curriculum and teaching materials with concentration, actively carry out teaching exploration and creativity with brevity, to learn professional basic knowledge, to participate in professional training, etc. Only with the holistic improvement of teachers' team, it can thoroughly improve the educational and teaching quality of Morality and Society curriculum to finally accelerate students' learning and to improve their academic achievement level.

5.6.3 To Transform the Beliefs and Approaches of Teaching and Learning and to Pay Attention to the Development of Students' Internal Thinking Level and the Ability to Comprehensively Solve Problems

The new curriculum has been carried out for more than ten years. The present survey particularly designed questions on the transformation of teaching and learning approaches to check whether new curriculum beliefs are really applied in practice. The results show that 47.3% of students think their teachers often "encourage students to propose questions", 35.0% of students think their teachers often "ask students to discuss questions in groups", 41.7% of students frequently feel that "they listen to teachers most of time in class", 35% of students think their teachers often "ask them to look for materials and to report for communication", etc. These data indicate that since the execution of Morality and Society new curriculum,

5.6 Countermeasures and Suggestions

certain changes do take place to teachers' teaching approach and there is certain of autonomy in students' learning approach. However, compared with that of Chinese and Mathematics, the degree is fairly low. That is to say, the traditional beliefs and approaches of teaching and learning still continue in Morality and Society curriculum.

The present survey finds out that teachers give more support for students' self-access learning, and then students' academic achievement level is higher. Thus, it could be said that the results of students' holistic performance of academic achievement in Morality and Society are slightly low, less than 5% of students like Morality and Society curriculum, and most students do not have interest in the curriculum and are directly related to the transformation degree of the curriculum teachers' teaching approach.

Development of students' abilities to think and analyze social subjects and phenomena and to solve social problems is one of the main teaching goals in Morality and Society curriculum. Through the test, it could be seen that there is quite some difference between students' performance on this aspect and the satisfying situation. Therefore, in the teaching and learning of Morality and Society, teachers' recognition of the aim and significance of new curriculum reform should be continuously improved further, accelerating teachers' deep transformation in the curriculum beliefs and teachers' role to practically transform teaching and learning approaches, to lead students to self-access learning and explore learning, in which students find and solve problems and gain the happiness of self-access learning. Teaching and learning should face society and life, and opportunities should be actively created for students to participate in social practice, to experience social life, to observe and think social phenomena, and to analyze and judge social problems. In this way, students' thinking level can be gradually improved and their social development can be accelerated.

5.6.4 To Build the Management Institution of Monitoring and Assessment on Subject Teaching and Learning Quality and the Sustainable Assessment System

Educational institutions and schools should strengthen the management of Morality and Society curriculum teaching process and semester evaluation to avoid the random teaching and perfunctory teaching, increase teachers' recognition and behavior of teaching researches, and to finally achieve the aim of improving educational and teaching quality and accelerating students' development. To supervise and urge schools' strengthening curriculum management, it is suggested that provinces and municipalities should build the supervision and direction system (teaching process) for the local teaching and regular sampling test system (school year test), etc. To macroscopically carry out effective monitoring of students' academic achievement, the national monitoring institution and system of educational quality should also be built. Various types of assessment methods should be explored and national monitoring and assessment of schools and students should be carried out continuously and traceably to guarantee the development and quality of national basic education.

Chapter 6
Survey Report on Factors Influencing Students' Academic Achievement

6.1 Introduction

Besides the subject tests in the present students' academic achievement survey, potential factors influencing students' learning outcomes are surveyed with questionnaire. The participants surveyed are students participating in tests and schools. Following the test, the students participating in the subject tests filled in a student questionnaire, with individuals' information including personal background information, family background information and family support, interest in learning, attitude to learning and self-efficacy, subject teaching and learning approach in class, self-access learning ability, out-of-school activities, learning load, etc. School questionnaire is filled in by the school principals, including school basic information, principal's basic information, quality of teachers' team of subjects, teachers' mobility, school running situation, educational and teaching activities, etc.

There are 372 schools participating in the survey, with 310 valid school questionnaires, in which 47.25% of schools are municipal, 11.3% of schools are in counties, 26.21% are in towns, and 15.21% are countryside schools. There are 272 primary schools, 20 9-year compulsory education schools, 11 junior high schools (Grade 1 in 5–4 system schools or schools with primary school high grades affiliated). In the comparative analysis between cities and towns, schools in counties are divided into the municipal category. The valid number of student questionnaires is 17,258 (18,226 students participated in the test). Student questionnaires come from 351 schools, with 303 schools corresponding with those from which school questionnaires come.

Data analysis methods include that descriptive analysis was first carried out for the factors related to academic achievement, presenting students' learning environment, and situation, and then univariate analysis was done with all factors influencing academic achievement to test the significance of the correlation with academic achievement. The factors with significance were involved with multivariate regression analysis, in which univariate multilevel linear model was employed, which could be read in the report. The statistical software programs are SPSS17.0 and MLWIN2.10.

6.2 Results and Findings

6.2.1 Holistic Distribution Feature of Students' Academic Achievement

6.2.1.1 Regional and City and Countryside Distribution Feature of Students' Academic Achievement

With the univariate nonparametric test, it has found that students' academic achievement in the east is significantly better than that of students in the west and in the middle, with insignificance between western and middle students' academic achievement. Among students in the east, the percentage of students with academic achievement at level 5 reaches 26.58%, with 9.4% and 10.07% higher than that in the middle and west, respectively. And among students in the middle and in the west, the percentage of students at level 1 is both approaching 1/4. City school students' academic achievement is significantly higher than that in town and countryside schools ($Z = -6.663$, $p < 0.01$) (Tables 6.1 and 6.2).

To reduce the influence of sampling error, the variables of region and city and countryside are both tested at the same time with multilevel model, in which only constant and variables of region and city and countryside are contained, with data divided into the three levels of sampling district or county, school, and student. The test result shows that students' academic achievement in the east is 1.755 (standard error = 0.718, $p < 0.05$, $n = 13,110$) and 2.134 (standard error = 1.024, $p < 0.05$, $n = 13,110$) standard scores significantly higher than that of students in the west and in the middle, respectively. Within the region, countryside students' academic achievement is 0.735 (standard error = 0.335, $p < 0.05$, $n = 13,110$) standard scores lower than that in city. And there is no significant difference between students' academic achievement in the middle and in the west, with 0.379 standard scores (standard error = 0.96, $p > 0.05$, $n = 13,110$) as the coefficient of variation.

Table 6.1 Regional distribution of students' academic achievement (%)

	Level percentage of students' academic achievement (5 is the highest level)					
	1	2	3	4	5	Total
East	11.26	18.97	20.06	23.13	26.58	100
Middle	24.04	20.32	19.55	18.92	17.17	100
West	23.40	21.12	21.17	17.83	16.48	100

6.2 Results and Findings

Table 6.2 City and countryside distribution of students' academic achievement (%)

	Level percentage of students' academic achievement (5 is the highest level)					
	1	2	3	4	5	Total
City	19.20	19.60	20.00	20.40	20.80	100
Countryside	23.00	21.50	19.70	17.70	18.10	100

6.2.1.2 Distribution Feature of Students' Academic Achievement by Gender

With the nonparametric test, it has found that there is no significant difference between male and female students' academic achievement in Mathematics ($Z = -0.10$, $p > 0.05$), while male students' academic achievement is higher than that of female students in Science ($Z = -3.86$, $p < 0.05$), and female students' academic achievement is higher than that of male students in Reading and Morality and Society ($Z = -11.48$, $p < 0.05$; $Z = -2.19$, $p < 0.05$). With the statistical effect size test, the difference between male and female students' academic achievement is not significant (Tables 6.3, 6.4, 6.5, 6.6, and 6.7).

Table 6.3 Distribution of students' academic achievement by gender—Reading (%)

Gender	Reading level of students' academic achievement (5 is the highest level)				
	1	2	3	4	5
Male	10.59	30.69	34.52	22.74	1.47
Female	7.16	26.48	36.65	27.14	2.58

Table 6.4 Distribution of students' academic achievement by gender—Mathematics (%)

Gender	Mathematics level of students' academic achievement (5 is the highest level)				
	1	2	3	4	5
Male	2.66	19.29	48.70	19.69	9.66
Female	2.28	19.00	50.14	19.25	9.33

Table 6.5 Distribution of students' academic achievement by gender—Science (%)

Gender	Science level of students' academic achievement (5 is the highest level)				
	1	2	3	4	5
Male	4.15	23.79	41.68	23.71	6.67
Female	4.54	25.43	42.52	20.83	6.68

Table 6.6 Distribution of students' academic achievement by gender—Morality and Society (%)

Gender	Morality and Society level of students' academic achievement (5 is the highest level)				
	1	2	3	4	5
Male	5.26	28.58	39.90	19.58	6.67
Female	4.36	27.44	41.70	20.04	6.46

Table 6.7 Statistical effect size test of gender difference (%)

	Cohen's (d)	Effect size (r)
Reading academic achievement	−0.2	−0.1
Mathematics academic achievement	0.01	0.00
Science academic achievement	0.05	0.02
Morality and Society academic achievement	−0.03	−0.02

6.2.2 Students' School Learning Situation and Environment

6.2.2.1 Students' School Learning Environment

Regarding the schools participating in the survey, there are 272 complete and incomplete primary schools and 31 9-year compulsory education schools. The average school size of students is 194, with the smallest size of 44 students and largest size of 5148 students.

1. Quality of Principals' Team

The percentage of female principals is 37.1%, with the average age of 43.79 years and the average teaching age of 23.82 years. 95.79% of principals have qualified certificate, and 59.55% of principals have undergraduate educational background or above (Table 6.8).

The average frequency of principals participating in training at or above county level is 2.82 times in the present school year, with 0 as the frequency for 12.5% of principals. 69.6% of principals in the sample schools also teach.

The frequency of principals' listening to classes each semester is 36.14 times (standard deviation is 17.3, n = 295) (Table 6.9).

2. Quality of Teachers' Team

Certificate

No matter in countryside or in city, the percentage of teachers' qualified certificate in sample schools is 99%. And the percentage of principals with undergraduate certificate or above reaches 45.51%. The certificate difference between countryside

Table 6.8 Distribution of principals' degree (%)

	Region			School location	
	East	Middle	West	City	Countryside
High school and below	0.00	0.00	0.00	0.00	0.00
Specialized secondary schools	0.90	7.50	0.00	1.11	8.59
Junior college	32.43	32.50	63.16	27.78	48.44
Undergraduate	61.26	51.25	36.84	60.56	42.19
Graduate and above	5.41	8.75	0.00	10.56	0.78

6.2 Results and Findings

Table 6.9 Classes principals listen each semester

	Classes principals listen each semester	
	Average	Standard deviation
East	39	14
Middle	37	18
West	23	14
City	39	17
Countryside	32	17

schools and city schools mainly represents in the high degree certificate, with the fact that the percentage of principals with undergraduate certificate or above is 50.39% in city schools, while 32.38% in countryside schools.

Regarding Grade 6 teachers with undergraduate certificate or above, the percentage is 40.80% for Chinese subject, with 42.59% and 35.89%, respectively, for city and for countryside; the percentage is 33.76% for Mathematics subject, with 35.98% and 27.92%, respectively, for city and for countryside; the percentage is 31.66% for Science subject, with 37.55% and 23.03%, respectively, for city and for countryside; and the percentage is 37.31% for Morality and Society subject, with 43.01% and 27.19%, respectively, for city and for countryside. Overall, Chinese teachers' certificate is fairly high no matter in countryside or in city, while Science teachers' certificate is fairly low.

Professional title

Regarding teachers' professional title, the percentages of Grade 6 teachers without intermediate or above professional title for Chinese, Mathematics, Science, and Morality and Society, respectively, are 12.8%, 14%, 32.7%, and 29%. And the percentages of Chinese teachers without intermediate or above professional title in city and in countryside, respectively, are 8.3% and 19.5%, with 11.3% and 18% for Mathematics, 32% and 32.8% for Science, and 27.1%, and 31.1% for Morality and Society.

Age structure of teachers' team

The main body of teachers for each subject is youth and middle-aged teachers. Especially for Chinese subject, the percentage of teachers at or below age 40 is 76.44%, with 12% higher than that of other three subjects. The percentage of teachers at or above age 51 in the west is fairly high, which is over 15% for each subject, higher than the average, with 8.33% for Chinese, 6.53% for Mathematics, 4.58% for Science, and 7.32% for Morality and Society. Regarding teachers' aging problem, the difference between city and countryside is not big (Fig. 6.1; Table 6.10).

Backbone teachers

The percentages of the schools without Grade-6 backbone teachers at county level or above for the subjects of Chinese, Mathematics, Science, and Morality and

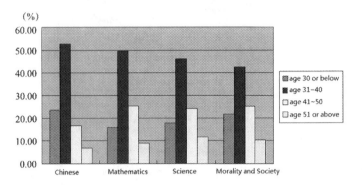

Fig. 6.1 Age distribution of each subject teacher

Table 6.10 Age distribution of each subject teacher (%)

	Age 30 or below	Age 31–40	Age 41–50	Age 51 or above
Chinese	23.74	52.70	16.65	6.91
Mathematics	15.97	49.47	25.53	9.03
Science	17.88	46.14	24.28	11.70
Morality and Society	21.63	42.63	25.32	10.42

Society, respectively, are 53.25%, 57%, 80.73%, and 79.8% of the total sample schools. The percentages for the city and countryside schools are 51.38% and 56.35% for Chinese subject, 54.44% and 61.11% for Mathematics subject, 77.65% and 85.95% for Mathematics subject, and 77.01% and 84.43% for Morality and Society subject.

Substitute teachers

The percentages of the schools with substitute teachers in Grade 6 for the subjects of Chinese, Mathematics, Science and Morality and Society, respectively, are 11.61%, 12.01%, 3.97%, and 6.04% of the sample schools.

Teacher training opportunities

The average training opportunities per teacher for Grade-6 teachers in the present school year for the subjects of Chinese, Mathematics, Science, and Morality and Society all are once, with the lowest training opportunities per teacher for Morality and Society subject. The training opportunities for countryside teachers are obviously fewer than that for city teachers, with the number of training opportunities per teacher for each subject lower than city. Especially for Science and Morality and Society, the training opportunities are almost half fewer (Table 6.11; Fig. 6.2).

3. Conditions for School Running

In the sampling districts, every 11 students share 1 computer, with the ratio of students versus computers 7.99 for the east, 13.67 for the middle, and 15.77 for the

6.2 Results and Findings

Table 6.11 Average training opportunities per teacher for Grade 6 teachers in the present school year for each subject

	Number of schools	Chinese	Mathematics	Science	Morality and Society
City	174	1.15	1.12	1.40	1.03
Countryside	124	1.11	0.95	0.73	0.54
Total	298	1.14	1.07	1.12	0.85

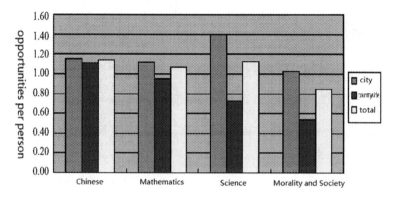

Fig. 6.2 Opportunities for each subject

west. And the ratio of students verse computers is 10.77 for the city and 11.85 for the countryside. Every 2.3 teachers share 1 computer to prepare classes in total, and the ratio is 1.4 for the east, 3.8 for the middle, and 5 for the west; 2.2 for the city; and 2.8 for the countryside.

The difference of functional classroom size for each student between schools is fairly large. The extreme values of some schools make the average value high. Actually, overall, the functional classroom size for each student of 75% of schools is below 1.36 m². The average value of the functional classroom size for each student is 1.31 m² (standard deviation = 2 m²), with the average value of 1.94 m² (standard deviation = 2.5 m²) for the east, 0.89 m² (standard deviation = 1.47 m²) for the middle, and 1.04 m² (standard deviation = 1.85 m²) for the west; 1.35 m² (standard deviation = 2.06 m²) for the city students; and 1.27 m² (standard deviation = 2 m²) for the countryside students.

The average number of books for each student is 15.89 (standard deviation = 12.82), with the average number of 21.03 (standard deviation = 10.22) for the east, 11.32 (standard deviation = 12.54) for the middle, and 19.62 (standard deviation = 14.02) for the west; 17.64 (standard deviation = 14.28) for the city; and 13.55 (standard deviation = 9.97) for the countryside.

The experimental equipment of 46% of sample schools cannot satisfy the requirements of grouping experimental teaching regulated in the textbooks. The percentages of schools choosing "basically can satisfy" in the east and in the west

Table 6.12 Whether experimental equipment can satisfy the requirements of grouping experimental teaching regulated in the textbooks (%)

	Total	City	Countryside	East	Middle	West
Fully cannot satisfy	20.62	16.87	25.00	7.62	30.26	17.65
Basically cannot satisfy	25.43	25.90	25.00	21.90	32.24	5.88
Basically can satisfy	41.58	44.58	37.90	52.38	31.58	52.94
Fully can satisfy	12.37	12.65	12.10	18.10	5.92	23.53

are similar, which are above 52%. It needs to discuss the reason that the school running condition has been improved a lot with the strong support of the nation or the similarity is caused by the misunderstanding of the grouping experimental teaching requirements regulated in the textbooks or their standard is fairly low. A small part of schools in the advanced east fully cannot satisfy the teaching requirements, with the percentage of 7.62%. The percentage of schools in the city choosing "basically and fully can satisfy teaching requirements" is 7.23% higher than that in the countryside (Table 6.12).

4. Teaching Research Activities and Family–School Communication

The average time for sample schools to carry out the new curriculum standards is 6.38 years (standard deviation = 1.18, n = 303), and all schools participate or organize various teaching research activities. The subject groups in 52.98% of schools organize teaching research activities at least once each week, and the grade groups in 42.23% of schools organize teaching research activities at least once each week, while the frequency for entire school teachers' teaching research activities or district teaching research activities is fairly low. However, 43.79% of schools organize entire school teachers' teaching research activities 2–3 times every semester and 62.25% of schools participate in activities at district level or above 2–3 times every semester. The frequency for the teaching research activities of schools in the east, in the middle, and in the west goes lower. And the percentages of schools with subject groups organizing teaching research activities at least once each week in the east and in the middle are 30 and 20% higher than that in the west. Regarding the participation in district activities, the percentages of schools choosing once every month both in the east and in the middle reach 30% above, while the percentage is only 8% in the west. The frequency for city schools' teaching research activities is obviously higher than that of countryside schools, and the percentage difference is 10% for the subject groups' teaching research activities at least once a week, and the percentage difference is 24% for that of grade groups. And for the participation in teaching research activities at district level or above 1–2 times each month, the percentage is 10% higher for city schools than for countryside schools (Table 6.13).

The class hours spent on class listening by teachers of the subjects surveyed from all sample schools are 16.99 class hours for Mathematics, 17.31 class hours for Chinese, 12.85 class hours for Science, and 12.83 class hours for Morality and

6.2 Results and Findings

Table 6.13 Research activities on teaching in school (%)

		Total	Region East	Region Middle	Region West	School location City	School location Countryside
Subject groups' teaching research activities	At least once a week	52.98	63.06	50.97	30.56	56.74	47.15
	1–2 times every month	38.08	34.23	34.84	63.89	37.64	39.02
	2–3 times every semester	8.94	2.70	14.19	5.56	5.62	13.82
	Never	0.00	0.00	0.00	0.00	0.00	0.00
Grade groups' teaching research activities	At least once a week	42.23	55.56	35.48	30.30	51.98	27.12
	1–2 times every month	35.14	37.04	36.77	21.21	35.03	35.59
	2–3 times every semester	16.89	5.56	21.29	33.33	10.17	27.12
	Never	5.74	1.85	6.45	15.15	2.82	10.17
Entire school teachers' teaching research activities	At least once a week	15.69	13.51	18.35	10.81	17.98	11.81
	1–2 times every month	39.87	43.24	33.54	56.76	38.76	41.73
	2–3 times every semester	43.79	42.34	47.47	32.43	42.13	46.46
	Never	0.65	0.90	0.63	0.00	1.12	0.00
Participation in district teaching research activities	At least once a week	4.64	6.48	4.43	0.00	6.21	2.42
	1–2 times every month	30.79	38.89	30.38	8.33	35.03	25.00
	2–3 times every semester	62.25	54.63	63.92	77.78	55.93	70.97
	Never	2.32	0.00	1.27	13.89	2.82	1.61

Table 6.14 Class hours spent on class listening by subject teachers every semester

		Mathematics	Chinese	Science	Morality and Society
Overall	Average	16.99	17.31	12.85	12.83
	Standard deviation	7.67	7.63	7.90	8.06
East	Average	19.07	19.98	14.92	14.72
	Standard deviation	7.66	7.62	8.07	8.20
Middle	Average	16.97	16.95	12.36	12.63
	Standard deviation	7.57	7.35	7.87	8.05
West	Average	11.03	11.05	8.73	7.97
	Standard deviation	4.21	4.17	5.26	5.21
City	Average	18.15	18.15	14.72	14.67
	Standard deviation	7.41	7.26	7.17	7.45
Countryside	Average	15.18	15.95	10.27	10.29
	Standard deviation	7.45	7.74	8.19	8.23

Society every semester. Overall, the class hours spent on class listening by teachers in the east, middle, and west gradually decrease. The number of class hours spent on class listening by teachers in the east is higher than that in the middle and in the west, with 2.11 and 8.05 class hours more for Mathematics, 3.03 and 8.92 class hours more for Chinese, 2.57 and 6.19 class hours more for Science, and 2.09 and 6.75 class hours more for Morality and Society. Compared with the east and the middle, there is a quite large gap for the west. The number of class hours spent on class listening by teachers in the city is higher than that in the countryside, with 2.97 class hours more for Mathematics, 2.20 class hours more for Chinese, 4.45 class hours more for Science, and 4.38 class hours more for Morality and Society. Compared between subjects, class hours spent by teachers of Chinese and Mathematics which are main subjects are similar and are more than the teachers of Science and Morality and Society, of which the class hours spent on listening classes are also similar. Schools in the east and in the middle pay more attention to the communication activities of Science and Morality and Society than schools in the west, and schools in the city also emphasize more than schools in the countryside (Table 6.14).

It could be seen that 95.8% of schools organize parent meeting once or more every semester, and there is no big difference between east, middle, and west, but 2.5% of schools in the middle never organize parent meetings. The percentage of city schools organizing parent meetings twice or more every semester is 10% higher than that of countryside schools, with 3.13% of countryside schools never organizing parent meetings (Table 6.15).

6.2 Results and Findings

Table 6.15 Frequency of organizing parent meetings (%)

	Total	Region			School location	
		East	Middle	West	City	Countryside
Twice or more every semester	38.19	36.94	38.13	42.11	42.78	32.03
Once every semester	57.16	61.26	55.63	55.26	55.00	60.94
Once every school year	2.91	1.80	3.75	2.63	2.22	3.91
Never	1.29	0.00	2.50	0.00	0.00	3.13

6.2.2.2 Educational and Teaching Factors

1. Teaching Ways

Among the four subjects, students assess the self-access learning supported by the mathematical teaching and learning ways highest, while assess the teaching and learning of subjects of Morality and Society and Science lowest.

Regarding the teaching and learning way for Science class, 29% of students think their Science teachers seldom or never encourage them to propose questions, 35% of students report that they never or seldom see teachers' demonstration experiment, 36% of students report that they never or seldom make Science experimental or survey plan with teachers' direction, 46% of students report that they never or seldom independently carry out Science experiment or survey, 38% of students report that they never or seldom do Science experiment or survey with classmates as a team, and 43% of students report that they listen to teachers most of time in class.

Regarding the teaching and learning way for Morality and Society class, 28% of students think their teachers seldom or never encourage them to propose questions, 20% of students report that their teachers often ask them to read books on their own, 14% of students report that Morality and Society class often change into self-learning class in which they do other subjects' schoolwork, 32% of students report that their teachers never or seldom organize students into groups to discuss questions or carry out various types of social survey, 63% of students report that they never or seldom pay visits or participate in social practice activities with the entire class together, 55% of students report that their teachers never or seldom organize students to do role-plays or practice based on the content learned, and 27% of students report that they listen to teachers most of time in class.

The higher the support degree from teachers' teaching way for self-access learning, the higher students' academic achievement is. From the perspective of region, compared with that of the east and of the west, the teaching way of teachers in the middle does not well support students' self-access learning, and the percentage of teachers' encouraging students to propose questions is lower than that in the east and in the west, with the serious phenomenon of cramming education. From the perspective of city and countryside, the teaching way of teachers in the

Table 6.16 Correlation between teaching way and students' academic achievement

		The support degree for self-access learning from Mathematical teaching way	The support degree for self-access learning from Chinese teaching way	The support degree for self-access learning from Scientific teaching way	The support degree for self-access learning from Morality and Society teaching way
Reading academic achievement	Product-moment correlation	0.172**	0.145**	0.091**	0.113**
	P value (two-tailed)	0.000	0.000	0.000	0.000
	Number of students	15,400	15,543	15,385	15,362
Mathematics academic achievement	Product-moment correlation	0.230**	0.169**	0.150**	0.165**
	P value (two-tailed)	0.000	0.000	0.000	0.000
	Number of students	16,511	16,679	16,501	16,475
Science academic achievement	Product-moment correlation	0.172**	0.140**	0.119**	0.142**
	P value (two-tailed)	0.000	0.000	0.000	0.000
	Number of students	15,025	15,180	15,018	14,985
Morality and Society academic achievement	Product-moment correlation	0.212**	0.189**	0.161**	0.193**
	P value (two-tailed)	0.000	0.000	0.000	0.000
	Number of students	16,577	16,743	16,567	16,538

Note ** means reaching significance level of 0.01

city better supports students' self-access learning, and the difference is not as large as that between the regions of east, middle, and west (Tables 6.16, 6.17, and 6.18).

2. Arrangement of class time

About 60% of students think teachers can follow the curriculum schedule. The percentage of students thinking the number of classes in accordance with that of the curriculum schedule is 61% for Mathematics, 57% for Chinese, 58% for Science, and 56% for Morality and Society. For Science and Morality and Society, there, respectively, are 40% and 42% of students proposing that the class time is reduced, while 36% and 41% of students, respectively, propose that Mathematics and Chinese class time is added. Compared with the east and the west, teachers in the middle region perform worst in following the class time plan, adding time to

6.2 Results and Findings

Table 6.17 Teaching ways (%)

	Never	Seldom	Sometimes	Often
About Math class, teachers encourage us to propose questions	2.26	8.90	28.80	60.05
About Math class, teachers encourage us to solve problems in different ways	0.99	4.21	18.89	75.91
About Math class, teachers encourage us to talk about our thoughts bravely even if we make mistakes	1.56	3.55	9.67	85.22
About Math class, teachers can elicit mathematical questions from our learning and living environment	1.99	8.24	27.68	62.09
About Math class, teachers divide us into groups for discussion	6.86	17.21	30.86	45.07
About Math class, teachers always tell us the key to the question in a hurry	65.09	25.87	5.32	3.72
About Math class, teachers ask us to find examples in daily life when delivering new knowledge	2.20	7.73	27.71	62.37
About Math class, in class, most of the time is devoted to listening to teachers	5.54	19.20	34.97	40.29
About Chinese class, teachers encourage us to propose questions	2.25	6.99	21.69	69.08
About Chinese class, teachers guide us to read out passages in textbooks in different ways	2.71	8.57	22.34	66.39
About Chinese class, teachers require us to silently read passages in textbooks independently	1.97	8.44	28.09	61.50
About Chinese class, teachers guide us to grasp key sentences or words to understand the main idea	0.75	2.30	10.85	86.10
About Chinese class, teachers divide us into groups for discussion	4.81	13.65	30.26	51.28
About Chinese class, a different understanding of the texts is allowed in class	4.59	9.41	26.29	59.71
About Chinese class, teachers give us instruction to read extracurricular books.	2.71	8.03	22.44	66.82
About Chinese class, in class, most of the time is devoted to listening to teachers	6.83	17.23	33.47	42.47
About Science class, teachers encourage us to propose questions	10.27	19.31	25.48	44.94
About Science class, we observe teachers conducting scientific experiments	13.69	21.59	27.85	36.87
About Science class, scientific experiments or investigation plans are made under teachers' guide	15.01	20.86	26.85	37.28
About Science class, we do experiments or investigations independently	18.32	27.29	28.36	26.03

(continued)

Table 6.17 (continued)

	Never	Seldom	Sometimes	Often
About Science class, we form groups with classmates to do experiments or investigations	17.35	20.68	25.62	36.35
About Science class, we make a note of the process and the result of experiments and investigations by ourselves	17.09	23.62	26.66	32.64
About Science class, we give a report and share our achievements in class.	15.91	20.35	24.55	39.19
About Science class, in class, most of the time is devoted to listening to teachers	7.73	17.82	31.86	42.60
About Morality and Society class, teachers encourage us to propose questions	10.49	17.61	24.65	47.25
About Morality and Society class, we learn this subject on our own by reading books	23.42	29.53	27.46	19.58
About Morality and Society class, we usually do self-learning or do homework of other subjects	44.73	25.40	16.34	13.54
About Morality and Society class, teachers ask us to look for materials and give a report and share with other students in class	13.87	18.29	31.21	36.63
About Morality and Society class, we form groups with classmates for discussion and for doing social investigations	18.65	21.66	24.68	35.02
About Morality and Society class, the entire class goes out for visits or does social practices together	38.51	24.11	18.50	18.88
About Morality and Society class, teachers organize students to do role-plays or practice according to what we learn	30.16	24.52	22.27	23.05
About Morality and Society class, in class, most of the time is devoted to listening to teachers	9.32	18.17	30.86	41.66

Mathematics and Chinese classes, higher than other regions by 10%, and the behavior of reducing time from Science and Morality and Society classes is serious, with class time reduction for Science class more than that in the east and that in the west by 16% and 14%, for Morality and Society class by 18% and 11%, respectively. In countryside schools, the behavior of adding time to Mathematics and Chinese classes and of reducing time from Science and Morality and Society is much (Tables 6.19 and 6.20).

3. School atmosphere

Most students feel safe in school, while there are still 10% of students do not feel safe in school. And 12% of students think they do not get equal treatments in school and 36.35% of students think that there is bully or insulting phenomenon among students. And the negative feelings are fairly obvious for the group of students with

6.2 Results and Findings

Table 6.18 Teaching ways by region and location (%)

		Region			School location	
		East	Middle	West	City	Countryside
		%	%	%	%	%
About Math class, teachers encourage us to propose questions	Never	1.86	2.69	1.62	2.16	2.30
	Seldom	8.16	9.18	9.69	8.14	10.27
	Sometimes	27.45	29.89	28.12	27.76	31.21
	Often	62.53	58.24	60.57	61.94	56.22
About Chinese class, teachers encourage us to propose questions	Never	1.46	2.93	1.70	2.29	2.10
	Seldom	5.96	7.69	6.94	6.48	7.87
	Sometimes	19.80	23.57	19.48	19.96	24.97
	Often	72.78	65.81	71.89	71.28	65.06
About Science class, teachers encourage us to propose questions	Never	7.14	12.98	8.07	10.06	10.57
	Seldom	17.62	20.47	19.26	17.52	22.60
	Sometimes	24.57	25.77	26.71	24.51	27.60
	Often	50.68	40.78	45.97	47.91	39.24
About Morality and Society class, teachers encourage us to propose questions	Never	7.56	13.05	8.34	10.64	9.79
	Seldom	15.98	19.21	15.73	16.53	19.43
	Sometimes	23.87	24.86	25.82	23.06	27.74
	Often	52.59	42.87	50.10	49.78	43.03
About Math class, in class, most of the time is devoted to listening to teachers	Never	6.64	4.64	6.13	6.29	3.90
	Seldom	22.16	15.75	24.55	19.89	18.37
	Sometimes	35.77	34.32	35.39	35.13	35.51
	Often	35.43	45.30	33.93	38.69	42.22
About Chinese class, in class, most of the time is devoted to listening to teachers	Never	7.27	5.64	10.13	7.95	4.81
	Seldom	20.46	14.49	19.25	17.40	17.63
	Sometimes	34.33	33.21	32.30	33.51	34.35
	Often	37.93	46.66	38.33	41.14	43.22
About Science class, in class, most of the time is devoted to listening to teachers	Never	7.97	7.83	6.79	8.46	5.30
	Seldom	19.88	14.96	23.20	18.64	17.23
	Sometimes	32.72	31.24	31.99	31.45	33.11
	Often	39.44	45.97	38.03	41.44	44.36
About Morality and Society class, in class, most of the time is devoted to listening to teachers	Never	9.36	9.53	8.42	10.27	7.21
	Seldom	19.72	15.48	24.22	18.88	16.94
	Sometimes	31.24	30.29	31.98	30.20	32.75
	Often	39.68	44.70	35.37	40.65	43.10

low academic achievement. Theoretically, negative feelings and unsatisfying academic achievement are correlational. However, this phenomenon reminds us of that when schools emphasize students' academic achievement, special attention to the negative feelings of students with low academic achievement should be paid, especially that the bully or insulting phenomenon among students should be dealt with as an important issue.

Table 6.19 Actual classes more or fewer than curriculum schedule every week (%)

	Mathematics	Chinese	Science	Morality and Society
Fewer	3.19	2.31	40.19	41.77
The same	60.93	57.03	57.95	56.36
More	35.87	40.66	1.86	1.87
Total	100.00	100.00	100.00	100.00

Table 6.20 Actual classes more or fewer than curriculum schedule every week by region and location (%)

		Region			School location	
		East	Middle	West	City	Countryside
		%	%	%	%	%
Mathematics actual classes versus curriculum schedule every week	Fewer	1.90	3.64	4.77	2.28	4.60
	The same	71.50	52.38	66.21	63.85	58.86
	More	26.60	43.98	29.03	33.86	36.53
Chinese actual classes versus curriculum schedule every week	Fewer	1.75	2.95	1.34	1.76	3.47
	The same	68.36	49.04	58.29	59.21	54.76
	More	29.89	48.01	40.38	39.03	41.77
Science actual classes versus curriculum schedule every week	Fewer	31.47	47.56	34.76	36.37	44.82
	The same	67.30	49.91	64.32	62.04	52.81
	More	1.23	2.53	0.92	1.58	2.37
Morality and Society actual classes versus curriculum schedule every week	Fewer	31.62	49.48	38.55	40.21	42.75
	The same	66.98	48.33	59.57	58.11	54.94
	More	1.40	2.19	1.88	1.68	2.30

Regarding the teacher–student relationship, most students hold fairly positive idea, with a small part of students assess negatively. 11% of students think that teachers cannot have conversations with students in an equal way, 6% of students think that teachers cannot give a hand promptly, 3% of students think that teachers do not take care of students, and 5% of students think that teachers cannot give students appropriate praise and encouragement (Table 6.21).

School atmosphere reflects students' personal relationship from another perspective. The more nervous students' personal relationship is, the worse their academic achievement for subjects, with the negative correlation. The correlation coefficients between the academic achievement of Reading, Mathematics, Science, and Morality and Society and teacher–student relationship, respectively, are −0.16, −0.21, −0.14, and −0.19, with the significance level of 0.001. The correlation coefficients between the academic achievement of Reading, Mathematics, Science, and Morality and Society and student–student relationship, respectively, are −0.03, −0.03, −0.04, and −0.05, with the significance level of 0.001 (Tables 6.22 and 6.23).

6.2 Results and Findings

Table 6.21 Students' view for school (%)

	Totally agree	Agree	Disagree	Totally disagree
I can easily make friends in school	61.90	30.92	5.68	1.49
It seems that my schoolmates like me very much	36.64	47.47	13.30	2.59
There is no bully or insulting phenomenon among students	33.07	30.57	26.63	9.72
I can get an equal treatment in school	53.67	34.19	8.99	3.15
I feel safe in school	58.60	30.90	7.86	2.64
I feel that I am an outsider in school	5.29	6.11	24.34	64.26
I like my school	64.51	32.26	2.31	0.93
On the whole, teachers care students much	65.21	31.66	2.33	0.80
On the whole, teachers can have conversations with students in an equal way	51.56	37.51	8.96	1.97
When I have difficulties, teachers can give a hand promptly	60.09	33.87	4.96	1.08
Teachers give me appropriate praise and encouragement	62.27	33.23	3.62	0.88

Table 6.22 Students' academic achievement and their feelings (%)

		Level of total academic achievement				
		1	2	3	4	5
I can get an equal treatment in school	Totally agree	14.51	17.51	19.84	23.49	24.65
	Agree	21.80	22.50	20.68	18.00	17.02
	Disagree	27.76	24.00	19.71	15.49	13.04
	Totally disagree	32.21	24.55	20.05	12.16	11.04
I feel safe in school	Totally agree	14.99	18.49	19.79	23.20	23.53
	Agree	22.50	21.44	20.88	17.84	17.33
	Disagree	26.73	24.51	20.07	15.03	13.66
	Totally disagree	34.39	24.07	17.72	11.38	12.43
There is no bully or insulting phenomenon among students	Totally agree	15.92	18.68	19.31	22.77	23.31
	Agree	18.85	19.79	20.00	19.77	21.60
	Disagree	21.21	21.67	20.75	19.43	16.94
	Totally disagree	22.39	21.39	21.54	17.27	17.41

Table 6.23 Students' academic achievement and their personal relationship

		Reading academic achievement	Mathematics academic achievement	Science academic achievement	Morality and Society academic achievement
Factorial value of the anxiety of student–student relationship	Product-moment correlation	−0.028 (**)	−0.029 (**)	−0.038 (**)	−0.046 (**)
	P value (two-tailed)	0.000	0.000	0.000	0.000
	Number of students	15,165	16,274	14,797	16,337
Factorial value of the anxiety of teacher–student relationship	Product-moment correlation	−0.160 (**)	−0.210 (**)	−0.143 (**)	−0.193 (**)
	P value (two-tailed)	0.000	0.000	0.000	0.000
	Number of students	15,165	16,274	14,797	16,337

Note ** means reaching significance level of 0.01

6.2.2.3 Students' Family Socioeconomic and Cultural Status

Large quantities of previous researches prove that students' family socioeconomic and cultural status has significant influence on students' learning outcomes. Therefore, the present survey designed questions on family cultural resources, materialistic resources and parents' education level and professional, etc., based on the reality of China, with the reference of survey on students' family socioeconomic and cultural status in international large-scale research programs, such as PISA and TIMSS.

1. Family Materialistic Condition

The number of books families have has positive correlation with students' academic achievement. The better the family materialistic condition is, the better students' academic achievement is. Variables including whether students' families have a desk specialized for their study, a quiet place for study, reference books beneficial for study, dictionaries, classical literature books, artworks, magazines or newspapers, Internet condition, audio player, and a car are integrated as the materialistic condition index of students' family educational support, and the analysis shows that materialistic condition of students' family educational support has significant positive correlation. The better the condition is, the better students' academic achievement is (Tables 6.24, 6.25, 6.26, 6.27, and 6.28).

2. Parents' Educational Background

Overall, the higher parents' education level is, the better students' academic achievement of each subject is. With the significance test of non-parameter difference, the difference in students' academic achievement levels is significant between students' groups of different parents' education levels (Reading

6.2 Results and Findings

Table 6.24 Level of family materialistic condition and students' academic achievement—Reading (%)

	Level of Reading academic achievement (5 is the highest level)				
	1	2	3	4	5
Low	14.45	35.72	30.98	17.63	1.24
Fairly low	9.77	31.14	36.00	21.60	1.49
Intermediate	7.51	29.84	37.20	23.69	1.76
Fairly high	5.01	25.12	38.27	29.50	2.09
High	3.18	21.60	37.69	34.16	3.37

Table 6.25 Level of family materialistic condition and students' academic achievement—Mathematics (%)

	Level of Mathematics academic achievement (5 is the highest level)				
	1	2	3	4	5
Low	3.99	29.34	48.68	11.94	6.05
Fairly low	2.03	23.23	50.99	15.42	8.33
Intermediate	1.51	18.77	53.35	17.81	8.56
Fairly high	0.78	14.29	50.16	22.96	11.80
High	0.73	8.18	47.34	29.84	13.90

Table 6.26 Level of family materialistic condition and students' academic achievement—Science (%)

	Level of Science academic achievement (5 is the highest level)				
	1	2	3	4	5
Low	6.30	32.64	41.42	15.14	4.50
Fairly low	4.94	28.03	41.67	18.58	6.79
Intermediate	3.26	24.64	43.71	20.85	7.54
Fairly high	2.12	20.99	42.45	26.47	7.96
High	1.72	15.55	42.97	32.03	7.73

Table 6.27 Level of family materialistic condition and students' academic achievement—Morality and Society (%)

	Level of Morality and Society academic achievement (5 is the highest level)				
	1	2	3	4	5
Low	8.44	41.44	36.04	10.56	3.52
Fairly low	6.06	33.37	39.43	15.82	5.33
Intermediate	3.84	29.38	43.06	17.86	5.87
Fairly high	2.78	21.99	45.32	23.32	7.58
High	1.17	15.41	43.35	30.42	9.65

$\chi^2 = 542.40$, $P < 0.05$; Mathematics $\chi^2 = 827.26$, $P < 0.05$; Science $\chi^2 = 524.05$, $P < 0.05$; Morality and Society $\chi^2 = 1065.00$, $P < 0.05$) (Tables 6.29, 6.30, 6.31, and 6.32).

Table 6.28 Family materialistic condition and students' academic achievement of each subject

		Reading academic achievement	Mathematics academic achievement	Science academic achievement	Morality and Society academic achievement
Materialistic condition of family educational support	Pearson correlation coefficient	0.231**	0.276**	0.201**	0.299**
	P value (two-tailed)	0.000	0.000	0.000	0.000
	Number of students	15,985	17,152	15,637	17,215

Note ** indicates $P < 0.01$

Table 6.29 Parents' education level and students' academic achievement—Reading (%)

The highest education level of parents	Level of Reading academic achievement (5 is the highest level)				
	1	2	3	4	5
Primary school level or below	19.53	35.94	22.66	21.09	0.78
Primary school level	13.40	37.47	32.35	15.58	1.20
Junior high school level	10.15	31.84	34.99	21.51	1.51
Senior high school level or technical secondary school level	6.78	27.90	36.79	26.38	2.15
Junior college level or vocational technical college	4.31	22.11	38.98	30.97	3.63
Undergraduate level	2.71	21.56	38.14	35.18	2.41
Postgraduate level	1.58	18.91	38.53	37.48	3.50

Table 6.30 Parents' education level and students' academic achievement—Mathematics (%)

The highest education level of parents	Level of Mathematics academic achievement (5 is the highest level)				
	1	2	3	4	5
Primary school level or below	6.80	33.33	44.22	10.20	5.44
Primary school level	4.18	31.18	48.31	10.66	5.68
Junior high school level	2.41	23.43	50.47	15.35	8.34
Senior high school level or technical secondary school level	1.42	16.49	51.41	20.60	10.09
Junior college level or vocational technical college	0.80	10.51	51.78	25.43	11.48
Undergraduate level	0.34	7.73	47.95	29.87	14.11
Postgraduate level	0.85	5.60	46.01	32.26	15.28

6.2 Results and Findings

Table 6.31 Parents' education level and students' academic achievement—Science (%)

The highest education level of parents	Level of Science academic achievement (5 is the highest level)				
	1	2	3	4	5
Primary school level or below	10.34	32.41	42.76	9.66	4.83
Primary school level	7.14	36.08	40.20	12.66	3.92
Junior high school level	4.69	27.94	41.83	18.45	7.09
Senior high school level or technical secondary school level	2.78	23.70	43.03	23.46	7.04
Junior college level or vocational technical college	1.76	15.47	45.41	29.05	8.31
Undergraduate level	1.13	14.41	43.18	33.87	7.41
Postgraduate level	2.02	12.78	42.83	34.08	8.30

Table 6.32 Parents' education level and students' academic achievement—Morality and Society (%)

The highest education level of parents	Level of Morality and Society academic achievement (5 is the highest level)				
	1	2	3	4	5
Primary school level or below	15.65	42.18	28.57	10.88	2.72
Primary school level	8.37	45.86	32.20	9.67	3.89
Junior high school level	6.38	33.79	39.50	15.06	5.28
Senior high school level or technical secondary school level	2.73	26.95	42.62	20.92	6.78
Junior college level or vocational technical college	1.42	17.46	47.45	25.91	7.77
Undergraduate level	1.42	14.18	45.26	30.31	8.82
Postgraduate level	1.16	9.60	42.72	35.26	11.26

3. Children of Floating Population

In the group surveyed, 6.31% of students are the "left-behind" children whose parent(s) go(es) to city to work and 12.28% of students study in city with their parents who leave hometown for the city to work. The non-parameter test finds that there is no significant difference between the "left-behind" children, children living with migrant workers and countryside children whose parents do not go out to work on Reading academic achievement. However, there is significant difference in academic achievement between the three types of children and city school children, with the former significantly lower than the latter (Table 6.33).

There is no significant difference between the "left-behind" children and children living with migrant workers on Mathematics academic achievement. However, there is significant difference on the academic achievement between the two types of children and countryside children whose parents do not go out to work and city

Table 6.33 Academic achievement distribution of floating population's children—Reading (%)

Student type	Level of Reading academic achievement (5 is the highest level)				
	1	2	3	4	5
"Left-behind" children	12.16	29.01	35.65	21.45	1.74
Children living with migrant workers	8.93	32.87	34.78	21.93	1.50
City school children of non-floating population	6.45	27.09	37.51	26.56	2.38
Countryside school children of non-floating population	10.61	29.87	31.65	26.19	1.68

Table 6.34 Academic achievement distribution of floating population's children—Mathematics (%)

Student type	Level of Mathematics academic achievement (5 is the highest level)				
	1	2	3	4	5
"Left-behind" children	2.95	23.87	48.76	14.93	9.49
Children living with migrant workers	3.09	24.41	48.62	16.10	7.79
City school children of non-floating population	1.38	15.55	51.32	22.21	9.54
Countryside school children of non-floating population	2.66	22.62	46.32	16.63	11.77

school children, with the former's academic achievement significantly lower than that of the latter. Meanwhile, the Mathematics academic achievement of countryside children whose parents do not go out to work is significantly lower than that of city school children (Table 6.34).

There is no significant difference between the "left-behind" children and children living with migrant workers on Science academic achievement. But there is significant difference on the academic achievement between the two types of children and countryside children whose parents do not go out to work and city school children, with the former's academic achievement lower than that of the latter. Meanwhile, the Science academic achievement of children living with migrant workers is significantly lower than that of city school children (Table 6.35).

There is no significant difference between the "left-behind" children and children living with migrant workers on Morality and Society academic achievement. But there is significant difference in the academic achievement between the two types of children and the other two types of children, with the former's academic achievement lower than that of the latter. Meanwhile, the Morality and Society academic achievement of countryside children whose parents do not go out to work is significantly lower than that of city school children (Table 6.36).

4. Time Spent on the Way to School

Time needed on the way to school is within half an hour for 91.5% of students surveyed. The time on the way is no more than 10 min for 42.5% of students. From

6.2 Results and Findings

Table 6.35 Academic achievement distribution of floating population's children—Science (%)

Student type	Level of Science academic achievement (5 is the highest level)				
	1	2	3	4	5
"Left-behind" children	4.01	24.70	45.11	20.69	5.50
children living with migrant workers	4.87	30.27	42.82	16.43	5.60
City school children of non-floating population	3.46	22.88	41.70	24.60	7.36
Countryside school children of non-floating population	4.05	26.60	43.50	19.69	6.16

Table 6.36 Academic achievement distribution of floating population's children—Morality and Society (%)

Student type	Level of Morality and Society academic achievement (5 is the highest level)				
	1	2	3	4	5
"Left-behind" children	5.73	34.29	41.13	14.60	4.25
Children living with migrant workers	6.32	34.76	35.57	16.07	7.28
City school children of non-floating population	3.55	24.76	43.00	22.02	6.67
Countryside school children of non-floating population	5.52	31.76	39.36	17.46	5.89

the perspective of school location, countryside students spend more time on the way, and students in the west spend more time from the perspective of region. Overall, the more time spent on the way to school, the worse students' academic achievement is. The percentage of levels 4 and 5 for each subject of students who need to spend over one hour on the way is lower than that of those students who spend less time on the way to school (Tables 6.37, 6.38, 6.39, 6.40, and 6.41).

5. Parent–Child Interaction

Students living with parents, with mother, with father or grandparents, and other people perform significantly differently on the academic achievement of Reading, Mathematics, Science, and Morality and Society. The difference mainly represents in that students living with parents and with mother perform better than those living with father or grandparents on academic achievement, with about 30% as the percentage of levels 4 and 5 of Mathematics, Science, and Morality and Society subjects' academic achievement, 10% higher than the latter.

Regarding parent–student interaction, as the requirement of devotion degree goes higher, the interaction frequency gradually decreases. 70.06% of students report that their families often encourage them to behave themselves in school, while the percentage of students reporting that their families often talk about the things happening in school with them is 42.01%, and the percentage of families talking about the national and international social affairs with students is only 26.8% and the percentage of families helping with homework is 11.22%. The

Table 6.37 Distribution of time needed on the way to school (%)

	Region			School location	
	East	Middle	West	City	Countryside
Within 10 min	41.55	43.99	39.13	44.40	40.32
10–30 min	49.86	48.69	47.93	47.77	49.98
30 min–1 h	7.71	6.38	10.71	7.00	8.02
More than 1 h	0.89	0.93	2.24	0.83	1.68

Table 6.38 Distribution of time spent on the way to school and students' academic achievement—Reading (%)

Time spent on the way to school	Level of Reading academic achievement (5 is the highest level)				
	1	2	3	4	5
Within 10 min	8.48	28.88	35.95	24.50	2.19
10–30 min	6.93	27.43	36.38	27.10	2.16
30 min–1 h	10.01	32.57	33.16	23.07	1.19
More than 1 h	15.38	34.91	32.54	15.98	1.18

Table 6.39 Distribution of time spent on the way to school and students' academic achievement—Mathematics (%)

Time spent on the way to school	Level of Mathematics academic achievement (5 is the highest level)				
	1	2	3	4	5
Within 10 min	2.23	19.11	49.49	20.12	9.05
10–30 min	1.58	17.27	50.10	20.48	10.58
30 min–1 h	1.89	21.62	51.81	16.12	8.57
More than 1 h	9.52	28.57	43.39	11.64	6.88

Table 6.40 Distribution of time spent on the way to school and students' academic achievement—Science (%)

Time spent on the way to school	Level of Science academic achievement (5 is the highest level)				
	1	2	3	4	5
Within 10 min	4.03	24.76	42.92	22.12	6.17
10–30 min	3.34	23.66	42.47	22.92	7.61
30 min–1 h	4.25	28.83	40.82	20.75	5.36
More than 1 h	13.89	37.22	33.33	12.22	3.33

6.2 Results and Findings

Table 6.41 Distribution of time spent on the way to school and students' academic achievement—Morality and Society (%)

Time spent on the way to school	Level of Morality and Society academic achievement (5 is the highest level)				
	1	2	3	4	5
Within 10 min	4.67	27.79	41.77	19.76	6.01
10–30 min	3.82	26.89	41.35	20.86	7.08
30 min–1 h	5.23	33.26	39.66	16.55	5.31
More than 1 h	15.34	43.39	30.16	8.99	2.12

Table 6.42 Parent–child interaction types (%)

	Never	Seldom	Sometimes	Often
My family or friends help me with my homework	24.47	34.75	29.56	11.22
My family encourages me to behave myself in school	2.99	7.20	19.75	70.06
My family talks about the things happening in school with me	8.30	18.38	31.32	42.01
My family talks about the national and international social affairs with me	18.32	27.40	27.49	26.80

non-parameter test finds that except that there is no significant difference for Mathematics academic achievement on the question of whether family often helps with homework, significant difference exists in every subject's academic achievement on the different degrees of every type of interaction between parents and students (Tables 6.42 and 6.43).

6.2.2.4 Students' Learning: Attitude, Devotion, and Efficacy

1. Favorite Subject and Subject with Time Spent Most

Out of the four subjects including Mathematics, Chinese, Science, and Morality and Society, 44.42% of students choose Mathematics as their favorite subject and 43.64% of students like Chinese, while the percentages of students enjoying learning Science and Morality and Society, respectively, are 7.38% and 4.56%.

Regarding the favorite subject, students are willing to read the books relevant to the subject, like attending classes of this subject, have interest in the knowledge learned from the subject, enjoy doing the exercises of the subject, and think that they can learn knowledge which could be used in life in the subject lessons.

Regarding the favorite subject, students most like the teachers of the subject. And teachers own these features: be very responsible for students' learning, can teach based on students' features, their classes are interesting and students are very

Table 6.43 Parent–child interaction types and students' academic achievement

		Reading academic achievement level	Mathematics academic achievement level	Science academic achievement level	Morality and Society academic achievement level
My family or friends help me with my homework	Chi-square	14.65	5.61	20.76	15.02
	df	3	3	3	3
	P value	0.00	0.13	0.00	0.00
My family encourages me to behave myself in school	Chi-square	166.31	201.02	125.20	195.22
	df	3	3	3	3
	P value	0.00	0.00	0.00	0.00
My family talks about the things happening in school with me	Chi-square	357.33	427.98	294.77	575.02
	df	3	3	3	3
	P value	0.00	0.00	0.00	0.00
My family talks about the national and international social affairs with me	Chi-square	370.86	524.54	367.49	777.49
	df	3	3	3	3
	P value	0.00	0.00	0.00	0.00

Table 6.44 Favorite subject and subject with time spent most (%)

| | | Subject you spend time most on ||||
		Mathematics	Chinese	Science	Morality and Society
Subject you like most	Mathematics	44.58	45.94	6.50	2.98
	Chinese	51.01	39.76	6.66	2.57
	Science	45.74	42.65	9.18	2.42
	Morality and Society	47.86	39.54	6.17	6.43

active in their classes, immediately give positive feedback for students' progress which raise students' confidence, pay attention to individuals' learning, give extra help to students only if they need, have patience, and seldom get annoyed to students.

Only 38.13% of students spend time most on their favorite subjects. Therefore, it is not totally consistent between students' favorite subject and the subject they spend most time (Tables 6.44 and 6.45).

6.2 Results and Findings

Table 6.45 Students' attitude to the subject with time spent most (%)

	Complete in accordance	Most in accordance	Partial in accordance	Little in accordance	Total
I like reading some books relevant to this subject	48.95	36.40	11.99	2.66	100
I like attending classes of this subject	54.78	34.53	8.67	2.02	100
I feel very interested in what I've learned from this subject	60.47	29.60	8.09	1.84	100
I like doing exercises of this subject	45.96	36.10	13.28	4.67	100

Table 6.46 Self-access learning ability and students' academic achievement (%)

		Reading academic achievement	Mathematics academic achievement	Science academic achievement	Morality and Society academic achievement
Self-access learning ability	Product-moment correlation	0.176**	0.237**	0.174**	0.224**
	P value (two-tailed)	0.000	0.000	0.000	0.000
	Number of students	15,332	16,469	14,975	16,522

Note ** means reaching significance level of 0.01

2. Self-Access Learning

Students' self-access learning ability has positive correlation with their academic achievement. The correlation coefficients between the academic achievement of Reading, Mathematics, Science, and Morality and Society and self-access learning, respectively, are 0.18, 0.24, 0.17, and 0.22, with the significance level of 0.001. Overall, students' self-access learning ability level is to be improved. Most students (73.59%) can actively review the reasons of mistakes in their exercises and test papers and modify them. Since new curriculum fairly emphasizes the combination of knowledge and life, only 43% and 34.98% of students, respectively, can find examples or evidence of knowledge learned in daily life and can manipulate what teachers deliver in class at home (Tables 6.46 and 6.47).

From the perspective of city and countryside, city students' self-access learning ability is significantly higher than countryside students (T = 8.12, df = 14,299, p = 0.00). From the regional perspective, students' self-access learning ability in the east is significantly higher than that in the middle and west and students' self-access learning ability in the middle is the lowest, significantly lower than that in the west (Tables 6.48, 6.49, and 6.50).

Table 6.47 Self-access learning ability (%)

	Never	Seldom	Sometimes	Often
When encountering questions I do not know, I will look them up in books first and think them on my own. And I will ask teachers or classmates if I really cannot work them out	1.53	7.30	30.47	60.69
For the content to be learned, I will do pre-reading even though teachers do not require	2.25	15.13	38.15	44.47
When learning new content, I will associate with the content learned and understand what I have learned from the perspective of new knowledge	1.70	11.60	35.83	50.88
When test papers or exercises are distributed, I seriously analyze the reasons for mistakes and modify the errors	0.71	5.21	20.48	73.59
I manipulate with hands what teachers deliver in class at home	7.81	22.12	35.09	34.98
I often list the outline to help to review	6.72	22.77	34.93	35.59
I actively look up and learn related papers or books to help to understand some questions	2.60	13.72	33.11	50.57
I look for examples or evidence of the knowledge I have learned in daily life	4.06	16.97	35.25	43.73
I actively discuss questions with classmates or others	3.02	14.88	32.37	49.73
I cooperate well with classmates when doing cooperative learning tasks.	3.69	12.63	31.14	52.54

Table 6.48 Self-access learning ability—city and countryside (%)

	Number of students	Average	Standard deviation	Standard error mean square
City	9917	0.05	0.99	–
Countryside	4384	−0.09	0.09	0.12**

Note ** means reaching significance level of 0.01

Table 6.49 Self-access learning ability—significance test of regional difference (%)

	Sum of mean square	Degrees of freedom	Mean square	F	Sig.
Between groups	503.470	2	251.735	259.586	0.000
Within groups	16,078.530	16,580	0.970		
Total	16,582.000	16,582			

6.2 Results and Findings

Table 6.50 Self-access learning ability—significance post hoc test of regional difference (%)

		Mean difference (I–J)	Standard error	Sig.	95% confidence interval	
					Lower confidence limit	Upper confidence limit
East	Middle	0.378**	0.017	0.000	0.345	0.411
	West	0.299**	0.0242	0.000	0.252	0.346
Middle	East	−0.378	0.017	0.000	−0.411	−0.345
	West	−0.079**	0.023	0.001	−0.124	−0.034
West	East	−0.299**	0.024	0.000	−0.346	−0.252
	Middle	0.079**	0.023	0.001	0.034	0.124

Note ** means reaching significance level of 0.01

3. Sense of Self-efficacy

The total score for sense of self-efficacy is 12, with 0 as the lowest score and the average is 9 for each subject. On the whole, Grade-6 students have quite good sense of self-efficacy with most students thinking that the subjects are not difficult and they have confidence to learn well, which indicates that the teachers do fairly successfully in building students' confidence. Compared between subjects, the sense of efficacy for Morality and Society is highest, with that for Science subject as the lowest (Tables 6.51 and 6.52).

4. Learning Load

Extracurricular time allocation

The school assignment takes over 1 h for 66.61% of students. And the load of school assignment for students in the middle is the heaviest, with 29.34% of students spending more than 2 h on school assignment, 15.63% and 7.95% higher than that in the east and in the west. And the load of school assignment for students in the city and in the countryside is similar.

12.59% of students do not do housework and 59.95% of students do not do sports or the time for doing sports is less than 1 h. 13.92% of students surf the Internet for more than 1 h with countryside students spending fairly less time on surfing the Internet, which is related to the family economic situation. 5.18% of students do not read extracurricular books, with the percentages for the middle and for the west are both 6%, 3% higher than that for the east. The percentages of students not reading extracurricular books and of students reading less than 1 h for the countryside, respectively, are 3% and 11% higher than that for the city (Tables 6.53, 6.54, and 6.55).

Out-of-school training and reviewing

Among the students surveyed, only 34% of students never participate in out-of-school training classes or reviewing schools. 71.14% of city students take

Table 6.51 Sense of efficacy for each subject (%)

	Complete in accordance	Most in accordance	Partial in accordance	Little in accordance
I can learn quickly in Math class	55.46	35.80	7.92	0.82
Compared with my classmates, I find Math difficult to learn well	9.39	16.74	28.72	45.15
In Math class, I can understand even the most difficult question	25.51	46.69	23.80	4.01
I am confident in learning Math well	67.64	23.72	6.73	1.92
I can quickly understand the authors' feelings or thoughts	48.03	42.93	8.00	1.04
I can understand difficult passages in the textbook	28.60	47.89	20.04	3.48
Compared with my classmates, I find Chinese difficult to learn well	6.86	13.79	29.76	49.59
I am confident in learning Chinese well	69.62	23.42	5.80	1.16
I can learn quickly in Science class	44.39	39.21	12.93	3.47
In Science class, I can fully understand the knowledge delivered by teachers	44.75	38.86	13.04	3.35
Compared with my classmates, I find Science difficult to learn well	8.24	16.67	34.05	41.03
I am confident in learning Science well	55.57	29.54	10.59	4.30
I can learn quickly in Morality and Society class	62.53	29.37	6.21	1.88
Since I took Morality and Society class, I have begun to pay more attention to the society and events taking place in the surroundings	59.33	30.86	7.66	2.15
Compared with my classmates, I find Morality and Society difficult to learn well	6.14	11.24	29.96	52.66
I am confident in learning Morality and Society well	64.43	26.23	6.97	2.37

training classes or go to reviewing schools, with 20% higher than that of countryside students. The percentages of students in the middle and in the west participating in out-of-school reviewing and training reach 70%, exceeding that in the east by about 15% (Tables 6.56 and 6.57).

6.2 Results and Findings

Table 6.52 Average of sense of self-efficacy for each subject

	Number of students	Average	Standard deviation
Sense of efficacy for Mathematics learning	17,233	9.01	2.50
Sense of efficacy for Chinese learning	17,224	9.16	2.27
Sense of efficacy for Science learning	17,195	8.87	2.64
Sense of efficacy for Morality and Society learning	17,205	9.76	2.25

Table 6.53 Students' extracurricular time allocation (%)

	None	Less than 1 h	1–2 h	2–4 h	More than 4 h
Doing housework	12.59	60.26	22.87	3.06	1.22
Doing sports	14.20	45.75	32.19	6.03	1.82
Reading extracurricular books	5.18	33.59	44.44	13.22	3.57
Surfing on the Internet	63.70	22.39	9.80	2.67	1.45
Doing homework	0.61	32.78	43.77	17.57	5.27

Table 6.54 Students' extracurricular time allocation by city and countryside (%)

		None	Less than 1 h	1–2 h	2–4 h	More than 4 h
Doing housework	City	14.15	60.14	22.28	2.34	1.10
	Countryside	9.81	60.45	23.71	4.47	1.56
Doing sports	City	12.21	43.34	35.72	6.73	2.00
	Countryside	18.05	50.92	25.26	4.43	1.35
Reading extracurricular books	City	4.20	29.82	47.42	14.70	3.86
	Countryside	6.98	40.71	39.40	10.06	2.86
Surfing on the Internet	City	57.47	26.39	11.39	3.12	1.63
	Countryside	75.96	14.64	6.64	1.83	0.93
Doing homework	City	0.58	32.42	44.13	17.42	5.44
	Countryside	0.64	35.87	43.19	16.10	4.20

Time of sleep

The sleeping time of 46.6% of students reach 9 h or more every day, 42% of students sleep 8 h every day, and about 13% of students cannot have 8 h sleep. The percentage of students sleeping 9 h or more in the east is higher than that in the middle and in the west by 15 and 5%, which is related to the reason that the quantity of school assignment is large in the middle. 16% of students spending 2 to 4 h on school assignment can only sleep as much as 7 h and 25.3% of students spending

Table 6.55 Students' extracurricular time allocation by region (%)

		None	Less than 1 h	1–2 h	2–4 h	More than 4 h
Doing housework	East	8.62	64.74	22.99	2.72	0.93
	Middle	15.64	57.85	22.31	2.91	1.29
	West	11.30	57.95	24.60	4.48	1.67
Doing sports	East	9.81	48.55	34.26	5.72	1.66
	Middle	17.35	45.02	29.71	5.98	1.95
	West	13.58	41.53	36.17	7.00	1.72
Reading extracurricular books	East	3.11	33.01	48.03	12.92	2.94
	Middle	6.34	33.62	41.91	13.92	4.20
	West	6.10	34.90	44.79	11.40	2.82
Surfing on the Internet	East	55.35	29.39	11.70	2.42	1.13
	Middle	67.53	19.67	8.46	2.80	1.55
	West	70.37	15.01	9.96	2.82	1.85
Doing homework	East	0.46	43.83	41.99	11.52	2.19
	Middle	0.72	25.47	44.47	21.78	7.56
	West	0.58	32.14	45.62	17.15	4.51

Table 6.56 Whether students participate in out-of-school reviewing or training (%)

	Region			School location	
	East	Middle	West	City	Countryside
No	44.89	28.33	30.86	28.86	48.24
Yes	55.11	71.67	69.14	71.14	51.76

Table 6.57 Time length of out-of-school reviewing or training (%)

	Never	Less than 1 h	1–2 h	2–4 h	More than 4 h
Relevant to Mathematics	62.50	8.67	16.78	8.31	3.73
Relevant to Chinese	65.10	10.84	15.79	6.10	2.17
Relevant to Science	83.08	9.77	5.12	1.49	0.54
Other	46.57	12.00	21.61	12.80	7.01

over 4 h on school assignment cannot sleep 8 h, while the percentage of students who spend less than 2 h on school assignment and sleep less than 8 h does not reach 10%. There is no significant difference between city and countryside students' sleeping time (Tables 6.58, 6.59, and 6.60).

6.2 Results and Findings

Table 6.58 Distribution of sleeping time (%)

		Number of students	Percentage	Effective percentage	Accumulative percentage
Effective data	6 h or less	406	2.2	2.4	2.4
	7 h	1481	8.1	8.7	11.1
	8 h	7214	39.6	42.3	53.4
	9 h or more	7953	43.6	46.6	100.0
	Sum	17,054	93.6	100.0	
	Miss value	1172	6.4		
Total		18,226	100.0		

Table 6.59 Distribution of sleeping time by region and school location (%)

	Region			School location	
	East	Middle	West	City	Countryside
	%	%	%	%	%
6 h or less	1.20	3.25	2.13	2.14	2.77
7 h	6.26	10.72	7.23	8.73	8.51
8 h	38.38	45.27	41.14	41.43	42.37
9 h or more	54.16	40.77	49.50	47.69	46.35

Table 6.60 Sleeping time and quantity of school assignment (%)

	No	Less than 1 h	1–2 h	2–4 h	More than 4 h
6 h or less	8.80	1.90	1.90	2.90	6.70
7 h	12.70	6.00	7.70	13.00	18.60
8 h	31.40	36.30	45.00	48.00	39.60
9 h or more	47.10	55.80	45.40	36.10	35.00

6.2.3 Factors Influencing Students' Academic Achievement —Analysis Based on Multilevel Model

6.2.3.1 Method

The present research employs multilevel regression model to test the factors influencing students' academic achievement. Two ways are usually used to analyze hierarchical data in general linear regression model. One is to calculate school-level data at student individual level, in which the calculation result of the school-level factor is influenced by the number of students. The other is to calculate student individual-level data into the average at school level and then to analyze, which loses the features at individual level. For the educational survey data with hierarchy, multilevel regression model can solve the problem that student-level variance is not independent in school, separating the variation at school level and student level.

The academic achievement sum of the four subjects is treated as dependent variable in the present section, with the four groups of variables including student individual and family background, students' devotion, attitude and self-efficacy, school education and teaching and management, etc. introduced to generate five models. Multilevel model analysis first makes variable comparison within group according to the predicted grouping structure, choosing the variables significantly related to students' academic achievement. Meanwhile, it analyzes the explanation degree of the model composed with the group variables to the variation of student and school academic achievement and compares the explanatory power of the grouping variables and the contribution to the total variance, etc.

Null model: only one constant term is added in null model to calculate the initial variance at student, school, and regional level.

Model 2: based on null model, the variables of individual background, family background, parent–child relationship, etc. are added.

Model 3: based on null model, the variables including students' devotion to learning, self-efficacy, attitude, etc. are added.

Model 4: based on null model, the variables of school education and teaching and management, etc. are added.

Model 5: significant variables from each group are added together into model to participate in the calculation, which is called complete model.

6.2.3.2 Result

Null model

1. Model comparison

Level-crossing correlation means the percentage of students' academic achievement variance which could be attributed to the school or regional variation. From Table 6.61, it could be seen that in the complete model, 38.73% of students' academic achievement variance can be attributed to school-level variance and 21.53% of students' academic achievement variance can be attributed to the districts or counties in which schools are located. However, the level-crossing correlation at student level reaches 39.75%, indicating that the variation of students' academic achievement is more caused by the individual and family variation.

Individual demography background and family support explain 13.76% of the variation between schools, 30.22% of regional variation, and 15.28% of total variance. Individual devotion, attitude, and self-efficacy explain 17.29% of the variation between schools, 34.21% of regional variation, and 21.00% of total variance. Compared with individual-level variable, the explanatory power of

6.2 Results and Findings

Table 6.61 Explanatory power of multilevel model (%)

	Null model	Model 2: individual background and family support	Model 3: individual participation, devotion, and attitude	Model 4: school education	Complete model
Level-crossing correlation at individual level	39.75	42.85	41.53	42.28	43.27
Level-crossing correlation at school level	38.73	39.42	40.55	35.46	36.40
Level-crossing correlation at regional level	21.53	17.73	17.93	22.27	20.33
Percentage of individual-level variance explained		8.66	17.47	8.36	22.67
Percentage of school-level variance explained		13.76	17.29	21.12	33.24
Percentage of regional-level variance explained		30.22	34.21	10.89	32.93
Percentage of total variance explained		15.28	21.00	13.84	28.98

school-level variable to school variance is higher, reaching 21.12%, but low-to-district or county-level variance, which is 10.89%, indicating that variables of students' family and individual devotion, etc. explain more regional variation.

Regarding individual-level variance, variables of individual background, family support, and school education all explain 8%, while the explanatory percentage of individual participation, devotion, and attitude reaches 17.47%, indicating that individual-level variation is more caused by individual factors.

With the integration of the variables of student family background variable, individual participation and devotion variable, and school education and teaching variable in complete model, variances at individual level, school level, and regional level are explained 22.67%, 33.24%, and 32.93%, and the percentage of total variance is explained 28.98%.

2. Variables reserved in complete model (more content could be found in Table 6.62).

Table 6.62 Analysis result of multilevel model

	Null model		Model 2: individual background and family support		Model 3: individual participation, devotion, and attitude		Model 4: school education		Complete model	
	Coefficient	Standard error	Coefficient	Standard error	Coefficient	Standard error	Coefficient	Standard error	Coefficient	Standard error
Fixed part										
Constant term	3.40	0.33	3.52	0.30	3.85	0.31	4.61	0.46	4.38	0.43
Age			−0.12	0.03						
Number of books in family (None as the reference)										
11–25 books			−0.03	0.07					−0.02	0.08
26–100 books			0.22	0.08					0.17	0.08
101–200 books			0.36	0.09					0.22	0.09
More than 200 books			0.45	0.10					0.41	0.10
Family socioeconomic support			0.08	0.01					0.07	0.01
Parents' education degree (Junior high school level as the reference)										
Primary school level or below			−0.63	0.20					−0.30	0.21
Primary school level			−0.25	0.08					−0.10	0.09
Senior high school level or technical secondary school level			0.06	0.05					0.11	0.05
Junior college level or vocational technical college			0.37	0.08					0.26	0.08
Undergraduate level			0.64	0.08					0.54	0.08
Postgraduate level			0.72	0.13					0.64	0.13
Unknown			−0.26	0.08					−0.15	0.08

(continued)

6.2 Results and Findings

Table 6.62 (continued)

	Null model		Model 2: individual background and family support		Model 3: individual participation, devotion, and attitude		Model 4: school education		Complete model	
	Coefficient	Standard error	Coefficient	Standard error	Coefficient	Standard error	Coefficient	Standard error	Coefficient	Standard error
Home–school distance (less than 30 min as the reference)										
30 min—1 h			−0.05	0.08					−0.12	0.08
More than 1 h			−0.59	0.19					−0.52	0.19
My family or friends help me with my homework (often as the reference)										
Never			0.29	0.07					0.17	0.07
Seldom			0.33	0.07					0.22	0.07
Sometimes			0.15	0.07					0.07	0.07
My family talks about the things happening in school with me (often as the reference)										
Never			−0.50	0.08					−0.35	0.08
Seldom			−0.32	0.06					−0.10	0.06
Sometimes			−0.24	0.05					−0.12	0.05
My family talks about the national and international social affairs with me (often as the reference)										
Never			−0.39	0.07					−0.19	0.07
Seldom			−0.06	0.06					0.03	0.06
Sometimes			−0.06	0.06					−0.01	0.06

(continued)

Table 6.62 (continued)

	Null model		Model 2: individual background and family support		Model 3: individual participation, devotion, and attitude		Model 4: school education		Complete model	
	Coefficient	Standard error	Coefficient	Standard error	Coefficient	Standard error	Coefficient	Standard error	Coefficient	Standard error
Live with whom (parents as the reference)										
Mother			0.22	0.07						
Father			−0.18	0.15						
Grandparents and others			−0.09	0.07						
Time of sleep (9 h or more as the reference)										
Less than 6 h					−0.71	0.12			−0.66	0.14
7 h					−0.13	0.06			−0.08	0.07
8 h					0.08	0.04			0.06	0.04
Mathematics learning efficacy					0.25	0.01			0.23	0.01
Science learning efficacy					0.06	0.01			0.03	0.01
Independently finish homework (often as the reference)										
Never					−0.56	0.18			−0.39	0.23
Seldom					−0.71	0.11			−0.49	0.13
Sometimes					−0.40	0.06			−0.34	0.07
Out-of-school reviewing related to Mathematics (none as the reference)										
Less than 1 h					−0.23	0.08			−0.37	0.08
1–2 h					0.13	0.09			−0.12	0.06

(continued)

Table 6.62 (continued)

	Null model		Model 2: individual background and family support		Model 3: individual participation, devotion, and attitude		Model 4: school education		Complete model	
	Coefficient	Standard error	Coefficient	Standard error	Coefficient	Standard error	Coefficient	Standard error	Coefficient	Standard error
2–4 h					0.53	0.13			0.14	0.08
More than 4 h					0.77	0.18			0.29	0.12
Out-of-school reviewing related to Chinese (none as the reference)										
Less than 1 h					−0.19	0.08			−0.37	0.07
1–2 h					0.10	0.09			−0.22	0.07
2–4 h					0.04	0.14			−0.34	0.09
More than 4 h					0.04	0.20			−0.51	0.16
Other out-of-school reviewing (none as the reference)										
Less than 1 h					0.04	0.07			−0.11	0.07
1–2 h					0.24	0.08			−0.17	0.06
2–4 h					0.66	0.11			0.09	0.07
More than 4 h					0.81	0.15			0.09	0.09
Time of doing housework (none as the reference)										
Less than 1 h					0.11	0.06			0.08	0.06
1–2 h					−0.01	0.06			0.02	0.07
2–4 h					−0.27	0.11			−0.35	0.13
More than 4 h					−0.52	0.17			−0.48	0.20
Time of doing sports (none as the reference)										

(continued)

Table 6.62 (continued)

	Null model		Model 2: individual background and family support		Model 3: individual participation, devotion, and attitude		Model 4: school education		Complete model	
	Coefficient	Standard error	Coefficient	Standard error	Coefficient	Standard error	Coefficient	Standard error	Coefficient	Standard error
Less than 1 h					0.02	0.05			−0.09	0.06
1–2 h					−0.07	0.06			−0.18	0.07
2–4 h					−0.30	0.09			−0.43	0.10
More than 4 h					−0.61	0.15			−0.80	0.18
Time of reading extracurricular books (none as the reference)										
Less than 1 h					0.29	0.08			0.30	0.10
1–2 h					0.38	0.08			0.38	0.10
2–4 h					0.49	0.10			0.42	0.11
More than 4 h					0.44	0.12			0.37	0.14
Time of surfing on the Internet (none as the reference)										
Less than 1 h					0.01	0.05			−0.10	0.05
1–2 h					0.03	0.06			−0.10	0.07
2–4 h					−0.28	0.11			−0.26	0.12
More than 4 h					−0.48	0.15			−0.55	0.17
Time of participation in out-of-school reviewing and training					−0.12	0.03				
Mathematics teaching and learning way							0.09	0.01	0.03	0.01

(continued)

6.2 Results and Findings

Table 6.62 (continued)

	Null model		Model 2: individual background and family support		Model 3: individual participation, devotion, and attitude		Model 4: school education		Complete model	
	Coefficient	Standard error	Coefficient	Standard error	Coefficient	Standard error	Coefficient	Standard error	Coefficient	Standard error
Reading teaching and learning way							0.04	0.01	0.02	0.01
Years as headmaster in this school							0.07	0.04	0.09	0.04
Number of Science classes teachers listen to each semester							0.05	0.02	0.04	0.02
Teaching and research activities of subject group (at least once per week as the reference)										
Once to twice per month							0.23	0.31	0.28	0.28
Twice to three times per semester							1.36	0.56	1.40	0.51
Never									0.00	0.00
Teaching and research activities of whole school teachers (at least once per week as the reference)										
Once to twice per month							−0.87	0.39	−0.75	0.36
Twice to three times per semester							−1.34	0.41	−1.22	0.38
Never							0.27	2.10	0.61	1.93
Actual classes compared with the classes planed in schedule (same as the reference)										
Actual classes of Mathematics are fewer than the curriculum schedule							−0.76	0.12	−0.50	0.12

(continued)

Table 6.62 (continued)

	Null model		Model 2: individual background and family support		Model 3: individual participation, devotion, and attitude		Model 4: school education		Complete model	
	Coefficient	Standard error	Coefficient	Standard error	Coefficient	Standard error	Coefficient	Standard error	Coefficient	Standard error
Actual classes of Mathematics are more than the curriculum schedule							0.16	0.05	0.05	0.05
Actual classes of Science are fewer than the curriculum schedule							−0.41	0.06	−0.33	0.06
Actual classes of Science are more than the curriculum schedule							−0.58	0.18	−0.50	0.18
Actual classes of Morality and Society are fewer than the curriculum schedule							−0.14	0.06	−0.06	0.06
Actual classes of Morality and Society are more than the curriculum schedule							−0.70	0.18	−0.50	0.18
Random part										
Regional level										
Constant term	2.51	0.79	1.75	0.59	1.65	0.55	2.24	0.73	1.68	0.56
School level										
Constant term	4.51	0.40	3.89	0.36	3.73	0.34	3.56	0.36	3.01	0.30
Student level										
Constant term	4.63	0.05	4.23	0.06	3.82	0.05	4.24	0.06	3.58	0.05

(continued)

Table 6.62 (continued)

	Null model		Model 2: individual background and family support		Model 3: individual participation, devotion, and attitude		Model 4: school education		Complete model	
	Coefficient	Standard error	Coefficient	Standard error	Coefficient	Standard error	Coefficient	Standard error	Coefficient	Standard error
Logistic likelihood function	66,722.52		53206.98		57838.28		47965.10		42948.44	
Sample quantity: districts or counties	28		27		27		27		27	
Sample quantity: schools	296		285		285		242		242	
Sample quantity: students	15,001		12,187		13,580		10,990		10,229	

Model 2: individual background and family support

Variables of individual background and family support reserved in complete model include number of books family owns, family economic and cultural resource support, parents' educational background, distance between home and school, parent–child interaction variables such as "My family or friends help me with my homework," "My family talks about the things happening in school with me," "My family talks about the national and international social affairs with me", etc.

There is no significant difference of students' academic achievement between those with 10 books or fewer in their family and those with 11–25 books in their family. However, the analysis result shows that the more books there are in families, the better students' academic achievement is. Family cultural possession and materialistic possession make the composed variable of economic and cultural support. And 1 mark increased to the variable, 0.07 mark (standardized score) is raised to students' academic achievement. The percentage of students whose parents have junior secondary school education is the highest, taken as the reference index, and their academic achievement is significantly lower than that of those whose parents have senior secondary school, junior college, undergraduate, and graduate education. The higher the parents' education degree is, the better the students' academic achievement is.

Home–school distance is still a significant variable. The more time spent on the way to school, the worse students' academic achievement is.

Parent–child interaction significantly influences students' academic achievement. About parents and children talking about the things happening in school and talking about the national and international social affairs, the academic achievement of students with the "often" frequency is higher than students with the frequency of "never", "seldom", or "sometimes". The family support, with the lack of the interaction such as "my family encourages me to behave myself in school," is not significant. The academic achievement of students with high frequency of help with homework from family is significantly lower than other students, which could be that the needs of family help is resulted from students' unsatisfying academic achievement. Therefore, in the model 3, the more the independence students have when finishing the homework, the better their academic achievement is.

Whether students are left-behind children by their parents or go to the city with their parents and study there and the influence of variables of city or countryside and region are explained by the effects of other factors. "Live with whom" is significant in model 2. Students living with parents are taken as the reference, and their academic achievement is significantly lower than that of those who live with their mother, by 0.22 standardized marks (standard error is 0.07), and there is no significant difference between the academic achievement of students living with father and those living with grandparents or others. However, the variable is no more significant with the variables of student individual attitude and school level, which indicates that the influence of students' academic achievement could be explained by other factors.

Model 3: individual participation, devotion, and attitude

Variables of individual participation, devotion, and attitude reserved in complete model include students' time allocation, such as time of doing housework, time of doing sports, time of reading extracurricular books, time of surfing on the Internet, and time of doing homework; participation of out-of-school reviewing, such as out-of-school reviewing related to Mathematics, Chinese and others; time of sleep; self-efficacy on learning (Mathematics, Reading, and Science) and independence of finishing school assignment, etc.

Time of sleep is a significant variable. The less the sleeping time is, the lower the students' academic achievement is. The academic achievement of students who sleep 6 h or less is significantly lower than those who sleep 9 h or more by 0.66 standardized marks.

The Mathematics and Science learning efficacy has significant correlation with students' academic achievement. With 1 mark raised for learning efficacy, the scores of students' academic achievement, respectively, are raised by 0.23 and 0.03 standardized marks.

Regarding the participation of out-of-school reviewing and training, the academic achievement of students not attending any out-of-school reviewing and training related to Mathematics is significantly better than that of those spending less than 1 h, significantly lower than those spending more than 4 h, but has no significant difference with that of those who spend time of other lengths. Reviewing related to Chinese has negative function, representing that the academic achievement of students participating the reviewing is significantly lower than that of those who do not attend the reviewing and training. There is no significant difference shown in the reviewing related to Science. Besides the fact that the academic achievement of students who spend 1–2 h on other out-of-school reviewing is significantly lower than that of those who do not participate reviewing, there is no significant difference between the academic achievement of students who participate the reviewing or training of different time lengths and that of those who do not attend any training or reviewing.

There is no significant difference between the academic achievement of students who do housework for less than 2 h and that of those who do not do housework, while the academic achievement of students who do housework for more than 2 h is significantly lower than that of those who do not do housework. The academic achievement of students who do sports for a long time is significantly lower than that of those who do not do sports.

The academic achievement of students who read extracurricular books every day is significantly higher than that of those who do not read extracurricular books.

The academic achievement of students who surf on the Internet for more than 2 h is significantly lower than that of those who do not surf on the Internet, while there is no significant difference between the academic achievement of students who surf on the Internet for less than 2 h and that of those who do not surf on the Internet. The time length of doing homework every day has no significant correlation with students' academic achievement, i.e., doing homework for a long time does not necessarily result in good academic achievement.

Out of expectation, students' learning autonomy has no significant influence to their academic achievement, which might be related to the reason that it is easy for students to be influenced by parents during primary school period or the free time and independent learning opportunities given by school to students are fairly few.

Model 4: school education and teaching

School-level variables significantly influencing students' academic achievement are school educational and teaching methods and the factor of management. The variables of the aspect of team building such as school running condition, teachers' educational background, age, professional title, etc. do not produce significant influence. Variables of school education and teaching reserved in complete model include working years of the headmaster in the school, teaching and learning methods (Mathematics, Reading), number of Science classes teachers listen to each semester, teaching and research activities of subject groups, teaching and research activities of whole school teachers, and actual classes compared with the classes planed in schedule (Mathematics, Science, and Morality and Society).

The higher the teaching method score is, the more it is in accordance with the requirements of self-access learning. To reduce the error of calculation, teaching method is centralized with the mean as the center. With Mathematics teaching method higher than the mean by every 1 unit, the standardized score of students' academic achievement goes up by 0.03 marks. And with Reading teaching method higher than the mean by every 1 unit, the standardized score of students' academic achievement goes up by 0.02 marks.

Teaching and research activity is an important approach to improve teachers' professional level and teaching quality. Regarding the number of classes teachers listen to each semester, only the activity of listening to Science classes produces significant influence to the total academic achievement. The academic achievement of students in schools with teaching and research activities of subject groups at least once each week is significantly lower than that of those in schools with teaching and research activities 2–3 times each semester. And the academic achievement of students in schools with at least once teaching and research activities of whole school teachers each week is significantly higher than that of those in schools with fairly few teaching and research activities of whole school teachers.

The statistical result of the relationship between class hours and students' academic achievement shows that actual classes more than the classes planed in schedule cannot bring the elevation of academic achievement and the academic achievement is the highest for schools with classes are given seriously based on curriculum schedule. That more actual classes of Mathematics are given does not elevate the total academic achievement, but the academic achievement of students in schools with fewer actual classes of Mathematics is significantly lower than that of those in schools in which the actual classes are the same as the classes planed in schedule. The academic achievement of students in schools with fewer or more actual classes of Science is significantly lower than that of those in schools in which classes are given seriously based on the schedule plan. The academic achievement of students in schools with more weekly actual classes of Morality and Society is significantly lower than that of those in schools in which the actual classes are the same as the classes planed in schedule by 0.5 standardized marks and the difference is significant.

Out of the headmaster variable, only the time of the headmaster working in the present school has significant influence on students' academic achievement. With every one year of the working time as headmaster in the school higher than the average time, students' academic achievement goes up by 0.09 standardized marks.

6.3 Conclusions

6.3.1 *Influence from Student Individuals and Family Is Stronger than That from Schools for Students' Academic Achievement*

About 28% of the total variation of students' academic achievement is explained with the variables as follows: gender, number of books in family, family socioeconomic support, parents' educational background, home–school distance, parent–child interaction, students' time allocation, condition of participation in out-of-school reviewing, self-efficacy on learning (Mathematics, Reading and Science) and independence of finishing school assignment, working years of the headmaster in the present school, teaching and learning methods (Mathematics, Reading), number of Science classes teachers listen to each semester, teaching and research activities of subject groups, teaching and research activities of whole school teachers, and comparison between actual classes and the classes planed in schedule (Mathematics, Science, Morality and Society).

In the complete model, the percentage of the total variation of students' academic achievement explained with student individuals and family variables is 43.27%, higher than the explanatory percentage from schools by 6.87%, which indicates that the difference of students' academic achievement is mainly caused by the reasons of individuals and family. The explanatory power of the variables of individuals' devotion, participation, and attitude is the strongest for the variation of students' academic achievement, reaching 21%, higher than the explanatory power of students' family and schools by 6–7%.

6.3.2 *Students' Learning Load Is Too Heavy and Their Learning Time Is Not in Direct Proportion to Students' Academic Achievement*

The homework quantity makes 66.61% of students study for more than 1 h and 59.95% of students do not do sports in their extracurricular time or the sports time is less than 1 h every day. Only 34% of students do not participate in any training classes or out-of-school reviewing and the percentage of city students taking training classes or out-of-school reviewing is 71.14%. The sleeping time of about 13% of Grade-6 students in primary school does not reach 8 h and 42% of students sleep 8 h every day.

The academic achievement of students who do homework for less than 1 h every day is significantly higher than that of those who do not do homework or do homework for a longer time. Except that Mathematics with the limitation of a certain time weekly is good for the improvement of students' academic achievement, the academic achievement of students participating in out-of-school training or reviewing is significantly lower than that of those who do not participate in out-of-school training; and the more the time of sleep is, the better students' academic achievement is. Therefore, to improve class efficiency and to limit students' learning time after school is an important method to improve the quality of education which is also a crucial way to improve school effectiveness.

6.3.3 The Education Efficiency of Middle and Western Regions Needs to Be Improved

Middle and western students' academic achievement is significantly lower than that of the East, but their learning load is heavier. The phenomenon that Chinese and Mathematics classes are added in middle and western schools is serious. The percentage of middle and western students participating out-of-school reviewing and training reaches 70%, higher than that of the East by 15%. The percentage of students sleeping 9 h or more in the east is higher than that in the middle and in the west by 15 and 5%. The load of school assignment for students in the middle is the heaviest, with 29.34% of students spending more than 2 h on school assignment every day, 15.63 and 7.95% higher than that in the east and in the west.

Although self-access learning ability is not added into the complete model, without significant influence for students' academic achievement, the development of self-access learning ability is one of the goals in education and teaching, which deserves the attention. Students' self-access learning ability in the east is significantly higher than that in the middle and west and students' self-access learning ability in the middle is the lowest, significantly lower than that in the west.

The teaching method of teachers in the middle does not support students' self-access learning, compared with that in the east and in the west, representing in the phenomena that the percentage of encouraging students to propose questions is lower than that in the east and in the west and it is serious for teacher to stuff the class, which might be one of the reasons for the low teaching efficiency. However, there are many factors resulting in that teaching efficiency is not high; thus, further research is needed to find the solutions.

6.4 Problems Found in the Survey

6.4.1 Some Teachers Do not Follow Curriculum Plan and the Academic Achievement of Students in Regions with Classes Added or Reduced Is Significantly Lower than That of Those in Regions Where Classes Are Given Seriously Based on Curriculum Schedule

About 40% of students report that teachers cannot follow the curriculum schedule, randomly adding or reducing classes. And the addition of classes is mainly for Chinese and Mathematics, while the reduction of classes is mainly for Science and Morality and Society.

6.4.2 The Aspects of Teaching Way for Self-access Learning and of Teaching Norms for Subjects of Science and Morality and Society Needs to Be Managed with Emphasis

The content, required in *Science Curriculum Standard*, of observing teachers' demonstration experiment, making Science experimental or survey plan with teachers' direction, independently carrying out Science experiment or survey and doing Science experiment or survey with classmates as a team is not realized. 35–46% of students report that the behaviors above never or seldom take place.

Regarding the teaching way for Morality and Society class, 20% of students report that their teachers often ask them to read books on their own and 14% of students report that Morality and Society class often change into self-learning class in which they do other subjects' schoolwork. The content, required in *Science Curriculum Standard*, of asking students to look up materials and then report for communication in class and organizing students into groups to discuss questions or carry out various types of social survey, etc., does not come true.

The classes of Science and Morality and Society are often reduced, especially in the western and middle regions. Management on the execution of curriculum schedule needs to be strengthened.

6.4.3 The Quality of Science Teachers' Team Needs to Be Strengthened

Regarding the percentage of Grade 6 teachers with undergraduate certificate or above, with the comparison between the four subjects, the certificate of Chinese teachers no matter in countryside or in city is the highest, while the certificate of Science teachers in countryside schools is the lowest. The total percentage is 40.80% for Chinese teachers with certificate, with 42.59% and 35.89%, respectively, for city and for countryside; while the total percentage is 31.66% for Science teachers with certificate, with 37.55% and 23.03%, respectively, for city and for countryside.

Regarding the percentage of the schools where Grade 6 teachers without intermediate or above professional title of the sample schools, Science subject is the highest, with 32% and 32.8%, respectively, for city and for countryside, higher than that of Chinese subject, which is the lowest, by 24% (city) and 13% (countryside).

Regarding the percentage without core teachers, Science subject is also the highest, with 77.65% and 85.95%, respectively, for city and for countryside, higher than that of Chinese subject by 26% and 30%.

6.4.4 There Is Aging Tendency for Teachers' Team in Western Schools

The percentage of teachers at or above age 51 in the west is fairly high, which is over 15% for each subject, higher than the average of every subject, with 8.33% for Chinese, 6.53% for Mathematics, 4.58% for Science, and 7.32% for Morality and Society.

6.4.5 Western and Countryside Teachers Lack Opportunities of Continuing Education

The training opportunities for teachers in countryside schools are significantly fewer than that for city teachers, with the people and times for training participation lower than that for city teachers of every subject. Especially for Science and Morality and Society subjects, the teachers' training opportunities are half fewer. The frequency of teaching and research activities in countryside schools is significantly lower than that of city schools, especially the percentage of participation in teaching research activities at district level or above 1–2 times each month, the percentage is 10% higher for city schools than for countryside schools.

The percentage of western teachers' teaching and research activities is lower than that of the east and of the middle by 30 and 20%. Regarding the participation in district activities, the percentages of schools choosing once every month both in the east and in the middle reach 30% above, while the percentage is only 8% in the west.

Appendices Sample Items of Assessment Instruments[1]

Appendix A Sample Items of Chinese Subject

Part I Accumulation and Application

Read the following questions carefully and choose the correct answer according to the requirement of each question.

Please choose the most appropriate answer from the four options of A, B, C, and D below each question, and write it in the corresponding bracket.

1. In the dictionary, there are four meanings of the character "*Ju*". Which one do you think is the correct meaning of "*Ju*" in the idiom "*Ju Shi Wen Ming* (being famous around the world)"? (　)

    A. to lift or hold upward
    B. to push
    C. to put forward
    D. totally, completely

2. Idioms such as "*Fu Jing Qing Zui*" (Carrying Vitex request to forgive), "*Wo Xin Chang Dan*" (to sleep on brushwood and taste gall), "*Wen Ji Qi Wu*" (to rise up upon hearing a rooster's crow and practice with the sword) and "*Ju Gong Jin Cui*" (Be loyal and devoted to the last) are frequently encountered in reading materials. The historical figures involved in these idioms are respectively (　).

---

[1]Annotation: The testing instruments of the four subjects including Chinese, Mathematics, Science and Morality, and Society are all sample items rather than the complete test papers, for reference only.

© Springer-Verlag GmbH Germany and Educational Science Publishing House 2019
H. Tian and Z. Sun, *Assessment Report on Chinese Primary School Students' Academic Achievement*, https://doi.org/10.1007/978-3-662-57530-7

A. Jing Ke, Gou Jian, Zu Ti, Zhuge Liang
B. Jing Ke, Lian Po, Gou Jian, Zhou Enlai
C. Lian Po, Gou Jian, Zu Ti, Zhuge Liang
D. Lian Po, Fu Chai, Zu Ti, Zhou Enlai

3. To complete the sentences cited from ancient poems, which one is the correct answer? ( )

   (1) Chun Chao Dai Yu Wan Lai Ji (On the flood of last night's rain), _____.
   (2) Xi Sai Shan Qian Bai Lu Fei (In front of western hills white egrets fly up and down), _____.
   (3) Quan Jun Geng Jin Yi Bei Jiu (I invite you to drink a cup of wine again), _____.
   (4) Ting Che Zuo Ai Feng Lin Wan (I stop my coach to behold the maple trees with joy), _____.

   A. Ye Du Wu Ren Zhou Zi Heng (The ferry—boat moves as though someone were poling)
   Tao Hua Liu Shui Gui Yu Fei (Over peach—mirrored stream, perches are full grown)
   Xi Chu Yang Guan Wu Gu Ren (West of the Yangguan Pass no more friends will be seen)
   Shuang Ye Hong Yu Er Yue Hua (Frosted leaves gleam more red than blooms of February)

   B. Mei Feng Jia Jie Bei Si Qin (I am twice as homesick on festive holiday)
   Bai Yun Sheng Chu You Ren Jia (Homesteads unveil in the floating white clouds)
   Shuang Ye Hong Yu Er Yue Hua (Frosted leaves gleam more red than blooms of February)
   Xi Chu Yang Guan Wu Gu Ren (West of the Yangguan Pass no more friends will be seen.)

   C. Tao Hua Liu Shui Gui Yu Fei (Over peach—mirrored stream, perches are full grown.)
   Ye Du Wu Ren Zhou Zi Heng (The ferry—boat moves as though someone were poling)
   Xi Chu Yang Guan Wu Gu Ren (West of the Yangguan Pass no more friends will be seen.)
   Qing Yan San Ru Wu Zhi Jia (Smoke scattered into five Hou's family)

   D. Xi Chu Yang Guan Wu Gu Ren (West of the Yangguan Pass no more friends will be seen.)
   Qing Yan San Ru Wu Zhi Jia (Smoke scattered into five Hou's family)
   Mei Feng Jia Jie Bei Si Qin (I am twice as homesick on festive holiday)
   Bai Yun Sheng Chu You Ren Jia (Homesteads unveil in the floating white clouds)

4. Choose the proper connectives to complete this paragraph: ( )
   Life is like a jade, and we ourselves are the craftsmen. ( ) through constant exploration, finding our own advantages and talents, carving and polishing the life with heart, ( ) it can present the inner luster. In this process, confidence plays an important role. With confidence, we ( ) have to work hard and try hard. We can accumulate experience from each try; we can gain wisdom from experience. ( ), when growing up along the time footprint, we can gradually get to know the value of life and enjoy the fruitful life.

   A. Because; so; what's more; Therefore.
   B. As; then; meanwhile; Of course.
   C. Only; may; also; Therefore.
   D. If; then; also; Since then.

5. The following sentences are from a disordered paragraph. What is the correct sequence of the recognization? ( )

   ① When the night comes, it moistens the seedlings just like a kind mother breeding her little baby.
   ② The dewdrop is small and its life is short, but it is extraordinary.
   ③ It hides itself in the air during the daytime and works silently in the darkness at night.
   ④ When the dawn comes, it is the earliest one to open the tireless eyes.
   ⑤ It works in silence and fades away without a word.

   A. ①④③⑤②
   B. ③①④②⑤
   C. ④②⑤③①
   D. ②⑤③①④

7. Choose the appropriate punctuations for the sentence below. ( )
   Mang ren zhong xia zhe xie hua xiang rang shi jie geng mei li ta xiang zi ji kan bu dao mei guan xi zhi yao zhou wei de ren kan le xi huan kan le gao xing ta jiu xin man yi zu le
   (The blind man has planted these flowers with an aim of beautifying the world. He thinks that it doesn't matter for his incapable of seeing them. As long as people around like them and feel happy to see them, he will be satisfied.)

   A. ，！，，，，。   B. ，。，，，，。   C. 。！：。、、！   D. 。。：。；；！

Part II Reading

Please read each essay (or poetry) carefully and answer the questions. Please choose the most appropriate answer from the four options of A, B, C, and D below each question, and write it in the corresponding bracket.

I The Winter of the Songfang Stream (Paragraph Three)
Song fang xi de dong tian (di san duan)

It has snowed.

(Xia xue le.)

The snow has visited the Songfang Village. The snow has fallen on the Songfang Stream. The snow has landed just like the willow catkin and the reed flower. The snow, resembling the fluffy seed of the dandelion flying in the wind, has come down to the earth. The snow has fallen on the Songfang Stream. The reed-flower-like snow has dropped onto the stones, big and small, in the stream.

(Xue jiang luo zai song fang cun le. Xue jiang luo zai song fang xi shang le. Xue jiang luo xia lai le, xiang liu xu yi ban de xue, xiang lu hua yi ban de xue. Xiang pu gong ying de dai rong mao de zhong zi zai feng zhong fei, xue jiang luo xia lai le. Xue jiang luo zai song fang xi shang le. Xiang lu hua yi ban de xue jiang luo zai xi zhong de da xi shi shang he xiao xi shi shang.)

Those stones in the stream have been covered by the white snow, like a flock of calves drinking in the river; like a couple of bears ready to leave the stream for the snow-covered-shore; like the stream breeding plenty of big white mushrooms.

(Na xi shi shang dou fu gai zhe bai xue le. Hao xiang you yi qun bai se de xiao niu, zai xi zhong yin shui le, hao xiang you ji zhi bai se de xiong, zheng zhun bei cong xi zhong mao xue zou dao fu xue de xi an shang le. Hao xiang xi zhong sheng chu xu duo bai se de da mo gu le.)

The snow has fallen down to the stone bridge above the Songfang Stream. The snow, like the willow catkin, like the flying seed of the dandelion, falls onto the stone bridge in succession. The bridge has been covered by the white snow: it seems that there stands a white jade bridge put up above the Songfang Stream.

(Xue jiang luo zai song fang xi de shi qiao shang le. Xiang liu xu yi ban de xue, xiang pu gong ying de fei qi lai de zhong zi ban de xue, fen fen luo zai shi qiao shang. Qiao shang dou fu gai zhe bai xue le: hao xiang song fang xi you yi zuo bai yu diao chu lai de qiao, da zai song fang xi shang le.)

10. When depicting the lightness of the snow, the author mentions the willow catkin, the reed flower and ( ).

    A. big mushrooms
    B. the dandelion seed
    C. the dandelion fluff
    D. white calves, white bears

11. How many "*le*" has been employed at the end of sentences in the passage? Read carefully and talk about the meaning conveyed by the usage of "*le*".

II One Piece of the Tang Poetry

Wang Dong Ting (Watching Dongting) ①

[Tang dynasty] Liu Yuxi

Hu Guang Qiu Yue Liang Xiang He ②,
(Lake light and moonlight integrate in harmony.)
Tan ③ Mian Wu Feng Jing Wei Mo ④.
(There is no wind and the surface of the lake is like a raw mirror)
Yao Wang Dongting Shan ⑤ Shui Cui,
(Looking at Dongting in distance, you will find mountain is green and water is clean.)
Bai Yin Pan Li Yi Qing Luo.
(The green mountain standing in the clean lake is just like a tender winkle ling on the silver plate.)

① Dongting: Dongting Lake, located in the present Hu'nan province.
② Xiang He: Integrate in harmony.
③ Tan: Dongting Lake.
④ Jing Wei Mo: The mirror in the ancient times is made of copper, which has to be polished before use. Here, the mirror unpolished symbolizes the quiet and misty lake.
⑤ It refers to Mountain Jun in Dongting Lake.

12. What does *"Tan Mian"* in the sentence "Tan Mian Wu Feng Jing Wei Mo" (There is no wind and the surface of the lake is like a raw mirror) refer to? ( )

    A. the surface of the deep pool
    B. the water of Dongting Lake
    C. the surface of Dongting Lake
    D. the deep pool in the lake.

14. What does "Hu Guang Qiu Yue Liang Xiang He" (Lake light and moonlight integrate in harmony) mean? ( )

    A. The lake light and the moonlight mix with each other harmoniously.
    B. The scenery of Dongting Lake is beautiful and in harmony.
    C. The moonlight is as bright as silver, making the lake very beautiful.
    D. The lake light and the water set off each other, beautifully and harmoniously.

III The Lily in My Heart

Lin Qingxuan

In a remote valley, there was a cliff a few 1000 feet high. Since nobody knows when, on the edge of the cliff, there grew a tiny lily. From the time it appeared, it hardly looked different from a weed, but the lily itself knew that it was not a weed by nature. In the innermost recesses of its heart, it had a singular belief: "I am a lily, not a weed, and the only way to prove this is to produce beautiful flowers." With this belief at heart, the lily made a great effort to absorb moisture and sunshine, to root itself into the earth deeply as it grew upright. And finally, on an early spring morning, it produced its first bud at the top of its stem.

The lily was happy, but the nearby weeds were scornful. They laughed at the lily behind its back. "It is a weed, and there is no doubt about it, but it insists it is a lily and is so deluded that it actually believes as much! I don't think that thing on its head is a bud. It must be a tumor growing out of its brain." They scoffed openly at the lily as well. "Stop dreaming. Even if you are able to bloom in the wild, you aren't' any more worthy than we are."

The lily responded, "I want to bloom because I know I can produce beautiful flowers; I want to bloom because I wish to fulfill my solemn life as a flowering plant; I want to bloom because I prefer to validate my existence with flowers. Whether or not there is anyone to appreciate me, and no matter how you look at me, I will bloom all the same!"

Under the scornful looks of the weeds, the wild lily strove to exert its inner will. One day, it finally began to produce flowers. Its dainty and erect stance in an inspiring pure white made it the most striking beauty on the cliff. At this point, no weed dared to laugh at it anymore.

(Selected from *Collection of Lin Qingxuan's Essays*)
(Translated by Xu Yingcai, from *Selected Works of Classical Chinese Prose*)

15. The lily doesn't think that it is a weed because (   ).

    A. it can produce beautiful flowers
    B. it can straight up her chest
    C. it grows on the cliff
    D. it produced its first bud at the top of its stem.

17. What is the reason that the weeds dared not to laugh at the lily anymore? (   )

    A. The weeds think that they are not as good as the lily.
    B. The lily is too proud.
    C. The weeds think it unnecessary to laugh at the lily any more.
    D. The lily has defeated the weeds' jeer and mockery.

18. Please summarize the main idea of this passage from the two aspects of the way of expression and the content.

_____

_____

_____

IV Students Also Need Anemia Prevention (An Excerpt)

Jian Nan

People with iron deficiency will suffer from anemia. In our country, a large percentage of anemia is caused by iron deficiency. Students suffering from anemia will get pale face and inappetence, and they tend to feel tired easily, with a decrease in responding and memorizing ability. Iron deficiency is unfavorable to students' growing and health. It is reported by experts from foreign countries that students with iron deficiency will be influenced in intelligence; while their academic performance will get enhanced with iron supplementation.

There are many reasons for anemia. Experts view that some are relevant to monophagia and insufficient intake of vegetables and fruits; some are caused by excessive intake of fried food and alkaline drinks; and some are primarily due to iron deficiency, with the accomplice of excessive lead (high level of blood lead).

Generally speaking, it is unnecessary for the common anemia. Keeping a balanced diet and properly taking more iron-rich foods work. Besides, it is beneficial to drink more water, to eat more vegetables and fruits, but less fried food.

Iron-rich food includes liver, blood of animals, bean products, sesame paste, agaric, kelp, seaweed, dried small shrimp, lean meat, longan, amaranth, celery, Chinese leek, cabbage, etc. It has been experimented that anemia morbidity in pupils drops from 41.88 to 5.13% after they take pig blood in meals for two months.

19. What is the illustration way in the fifth paragraph? ( )

    A. Examples
    B. Examples and data
    C. Analogy'
    D. Comparison.

20. What is the main reason causing iron-deficiency anemia? ( )

    A. Inadequate participation in physical exercises.
    B. Monophagia and insufficient intake of vegetables and fruits.
    C. Excessive intake of fried food and alkaline drinks.
    D. Unbalanced diet with iron deficiency and excessive lead.

22. Can anemia affect students' study? Please give reasons.

    A. Anemia will affect students' study and the reason(s) is (are) _____.
    B. Anemia will not affect students' study and the reason(s) is (are) _____.

Appendix B Sample Items of Mathematics Subject

Please choose the most appropriate answer (here the complete expression is "the most appropriate answer") from the four options of A, B, C, and D below each question, and write it in the corresponding bracket. Reasoning process could be written in the blank.

1. What number is composed of six ten million, two hundred thousand, eight hundred and five ten? ( )

    A. 6000200850
    B. 60200850
    C. 62000850
    D. 600002850.

2. What number will 62870050789 be around by omitting the mantissa after the hundred million? ( )

    A. 6287 hundred million
    B. 628.7 hundred million
    C. 629 hundred million
    D. 628 hundred million.

3. The number made up by one hundred, six ten, nine one and three one percent can be written as ( ).

    A. 169.003
    B. 169.03
    C. 169.3
    D. 169.300.

4. Starting from Mingming's home, it is positive to go east and negative to go west. If Mingming goes +30 m from his home, and then −30 m, where he is now?

    A. At the place 30 m away east from his home.
    B. At the place 30 m away west from his home.
    C. At a place 60 m away from his home.
    D. At his home.

6. Which number is the nearest to your heartbeat per day? ( )

    A. 100
    B. 100000
    C. 1000
    D. 60.

7. Which number cannot be transferred into a finite decimal? ( )

    A. $\dfrac{5}{12}$

    B. $\dfrac{4}{32}$

    C. $\dfrac{3}{16}$

    D. $\dfrac{7}{35}$.

8. The decimal point of 8.09 is firstly moved to the right by three digits, then to the left by four digits. The new number will ( ).

    A. enlarge to be 10 times of the original,

    B. reduce to be $\dfrac{1}{10}$ of the original,

    C. enlarge to be 1000 times of the original,

    D. reduce to be $\dfrac{1}{1000}$ of the original.

10. If 143 yuan is divided by a proportion of 2:4:5, then the difference between the largest and the smallest amount of money is ( ) yuan.

    A. 3
    B. 39
    C. 52
    D. 13.

11. If the boys are $\dfrac{9}{16}$ of the students in a school, then the proportion of boys to girls is ( ).

    A. 9:16
    B. 9:7
    C. 16:7
    D. 25:16.

12. Li went to buy some stationery, and the shopping receipt (as shown below) was torn out carelessly.

    Shopping receipt

Issue	Number	Unit price (yuan)
Pencil	8	1.5
Eraser	5	

    Total: 16 yuan

    So the unit price of the eraser is ( ) yuan.

A. 12
B. 3.2
C. 4
D. 0.8

15 For the two numbers "a × b" and "b × c", what is their least common multiple?

A. a × b × b × c
B. b
C. a × b × c
D. 1.

16. Between two natural numbers smaller than 10, one is a composite number and odd number and the other one is a prime number and even number. What two-digit number, divisible by 2, will be composed of these two numbers? ( )

A. 22
B. 71
C. 38
D. 92.

19. In the activity of collecting tree seeds to green the country, each class of the 5 classes in Grade Four collected 20 kg and each class of the 3 classes in Grade Five collected 30 kg in a school. The average amount of tree seeds collected by each class was ( ) kilograms.

A. 25
B. 16.25
C. 23.75
D. 190

20. A farmer has harvested wheat 2500 kg this year, 500 kg more than last year. By how much does the amount go up? ( )

A. 20%
B. 25%
C. 16%
D. 5%

23. In the activity "Saving one piece of paper" carried out in a school, each student out of the 40 students in Class Two Grade Five recycled 1.5 kg of waste paper on average. And the waste paper they had collected produced 48 kg of recycled paper. Thus, 1 kg of waste paper can produce ( ) of recycled paper.

A. 0.8 kg
B. 1.2 kg
C. 1.25 kg
D. 60 kg

24. A pass can be given if 60% of the full score is achieved in an exam. Xiao Hong got 23 marks in an exam with the full score of 40 marks. ( ).

   A. Xiao Hong has passed the exam.
   B. She could pass the exam with a minimum of 60 marks.
   C. She could pass the exam with a minimum of 30 marks.
   D. She could pass the exam with a minimum of 24 marks.

25. As shown on the right, the triangle has been divided into two parts with equal area. The area of the shaded part is ( ).
   (Unit: cm²)

   A. 14 cm²
   B. 26 cm²
   C. 52 cm²
   D. 20 cm².

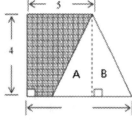

26. As shown on the right, the circumference of the rectangle is 80 cm. Its length and width respectively are ( ).

   A. 5 cm and 3 cm
   B. 50 cm and 30 cm
   C. $\frac{200}{7}$ cm and $\frac{120}{7}$ cm
   D. 25 cm and 15 cm.

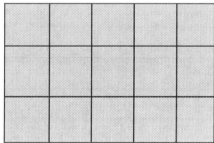

27. The table below shows scores of five athletes in a game.

Name	Round 1	Round 2	Round 3
Wang Jun	87	104	99
Li Wei	108	107	94
Zhao Gang	94	83	100
Feng Jun	116	92	119
Zhou Qiang	103	94	120

The difference between the median and the mode of all the scores is ( ).

   A. 100
   B. 6
   C. 37
   D. 94.

28. Known that the Electricity Company is located 200 m south of Heping Square, and the Jiankang road is about 120 m the north of Heping square and parallel with Heping road, which figure below is accurate? Note: the dotted line represents Jiankang road.

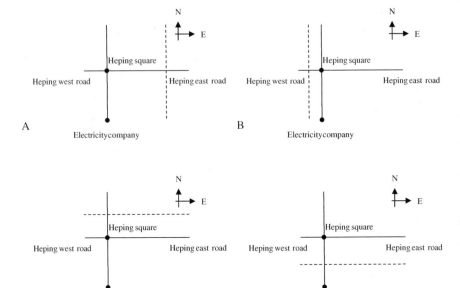

29. View this three-dimensional graph from the front, the above and the left respectively. Which is correct? ( )

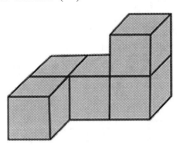

Appendices Sample Items of Assessment Instruments   315

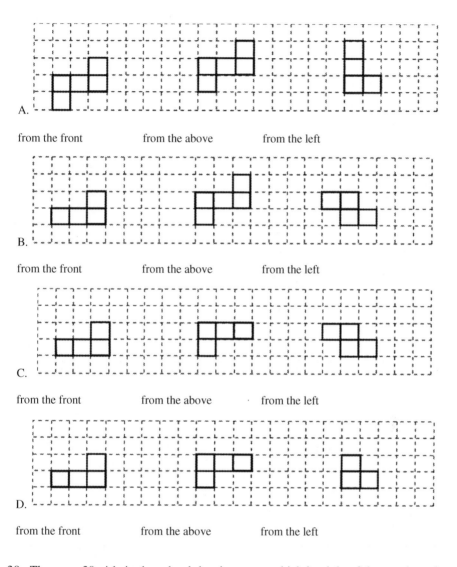

A.
from the front   from the above   from the left

B.
from the front   from the above   from the left

C.
from the front   from the above   from the left

D.
from the front   from the above   from the left

30. There are 30 girls in the school dancing team, which is triple of the number of boys if added 6 more. How many boys in this team? ( )

　　A. 8
　　B. 2
　　C. 16
　　D. 12.

37. The statistical graphs show the total number of students at school each year and the per capita book amount in the library each year.

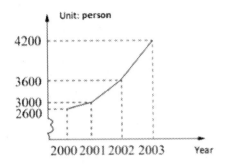 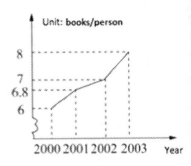

Statistical chart of students at school each year   Statistical chart of books per person

How many books have been increased by at the end of Year 2002, compared with the end of Year 2000? ( )

A. 1000
B. 1
C. 9600
D. 22600.

Appendix C Sample Items of Science Subject

Multiple Choice: Please choose the most appropriate answer to each question, and write the answer in the corresponding bracket.

1. Which organism below does not belong to plant or to animal? ( )

    A. Corn
    B. Dandelion
    C. Mushroom
    D. Locust.

2. Adapted to the desert, the leaves of cactus specialize into sharp and hard needles, which can ( ).

    A. protect itself from being eaten by other animals,
    B. adapt itself to the desert by reducing water evaporation,
    C. make cactus more unique and beautiful,
    D. attract insects.

Appendices Sample Items of Assessment Instruments 317

4. The graphs below show the growth change process of the cabbage butterfly and the locust. What is the main difference between them? ( )

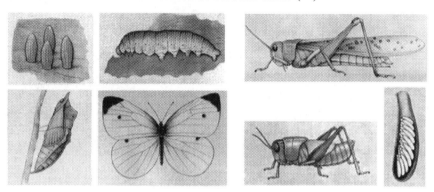

   A. The cabbage butterfly's eggs are larger than the locust's.
   B. The cabbage butterfly flies high while the locust flies low after growing up.
   C. The cabbage butterfly needs nymphosis in growth while the locust does not.
   D. The adult cabbage butterfly is bigger than the adult locust.

   Cigarettes contain tar, nicotine, and many other harmful substances. When people smoke, some harmful substances deposit in the lung, hampering its normal function.

5. The main function of lung is to ( ).

   A. send the blood full of oxygen to every part of the body,
   B. send some oxygen inhaled to the blood,
   C. purify the blood by reducing carbon dioxide to zero,
   D. transform the carbon dioxide molecules into the oxygen molecules.

6. Smoking a lot is most likely to enhance the risk of suffering from ( ).

   A. chicken pox
   B. rhinitis
   C. bronchitis
   D. gastritis.

7. Various ways have been tried to help people give up smoking. Among the methods bevlow, which is based on technology? ( )

   A. Prohibiting smoking in public.
   B. Increasing the price of cigarette.
   C. Reducing tobacco planting area.
   D. Researching and producing quitting smoking patch.

8. Among the following options, ( ) can be inherited from parents by children.

   A. height and weight
   B. hobby and hairline

C. skin color and hair color
D. saprodontia.

This graph above shows the process of purifying water and the technique needed.

9. In the second step, the aim of collecting water within an impounding reservoir is to ( ).

   A. kill the bacteria in water
   B. add oxygen into the water
   C. make sands and stones precipitate
   D. decompose poisonous substances.

10. In the fourth step of water purifying process, chlorine is added in order to ( ).

    A. kill the bacteria in water
    B. add gas into the water
    C. make sands and stones precipitate
    D. decompose poisonous substances.

11. It is most likely to cause ( ) if people drink polluted water.

    A. diabetes
    B. diarrhea
    C. flu
    D. AIDS.

12. The soil is composed of ( ).

    A. water, sand, rock and air
    B. water, air, stone, earth and humus
    C. water, air, sand and clay
    D. water, air, sand, clay and humus.

13. Smooth cobblestones are formed under the functions of ( ).

    A. weathering, running water transportation, rolling by wind,
    B. weathering, running water transportation, friction and striking,
    C. weathering, running water transportation, erosion,
    D. weathering, friction and striking, rolling.

16. Which one is the correct statement about describing the constitution of the earth surface? ( )

    A. The earth is composed of major part of land and the minor part of water.
    B. The earth is composed of minor part of land and the major part of water.
    C. The earth is composed of half land and half water.
    D. The earth is composed of half ice mountain and half water.

17. Observe the pictures below. The Big Dipper is likely to exist in ( ).

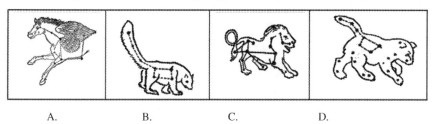

A.　　　　　　　B.　　　　　　　C.　　　　　　　D.

18. Different types of soil and same amount of water were put in three bottles. Thirty minute later, the water seeped from each bottle was shown in the picture. Please infer the capacity of water retention based on their water infiltration and the sequence of their capacity of water retention from strong to weak is ( ).

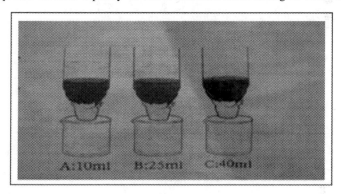

A. A-B-C
B. B-C-A
C. C-B-A
D. C-A-B

19. Jiajia thinks that green plants need sand in the soil for healthy growth. She uses two plants to verify her opinion, and one is put as shown in the picture below.

　　　　　　　Sand, soil and water

The other plant should be handled as shown in ( ).

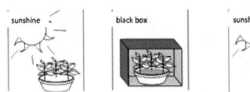

A. Sand and water
B. Sand, soil and water
C. Sand and soil
D. Soil and water.

20. An astronaut carries an apparatus to the moon for investigation. On the earth, the weight of the apparatus is measured 24 kilograms. On the moon, the weight of the apparatus is measured ( ).

   A. 36 kg
   B. 24 kg
   C. 6 kg
   D. 4 kg.

23. A deflated table tennis will get inflated when put into the hot water. The main reason is that ( ).

   A. the surface of the table tennis expands in volume when heated,
   B. it is affected by the air pressure,
   C. the air inside of the table tennis expands in volume when heated,
   D. the hot water flows into the table tennis to make it expand in volume.

24. In order to reach the same effect heat insulation, the materials below are required to be as thick as:

Air	8mm
Feather	8.5mm
Rabbit fur	9mm
Wool	12mm

Different materials have different heat insulation effect. Based on the information above, these four materials could be rearranged according to their heat preservation from strong to weak as ( ).

   A. air-feather-rabbit fur-wool,
   B. wool-rabbit fur-feather-air,

C. feather-rabbit fur- wool-air,
D. rabbit fur-wool-air-feather.

25. The boiling temperature of alcohol is 78 °C, quicksilver 357 °C, and kerosene 150 °C. The last choice to measure the temperature of drinkable water is ( ).

   A. an alcohol thermometer
   B. a quicksilver thermometer
   C. a kerosene thermometer
   D. a clinical thermometer.

26. Among the options below, ( ) is made under the rationale that hot air rises.

   A. A water gun
   B. A kite
   C. A Kong Ming lantern
   D. A bamboo dragonfly.

28. It is less possible to see fog in a desert city than in a coastal city, because ( ).

   A. it hardly rains in the desert,
   B. the temperature is very high in a desert,
   C. there are few plants in a desert,
   D. there is little vapor in the air in the desert.

Constant heating up a metal for several minutes will melt it. Keep heating for a while, it will boil. The graph below shows the temperature change when the metal is kept on heating.

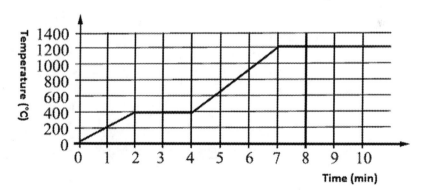

29. From the curve graph, it can be analyzed that this metal starts to melt at the temperature of ( ).

   A. 200 °C
   B. 400 °C
   C. 800 °C
   D. 1200 °C.

30. From the curve graph, the time it takes for the metal from the end of melting to the beginning of boiling is ( ).

   A. 3 min
   B. 4 min
   C. 6 min
   D. 7 min.

34. From the tools below, the one applying the lever principle is ( ).

   A. the steering wheel of a car
   B. the balance
   C. the burton
   D. the screw.

35. There are four students respectively using a thermometer to measure the temperature of hot water in the cup. The correct way to measure and to read number is ( ).

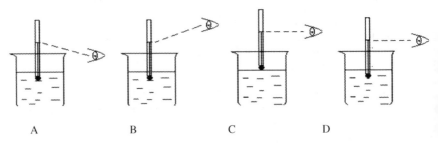

   A   B   C   D

Xiaojie is studying the change principle between depth and temperature of dry sand and wet earth. The experimental device is shown below:

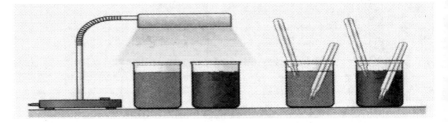

She uses a lamp to heat the dry sand and the wet earth at the same time, then she measures their temperatures at different depths. Two pairs of experiments have been conducted and the result is shown as follows.

	Temperature of dry sand (°C)		Temperature of wet earth (°C)	
The surface	20	28	20	24
2 cm deep	18	20	20	22
4 cm deep	16	17	19.5	21
6 cm deep	15	15	19	20.5

36. Which statement is correct according to the table above? ( ).

    A. On the surface, the temperature of the dry sand is lower than that of the wet earth.
    B. At the 2 cm deep, the temperature of the dry sand is higher than that of the wet earth.
    C. At the 4 cm deep, the temperature of the dry sand is lower than that of the wet earth.
    D. At the 6 cm deep, the temperature of the dry sand is the same as that of the wet earth.

37. According to the result, Xiaojie makes some inferences. Which one is incorrect? ( ).

    A. The temperature of the dry sand goes down with the increment of the depth.
    B. The temperature of the wet earth goes down with the increment of the depth.
    C. The surface temperature of the dry sand goes up faster than that of the wet earth.
    D. With the increment of the depth, the temperature of the wet earth goes down faster than that of the dry sand.

38. Look at the map below. Which statement is wrong? ( ).

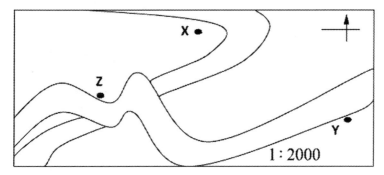

    A. X is at the northwest of Y
    B. X is at the northeast of Z
    C. Y is at the southwest of Z
    D. Z is at the northwest of Y.

40. The picture below shows temperatures of four cups of liquids. According to the temperature of these liquids from low to high, the correct sequence is ( ).

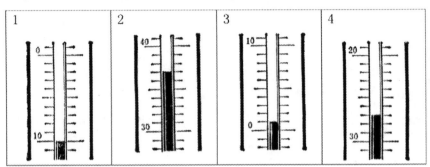

A. 2 3 1 4
B. 4 1 3 2
C. 2 4 3 1
D. 1 3 2 4.

Here is a food chain composed by four types of creatures.

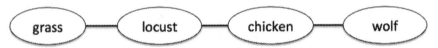

41. In this food chain, if a large number of chickens die, then the number of wolves will ( ).

    A. greatly increase
    B. greatly reduce
    C. not change obviously
    D. be hard to judge.

42. In this food chain, if a large number of wolves die, then the number of grass will ( ).

    A. greatly increase
    B. greatly reduce
    C. not change obviously
    D. be hard to judge.

Appendices Sample Items of Assessment Instruments 325

Appendix D Sample Items of Morality and Society Subject

Multiple Choice: Please choose the most appropriate answer to each question, and write the answer in the corresponding bracket.

1. The symbol of the United Nations is ( ).

 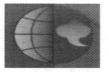 

     A   B   C   D

2. Li Ming is 9 years old, and his cousin is 13 years old. They want to ride bikes on the road. Which way is correct? ( ).

    A. Li Ming's cousin can ride independently on the road and she can take Li Ming on her bike.
    B. Li Ming's cousin can ride independently on the road, but she can't take Li Ming on her bike.
    C. Li Ming can ride independently on the road, but he can't take anyone on his bike.
    D. Li Ming cannot ride independently on the road, but he can be taken by his sister.

3. When fire accident happens, toxic fume will be produced and too much inhalation will make one suffocate to death. Therefore, in the following statements, which way is correct in an unexpected fire? ( ).

    A. Screaming loudly and thinking ways to evacuate.
    B. Trying to evacuate as quickly as possible in the pose keeping body down as much as possible.
    C. If people live in high buildings, they should go to a higher position.
    D. If there is no way out, people should lie down under the bed or get into the closet, waiting for rescue.

4. Thunderstorm happens frequently in our daily life. When lightning flashes and thunder rumbles, we are supposed to ( ).

    A. get the clothes hung on the iron wire back,
    B. go near to the door or the window if we are at home,
    C. hide under a big tree for shelter if we are in an open area,
    D. crouch down in a low-lying place if we are in an open area.

5. The picture below is a relief sculpture on the Monument to the People's Heroes erected in Tiananmen Square in Beijing. What historical event of our country does it reflect? ( ).

   A. Burning Old Summer Palace.
   B. Burning of Opium Stocks in Humen.
   C. War of Resistance Against Japan.
   D. Nanchang Uprising.

7. Zhang Hua is always maltreated by his father because of his poor academic performance. His father hits, abuses him or starves him. When he is in Grade Six, his father makes him quit school and work in a restaurant in town. His father's behavior has offended ( ) and should receive corresponding punishment.

   ① General Principles of the Civil Law of the People's Republic of China.
   ② Compulsory Education Law of the People's Republic of China.
   ③ Law of the People's Republic of China on Protection of Minors.
   ④ Criminal Law of the People's Republic of China.

       A. ①②
       B. ②③
       C. ②④
       D. ③④.

8. The picture on the right is a paper money pattern of 2 Jiao RMB. The portraits in the picture represent Buyi nationality and ( ).

   A. Monggolia nationality
   B. Chaoxian nationality
   C. Hui nationality
   D. Gaoshan nationality.

10. Liu Chang passed by a store yesterday after school, finding that the biscuit he always bought was 2 RMB cheaper than normal. He then saw the package printed "Produced on Nov. 10, 2008; Quality guarantee period: 6 months". Should he buy the biscuit? ( )

   A. Yes. The biscuit is still within its quality guarantee period, and it is cheap. So he can buy and eat it.
   B. No. The biscuit has already passed its quality guarantee period.
   C. Yes. The biscuit has just passed its quality guarantee period but it is cheap. So he can buy and eat it.
   D. No. He should also suggest the shopping assistant not sell it any more.

12. Which one of the pictures below can represent the building of ancient Rome? ( )

      A   B   C   D

13. Based on the distribution of the harmful substance during the burning of a cigarette shown in the table below, what can be inferred? ( )

The harmful substance is broken when it is burnt	25%
The harmful substance spreads around in space	50%
The harmful substance remains in butt	5%
The harmful substance is taken in by the smoker	20%

   A. Half of the harmful substance spreads, so air pollution is the main danger of smoking.
   B. Only 20% of the harmful substance is taken in by the smoker, so smoking does not do much harm to smokers.
   C. Smoking does harm to smokers, but doesn't do harm to nonsmokers.
   D. Passive smokers may take in more harmful substance than smokers.

14. When earthquake happens in a sudden, while we are in a high building, we should ( ).

   A. take an elevator downstairs quickly,
   B. hide at a place near window in the living room,
   C. run down the stairs to the open area outside the building,
   D. hide in the bathroom or in the kitchen.

15. At the beginning of the new semester, students are talking about their Spring Festival in hometown. Liu Pai says "This year, my four uncles came back home. I got much lucky money from them together with my grandparents." Guo Rui says "That's true! But I got confused sometimes because I have so many uncles." Li Xin replies "However, most of us do not have that many sisters or brothers, so the next generation will not have such trouble. Also, there will be fewer people giving them lucky money."

    According to this conversation, what phenomenon can be reflected to the population of our country? ( )

    A. The family birth rate decreases.
    B. The birth rate of the whole country decreases.
    C. People living in rural area are moving to cities.
    D. Mortality decreases.

17. Since long ago, products made in China, due to low price and high quality, have been sold all over the world. At the same time, we can enjoy American Coca Cola and Japanese digital camera in our daily life. What phenomenon does this indicate? ( )

    A. China's economy grows stronger.
    B. Globalization of economy.
    C. Difference in labor division.
    D. A balance between import and export.

18. A batch of ancient cultural relics have been found in an archeological discovery. Each piece of the cultural relics has been examined.

    ① Copper ware—AD 1150
    ② Coin—BC 221
    ③ Seed—AD 910
    ④ Porcelain—BC 900.

    If these cultural relics are arranged in time order from near to far, the accurate sequence is ( ).

    A. ①-③-④-②
    B. ④-②-③-①
    C. ①-③-②-④
    D. ②-④-③-①.

22. Which one can correctly reflect the relationship between human being and natural environment? ( )

   Illustration: Human society ■   Nature □

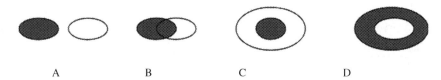

   A   B   C   D

24. "... at present, the ski field is located at the height of 1200 m in the Alps. However, in ten years, people who want to ski have to climb up to 1500 m high where there will be enough snow for skiing." Which reason below can explain this phenomenon? ( )

   A. A decline in rainfall
   B. Ground subsidence
   C. Global warming
   D. Water and soil loss.

25. It is said that Santa Claus distributes Christmas gifts to children around the world on Christmas Eve (December 24th) every year. In which place, indicated in the map on the right, when he arrives, is Santa Claus most likely tvo take off his heavy coat because of the hot weather? ( )

   A. London
   B. New York
   C. Sydney
   D. the South Pole.

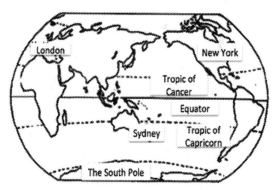

26. Garbage bins in the street corner often labeled "Recycling", "Poisonous/Harmful Substances", and "Others". Below are waste products to be put into corresponding garbage bin:

   ① plastic bags ② worn-out fur shoes ③ foam food boxes
   ④ fluorescent tubes ⑤ a used-up battery ⑥ a paint pot
   ⑦ a useless thermometer ⑧ overdue medicines

Which ones should be put into the "Poisonous/Harmful Substances" labeled garbage bin? ( )

A. ①②③④⑤
B. ②③④⑤⑥
C. ③④⑤⑥⑦
D. ④⑤⑥⑦⑧.

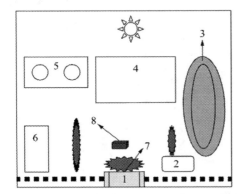

1. The school gate
2. The reception office
3. The sports ground
4. The teaching building
5. The basketball playground
6. The dining hall
7. The flowerbed
8. The flag-raising place

Answer the following questions based on the plan of Guangming Primary School.

27. The sun shown in the picture represents the location of sunrise in the morning. If Xiao Ming, on the basketball playground now, is going to answer phone call in the reception office, how can he get there in the shortest way? ( )

    A. Go southwards directly to the dining hall first, and then go eastwards along the flowerbed.
    B. Go westwards directly to the dining hall first, and then go southwards along the flowerbed.
    C. Go southeastwards passing by the flag-raising place.
    D. Go southwestwards passing by the flag-raising place.

29. The Mid-autumn Festival, the Lantern Festival, the Dragon Boat Festival and the Spvring Festival are important traditional days in our country. If the special representative food of these festivals are arranged in the order of time, the correct sequence is ( ).

    A. the Spring Festival—the Lantern Festival—the Dragon Boat Festival—the Mid-Autumn Festival
    B. the Lantern Festival—the Dragon Boat Festival—the Spring Festival—the Mid-Autumn Festival
    C. Chinese New Year's Eve dinner—Yuanxiao/Tangyuan (glutinous rice balls)—Zongzi (rice dumpling)—Mooncake
    D. Mooncake—Chinese New Year's Eve dinner—Yuanxiao/Tangyuan (glutinous rice balls)— Zongzi (rice dumpling).

Appendices Sample Items of Assessment Instruments

30. Since the year 1998, our country has expanded the scale of university (Junior college level and above), so more and more opportunities are available for people to go to university.

Year	Junior college level and above	Senior high school level and technical secondary school level	Junior high school level	Primary school level
1964	416	1319	4680	28,330
1982	615	6779	17,892	35,237
1990	1422	8039	23,344	37,037
2000	3611	11,146	33,961	35,701

The population receiving types of education every 100 thousand people in China's previous census

Based on the table above, please make a prediction on the educated population condition in the next round of census (around in Year 2010). ( )

A. Population of all education levels will largely increase.
B. The proportion of population receiving university education grows the most.
C. The total number of people receiving types of education will reach 80% every 100 thousand people
D. Population receiving middle school education will outgrow that of elementary school education; population of college level education will surpass that of senior high school education.

Answer the questions according to the map of Happy Island on the right.

31. On the Happy Island, which river flows to the northeast? ( )

   A. Chang River.
   B. Blue River.
   C. Black River.
   D. Red River.

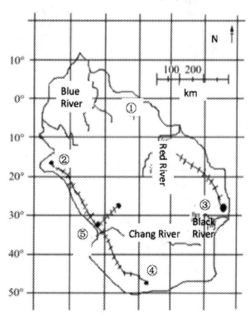

Map of Happy Island

32. Somebody is leaving the second city to the next for travel. It is known that these two cities are 750 km away from each other. Based on the map scale, the city should be ( ).

   A. ①
   B. ③
   C. ④
   D. ⑤

33. The busiest port city is ( ).

   A. ④
   B. ⑤
   C. ①
   D. ③

35. Looking at a scenery picture of Africa, Xiao Gang finds that the top of the mountain is covered by ice and snow. He feels strange. Why is there ice and snow on the mountain located in the tropical region? Your explanation is that ( ).

   A. it might be related to the nearness to the ocean,
   B. it might be related to the height in altitude,
   C. it might be related to that Africa is far away from the equator,
   D. it might be related to the wind direction.

Answer the questions according to Pictures 1–3.

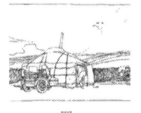

Picture 1　　　　　Picture 2　　　　　Picture 3

36. People in different regions have different living ways. For example, Picture 1 shows the Mongolian yurt, Picture 2 is the bamboo house of Dai nationality, and Picture 3 represents quadrangle dwellings in Beijing. People adopt different styles and structures to make their own buildings, indicating how people rely on ( ).

   A. the environment
   B. the customs
   C. the landform
   D. the climate.

41. The picture on the right reflects the theme of World Environment Day in 1989: Earth sweats. The most directly related factor causing this phenomenon is ( ).

A. that carbon dioxide in the air sharply increases,
B. the that ecological environment is polluted increasingly,
C. the reduction of forest size with high speed,
D. the increase of world population with high speed.

Appendix E Student Questionnaire

Name _____

Student code

        District or county   School   Class   Student

Dear students:

Here are some questions for you to answer in order to know some of your situation and thoughts. If something puzzling occurs to you, you can ask your teachers for help. Please make sure that you answer each question after clearly understanding its requirement. Some questions can be answered directly, and the others followed by options for you to choose. Please use your pen or pencil to color the option that can represent your real situation, thought or behavior.

Only one option can be chosen to each question except for special cases.

E.g. To what extent the descriptions below are in accordance with your situation (choose one code and color it)

  Complete   Most   Partial   Little

I like going to school................①...........②.........③............④..

Please read each question carefully and give your answer based on your real situation. Please make sure of answering all of the questions. Thanks for your cooperation!

National Institute of Education Sciences

Research Group of Primary and Middle School Students' Academic Achievement

May, 2009

Appendices Sample Items of Assessment Instruments

I About Yourself and Your Family

Q1. Your birthday is 19_____ (year) _____ (month) (keep in accordance with the Gregorian calendar)
Q2. Your gender
　　Male ....① Female ....②
Q3. Your nationality
　　Han .... ① Minority .... ②
Q4. How many books are there in your home?
　　A bookshelf usually can hold 40 books (excluding magazines, newspapers or textbooks) every meter.
　　0–10 ....① 11–25 .... ②
　　26–100 .... ③ 101–200 .... ④
　　More than 200 ....⑤
Q5. Do you have things below in your home? (Choose Yes or No and color your choice)
　　Yes　No

　　5.1 A desk specialized for your study .... ① .... ②
　　5.2 A quiet place for study .... ① .... ②
　　5.3 Reference books beneficial for your school study .... ① .... ②
　　5.4 Dictionaries .... ① .... ②
　　5.5 Classical literature books (e.g. *Romance of the Three Kingdoms*)
　　　　................ ① .... ②
　　5.6 Art works (e.g. a painting) .... ① .... ②
　　5.7 Poems or poetries .... ① .... ②
　　5.8 Magazines or newspapers subscribed for you .... ① .... ②
　　5.9 A computer (excluding the game player) .... ① .... ②
　　5.10 A computer with which you can surf on the Internet .... ① .... ②
　　5.11 A recorder, a monoplayer or a MP3 .... ① .... ②
　　5.12 A car .... ① .... ②

Q6. The highest education level of your parents is:

　　Primary school level or below ....①
　　Primary school level .... ②
　　Junior high school level .... ③
　　Senior high school level or technical secondary school level .... ④
　　Junior college level or vocational technical college .... ⑤
　　Undergraduate level .... ⑥
　　Postgraduate level .... ⑦
　　Unknown .... ⑧

Q7. What is your situation?

I am living in my hometown, and my parent(s) leave(s) hometown for the city to work .... ①
My parent(s) leave(s) hometown for the city to work, and I also come here studying ....②
Neither .... ③

Q8. How long does it take from the place where you live to school?

Within 10 min .... ①   10–30 min .... ②
30–60 min .... ③   More than 1 h ....④

II School Study

Q9. What is your favorite subject?

Math .... ①   Chinese .... ②
Science .... ③   Morality and Society .... ④

Q10. As for your favorite subject, to what extent are the descriptions below in accordance with your real situation?

Complete   Most   Partial   Little

10.1 I like reading some books relevant to this subject.
.... ① .... ② .... ③ .... ④
10.2 I like attending classes of this subject.
.... ① .... ② .... ③ .... ④
10.3 I feel very interested in what I've learned from this subject.
.... ① .... ② .... ③ .... ④
10.4 I like doing exercises of this subject.
.... ① .... ② .... ③ .... ④

Q11. Which subject takes most of your time to learn?

Math .... ①   Chinese .... ②
Science .... ③   Morality and Society .... ④

Q12. To what extent are the descriptions below in accordance with your real situation?

Complete   Most   Partial   Little

Math

12.1 I can learn quickly in Math class.
.... ① .... ② .... ③ .... ④
12.2 In Math class, I can understand even the most difficult question.

.... ① .... ② .... ③ .... ④
12.3 Compared with my classmates, I find Math difficult to learn well.
.... ① .... ② .... ③ .... ④
12.4 I am confident in learning Math well.
.... ① .... ② .... ③ .... ④

Chinese

12.5 I can quickly understand the authors' feelings or thoughts.
.... ① .... ② .... ③ .... ④
12.6 I can understand difficult passages in the textbook.
.... ① .... ② .... ③ .... ④
12.7 Compared with my classmates, I find Chinese difficult to learn well.
.... ① .... ② .... ③ .... ④
12.8 I am confident in learning Chinese well.
.... ① .... ② .... ③ .... ④

Science

12.9 I can learn quickly in Science class.
.... ① .... ② .... ③ .... ④
12.10 In Science class, I can fully understand the knowledge delivered by teachers .... ① .... ② .... ③ .... ④
12.11 Compared with my classmates, I find Science difficult to learn well.
.... ① .... ② .... ③ .... ④
12.12 I am confident in learning Science well.
.... ① .... ② .... ③ .... ④

Morality and Society

12.13 I can learn quickly in Morality and Society class.
.... ① .... ② .... ③ .... ④
12.14 Since I took Morality and Society class, I have begun to pay more attention to the society and events taking place in the surroundings.
.... ① .... ② .... ③ .... ④
12.15 Compared with my classmates, I find Morality and Society difficult to learn well .... ① .... ② .... ③ .... ④
12.16 I am confident in learning Morality and Society well.
.... ① .... ② .... ③ .... ④

Q13. How do you usually have Math class?

Never   Seldom   Sometimes   Often

13.1 Teachers encourage us to propose questions.

.... ① .... ② .... ③ .... ④
13.2 Teachers encourage us to solve problems in different ways.
.... ① .... ② .... ③ .... ④
13.3 Teachers encourage us to talk about our thoughts bravely even if we make mistakes .... ① .... ② .... ③ .... ④
13.4 Teachers can elicit mathematical questions from our learning and living environment .... ① .... ② .... ③ .... ④
13.5 Teachers divide us into groups for discussion.
.... ① .... ② .... ③ .... ④
13.6 Teachers always tell us the key to the question in a hurry.
.... ① .... ② .... ③ .... ④
13.7 Teachers ask us to find examples in daily life when delivering new knowledge .... ① .... ② .... ③ .... ④
13.8 In class, most of the time is devoted to listening to teachers.
.... ① .... ②............... ③ .... ④

Q14. How do you usually have Chinese class?

Never   Seldom   Sometimes   Often

14.1 Teachers encourage us to propose questions.
.... ① .... ② .... ③ .... ④
14.2 Teachers guide us to read out passages in textbooks in different ways.
.... ① .... ② .... ③ .... ④
14.3 Teachers require us to silently read passages in textbooks independently
.... ① .... ②............... ③ .... ④
14.4 Teachers guide us to grasp key sentences or words to understand the main idea .... ① .... ② .... ③ .... ④
14.5 Teachers divide us into groups for discussion.
.... ① .... ② .... ③ .... ④
14.6 Different understanding of the texts is allowed in class.
.... ① .... ② .... ③ .... ④
14.7 Teachers give us instruction to read extracurricular books.
.... ① .... ② .... ③ .... ④
14.8 In class, most of the time is devoted to listening to teachers.
.... ① .... ② .... ③ .... ④

Appendices Sample Items of Assessment Instruments   339

Q15. How do you usually have Science class?

   Never   Seldom   Sometimes   Often

   15.1 Teachers encourage us to propose questions.
   .... ① .... ② .... ③ .... ④
   15.2 We observe teachers conducting scientific experiments.
   .... ① .... ② .... ③ .... ④
   15.3 Scientific experiments or investigation plans are made under teachers' guide .... ① .... ② .... ③ .... ④
   15.4 We do experiments or investigations independently.
   .... ① .... ② .... ③ .... ④
   15.5 We form groups with classmates to do experiments or investigations.
   .... ① .... ② .... ③ .... ④
   15.7 We give a report and share our achievements in class.
   .... ① .... ② .... ③ .... ④
   15.8 In class, most of the time is devoted to listening to teachers.
   .... ① .... ② .... ③ .... ④

Q16. How do you usually have Morality and Society class?

   Never   Seldom   Sometimes   Often

   16.1 Teachers encourage us to propose questions.
   .... ① .... ② .... ③ .... ④
   16.2 We learn this subject on our own by reading books.
   .... ① .... ② .... ③ .... ④
   16.3 In this class, we usually do self-learning or do homework of other subjects .... ① .... ② .... ③ .... ④
   16.4 Teachers ask us to look for materials and give a report and share with other students in class .... ① .... ② .... ③ .... ④
   16.5 We form groups with classmates for discussion and for doing social investigations............... ① .... ② .... ③............... ④
   16.6 Paying a visit or doing social practices with the entire class together.
   .... ① .... ② .... ③ .... ④
   16.7 Teachers organize students to do role-plays or practice according to what we learn.
   .... ① .... ② .... ③ .... ④
   16.8 In class, most of the time is devoted to listening to teachers.
   .... ① .... ② .... ③ .... ④

Q17. Generally speaking, the actual classes of the following subjects, compared with the curriculum schedule every week, are more or fewer?

Fewer   The same   More

17.1 Chinese .... ① .... ② .... ③
17.2 Math .... ① .... ② .... ③
17.3 Science .... ① .... ② .... ③
17.4 Morality and Society .... ① ....② .... ③

III About Your School

Q18. How do you think of your school?

	Totally agree	Agree	Disagree	Totally disagree

18.1 I like my school............... ① .... ② .... ③ .... ④

18.2 On the whole, teachers care students much.
.... ① .... ② .... ③ .... ④

18.3 On the whole, teachers can have conversations with students in an equal way.
.... ① .... ② .... ③ .... ④

18.4 When I have difficulties, teachers can give a hand promptly.
.... ① .... ② .... ③ .... ④

18.5 Teachers give me appropriate praise and encouragement.
.... ① .... ② .... ③ .... ④

18.6 I can easily make friends in school.
.... ① .... ② .... ③ .... ④

18.7 Schoolmates can help each other.
.... ① .... ② .... ③ .... ④

18.8 It seems that my schoolmates like me very much.
.... ① .... ② .... ③ .... ④

18.9 There is no bully or insulting phenomenon among students.
.... ① .... ② .... ③ .... ④

18.10 I can get an equal treatment in school.
.... ① .... ② .... ③ .... ④

18.11 I feel safe in school .... ① .... ② .... ③ .... ④

18.12 I feel that I am an outsider in school.
.... ① .... ② .... ③ .... ④

Appendices Sample Items of Assessment Instruments   341

IV After School

Q19. How long does it take you to do the following things after school every day?

| None | Less than 1 h | 1–2 h | 2–4 h | more than 4 h |

    19.1 Doing housework .... ① .... ② .... ③ .... ④ .... ⑤
    19.2 Doing sports .... ① .... ② .... ③ .... ④ .... ⑤
    19.3 Reading extracurricular books .... ① .... ② .... ③ .... ④ .... ⑤
    19.4 Surfing on the Internet .... ① .... ② .... ③ .... ④ .... ⑤
    19.5 Doing homework .... ① .... ② .... ③ .... ④ .... ⑤

Q20. How do you usually finish your homework?

Never Seldom Sometimes Often

    20.1 Independently .... ① .... ② .... ③ .... ④
    20.2 Under supervision .... ① .... ② .... ③ .... ④
    20.3 With family's help .... ① .... ② .... ③ .... ④
    20.4 With classmates' help .... ① .... ② .... ③ .... ④

Q21. Does your family do the following things with you?

Never Seldom Sometimes Often

    21.1 My family or friends help me with my homework. .... ① .... ② .... ③ .... ④
    21.2 My family encourages me to behave myself in school. .... ① .... ② .... ③ .... ④
    21.3 My family talks about the things happening in school with me .... ① .... ② .... ③ .... ④
    21.4 My family talks about the national and international social affairs with me .... ① .... ② .... ③ .... ④

Q22. How long do you sleep every day?

    Less than 6 h .... ① 7 h .... ② 8 h .... ③ More than 9 h .... ④

Appendix F School Questionnaire

Fullname of the school: _____ District or county _____ School _____

Name of headmaster: _____

Respectable headmaster:

Some factors influencing students' learning quality are to be studied in this investigation, as a reference for the Research on Students' Academic Achievement in Primary and High Schools, an important national project in "The 11th Five-Year Plan "of National Education Sciences Planning. Your participation and the participation of your school are of great importance. We promise to keep your answer secret.

Thanks for your cooperation!

National Institute of Education Sciences

Research Group of Primary and Middle School Students' Academic Achievement

May, 2009

Only one option can be chosen to each question except for special cases.

Choose the code that can represent the real condition of your school, use a pen to color it or write down the number in the corresponding blanket.

I Basic Condition of the School

Q1. Our school is located in

① a city
② a county
③ a town
④ a township
⑤ a village

Q2. Our school can be categorized as

① The primary school with all grades.
② The primary school without all the grades.
③ Nine-year education school.
④ Independent junior middle school.
⑤ Middle school with junior and senior.

Q3. At the beginning of this school year, the school scale includes

Q3.1 Total number of grades _____
Q3.2 Total number of classes _____

Q3.3　Total number of students _____
Q3.4　Number of boarding students _____
Q3.5　Number of minority students _____

Q4. At the beginning of this school year, the condition of Grade Six includes

Q4.1　Number of classes _____
Q4.2　Number of students _____
Q4.3　Number of boarding students _____
Q4.4　Number of minority students _____

II Basic Information of Headmaster

Q5. Your gender ① Male　② Female

Q6. Your age _____
Q7. Your highest education level

① Senior high school or below.
② Technical secondary school level.
③ Junior college level.
④ Undergraduate level.
⑤ Graduate or above.

Q8. How many years have you worked as headmaster in this school? _____ year(s).
Q9. How many years have you worked as headmaster (including in this school)? _____ year(s).
Q10. You have been teaching for _____ year(s).
Q11. How many classes delivered by teachers in your school do you attend on average a semester? _____ classes.

III Condition of Teachers' Team (Including Impermanent Teachers)

Q12. There are _____ teachers altogether in our school.

Q13. Teachers' education level:

Q13.1　Number of teachers with qualified education background _____

Q13.2　Number of teachers with undergraduate level or above _____

Q14. Basic condition of teachers in Grade Six within this school year so far

	Chinese	Math	Science	Morality and Society
Total number of teachers				
Average amount of work (weekly class hours)				
Number of teachers with intermediate professional title or above				
Number of backbone teachers at county level or above				
Number of substitute teachers				
Number of people and times attending the training at county level or above this year				

Q15. The highest education level of Grade Six teachers so far (unit: person)

	Senior high school or below	Secondary normal school	Junior college	Undergraduate	Graduate
Chinese					
Math					
Science					
Morality and Society					

IV Conditions for School Running

Q16. About computers

    Q16.1 Total number of computers in school (If there is no computer, please write "0".): _____

    Q16.2 Number of computers used for teaching: _____

    Q16.3 Number of computers that can be connected to the Internet: _____

    Q16.4 Number of computers specialized for teachers to prepare classes: _____

Q17. The size of functional classroom per student is _____ (m^2) (If there is no functional classroom, please write "0".)

Q18. Can the experimental equipment satisfy the requirements of doing experiments in groups regulated by textbooks?

    ① Totally cannot
    ② Cannot fully
    ③ Basically can
    ④ Fully can

V Education and Teaching

Q19. The new curriculum standard has been conducting for _____ years in our school.

Q20. How many classes of other teachers on average do teachers listen teach semester?

    Q20.1 Math _____ classes
    Q20.2 Chinese_____ classes
    Q20.3 Science_____ classes
    Q20.4 Morality and Society _____ classes

Q21. Conditions of teaching and research system (choose one and color it)
At least once per week............① Once to twice per month......②
Twice to three times per semester......③ Never......................④

    Q21.1 Teaching and research activities of subject groups: _____
    Q21.2 Teaching and research activities of grade groups: _____
    Q21.3 Teaching and research activities of all the school teachers: _____
    Q21.4 Teaching and research activities of the district (or township level): ___

Q22. How many classes of different subjects do Grade 6 students have per week?

    Q22.1 Math _____
    Q22.2 Chinese_____
    Q22.3 Science ① _____ ② unfixed classes
    Q22.4 Morality and Society ①_____ ② unfixed classes ③ without independent classes

Q23. What is the educational system of your school?

    ① Six-three system (Primary school education is six years and junior middle school education is three years.)
    ② Five-four system (Primary school education is five years and junior middle school education is four years.)

References

Assessing scientific, reading and mathematical literacy: a framework for PISA 2006. Retrieved May 24, 2012, from http://www.pisa.oecd.org.

Cai, Y. H. (2006). SOLO taxonomy theory and its application in teaching. *Teacher Education Research, 1*, 34.

Chen, H. C. (1994). Construction of children's social development scale and norm design. *Psychological Development and Education, 4*, 62.

Cui, Y. H., Wang, S. F., & Xia, X. M. (2007). *Standards-based assessments of students' academic achievement*. Shanghai: East China Normal University Press.

Dong, P. F. (2009). 2009 international student assessment on reading literacy. *Global Education, 10*, 91.

Hu, J. (2008). How to assess students' science learning achievement—enlightenment from TIMSS science assessment framework. *Science Lesson, 6*, 26.

Huang, X. T. (1988). *Personality psychology*. Taipei: Tung Hua Book Company Limited.

Husen T (1991) In: T.S. Ding et al. (trans.) *International encyclopedia of education*, Vol. 8. Guizhou Education Publishing House, Guiyang.

Li, Y. J. (2008). British students' science achievement assessment. *Asia-Pacific Forum on Science Learning and Teaching, 6*, 30.

Lin, C. D. (2002). *Education and development*. Beijing: Beijing Normal University Publishing Group.

Ministry of Education of the People's Republic of China. (2001). *Full-time compulsory education science (grades 3–6) curriculum standard (experimental version)*. Beijing: Beijing Normal University Publishing Group.

Ministry of Education of the People's Republic of China. (2001). *Full-time compulsory education morality and society curriculum standard (experimental version)*. Beijing: Beijing Normal University Publishing Group.

Shen, B. Y., Meng, H. W. (1996) The present situation of our country' primary school students' learning quality. *Yunnan Education, 5*, 20 (Page quoted. Ditto).

Su, Y. M. (2008). Look into the primary school science learning in Hong Kong from TIMSS. *Asia-Pacific Forum on Science Learning and Teaching, 6*, 16.

Wang, L. (2007). *New exploration on educational assessment*. Xi'an: Xi'an Jiaotong University Press.

Wang, L., & Jiao, L. Y. (2006). Brief introduction to PISA and re-assessing Hong Kong PISA 2003 assessment report. *China Examination, 9*, 10.

Wang, Y. C., Hao, Y., & Hu, J. (2009). Assessment results analysis on Beijing 2007 compulsory education period academic achievement. *Educational Science Research, 9*, 43.

Wu, Z. J., et al. (1997). *Modern sociology*. Shanghai: Shanghai People's Publishing House.

Wu, H. L., Yang, Y. Y., & Zheng, M. H. (2008). Science assessment in American national assessment of educational progress. *Asia-Pacific Forum on Science Learning and Teaching, 6*, 23.

Xin, T. (2006). Academic achievement against the background of new curriculum: value of measurement theory. *Journal of Beijing Normal University (Social Sciences), 1*, 56.

Xu, Y. B. (2001). *Mathematics education outlook*. Shanghai: East China Normal University Press.

Yang, B. S. (2008). The execution of science academic achievement survey. *Asia-Pacific Forum on Science Learning and Teaching, 6*, 1.

Zhang, W. X. (1999). *Children's social development*. Beijing: Beijing Normal University Publishing Group.

Zhou, Y. R. (1999). *Primary school math pedagogy*. Beijing: China Renmin University Press Co. Ltd.

Printed in the United States
By Bookmasters